CONSTITUTION.

PREAMBLE.

WHEREAS : The Israelites of this City, being desirous of procuring a piece of ground suitable for the purpose of a Burying Ground for the deceased of their own faith, and also to appropriate a portion of their time and means to the holy cause of Benevolence—unite themselves, for these purposes, under the name and style of "THE HEBREW BENEVOLENT SOCIETY" of Los Angeles.

ARTICLE I.

The government of this Society shall be administered by a President, Vice President, Secretary and Treasurer, and three Trustees.

ARTICLE II.

The President, Vice President and the three Trustees shall constitute a Board of Trustees.

ARTICLE III.

The Election of Officers of this Society shall take place annually, on the first Sunday in the

(See pages following 362 for complete text)

HISTORY OF THE JEWS OF LOS ANGELES

Regional History Series
of The American Jewish History Center
of The Jewish Theological Seminary of America

EDITORS
SALO WITTMAYER BARON
MOSHE DAVIS
ALLAN NEVINS

.... ודרשו את שלום העיר

כי בשלומה יהיה לכם שלום.

"And seek the peace of the city . . .
for in the peace thereof shall ye have peace."

JEREMIAH 29.7

History
of the Jews
of
Los Angeles

BY MAX VORSPAN

AND LLOYD P. GARTNER

THE JEWISH PUBLICATION SOCIETY OF AMERICA

5730 Philadelphia 1970

THIS VOLUME WAS PREPARED UNDER THE DIRECTION OF THE AMERICAN JEWISH HISTORY CENTER OF THE JEWISH THEOLOGICAL SEMINARY OF AMERICA, IN COOPERATION WITH THE JEWISH FEDERATION-COUNCIL OF GREATER LOS ANGELES AND THE SOUTHERN CALIFORNIA JEWISH HISTORICAL SOCIETY.

This edition produced by arrangement with The Henry E. Huntington Library and Art Gallery

PREFACE

———————————————❧———————————————

"CHARACTER STUDY" according to Allan Nevins, "is the essence of biography." In that sense, the character of a city may be conceived as the biography of its spiritual and cultural components. For the city is what man makes of his environment for himself and his society, how he fashions its material strength in his own design. To study a city involves more than the detail of its ecology. It calls for the broadest analysis of the continuing interplay between the psychological and social facets of urbanization as they relate to human aspiration in a given time and place.

This is the central idea which pervades the Regional History Series of the Seminary's American Jewish History Center even as it is concerned primarily with American Jewry's role in urban communities. In our time, when the nature of the American city dominates national thought, the Center's legend assumes special meaning as it hearkens back to Jeremiah's teaching: "Seek ye the peace of the city."

In America's widening social and economic frontiers, the lure of the West has remained a potent force. Within this very decade, according to the July 1, 1969 Census Bureau report, the average population gain of the Pacific states was more than 22%, far greater than any other region; and the state of California was augmented by 23.7%. On the scale of American Jewish community development, Los Angeles (now numbering some 510,000 Jews), represents America's second largest Jewish center, having outstripped the communities of Philadelphia (330,000), and Chicago (269,000). On the Jewish world scene, Los Angeles Jewry has surpassed Buenos Aires (360,000), Paris (300,000), and London (280,000). The Los Angeles community may emerge by the close of the century as the largest Jewish community in the world, except, of course, for megalopolitan New York, which in the expanse of suburbia has lost its cohesive city character. What makes this projection particularly significant is the relative youth of the Jewish community of Los Angeles; most of its important cultural, religious, social service and educational institutions are of post-World War I growth.

v

The destiny of the city and its Jewish community are intertwined. From its earliest beginnings, the Jews contributed greatly to the welfare of Los Angeles as they shared in its growth and prosperity. It is no coincidence that the early Jewish historical record about California included an illuminating statement on this very theme. Thus wrote the traveler Benjamin II (Israel Joseph Benjamin) in the Preface to the second volume of his *Drei Jahre in Amerika* (1862) after his visit to the New World (1859-1862):

> Every land, every race, has sent its children to share in this gigantic task and, if the civilized world did not send the best of its sons, the work itself improved the rude, so that civilization need not be alarmed of its children in California. Law and morality have, on the whole, conquered everywhere, and many a man who in Europe found himself at odds with human and divine laws, has in the depths of the mine, or upon the prairies, regained his lost faith in God, learned to adjust himself to the laws of society, and become a respected member of the new State. [Charles Reznikoff, trans., *Three Years in America, 1859-1862* (Philadelphia, 1956).]

Benjamin II's California pastorale, it turned out, was more a prevision than reality. The century's course brought forth radical and sometimes violent manifestations: ethnic strain, economic friction, social imbalance, and, latterly, racial conflict. As the present *History of the Jews of Los Angeles* reflects, the Jews participated in virtually every sphere of civic endeavor, whether in the economics of banking, brokerage, transportation and agriculture, or in the social and cultural areas of hospitals, public education, libraries, and centers of art. Individually and collectively, they worked hand in hand with progressive forces for "civic virtue," social elasticity, economic improvement and the achievement of social justice.

But Los Angeles Jewish history enters into areas beyond civic and even national enterprise. It is also the delineation of a distinctive group life. The ultimate test of creative experience is its qualitative contribution to the spirit of the real society in which it lives and thrives. In the American pattern, the organized Jewish community of Los Angeles is deepening its spiritual roots through its network of social welfare, religious, cultural and educational institutions. This is the special value of this volume as it traces, for the first time, the transplantation of European and eastern American religious, educational and communal experiences into Southern California soil. By explaining the environmental and social forces which were indigenous to the western state, local personalities—immigrant and native born—come forth with their special flavor. Not all men make history; but they are all *of* history. A host of seemingly secondary figures walk across the pages of the book. Yet, in their total image they offer a fresh portrait of a singular Jewish community in the American West.

In the process of searching and sifting archives and periodicals, Vorspan and Gartner have gathered and organized a remarkable collection of documents, which can become the backbone of an active center for the further collection and study of materials on Jewish immigration, community life, and institutions. Precisely because it is arranged in larger perspectives, the collection can also serve future study of American and world Jewish community history. It was this comprehensive objective—to create a documentary collection as part of the writing of the Los Angeles history—which guided the Center's editorial directorate together with Professors Louis Finkelstein and Simon Greenberg, from its inception. In this regard we express our gratitude to the founding members of the Center's Board: Daniel G. Ross, Dr. Joel S. Geffen, Reuben Kaufman, Richard K. Manoff, Irving Neuman, Herbert Salzman, and Dore Schary. The memory of the Center's first two chairmen—Louis M. Rabinowitz and Sol Satinsky—shall ever be reverently recorded.

As the Center's program in New York began to move forward, its general aim to combine local focus with national outlook took shape. Happily, Dr. Gartner, of the History Center, and Dr. Vorspan of the University of Judaism joined hands in the research and writing. Dr. Samuel Dinin, Chairman of the university's faculty, and Dr. David Lieber, now the university's President, encouraged the entire enterprise; and the university's Board of Overseers, under the chairmanship of Julius Fligelman and his able successor, Jack M. Ostrow, supported this effort as part of the university's expanding program. Following these internal Seminary-University of Judaism arrangements, the thoughtful and energetic Dr. Justin Turner created indispensable liaison with the Los Angeles Jewish Federation-Council of Greater Los Angeles and the Southern California Jewish Historical Society. The Jewish Federation-Council through Mr. Julius Bisno, its Associate Executive Director, not only helped substantially to sponsor the research, but also involved specialists in the community's history in sub-sections of the work as it proceeded. The Historical Society, of which Mr. William R. Blumenthal is President, kept the project in the forefront of local historians' interest. Withal, and always with an eye on the goal of establishing a research and teaching department in western Jewish Americana at the University of Judaism, collaboration was effected with the Huntington Library. The fortuitous circumstances of Professor Nevins' devoted guidance both at the Huntington Library and the Seminary's History Center established the basis for this partnership, with the Library's former Director, Dr. John E. Pomfret, and its Senior Associate in Western America, Professor Ray Billington. Together with Dr. James Thorpe, the present Director, plans for the publication of the History by the Huntington Library were completed. The entire collective project was coordinated with characteristic perspicacity and devotion by Dr. Gladys Rosen, the History Center's Executive Associate. Professor Bernard Mandelbaum, Seminary President, has taken interest in the development of this project for which we are grateful.

The combination of scholarship, disciplines, and backgrounds in this historical enterprise is in itself a tribute to the persons and institutions involved. It also illustrates the meaning of *The History of the Jews of Los Angeles:* universal history is local history writ large.

MOSHE DAVIS

Jerusalem
Tishri, 5730
October, 1969

CONTENTS

ACKNOWLEDGMENTS

>:<

THE OBLIGATIONS incurred in the preparation and writing of such a book are manifold. We would like to acknowledge the numerous persons and institutions which were of service at many stages of this work.

Of libraries and archives, thanks are due to U.C.L.A., the Los Angeles County Museum, the *Los Angeles Times*, Henry E. Huntington Library and Art Gallery, University of Southern California, Los Angeles Jewish Community Library, Masonic Library, Los Angeles County Hall of Records, the Council of Jewish Federations and Welfare Funds, YIVO Institute for Jewish Research, the Welfare Planning Council of Los Angeles, and their devoted staffs.

Historians of Los Angeles who added their personal knowledge and reminiscences to their published writings include Messrs. Remi Nadeau, W. W. Robinson, Frank B. Putnam, and the late Oscar Lawler. Dr. Fred Massarik, of U.C.L.A. and the Research Service Bureau of the Jewish Federation-Council, has been endlessly helpful in criticizing early drafts, and in making available statistical and quantitative data of which he is both pioneer and master interpreter.

Not only has the Jewish Federation-Council generously sponsored this book and patiently awaited its completion, but its staff and that of its affiliates have been careful in keeping historical records and generous in making them available. Our particular thanks go to Mr. Julius Bisno, Associate Executive Director of the Jewish Federation-Council, his former colleague Mr. Charles Zibbell (now with the Council of Jewish Federations and Welfare Funds), Mr. Charles Mesnick of the Jewish Centers Association, and Mr. Joseph Roos of the Community Relations Committee. Mr. Aaron Riche had much to do with the creation and preservation of these records.

The many men and women who have provided personal reminiscences are mentioned individually when their statements are cited in the text. We would like to mention thankfully our general obligation to them as a group.

Our secretaries, Mrs. Sylvia Zuckerman and Mrs. Diana Rosenberg, have been resourceful and long-suffering.

The administrative support and friendly help of Dr. Gladys Rosen, Executive Associate of the American Jewish History Center, is gratefully remembered. Dr. Simon Greenberg and Dr. David Lieber of the University of Judaism were constantly helpful. The interest of Mr. Harry Friedman and the late journalist and trade union leader Harry Lang is deeply appreciated.

With his characteristic graciousness, Professor Allen Nevins observed and encouraged the writing of this book and made numerous practical suggestions for its improvement. From Jerusalem, Professor Moshe Davis kept a watchful eye and a tireless concern for the progress of this history, repeatedly reading, suggesting, and stimulating. Many of this book's better qualities, such as they are, we owe to him.

MAX VORSPAN
LLOYD P. GARTNER

PART I

Early Decades

Castelar St., now North Hill St., looking north from Fort Moore Hill, circa 1890. Jewish cemetery near top left, surrounded by grove of trees, in Chavez Ravine. Dirt ravine in foreground is now Sunset Blvd. (Courtesy Los Angeles County Museum History Department.)

CHAPTER 1

The Gold Rush Days: 1850-1858

A Spanish-American Town

Los Angeles is not a new city. It is as old as most cities in the United States. Unlike most towns, however, it was founded for a purpose and on a specific date: September 4, 1781. On that day the Spaniards dedicated a pueblo (town), in a planned series of pueblos along the California coast to complement a parallel series of presidios (forts) and missions. Its imposing name was El Pueblo de Nuestra Señora la Reina de los Angeles: the Town of Our Lady the Queen of the Angels.

From the beginning, the city was polyglot and multiracial. The first forty-four citizens were brought from Sonora, Mexico—eleven men, eleven women, and twenty-two children. The adults consisted of two Spaniards, nine Indians, one mestizo, eight mulattoes, and two Negroes. None could read or write, and only one, a tailor, had a trade.[1] The surrounding land, comprising perhaps one and a half million acres, was under the control of San Gabriel Mission, founded ten years before. When the missions were secularized during 1834-1836, the land was parceled out and given away in the form of grants. Land was handed over by Mexican governors to favored claimants: retired soldiers, ex-governors or other Mexican officials, and friends. Some administrators sent from Mexico to wind up the affairs of the mission ended as well-to-do ranchers. Grants of land in the Los Angeles area were made very sparingly during the last forty years of Spanish rule, which ended in 1822. However, the taking over of the missions by independent Mexico in 1833 brought radical changes. Land was quite indiscriminately parceled out in enormous grants to private petitioners, often for the mere asking. Boundaries were vague, but no one paid attention at the time. The recipients of the grants used the land for grazing. Without water and manpower, and given the undeveloped technology of the period, a pastoral economy was the sole practical use for the huge tracts.[2]

Thus begins the fabled rancho period in California history. Much of the early California romance clusters about the hacienda, the fiesta, the corrals, the cattle roundup called rodeo, and the hospitable, carefree life of the early Californians. White trappers began to infiltrate in the 1830's. They settled down, took beautiful Spanish daughters to wife, adopted the Catholic religion, and soon became noted ranchers, as though to the rancho born. The rancho era also had its dark side. The Mexicans and Indians, the wards of the now abolished missions, were left to their own devices. They became poor peons on the ranchos and rapidly deteriorated as their fiber was destroyed by a system which could only exploit them. Drunkenness and crime became habitual with them as they sank to the bottom of society.[3]

By 1840 the town's population was perhaps 1,100.[4] One year later, the first overland group of pioneers to set out for California, about half of whom had the avowed purpose of establishing homes, reached Los Angeles. They were the Rowland-Workman party, who had come through today's New Mexico. When the Mexican authorities had them register they thereby recorded for history the name of the first known Jew in Los Angeles: Jacob Frankfort, with a variant spelling of "Frankford." A tailor by profession, he was obviously a wanderer and adventurer by inclination, who did not stay long in Los Angeles on this first visit. When some members of the expedition decided to travel on to the Philippines and China, possibly he went with them. Frankfort is mentioned again as having been in Los Angeles in 1846. He traveled up and down the coast in 1847 and 1848 and in the first census of Los Angeles (1850) is listed as a resident, native of Germany, aged forty. Subsequently, he settled down in San Francisco.[5] We do not have proof positive that Frankfort was Jewish, but his name, place of origin, and trade make the assumption a valid one.

During the 1840's the small but growing number of Americans in California felt increasingly restive under Mexican rule. The outbreak of the Mexican war in 1846 gave them the opportunity to take part in the conquest of this vast province and to incorporate it into the United States. Shortly after open hostilities with Mexico commenced, John C. Frémont and Commodore Robert F. Stockton moved on southern California. Los Angeles was taken, unopposed, on August 13, 1846, and rudimentary American civil government was installed. When a Mexican rebellion broke out in the temporary absence of the conquerors, Frémont's return led to immediate capitulation on January 13, 1847. One year later, the peace treaty between Mexico and the United States, ratified by the Senate on May 30, 1848, made California part of the United States. It became a state of the Union on September 9, 1850. The gap of two years between American conquest and statehood was filled by makeshift, de facto government; California was never a United States Territory.

At the same time as these epochal political events unfolded, gold was discovered in January 1848 at Sutter's mill, in north central California. The gold rush which ensued revolutionized California and "profoundly affected the whole United States and the civilized world."[6] The discovery and mining of gold, while confined to the northern section of the state, also had sharp effects upon the south. The little village of Los Angeles, which in 1850 possessed 1,600 inhabitants, together with its ranching hinterland, was now called upon to feed the miners of the north. The cattle of the southland, hitherto useful only for hides and tallow, were in demand as food. The placid ranchos of the 1830's and 1840's, with their self-sufficient, patriarchal mode of life, were caught up in a cattle boom. With the swelling population in the north requiring meat for its food and tallow for light, the market price of a steer multiplied perhaps fivefold in two years. On the ranchos, cash was needed to pay the no longer servile Indian laborers. Newly imposed taxes, and legal fees in connection with litigation over loosely held land titles, also required money. However, the economically inexperienced rancheros of southern California improvidently consumed the profits of these fat years. When competition came from Texas and Missouri, and the gold rush declined, they had little to show for their good years.[7]

The First of the Jews

While the gold rush was achieving momentum and Los Angeles was being incorporated as an American city on April 4, 1850, a census was taken of Los Angeles County.[8] It showed a total population of 8,624, of whom only 295 were "foreigners"—that is, non-Mexican whites. The white native population and the Indian population were about equal, occupying a total of 518 residential structures. Eight persons recognizably Jewish were: Abraham Jacobi (or Jacoba, or Jacoby), aged 25—Poland; Morris Michaels, aged 19—Poland; Morris L. Goodman, 24—Germany; Phillip Sichel, 28—Germany;

Augustine Wasserman, 24—Germany; Felix Bachman, 28—Germany; Joseph Plumer, 24—Germany; Jacob Frankfort, 40—Germany. All were unmarried merchants, except for Frankfort, the tailor, and all resided in four adjacent dwellings. Frankfort lived with the Alexander Bell family, one of the most important in the state, which dwelt in an imposing home, a $70,000 mansion of two stories, with a walled garden. General Frémont and General Stockton had occupied it during the war.[9] Since it is not likely that Bell took in boarders, Frankfort either was a guest or perhaps did the family's tailoring. In the home adjacent lived Michaels and Jacobi; next door were Sichel, Plumer, and Goodman; Wasserman and Bachman occupied the following house.[10]

These men were soon joined by numerous coreligionists, eager to seize the chance for quick wealth. They were youthful Jews mostly from Germany, some from Poland; tough, self-reliant, enthusiastic. They formed part of the great migration of German Jews to the United States. They came to escape the constrictions on their life in Germany, Bohemia, German Poland, and Hungary: limitations on occupation and even on marriage, not to mention the general oppressiveness of the political and economic regime in the lands of their birth. Mostly on this account, the number of Jews in the United States increased from 6,000 in 1825 to about 280,000 by 1880. The majority lived in the Northeast and Middle West, but a large number made their way to California, drawn by the gold rush and the quick development of the state. The traveler I. J. Benjamin estimated their number in 1860 at 10,000, half of whom lived in San Francisco.[11] An adventurous handful of young men found their way to Los Angeles. There could be no further remove from the confined life of German and Polish Jewry in which most of them were living five years earlier. They traversed the dusty streets, into hole-in-the-wall store fronts, traveling by wagon from rancho to rancho loaded with tempting merchandise, setting up businesses, establishing partnerships, dissolving them with disconcerting frequency, moving into town and out again with the easy flexibility of the unmarried, who formed a substantial proportion of the white non-Mexican population.

Horace Bell comments on Los Angeles in the early 1850's: "The business of the place was very considerable; the most of the merchants were Jews, and all seemed to be doing a paying business.

The fact was, they were all getting rich."[12] Actually, there was very little incentive for anybody to live in the town except economic advantage. Isolated from the world save by arduous trip in stagecoach and steamer, Los Angeles from 1850 to 1870 is described as one of the roughest, crudest cities in the United States. Gamblers and outlaws had followed the gold southward, while the backwash of the vigilante operations in the northern mines and San Francisco spilled into Los Angeles. A murder a day was normal. The short street from Aliso to the Plaza was filled door by door with gambling halls, saloons, and houses of prostitution. In the course of twenty years there were forty legal hangings and thirty-seven lynchings. A typical coroner's jury reported that "the victim came to his death by the discharge of a gun loaded with powder and bullets."[13]

Protestant ministers intermittently came and quit. When the Reverend T. N. Davis, Presbyterian, left in 1856, "for want of appreciation of his services by the community," he excoriated in his valedictory sermon the "torrents of vice and immorality which obliterates [sic] all traces of the Christian Sabbath—to live where society is disorganized, religion scoffed at, where violence runs riot, and even life itself is unsafe. . . . Moreover a clergyman can as ill support his family without funds, as any other member of the community, and in this Los Angeles presents an uninviting field for a minister dependent solely on his congregation for support."[14] Nine years later there was still no Protestant minister in town, and it was regarded as "a burning shame that at this moment Los Angeles cannot boast of a full thoroughgoing congregation who can spend one hour each Sabbath from a 'busy life' without being drummed up by handbill or some other method extraordinary, to hear an able or eloquent discourse."[15]

Horse racing, cockfights, bullfights, bear hunting, and card playing were the diversions of the day. The streets were dusty and dirty, with carcasses lying unburied and myriads of dogs running wild. The fanciest hotel, the Bella Union, was graphically described as a "corral" with "numerous pigeon-holes, or dog-kennels."[16]

Into this environment, in which they learned quickly to carry a gun and to speak Spanish sometimes even before mastering English, trickled some Jews.[17] During the hectic first decade, numerous Jewish merchants established themselves in business and in the life of the Los Angeles community.

Like most Americans, few Jews who came to Los Angeles during its early years remained permanently. Those who settled, however, contributed in large measure to the economic growth of the town, where they constituted a large proportion of the commercial class. In primitive Los Angeles, the trader's customary tasks of supplying wants and marketing local production imposed the further responsibility of creating trade routes and instruments of credit. The little town had to be drawn out of its isolation, and lacking a class of professionals and even a clergy, early Los Angeles also depended heavily upon its merchants for civic leadership. The Jews were prominent in these efforts, joining projects for the economic, civic, and cultural development of the newly American town.

The following are some of the Jews of whom we have recorded knowledge: In 1851, Solomon Lazard was in business with H. Bauman.[18] A few months later, when his cousin Maurice Kremer arrived from their home town in Alsace, Lazard immediately dissolved partnership and established the firm of Lazard and Kremer, wholesale and retail dealers in clothing, groceries, boots, shoes, etc. They have the distinction of being the first Jewish advertisers in the *Los Angeles Star*, which began publication on May 17, 1851.[19] Both Lazard and Kremer were to live out their lives in Los Angeles as esteemed figures in the civic and business, as well as the Jewish, community. Their partnership, however, was shorter lived, being terminated in 1856.[20] Lazard's entry into partnership with Louis Wolfskill, a non-Jew, was relatively unusual, as the Jews tended to associate with each other in the intimacy of partnerships.[21] In August 1858 this partnership was also dissolved.[22]

John Jones, an English Jew, came to Los Angeles via Australia in 1851 and established a wholesale grocery business.[23] He soon amassed a fortune. He married a Christian, Doria Deighton of San Francisco, while remaining prominent in the Jewish community. Jones's wife became a leading member of the Ladies' Hebrew Benevolent Society when it was established in 1871.[24] Their daughter married the son of Isaac Lankershim, a leading citizen of Los Angeles. Of Jewish birth, Lankershim had been converted to Baptist Protestantism, and his descendants were lost to Judaism. As for Jones, by 1854 he had enough money to retire. He sailed to San Francisco with a view to remaining there but returned a few years later and lived out his life in Los Angeles.[25]

Jacob Elias, a doughty merchant and hard competitor, was in business with his brothers Raphael and Israel in 1853. In 1855 Israel withdrew, and Raphael in 1857.[26] Jacob Elias remained, to become one of the leaders of the Jewish community and a pioneer in the Masonic order.

Samuel Meyers, who gained the distinction of serving the Los Angeles Masonic Lodge No. 42 as treasurer for fifty years, entered business with Hilliard Lowenstein in 1853. When the partnership dissolved, Meyers went into the crockery business with his father-in-law, S. C. Davis.[27]

Success and a lifetime spent in Los Angeles were the exception rather than the rule. Far more typical were the ups and downs of such merchants as Baruch Marks, Louis Schlesinger, and Hyman Tischler, who did general merchandising as B. Marks and Company in the early 1850's.[28] All three fared badly. Marks returned to Germany, lost his fortune in speculation, and came back to Los Angeles. Schlesinger lost his life in the explosion of the steamer *Ada Hancock* in 1863, and Hyman Tischler a short time later fled town for fear of being assassinated.

Herman Schlesinger was in Los Angeles in 1851 and engaged in dry goods business with Tobias Sherwinsky. His brother Moritz arrived from Germany in 1855 and joined the firm. In 1857 the two original partners, longing for their fatherland, sold out to the late arrivals and returned there. Sherwinsky, however, lost his competence and was compelled to return, settling in San Diego, but Schlesinger remained in Germany.[29] A. Portugal, who owned a general store, also sold out and returned to the old country. There he lost all, but he came back to Los Angeles, where he tried unsuccessfully to recoup his fortunes.[30]

Felix Bachman and Phillip Sichel were both in Los Angeles by 1850. In partnership with Ben Schloss and Samuel Laubheim, they carried on the largest wholesale merchandising and trading business in the Southwest, which in those pre-railroad days dominated the flourishing trade with Salt Lake City. The enterprising Bachman also became treasurer of a German syndicate centered in San Francisco, which purchased 1,200 acres near the Santa Ana River in 1857. Land was laid out in twenty-acre plots, on each of which it was planned to plant ten thousand vines. Shares were sold at $750. Local investors included Charles Kohler and Louis Jaszynsky, and there were fifty stockholders in all. The enterprise was called the Los Angeles Vineyard Society. To encourage German farmers to settle, the Society even gave the Santa Ana area a German name—Anaheim.[31] Morris L. Goodman moved there to become a founder and community leader.[32] But for all this impressive record of enterprise, Felix Bachman was to suffer bad years and quit the city in 1864.[33]

In 1854 the three brothers I. M., Samuel, and Herman Hellman arrived and opened a flourishing book, stationery, and notion business.[34] They were cousins of the Hellmans who were to arrive in 1859 and mold the economic life of the city.

Harris Newmark (1834-1916), early leader and later patriarch of the Jewish community, and author of the classic personal history *Sixty Years in Southern California,* arrived in 1853. He entered business with his brother, J. P. Newmark, and then with Jacob Rich and Elias Laventhal in Rich, Newmark & Company; later with Maurice Kremer, a cousin by marriage, in Newmark and Kremer; ultimately with other partners in the noted wholesale grocery firm of H. Newmark and Company.[35]

Los Angeles merchants were always alert for commercial opportunities with the army. When a fort was established in El Tejon in the Sierra in 1854, among the merchants who came to supply the military were C. Whitkosky and Harris Newmark. Newmark established a general store at El Tejon and placed the penniless John Philbin in charge. Philbin made $20,000 in eight months and then withdrew because of ill health. Newmark replaced him with a man named John, who gambled away all the profits, and then a nephew, Kaspare Cohn, took his place. In 1861 the army moved nearer Los Angeles to keep a closer eye on that potentially hostile population, and the fort was closed. Harris Newmark sold his $3,000 investment for $50.[36]

The brothers-in-law Moses Norton and Ephraim Greenbaum arrived late in 1851 or early in 1852 and opened a clothing store. Mrs. Ernestine Greenbaum was one of the first Jewish women in Los Angeles and was reportedly the mother of the first non-Mexican child born in Los Angeles.[37] As the operator of a boarding hotel during the 1870's, she was a motherly friend to many a young and homeless Jewish boy seeking his fortune in the West.[38]

Among Mrs. Greenbaum's boarders there were probably many who never found their way into the scanty records of those days.

Some were peddlers, who in all likelihood found a welcome reception among the señoritas and the vaqueros of the ranchos, to whom the wagons filled with goods and finery must have irresistibly appealed. The shop owners of the city, too, did not scorn to fill their carts and travel about the countryside, bringing the store to the customers. Harris Newmark tells of Schlesinger and Sherwinsky, traders in general merchandise, who in 1853 bought a wagon in San Francisco, sent it by steamer to Los Angeles, loaded it with attractive wares, and brought it to the easygoing ranchero Don Bernardo Yorba. During those days of the cattle boom, they persuaded him to buy not only the contents but also the horse, wagon, and harness. They did so well that they performed the same feat on the Don several times.[39]

It was not easy, however, to be a businessman in Los Angeles. Merchandise had to be shipped from San Francisco, and sometimes from New York, by steamer. It was hard to get help, and clerks often were younger brothers, relatives, or friends. It was valuable to have a partner to tend the store while one traveled to San Francisco or even to New York to buy a load of goods. When he was without a partner, John Jones had to close for six weeks while he laid in his new season's merchandise from San Francisco.[40] One partner could also keep store while the other went peddling. Partnerships were not stable, and were constantly formed and dissolved. By a notice in the paper and an inventory of goods, one partner might buy out the other and then continue "at the old stand."[41]

With a group of lively merchants competing in business there was bound to be friction. Some dissolutions of partnership were acrimonious and led to occasional lawsuits between Jew and Jew. The only dispute which became public was a bitter and revealing exchange of letters between S. K. Labatt and diminutive Moritz Michaels. It started with a curt notice in the *Star* of March 31, 1855, announcing that a note for $700, drawn in favor of H. C. Labatt and signed by M. Michaels, was obtained under false representation and would not be honored. Labatt replied in the *Southern Californian* with a long explanation. He referred to Leopold Hart, a peddler who owed him a goodly sum of money. In order to avoid payment Hart had sold his stock to Lazard and Kremer. Labatt had Hart jailed for fraudulent transfer of property, but Lazard protected Hart by guaranteeing the loan. Eventually Lazard sold Hart's note, payable to Labatt, to Moritz Michaels. Michaels was told by Labatt that the note from Hart carried interest of 3% per month, and so gave Labatt a note for 3% a month interest. When Michaels found that Hart's note was for 10% a year only, the legal interest, he was furious and announced that he would not pay. Michaels let the matter rest with the statement: "There is one assertion that I will make, and I trust that my residence of more than five years in this community will bear me out. I have never contracted a debt that I have not made arrangements to pay. I have strictly minded my business and what I have lacked in show or bauble, I have made up in honesty and sobriety. I would respectfully call attention of this community to these parts and beg them to compare my action with those of this extraordinary youth who would vilify me at the expense of truth." (Michaels was himself twenty-four years old.) Not long after their clash, Labatt moved to San Francisco and Michaels departed for South America.[42]

This involved affair illustrates the prevalence of notes as a form of cash. They were bought and sold freely among the merchants at high rates of interest and were used to pay creditors. It also shows that partnerships were readily dissolved. Some partners wanted to move to San Francisco with its opportunities for business and more gracious living, or to return to their homeland with new-found fortune, or to seek a wife. Quite a few returned to Germany, but some of these, as we have noted, were constrained to come back to Los Angeles when they lost their money in the old country. There was also constant movement between Los Angeles, San Bernardino, El Monte, and other hamlets. A merchant might try his fortune by opening a store in San Bernardino or El Monte or Anaheim; if he failed, he might soon be back in business in Los Angeles.

Travelers of note periodically visited the local Jews. They gave of their experience and advice and extracted what they could of income and sustenance. In the 1860's it was I. J. Benjamin ("the Second"), and during the 1870's, Rabbi H. Z. Sneersohn; the first such visitor was S. N. Carvalho, in 1854.

Solomon Nuñes Carvalho (1814-1897), of a noted family of rabbis, merchants, and writers, became at the age of twenty a professional portrait painter. In 1853 he crossed the Rockies in Colonel John C. Frémont's fifth expedition, to survey a course for a projected railroad.[43] Carvalho reached Los Angeles in June 1854 and gained the friendship of Samuel Labatt, whose store Tiende de China was "the most pretentious and certainly the most specialized of its day in town."[44] Carvalho acknowledged that "To the brothers Samuel and Joseph Labatt, merchants of Los Angeles, I am indebted for many acts of kindness; men who anticipate the necessities of their fellowman, and spontaneously offer *money advances* to a perfect stranger, I have not often met with, 'but when found, I make a note of it.' "[45] Carvalho may have influenced Sam Labatt to be a founder of the Hebrew Benevolent Society, and to serve as its president. For his part, Sam helped Carvalho set up in business and earn some badly needed money during his stay in Los Angeles. In August 1854 the Labatt brothers moved their store to a new location. It was called the "New Tiende de China," where the dry goods business was expanded to include such items as India rubber combs, soap extracts, gold hunting watches, accordions, oils and essences such as rose pomatum, ox marrow, bear oil, poincine soap, etc.[46] In the new store's unoccupied second floor Carvalho and a partner, A. M. Johnson, opened the first photography shop in Los Angeles. An advertisement described the business: "Daguerrotypes taken in all styles. Particular attention is paid that none but first rate pictures emanate from this establishment. Pictures taken after death if required. Portraits in oil, and daguerrotypes copied in the first style of the art. A reception room has been arranged expressly for the ladies. . . . Carvalho and Johnson."[47]

To make ends meet, Carvalho undertook another fund-raising scheme. He painted three pictures and raffled them.[48] The pictures were displayed at his Daguerrean Gallery in an exhibition of pictures he had painted since his arrival in Los Angeles.[49] One was of Pio Pico, the Mexican ex-governor of California. Others were painted during his trip from Salt Lake City to Los Angeles and included paintings of the Utah Indian chiefs as well as general views of the country. People were invited to sit for their portraits.[50]

When he fell ill, Carvalho stayed at the hospitable Dominguez ranch. He states that had he languished in Los Angeles instead of resting with the Dominguez family, he might not have regained his health. While recuperating at the ranch, he excavated a mastodon and wrote a full report of it for the local paper.[51] Carvalho remained in Los Angeles from about June 12 until September 21, 1854, when his departure was noted in the *Los Angeles Star*: "Announcement— Dissolution of Partnership: S. N. Carvalho, A. M. Johnson."

Early Los Angeles' population, while small, was very diverse. To the Mexicans and Indians speaking Spanish or native tongues, many of whom were only recently and imperfectly Christianized, Americans, the "gringos," were foreigners. The Americans, too, were variegated, including Yankees, Germans, French, and others. In fact, the effigy of Judas Iscariot hanged by the local Mexicans during their riotous Easter celebration was fashioned to resemble the "gringo" whom they feared and disliked. Indians and Mexicans, forming the large majority of the population, did not "need" the Jew as a target; it was the "gringo," whatever his origin, whom they regarded as the enemy. Actually, Jews were prominent among the white settlers in the city. Yet no evidence points to their exclusion from the American settlers' community, nor does any sign indicate that the Jews were outsiders to those who, after all, were themselves outsiders in the town of the 1850's. This simple acceptance of Jews at all levels may hold true during the founding period of other nineteenth-century American cities.[52]

Jews moved freely in the hectic, unsettled society of the period. They did not seek protective coloration by imitating the appearances of the general environment. Louis "Chino" Phillips, whom Horace Bell described as a Jew more Mexican in his behavior than the Mexicans, was a violent exception.[53] The Jew himself remained a fully accepted but sharply defined and identifiable person. Judge Benjamin Hayes referred to his fellow passengers aboard a stage coach for San Bernardino as "Letha, Alice Ballou, Grewald and child, and two Jews." On his return Hayes again listed his companions, this time noticing that "a Jewess on the stage was Mrs. Cohn."[54] They were immediately identifiable as Jews without further embellishment. A traveler in the early 1860's described Los Angeles as "a city of 3,500 or 4,000 inhabitants . . . a mixture of old Spanish, Indian, American, and German Jews."[55] Presumably the French, Italians, and Germans were subsumed as "Americans," but not the French and German Jews. The townsfolk's interest in the Jew, as well as the respect of the local editors for their Jewish clientele, is indicated by the coverage given to news about Jews or news of

Jewish interest. In 1853 the *Star* somewhat foreshadowed Zionism when it reported in garbled fashion that "remarkable change is in progress among the Jews in every country, owing to a manuscript being largely circulated by an influential rabbi, proving from the scriptures, that the time has come when the Jews must set about making preparations for returning to the land of their fathers."[56]

Agitation for a Sunday closing law, which would give some legal semblance to a Christian Sabbath in the rough communities of California, began in 1853. A Jewish newspaper observed with displeasure "that the spirit of religious aggrandizement on the part of certain sects, is witnessed also in California which manifests itself in a compulsory observance of the Sunday. We hope that no obstacles will be fastened on Jews who keep holy the Sabbath Day."[57] Assembly Speaker William W. Stow's contribution to the debate in 1855 on a bill to close all stores on Sunday in Santa Clara and Santa Cruz counties was most disturbing. Stow, a resident of Santa Cruz, attacked the Jews as undesirable citizens, and suggested that measures be taken to drive them out of the state. He declared that Jews came to California only to make money and then leave, not to invest their money within the state nor build fine stores. He proposed that they be taxed so highly that they would be forced out of business.

The Speaker's diatribe aroused a storm of protest in San Francisco and in Sacramento but apparently not in Los Angeles. True, Henry Labatt, an attorney and brother of S. K. Labatt, replied in the *Los Angeles Star*, which also commented editorially: "Such bigoted views show an intolerance entirely adverse to the spirit and character of our institutions." It supported Sunday closing, however, and had "no doubt that a large portion of our Jewish citizens here and throughout the state would sanction and support a bill that was uniform in its operations."[58] Yet there is no record that the Jews of Los Angeles took any notice of Stow's performance, although his words and proposal must have outraged them. The only local allusion is in Michaels' letter to the local paper during his dispute with Labatt.

The *Star* continued its catering to the interest in Jews when it explained to its readers at length the differences between the terms Israelite, Hebrew, and Jew. After mentioning that "Hebrew" came from "passing over," and "Israel" from the "wrestling of the angel with Jacob," and "Jew" from "Judah," it concluded that "Hebrew" today refers mostly to the language, and that "Jew" is generally a term of reproach, while "Israelites" is used in "a respectful address to the nation."[59] Next the *Star* reprinted a long panegyric upon the Jews, confident that "the following just and beautiful tribute to our Jewish fellow citizens will be read with admiration by every person possessing the enlarged ideas, the generous impulses, that constitute the true American."[60] One can assume from the fulsome introduction that some in Los Angeles were lacking in the "generous impulses," the "enlarged ideas." The *Southern Vineyard's* reprint of an article entitled, "What Jews Can Do Besides Make Money," also might well have reflected local attitudes.[61]

Lewis Franklin of San Diego wrote to J. L. Morris in Los Angeles of an "anti-Semitic" incident in his town, whose significance lay not in the act but in the Jewish reaction which it provoked. The letter began: "I know not what feeling mostly activates me in recapitulating to you the occurrences which have disgraced civilization in this remote little town of San Diego. Were I to say that unmitigated disgust fills my bones I would scarcely express myself, as a wrong I shall here relate to you, *knows no parallel in the annals* of the civilized world—and I, in common with all my co-religionists, call upon you to give publicity in the matter, so that the perpetrators may be marked with the rebuke of scorn by a free and independent press." The letter described a group at worship on Rosh Hashanah 1858, which included one Moses Menasse, a pioneer agriculturist of the San Diego territory engaged in grape growing, who had traveled fifty miles to attend. A deputy sheriff appeared and requested Menasse to testify before the grand jury. Menasse replied that he was engaged in worship. The deputy shortly returned with a subpoena, but the assemblage insisted that Menasse was needed for the prayer quorum and that serving a subpoena in a synagogue was improper. The deputy presently reappeared with a posse, forced the door, and took Menasse. He was brought before the grand jury but refused to be sworn, and was put in custody of the sheriff, who released him on his own recognizance. Menasse returned after sundown and answered the routine questions. "We lay this communication before our readers to acquaint them with one case out of several of a similar nature which lately transpired in California."[62]

The unrestrained anger of the Jewish citizenry over this minor incident exemplifies the forthright self-assertion of the Jew in frontier society. He expected to be identified as a Jew but vigorously resented and resisted any invidious consequences which might stem from this distinction. Lewis Franklin was not aware of hyperbole in declaring that this case "had no parallel in the annals of the civilized world." In their righteous indignation these Jews were worthy inhabitants of the egalitarian Western frontier.

The Political Arena

The Jews' economic interests led them naturally into the political life of the community, the fraternal life of the lodges, and the social life of the clubs. They were active in politics, for the most part as ardent Democrats. As early as 1852 a public meeting called to ratify the presidential nominees of the Democratic Party, Pierce and King, had as its vice-presidents Moses Norton and Arnold Jacobi.[63] This sympathy of Los Angeles Jews for the Democrats was to become a public issue during the tense days of the Civil War.

Jews were especially prominent in local politics. In the very first city council elected in 1850 sat M. L. Goodman, one of the first eight Jews.[64] In 1853 Arnold Jacobi, another of the original eight, was also elected to the council. One year later, Solomon Lazard (1826-1916), who was to combine business with civic interests through a long and full life, was elected for the first of many times. Lazard, born in Alsace in 1826, left France at the age of seventeen. He clerked in New York for two years, then went to New Orleans and remained in business there until 1851, when he and four friends sailed for California by way of the Isthmus of Panama. From San Francisco he proceeded to Sacramento and thence to San Jose, sojourning briefly in San Diego and Stockton before he reached Los Angeles, where his wanderings ended. He opened a dry goods store on the corner of Aliso and Los Angeles Streets, where he began his successful mercantile career.[65] In the city elections of 1858, Solomon Lazard was appointed inspector of elections, a far from honorary position. Considering how votes were bought and sold, how Indians were corralled and served intoxicants until the polls opened and then delivered in carts to vote, only a man of courage and integrity could serve.[66] When the first military company was formed in 1853 to bring law and order into the wild city, Lazard was third lieutenant. After the Mountain Meadow massacres of 1857, when fear of a

Mormon invasion from Salt Lake City gripped Los Angeles, the Union Guards were formed and Lazard became first lieutenant.[67]

In 1859, Maurice Kremer (1826-1907), a cousin of Lazard, began his long political and civic career by winning election as treasurer of Los Angeles County, holding office until 1865. In that year, he paid $1,239 income tax, the highest of any Los Angeles Jew. It may be he really had the highest income, or that in his exposed position he was most scrupulous.[68] Also in 1865 Kremer was elected a county supervisor, and a year later, president of the board. In 1868 he ran successfully for the city council and subsequently became city clerk.

Kremer was one of several Jews who were politically prominent during the Civil War years. From 1850 until 1880, in fact, there was hardly a year without one Jew and sometimes two serving on the city council or the board of supervisors of Los Angeles County,[69] not to mention those who ran for office unsuccessfully. Jews did not function in politics as Jews. Many had links with the German group which at times operated a political caucus. In 1855, for example, the Germans met and officially nominated Felix Bachman to the city council and Charles Schachno as county assessor.[70]

Several reasons may explain Jewish political leadership. They were among the respected elements of society, merchants and men of affairs well-known and respected by the Mexican population. For business reasons many Jews learned Spanish, which further attracted the Spanish-speaking voter. Furthermore, the Jews' not insignificant numbers could mean a certain number of votes when, as during the Civil War period, three hundred votes could elect a city councilman and seven hundred to eight hundred could bring into office a supervisor of Los Angeles County.[71] Finally, the ancient rabbinic principle, "where there is no man one must strive to be a man," had its application on the Western frontier. The community was rough, lawless, untutored in government. The Jews were peaceable, intelligent, literate. They were needed in city government, and filled a vacuum which lasted until a later surge of immigration from the Midwest and the East changed the ethnic and civic complexion of the community.

The Hebrew Benevolent Society

Jewish religious services are believed to have begun some time in 1851 when the first minyan (quorum for public worship) was held.[72] One tradition states that services were held Friday nights and Saturday mornings at the home of Ephraim Greenbaum, and later at an adobe saloon owned by John Temple.[73] Marco Newmark includes in the first minyan Ephraim Greenbaum, Wolf Kalisher, Morris L. Goodman, Maurice Kremer, Solomon Lazard, Joseph P. Newmark, Herman Schlesinger, and Tobias Sherwinsky—obviously not all the known Los Angeles Jews. The Census of 1850 lists eight Jews, of whom only M. L. Goodman is mentioned by Newmark.[74] Newmark's list is either incomplete or, as likely, some Jews were not worshippers.

Religious services and Jewish life were formally organized with the arrival of Harris Newmark's uncle Joseph Newmark (1799-1881) and his family in 1854. (They brought a servant who was the first Chinese person to reside in Los Angeles.) Joseph Newmark, who had arrived in America in 1824 and resided in New York, St. Louis, and San Francisco before coming to Los Angeles, was a devout person who pioneered in organizing Jewish life wherever he was. In New York he had helped to establish the Elm Street Synagogue and later the Wooster Street Synagogue.[75] As a nonpracticing ordained rabbi, he helpfully performed rabbinical functions when necessary, and he officiated at religious services until the establishment of the B'nai B'rith Congregation in 1862 and the arrival of Rabbi A. W. Edelman to occupy the pulpit.

In Los Angeles, considering especially the physical insecurity and high infant mortality, the immediate need was a cemetery. The society which would maintain it could also look to the welfare of the rapidly growing Jewish population. S. N. Carvalho also interested himself in the establishment of a Jewish society. The Jews of the area were invited to meet at the home of Joseph Newmark, where on June 24, 1854, they formed a Gemilat Chesed, modeled after its counterparts all over the world. The name was rendered in English as Hebrew Benevolent Society. The incorporation records of Los Angeles County preserve the following record of the founding:

I, Samuel Labatt, do hereby certify that the following named persons, to wit: Samuel K. Labatt, Charles Schachno, Jacob Elias, H. Goldberg, J. L. Morris, J. J. Labatt, H. J. Labatt, E. Laventhal, C. Behrendt, H. Newmark, A. Brun, L. Brun, Alexander Ephraim, Moritz B. Ephraim and Simon Ferner, Israelites of the city of Los Angeles, have formed themselves into a society for the purpose of procuring a piece of land for the burying ground for the deceased of their own faith, and also to appropriate a portion of their time and means to the holy cause of benevolence under the name and style "Hebrew Benevolent Society of Los Angeles," to be managed by a president and vice-president, and three trustees, who together shall constitute a Board of Trustees.

And I further certify, that the 2nd day of July, 1854, the above named persons in the city of Los Angeles, proceeded to organize said society by the appointment of Samuel K. Labatt, as Chairman of said meeting and unanimously adopted by-laws and constitution, and in pursuance thereof, proceeded to elect officers and trustees of said society, and that said Samuel K. Labatt, Chairman as aforesaid, acted as Judge of said election.

And I also certify that at said election, Samuel K. Labatt was chosen president of said society, Charles Schachno was chosen vice-president, and S. Lazard, H. Goldberg, and Isaac Elias were chosen trustees, who were duly elected a Board of Trustees for said society the ensuing year, and that Jacob Elias was also chosen secretary and treasurer.

In testimony whereof, I have hereto as Chairman of said meeting and judge of said election, set my hand and seal, this 2nd day of July, 1854.

[Here the signature of S. K. Labatt is affixed.]

The *Los Angeles Star* of July 8, 1854 published a laconic notice: "The Israelites of this city have formed themselves into a society under the name of Hebrew Benevolent Society. At a meeting held on the 21st inst., the following gentlemen were elected, the first officers of the society: S. K. Labatt, president, Charles Schachno, vice-president, Jacob Elias, secretary and treasurer, S. Lazard and H. Goldberg, trustees." Thirty names are appended to the published constitution and by-laws.

At least twenty-eight other Jews who lived in Los Angeles did not become charter members.[76] Why did so many not join this first association of Jews in southern California? The initiation fee and the monthly dues may have deterred them, but this is doubtful in view of the prosperity of the time. Probably more important was the lack of urgency in an institution created, in a community of the young and unmarried, to meet the costs of death. For parents, however, the need for a cemetery was more poignant. Thus, from 1854 until 1873, only three of the twenty-eight burials were of persons twenty-one years and over, and the oldest was only forty years of age. Although charity during good times would be of minor interest, the purchase of burial ground symbolically indicates that a person has decided on his home town. Jews, therefore, probably joined the Hebrew Benevolent Society only when they married or felt "settled." The listing of Jewish residents also indicates how considerable was the proportion of Jews in the total population of the town. A community of at least sixty male adults and an unknown though much smaller number of wives and children comprised a sizable portion of the white population and an even more substantial proportion of its "gringo" element.[77] The list of founders of the Hebrew Benevolent Society also demonstrates that residents of San Bernardino and neighboring hamlets became members until they founded their own society in 1861. It is notable that the founding members felt themselves, even in the remotest West, part of the American Jewish community. They announced their establishment not only in Los Angeles but in Isaac Leeser's *Occident,* published in Philadelphia. They added their thanks to S. N. Carvalho for his valuable services in organizing the society, to which they elected him an honorary member. The hope was expressed by Leeser that other Israelites, "who are said to be quite numerous in the neighborhood of Los Angeles, will soon join in fellowship with their brethren who had for the first time associated for the purpose of charity and benevolence. We trust to hear soon of religious progress likewise."[78] It could be called progress when, in April 1855, S. K. Labatt invited bids to build a solid wall around the cemetery plot which the Hebrew Benevolent Society had purchased.[79]

The first Jewish organization inched ahead yearly. Jacob Elias became president of the Hebrew Benevolent Society in 1857, Solomon Lazard, vice-president, and Harris Newmark, secretary; Newmark, S. Meyer, and S. Prager were trustees. With the collapse of the boom in 1857, two committees became active, one for charity and another on accounts.[80] In 1859 Lazard became president and Henry Wartenberg secretary, with W. Kalisher, P. Sichel, M. Schlesinger, and Wartenberg serving as trustees.[81] A financial report for the year ending August 1859 shows that the Society began the year with $87.20 and took in eleven members during the year at $5.00, so that dues brought in $475.50. The committee on charity spent $233.50, leaving cash on hand of $384.20.[82]

The Hebrew Benevolent Society was Los Angeles' original welfare organization, the predecessor of all benevolent societies and charitable institutions, followed in order by the Masonic Lodge, Odd Fellows Lodge, Sisters of Charity, French Benevolent Society, and German Turnverein.[83]

Fraternal, Social, and Cultural Outlets

In the rough but uncomplicated life of the 1850's, the desire for an element of secrecy and color in social relationships was met by fraternal orders. The first, formed in Los Angeles on May 16, 1854, was the Masonic Lodge Number 42, whose first officers included the ubiquitous Jacob Elias as senior warden and Jacob Rich as senior deacon.[84] Elias soon became worshipful master; J. C. Morris, treasurer; and S. Prager, senior deacon.[85] When Sheriff Barton and three deputies were killed by a band of Mexican outlaws that year, Worshipful Master Elias helped to officiate at the melancholy funeral. Since there was no Protestant minister in Los Angeles at this time, Masonic rites were extended to include the non-Masonic dead. When a Vigilante Society was formed against marauding bandits, Elias was appointed to the important committee on resolutions.[86]

The Masonic Lodge provided some desirable social activities in a town all too full of dubious diversions. In June 1855, for example, the Masons celebrated St. John's Day. The members proceeded from the lodge room in full regalia and marched through Principal, Commercial, and Los Angeles Streets to the home of J. P. Newmark. There they sat down to a supper which for "elegance, taste and delicacy reflected highest credit on Mr. and Mrs. Newmark and would have won the praise of the most fastidious."[87] The Jews continued in Los Angeles, as elsewhere in the United States, to be active in Masonic life.[88] One year after the Masons organized, the first local lodge (No. 35) of the Independent Order of Odd Fellows was formed, of which Morris L. Goodman was a founder; Jews for years were also prominent in the I.O.O.F.[89] In 1859 the first German society was organized, called the Teutonia Verein. Among the charter members were M. Kremer, V. Cohn, and I. Fleishman. Germanic qualifications must have been subordinated to choral requirements, because M. Kremer was a Frenchman.[90]

Although most inhabitants of Los Angeles were unlettered, there were some "whose literary tastes were both catholic and discriminating; and the few newspapers published in southern California, notwithstanding novel and at times insuperable handicaps, maintained a higher standard and reflected a far more cosmopolitan point of view than most small town newspapers of the East and Middle West."[91] This intellectual and literary core founded a Library Association in 1859. Reading rooms were opened, and townspeople could join upon the substantial contribution of five dollars, and one dollar a month as dues. Books were to be contributed by members. Among the leading sponsors of the project were Felix Bachman, M. J. Newmark, and Israel Fleishman, who served as secretary of the Association.[92] However, the demand for cultural facilities was premature, failing to gain community support, and the project was abandoned until a later date. The circulating library store sufficed for the intellectuals of the town.

Social life in town was as full-blooded and intense as could be expected of a vigorous, variegated citizenry. Here is a vivid description from the pen of Horace Bell:

The Fandango is in full blast. The musicians seated in one corner of the room perform on the harp, guitar, violin, and flageolet, and make very good music for the initiated; but to the *gringo,* somewhat discordant. . . . The room is packed to its utmost capacity, a waltz is going on, gaudily dressed *rancheros,* fashionable and unfashionable gamblers, store clerks, county officials, and well-to-do merchants, with representatives from all lands under the sun, except China. . . . a brilliant array of Rangers, with quite a sprinkling of Jews and one or two young army officers, went to make up the male part of the fandango, while the female part of the house consisted of a brilliantly gaudy crowd of *señoritas* of various hues, ranging all the way from a beautiful brunette to the regular black diamond.[93]

In 1857 the Harmony Club was established, consisting of unmarried men. One of its by-laws provided a "sudden death"—the first member to marry would automatically terminate the club. By 1862 E. Laventhal could no longer restrain his romantic impulses, and upon his marriage the club dutifully disbanded.[94]

Despite this easygoing social life and a predominance of male Jews and shortage of Jewish girls, the records indicate that there was little marriage with Gentiles. There were cases of Jewish men marrying non-Jewish girls, but by and large, the Jewish opposition to intermarriage made this act unusual. The marriage records of Los Angeles County from 1858 to 1876 show seventeen marriages involving Jews. Seven were performed by Joseph Newmark, six by Rabbi Edelman, and four (obviously intermarriages) by pastors or justices of the peace. Those who went east or to San Francisco to marry almost always wedded Jewish girls.[95] There is also evidence that some men kept mistresses. This was not extraordinary in the free life of the times, but these liaisons only infrequently led to marriage. There are also indications that ardent Gentile suitors were stung by rebuffs from Jewish maidens, who had, after all, many eligible Jewish suitors. Jewish restraints were evidently still effective even on the wild frontier.

CHAPTER 2

Disaster and Recovery: 1860-1880

———————————————————>•<———————————————————

Los Angeles prospered during its first years as an American city. But this auspicious early period ended in 1857, as the inhabitants were stricken by a series of natural and man-made afflictions which blighted the town until 1865. Los Angeles emerged from this time of troubles spent and virtually bankrupt.

The cattle boom ended in 1857 as demand dropped and animals began to be brought to northern California from Missouri and Texas. A regional drought decimated the herds. The economically inexperienced rancheros lay deep in debt, most of it contracted during flush times to meet the costs of litigation over vague land titles and to pay taxes imposed by the new state legislature. At the exorbitant interest required of them in the cash-short region, it was not long before the rancheros were ruined and lost their lands to their creditors, a few of whom were Jews. The collapse of the cattle economy was soon followed by a series of debilitating natural disasters. While the Civil War was being fought thousands of miles to the east, California underwent a prolonged flood at the beginning of 1862 which also devastated the Los Angeles area, carrying away hundreds of homes, gardens, and vineyards. The year closed, and 1863 continued, with a smallpox epidemic which ravaged the town, especially its Mexican and Indian population. The iron chain of disaster continued with a drought lasting three years. When the inhabitants who had not quit the town in fear and despair at last saw rain, the cattle were dead and the pastoral economy ended forever.

From its nadir of 1865, Los Angeles began the slow climb upwards. Immigration resumed with the end of the Civil War, and very gradually an agricultural economy, and especially viticulture, developed. The beginnings of responsible commercial banking date to the 1870's, about the same time the railroad came to Los Angeles. These two accomplishments gradually ended the town's anarchic business conditions and its isolation from the rest of the country.

Needless to say, Los Angeles' Jews were affected by these misfortunes, as depression, epidemic, and drought struck them also. On the other hand, the contribution of Jewish citizens to the advent of banking and railroads was of conspicuous importance.[1]

Depression, Epidemic, and Drought

During the cattle boom there had been plenty of cash to keep the rancheros in the expansive, carefree life they knew. But their ignorance of money as a weapon proved their undoing when times became bad. They borrowed money from the "gringo" at rates from 3% to 10% a month, compounded monthly, mortgaging their properties. When the seductively easy credit reached mountainous heights of debt, the rancheros uncomprehendingly saw their millions of acres taken from them.

Some Jewish "gringos" were among the creditors. Julio Verdugo's Rancho San Rafael, covering 36,000 acres (approximately today's Glendale), stood behind its owner's note for $3,445 in favor of Jacob Elias, signed January 2, 1861. The rate was a relatively low 3% monthly. Eight years later, judgment was secured in the amount of $56,000, and Rancho San Rafael was auctioned.[2] Ricardo Vejar, owner of the San José ranch around today's Pomona, found himself $28,000 in debt to Isaac Schlesinger and Hyman Tischler in 1864. After years of disasters, Don Ricardo despairingly deeded his lands to the two creditors, as "bitterness swept the whole Pomona Valley."[3] Schlesinger and Tischler never enjoyed their prize. The former had died in a steamship explosion in 1863, and the latter, to whom Schlesinger's heirs turned over the rights, narrowly escaped being murdered, and sold out to Louis "Chino" Phillips.[4] Rancho San José was the basis of Phillips' wealth, which ultimately earned him the reputation of the richest man in the city.[5] For a mere $1,528 debt to Bachman & Co., Henry Dalton's 8,000-acre Rancho San Francisquito was auctioned off in 1865.[6] Years later, Bernard Cohn moved to foreclose the Pio Pico ranch; that is discussed elsewhere. These are all the known cases of Jewish participation in the expropriation of the rancheros. If Horace Bell's observation is true, that "any of the alien population would credit [the rancheros], especially the Jew peddler and shopkeeper,"[7] Jewish lending must have been in small amounts soon paid, or the Jewish lenders remarkably forgiving men. An encomium upon the Jews in 1869, which notwithstanding its eulogistic tone deserves to be taken seriously, referred to the expro-priation: "Mercilessly and remorselessly have confiding Californians been plucked of their substance in this city but it is not the Jew under guise of favor and friendship who has wrested from them fair and hereditary possessions by extortionate rates of interest—rates that have absorbed valuable ranches in a year or two."[8]

During the difficult days in the late 1850's and early 1860's every merchant was struggling to survive. Some gave up and left town. Thus, Jacob Elias advertised in 1857: "Last Call! Persons indebted to Jacob Elias will please make settlement within thirty days or otherwise they will find them in the hands of an attorney for col-lection. Any person having claims against him will present them for payment as he will be leaving for the Atlantic states."[9] In July 1861, Elias was back from New York with a supply of goods at all prices, "which if we are to judge by the hardness of the times and the stringency of the money market, must be low indeed."[10] His adver-tisement six weeks after his return poignantly reflects the local state of affairs: "I will take almost anything in exchange for goods, gold dust, silver, woolhides, wheat, corn, barley, U.S. drafts, state, county and city script, and bonds, horses, mules, and sheep. Will transact a brokerage and commission business and will make liberal cash advances on real estate and personal property."[11]

While Jacob Elias was still in New York, notices of liquidation con-tinued to appear with distressing frequency.[12] Felix Bachman held out longer, but adversities and the alleged influence of his wife at last made him give up in 1864: "For many years Bachman and Com-pany was the leading mercantile house of this city. Mr. Bachman, head of the firm, now leaves on a visit to his friends and his early home. . . . his temporary absence is regretted by a host of friends who united in wishing him a happy sojourn and a quick return."[13] But Bachman finally settled in San Francisco and died a poor man.[14] David Solomon, selling out in 1865, publicly explained that he was "selling his goods cheap on account of his health being so poor and wishing to take his family to San Francisco."[15]

There were certainly many who feared for their own and their families' health after the smallpox epidemic. During its duration, a pesthouse was established in Chavez Ravine which overflowed with patients brought in and drawn out. In March 1863 the disease abated, "for want of further material to work upon."[16] The Hebrew

Benevolent Society undertook charitable collections and turned over its own treasury to provide nourishment for the indigent sick,[17] winning commendation for "practical philanthropy.... This unostentatious charity reflects highest credit on the members of the society."[18] In the same vein, the Board of Health thanked it for "materially mitigating the suffering of the indigent sick." How many Jews fell victim to the plague is not known. Years later, the *Star* reported, "It may not be generally known to either the Hebrew or the other population of this city that the Jews as a race [thanks to the hygienic and dietary habits] have hardly ever lost any lives by the smallpox, although there have been two Jewish lives lost by that fell complaint in this city."[19]

Most merchants did not give up, but reshuffled their partnerships and started again. At least thirty-three dissolutions of partnership between 1851 and 1859 involved Jews, and twenty more occurred between 1860 and 1869. The index of civil cases from 1854 through 1863 records over one hundred suits with Jews as plaintiffs—a strong suggestion of commercial strain and tightness.[20] During the drought years, when land was the cheapest, least needed commodity, tracts later worth millions were sold at auction for the few dollars of tax lien. An oft-repeated story tells of Mayor Joel Turner auctioning lots on the steps of City Hall when Harris Newmark, a passer-by, heard a bid of $7.00 and playfully bid $7.50, not even knowing what he was bidding for. Newmark found himself possessor of twenty acres in the Wilshire district, which he subsequently sold for $10,000.[21] Dr. John Griffin accepted 2,000 acres as payment in full for his services during the epidemic.[22] When he later sold part of his holdings at $7.50 an acre to a group of Indiana colonists bent on establishing a town to be called Pasadena, this ex-Southerner gloated, "This is once where I got the best of those damn Yankees."[23]

Civil War

The Civil War was fought far from California, but it rent the state. Northern California was Unionist in sympathy, while southern California favored the South. The *Los Angeles Star* spoke for most of the townspeople: "We are on the highway to and from the south. Our emigration came from the south; our population is of the south and sympathizes with her. Why then should we turn our backs on our friends and join their enemies to invade, impoverish and despoil them?"[24] The secessionist *Star*'s viewpoint was countered by the Unionism of the *Semi-Weekly Southern News*, which had the field to itself while the *Star* ceased publication from 1864 to 1868.

Unionists were active in keeping an eye on the citizenry of dubious loyalty. As each element of the "gringo" population (Mexicans and Indians did not count) was scrutinized for its attachment to the Union cause, the local Jews also came under examination. Edwin A. Sherman, editor of the short-lived Unionist *Weekly Patriot* in San Bernardino, reported confidentially to General Sumner of the Pacific Division of the Union Army on the composition of local secessionist sentiment. They were mostly "Mormons, Mormon Apostates (who are even worse), gamblers, English Jews and the devil's own population to boot."[25] Sumner responded to Sherman's pleas for a show of Union force by dispatching a Major Carleton to San Bernardino. Carleton reported that of the approximately 1,500 inhabitants of the town about 1,000 were Mormons. "The remainder consisted of a few respectable Americans, and a good many Jew merchants *who control the business of the town and go along with any side that pays best for the time being.*"[26] To omit his prejudice, Carleton was reporting that neither Union nor disunion, much less slavery or freedom, was the issue with the Jews. They were devoted citizens less of their country than of their town, and like the majority of American Jews during the Civil War period, took the side of the area in which they lived.[27]

In Los Angeles, where the Jews were a valued and substantial segment of the American population, it was important if possible to stir their patriotic feelings for the Union cause. Thus on July 24, 1861, the *News* printed a melodramatic story of a Jew who disowned one of his two sons when he took up Confederate arms. It concluded with the father's declaration: "'I disown you. No traitor shall bear my name. I have but one wish left—that if my loyal son goes into battle, the first bullet he shall send against the enemy may pierce you to the heart.'" Such lurid fiction failed of its purpose, for the state and county elections in the fall of 1861 fulfilled the Unionists' fears as the Democrats swept to victory in Los Angeles. The *News* (September 6, 1861), appalled at the outcome, turned in anger upon Jewish Democrats:

The Union party has been utterly defeated in this country. Secession and disunion have carried the day and years of repentance cannot wash away the stain. . . . Nearly the whole of the Jewish population of this city voted the secessionist ticket, and we sincerely believe many of them will live to rue the day they did so. That a foreigner should come from a land of tyranny and oppression to a free and enlightened republic, from a land where he is no better than a serf, having no choice in the selection of his rulers; should come here and give his vote and influence against our government and in favor of the same state of affairs he left behind in the old world, seems passing strange.

One can imagine the anger this editorial aroused, especially among the Jews. Next day the Democratic *Star* reproved the *News:*

The glorious result of the late election has not been allowed to pass without an attempt, a weak one it is true, to awaken prejudice against a religious sect of our fellow citizens. This effort to add religious animosity to political partisanship meets with the disapprobation of the community at large. Why Jews more than Protestants, Catholics or Presbyterians should be stigmatized for voting the Democratic ticket is more than we can imagine; and we merely notice the matter here to give expression to the general feeling of disapproval and contempt which the silly remark has called forth.

Jews and other "foreigners" were determined to pursue the matter, and a serious course of action was decided upon. As the *News* itself curtly announced:

On Saturday last we received the following document by the hands of Mr. F. Lecouver, clerk of the house of Bachman and Company:—

Editor, Southern News: We, the undersigned, herewith withdraw our subscriptions to the Southern News and any and all of our respective advertisements from and after today.

Thirty German and Jewish names were affixed to this damaging statement. But the *News* stood its ground, warning and exhorting:

It is not denied that nearly the whole of the Jewish population voted the disunion ticket. . . . How strange does it seem then, that foreign born citizens should give their newly acquired vote and influence against the free and liberal government now in existence, and favor the schemes of Davis and his co-conspirators. . . . The charge that we have desired to awaken religious persecution against those of the Jewish faith is false. We mention them because, *comprising so large a body of our voting population, they had nearly all voted the disunion ticket.* We chronicled the fact and it has not been nor cannot be denied. We advocate the rights of all men under the Constitution and Government of the United

States, but when the foreign born citizen violates his most solemn oath; when he turns against the Constitution which he has solemnly sworn to support, then he is to be despised.

The *News* flung before its thirty boycotters a list of thirty San Francisco bankers and merchants, twenty-two of them apparently Jewish, "who had closed their business on election day to devote themselves to the polls, to the interest of their country, their creed being the Constitution, the Union. . . . What a contrast did our city present on the day of election, many of the merchants voting for the secession ticket."[28]

Flood, epidemic, and withering drought had to be survived, and the Civil War seemed remote and lacking in interest. Men held to their sympathies but did little if anything to further the cause, particularly with a Union garrison close at hand. Some secessionists' joy at the news of Lincoln's assassination was muted by the presence of troops. Young Henry Baer dashed into the street cheering when he heard the news, for which his father thrashed him, "an act nearly breaking up the Baer family, as Mrs. Baer was a pronounced secessionist."[29]

On April 17, 1865, the city council passed appropriate memorial resolutions, and on the following day the officers of the Jewish congregation met to plan their participation in the next day's public exercises. They also arranged a Jewish service for that day in Rabbi Edelman's house. Evidently this was a rarely conducted weekday service, with special mention of the assassinated President. A fitting resolution was also drawn up:

RESOLVED, That with feelings of deepest regret, we deplore the loss that our country has sustained in the untimely end of our late President, but as it has pleased the Almighty to deprive this country of its Chief and great friend, we have to bow with submission to his Divine Will.

RESOLVED, That the great calamity, the death of Abraham Lincoln, leaves a void which is not easily filled.

RESOLVED, That we will, in a body, join the procession.

RESOLVED, That the above proceedings be published in the Los Angeles News and the Wilmington Journal.

M. Kremer
Secretary, pro. tem.[30]

Thus, on Tuesday, April 18, 1865, Los Angeles Jews first held services and then joined in procession with city officials, patriotic and benevolent societies, and the United States mounted cavalry.[31] This was the solemn end of the Civil War.

Sympathy for the South continued in Los Angeles, with Jewish participation. Jews stood in the forefront of the 1867 drive for the Southern Relief Fund, and their ladies were prominent in arranging a fair for it. $2,000 in gold was raised, a sum which the treasurer, Phillip Sichel, rightly described as a "very creditable showing for the community, which has labored for many years under serious disadvantages and difficulties threatening at times to retard our program forever and cause our city to sink into utter insignificance. Our dark days seem to be over, and we acknowledge the dawning of our prosperity upon our valley by giving of our worldly goods to aid those of our countrymen in the south who are suffering want."[32]

Post-War Revival

Sichel rightly viewed the fine showing of the Southern Relief Fund not only as a sign of the townspeople's generosity, but also as thankfulness for the renewed "dawning of our prosperity."[33] The close of the Civil War coincided with the end of the three-year drought. Immigration resumed, especially from the defeated South. Already there was publicity in the East, even reaching Europe, about southern California's wondrous climate and soil. Huge overland trains, containing as many as five hundred persons and a hundred wagons, started the trek to Los Angeles in 1868. This influx of settlers, most of them small farmers, helped to revive business and real estate. Irrigation and diversified farming constantly increased, while an ampler supply of money lowered interest levels. Of the 5,600 persons in the city and 15,000 in the county in 1870, perhaps 150 were Jewish.[34]

Despite this progress, Los Angeles was far from being a civilized city. The wine and brandy produced in the area, and whiskey as well, were sometimes more available than water; drunkenness was extremely common. Gambling and prostitution and a hell-roaring time were available to all who wanted them, while robbery and theft were frequent. Small wonder that men wore arms as part of their daily attire, disregarding city council ordinances to the contrary.[35] Merchants were always on guard against "light fingered gents" who prowled among stores at night. Malefactors had been warned that unless they "keep a sharp lookout, the vigilance and perseverance of the sheriff will yet overcome them and bring them to justice."[36] This did not always deter criminals. Thus, Moritz Morris, who owned reputedly the largest vineyard in Los Angeles, found his house plundered down to the bedding when he returned with his family from worship on Rosh Hashanah, 1865. One culprit was seized while wearing one of Morris' suits, complete with monogrammed shirt. Another was apprehended in San Francisco, while attempting to dispose of a silver pitcher engraved "Congregation B'nai B'rith" to a pawnbroker who had been one of the congregation that had presented this pitcher to Morris several years before.[37] Still more serious was the matter of the Brun brothers, charter members of the Hebrew Benevolent Society, one a merchant in San Bernardino and the other a peddler. The latter was murdered one day and J. R. Brun, the surviving brother, devoted years to searching vainly for the murderer.[38]

As citizens profoundly interested in the security of their property and the safety of their persons, Jews regularly served on grand juries. Year by year, usually three Jewish Los Angelenos could be found sitting. Perhaps it is significant that the grand jurors after the infamous Chinese massacre of 1871 included five Jews.[39] Los Angeles Jews' main interest, of course, remained business. After the Civil War, real estate could no longer be had almost for the asking, as land purchases for home building and farming surged. Five Jewish businessmen established the Aliso Homestead Association in 1869, selling off building lots of 50' x 140' for $480, payable at $10 monthly, interest-free.[40] I. W. Hellman bought and subdivided a 2,000 acre tract.[41] While these men were looking forward to immigrants erecting dwellings, Wolf Kalisher sought to profit from converting ranch land to farming. He bought a section of the Rancho Santa Gertrudes consisting of 800 acres and an adobe house. A few years later, however, he offered it for sale "on account of the owner having large bands of wild mares and horses which he can no longer keep running at large as heretofore and therefore [is] obliged to remove them to some remote, unsettled place."[42] Next year, in 1871, Kalisher established Los Angeles' first tannery; perhaps we may infer from this his disposition of the troublesome horses.[43] In 1869, a syndicate of San Francisco Jews together with Isaac Lankershim, the convert to Christianity, entered the Los Angeles land market on a grandiose scale by buying for $115,000 part of the San Fernando Ranch. They stocked their land with sheep, but Lankershim later rented land from his partners to become southern California's first large wheat rancher.[44]

The pursuits of Los Angeles Jews during the decade between the close of the Civil War and the brief depression of 1875 may be seen from data in *An Historical Sketch of Los Angeles County, California,* published by Louis Lewin in 1876. The *City Directory* of the previous year listed 103 apparently Jewish businessmen, while Lewin estimated about 600 Jews in the town and specified the occupations of 98:

Dry goods, clothing, general merchandise retail stores	31
Commission merchant, wholesale	11
Clerks and salesmen	20
Liquor, wine, saloon	7
Tailoring	6
Cigars and tobacco	5
Books and stationery	2
Furniture	2
Hotel keeper	2
Paint and oils	2
City Clerk	2
Banker, pawnbroker, clergyman, attorney, newspaper man, shoe store, milliner, capitalist (one of each)	8

It is instructive to compare this Jewish list with that for the population as a whole:[45]

Carpenters	107
Fruit dealers	72
Attorneys at law	50
Blacksmiths	43
Clothing, dry goods	37
Printers	33
Physicians	32
Boots and shoes	30
Butchers	30
Teachers	28
Wagon and carriage makers	28
Saddle and harness makers	27
Upholsterers	23
House and sign painters	23
Clergymen	22
Livery feed and sale	22

The Jews thus ·dominated the occupational classifications in which
they were found. Simply, they were the merchants on Main Street.

Jewish business and partners changed frequently, as had indeed
been true from the earliest days, but clothing, most of it made in
San Francisco, was usually the Jewish merchant's main stock. Nathan
Jacoby, who had come to Los Angeles with his brothers Lesser,
Charles, Abraham, Herman, and Morris, joined Leopold Harris in
1870 in purchasing H. W. Hellman's clothing store, and set up in
business as Harris and Jacoby.[46] Harris left the firm five years later
and founded the Quincy Hall Clothing Company. Eventually his
son-in-law H. W. Frank joined him, and the Harris and Frank chain
of clothing stores was thus born.[47] The firm which Leopold Harris
had quit, now called Jacoby Brothers, prospered greatly; it employed
more than twenty clerks.[48] A. Portugal and H. Kraushaar, who had
left town during bad times, now returned and reentered the clothing
business.[49] J. Strelitz, a merchant tailor, opened his shop in 1870, and
later built a block of stores.[50] In 1874, Emanuel Cohen and Alexander
Davis opened their "identical" clothing store with brass band and
panoply, and included cigars and tobacco in stock.[51] There were
many more Jews in the clothing business, singly or in partnership.

In the remote, dusty town, merchants attempted to add a dash of
fashion and glamor to attract customers. Sometimes they named
their store after a great European city. The first and largest to be
renamed was Lazard and Company, which became the City of Paris
when Solomon Lazard retired from it in 1874. His former partner
Eugene Meyer and brother Constant Meyer made theirs one of the
leading stores of Los Angeles.[52] Joseph Cohn, who bought out the
distressed David Solomon in 1865, tried to compete with his City of
Lyons, and M. Hoff was proprietor of a City of Berlin a few years
later.[53] Mendel Meyer, who for a while tried to earn his livelihood as
a local violinist, was proprietor of the Vienna Exposition Store,
purveying dress goods.[54]

There were businesses operated by Jewish women. Flora Cohn
petitioned for the legal right to function as a Sole Trader, while
Mrs. H. Cohn had a ladylike trade in "fashionable millinery, dress,
cloak maker and dealer in fancy goods."[55] A Mrs. Goldstein's private
boarding house was also popular as a meeting place for organizations
and parties—probably a forerunner of today's catering establishment.
She opened a candy, fruit, and cigar stand in 1874 and then joined

Ephraim Greenbaum and his wife in operating the newly-opened White House Hotel in 1875.[56] Greenbaum was for a time proprietor of the California Loan and Brokers Office, where he pawned, bought and sold greenbacks, gold, and silver, and advanced cash on commission.[57] This business failed to develop into a real bank, however.

Jewish businessmen also traded in foodstuffs. When John Jones and Bernard Cohn dissolved their partnership in 1871, Cohn joined Jacob Haas and H. W. Hellman in the wholesale grocery firm of Hellman, Haas and Company.[58] There were further changes among the partners before Haas, Baruch and Company emerged as one of the city's leading firms in its branch. Eugene Germain's fruit and poultry market eventually made its owner one of the foremost agricultural produce dealers in the Far West. The scope of Germain's business is suggested by his purchase in 1874 of Louis Wolfskill's entire orange crop for $250,000.[59] Some Jews became substantial agricultural producers. Simon Levy, an arrival of 1865 who was once in the cigar trade, in 1875 offered for sale at his ranch 3,000 sheep and twenty thoroughbred rams.[60] Harris Newmark, too, was a sheep rancher for a short time, but the collapse of wool prices induced him to sell out to E. J. (Lucky) Baldwin.[61] Jews participated in wine production both as growers and shippers. One Los Angeles Jewish wine merchant, Charles Stern, was the partner of L. J. Rose in Sunnyslope, a 2,000-acre vineyard near San Gabriel Mission.[62] The county's largest grape grower was the Anaheim pioneer Benjamin Dreyfus, who had 170,000 vines planted.[63] During the short-lived southern California silk boom, Jews were also involved in this fruitless venture.[64]

Various small mining enterprises in the San Gabriel Valley also found such Los Angeles Jewish merchants as Eugene Meyer, Charles Jacoby, and Solomon Lazard among the investors.[65] A more typical investment opportunity during a period of immigration was real estate in town. Louis Lewin, the printer, and Charles Jacoby were organizers of the Pioneer Lot Association, which developed the area later known as Boyle Heights.[66] Downtown, I. W. Hellman built a block in 1870 which contained three basement rooms for a saloon, three store fronts, and eighteen rooms upstairs.[67] The largest real estate purchase until its time was recorded when the Newmarks bought the Temple Block at auction in 1877, in the aftermath of the Temple-Workman bank failure. The price exceeded $131,000.[68]

The Hellmans and the Birth of Banking

In 1859 two brothers from Bavaria, aged sixteen and fifteen, who were destined to mold the financial destiny of Los Angeles, arrived in town. They were Isaias Wolf Hellman (1843-1920) and Herman Wolf Hellman (1843-1906). Their cousins I. M. and Sam Hellman, who had preceded them by a few years, met the boys and took them home. Young Isaias went to work in I. M. Hellman's general mercantile business, while his brother Herman found a job with Phineas Banning's forwarding and warehousing business, which shipped from Wilmington to Los Angeles. Drought and depression notwithstanding, I. W. Hellman saved enough money within six years to buy out Adolph Portugal, who, as we have seen, was returning to Germany. Portugal invited his patrons to call on the new proprietor for their men's clothing and haberdashery.[69]

This store was the birthplace of banking in Los Angeles. As long as it was unsafe to keep gold dust and other valuables in private houses, trusted merchants were customarily asked to act as custodians and did so as a favor. On visits to town, miners and sheepherders would often request a local friend to care for their gold while they went "on the town." Isaias Hellman was one such trusted merchant, and he had the advantage of possessing a safe. This friendly but haphazard method of safeguarding valuables could cause embarrassing incidents, one of which helped to persuade Hellman toward his career as a banker. As described by Jackson A. Graves, a long-time Hellman associate, who probably heard it from the protagonist:

These miners would get gloriously drunk and gamble. When out of funds, they would come back to him, get out the purses deposited in their respective names, take out gold dust, tie the purse up again and put it back. Finally a great big double-jointed Irishman, who had been on a glorious drunk and spent money freely, came to get the remnant of his deposit. His purse was nearly empty. He was now sober. He looked at it and, with an oath, he said: "You dirty Jew, you have stolen my gold." Fortunately, a companion, who had stayed sober, was with him, and that companion had been with him every time he opened his sack. He put his hand on Pat's arm, and said: "Pat, that will not do. It is not true. I have been with you. I told you not to drink and gamble, but you would do it. You took this gold out yourself, and you must apologize to Mr. Hellman," which he did. Mr. Hellman told me that it was against his commercial instincts to have so much gold not earning anything, and that, after this incident with the Irishman, he said to himself, "What is to prevent one of those fellows from cracking me over the head, sticking a knife into my ribs, or shooting me," and, as he was a man of peace, he cudgeled his brains what to do. This was on a Saturday. He got hold of a good friend who was running a paper, and between them they fixed up some pass-books and some deposit slips marked "I. W. Hellman, Banker." He had a carpenter fence off a corner of his store, in which he put the safe, and hung up the sign, "I. W. Hellman, Banker." The next miner who came along with gold dust was told he could not leave it there, "but," said Mr. Hellman, "I will buy your gold dust, at current rates, and I am running a bank. Here, see this book. After I buy your gold you can deposit the money with me, take this book and check it out as you please. All checks drawn on me, while your money lasts, will be paid." The scheme took and, strange to say, the miners spent much less money after they began to make the bank deposits, than they did before. Many of them left thousands and thousands of dollars with him, and when the mines gave out a great many of them bought land, built houses, barns, etc., and became prosperous farmers, and always had a high regard for Mr. Hellman.[70]

Graves concludes, "Such was I. W. Hellman's introduction to banking, without any banking training, and nothing but his hard sense and commercial instincts to guide him." Soon after, Hellman joined William Workman and F. P. F. Temple actually to enter the banking business in a building which they planned to erect.

Yet Hellman did not neglect his clothing business. In 1868 he enlarged its premises, announcing: "Most of my stock has been bought since the late decline in goods, and I am therefore enabled to sell cheaper than any house south of San Francisco."[71] But his skill in banking was becoming well known. "Mr. Hellman will, I suppose, be the business manager under whom the affairs of the [banking] establishment will no doubt be most ably conducted."[72] This was not the first bank in town, for earlier in 1868 James A. Hayward and former governor John Downey had started one. On September 1, 1868, Hellman, Temple and Company opened their doors, and next day the respectable citizenry assembled in the "bank parlor" for a grand opening, and "quaffed generous wine" to the prosperity of the new institution. They may also have admired the new building, which "marks a new era in our architectural designs, or rather it is the first building erected here with any regard to elegance."[73]

Hellman invested $25,000; each of his partners, $50,000. Hellman, Temple and Company had eighteen accounts and deposits of $38,000 on opening day, many of them carried over from the corner of Hellman's clothing store. The first religious organization to open an account was the African Methodist Episcopal Church. The bank prospered from the first: between September 1, 1869, and April 8, 1871, Hellman, Temple and Company gave 690 loans totaling $788,000. As a result of having two competing banks, the formidable rates of interest in Los Angeles were forced down to a comparatively moderate 1½% and 2½% per month.[74]

Isaias Hellman, able and ambitious, soon moved to the forefront of Los Angeles' banking scene, selling out his clothing business to Polaski and Goodwin. Neither of Hellman's partners, however, displayed his financial acuity or his prudence. John Downey at Los Angeles' other bank was meanwhile also dissatisfied with his partners. The outcome was a general shuffle by which Hellman and Downey together founded the Farmers and Merchants Bank of Los Angeles, while the combination of Temple and Workman established "The Bank, Temple and Workman." Downey was president and I. W. Hellman cashier of their new enterprise. Of the Farmers and Merchants' nine founding directors, only I. W. and his cousin I. M. Hellman were Jews; David Solomon served in 1872-1873, and Eugene Meyer from 1877 to 1879. Isaias W. Hellman thus commenced a business career unsurpassed in importance during the nineteenth-century history of Los Angeles. He was to become a director or major stockholder of twelve other local banks and was to hold innumerable other interests in commerce, real estate, and public utilities.[75] The Farmers and Merchants Bank did, however, endure a crisis during the economic slump of 1875.

Jews in the Mercantile Community

During Los Angeles' optimistic decade which ended in 1875, its merchants developed a sense of solidarity in advancing the economic fortunes of their class and city. Politics came under the lengthy domination of local business interests, especially those such as railroads and public utilities, which were affected by governmental decisions. The great need was a railroad. The all but omnipotent masters of the rails were implacable, however, in driving a bargain before bringing their lines to town. This and other mercantile interests were represented in the short-lived Board of Trade, organized in August 1873, which over one hundred merchants joined as charter members. It was renamed the Chamber of Commerce, and its president was Solomon Lazard, with M. J. Newmark and H. W. Hellman among the eleven directors. The Chamber of Commerce undertook to stimulate interest in San Pedro as a possible harbor for Los Angeles, to further trade with Arizona, and to introduce new varieties of fruit which southern California could grow.[76] For the Centennial celebrations at Philadelphia in 1876 a persuasive pamphlet was published. Its editor, Harris Newmark, believed that his effort "certainly led many Easterners to migrate West and to settle in Los Angeles and vicinity."[77]

All this was subordinate to the merchants' great purpose of bringing the railroad to Los Angeles. In 1872 Harris Newmark and John Downey met in San Francisco with Collis P. Huntington of the Southern Pacific and learned his terms.[78] A bitter local electoral contest was waged that year over the proposal that Los Angeles float twenty-year bonds, bearing 7% interest, to finance its share of the railroad bargain. On election day Dr. John S. Griffin and I. W. Hellman had an altercation during which the physician struck the banker with a cane, inflicting a deep gash. Mrs. Hellman insisted that a doctor be called, and her husband finally consented. "Whom shall I get?" she inquired. Hellman answered, "Send for old Doc Griffin, of course!"[79] Hellman healed, and the town's voters approved the flotation. When the Southern Pacific was ready to come into Los Angeles and a golden spike was to be driven at Newhall where its two sections met, Harris Newmark and Solomon Lazard well merited their membership in the city's delegation.[80]

The isolation of Los Angeles was ended, but not the city's problems with the lordly railroad. Now began a struggle against rate discrimination, for the Southern Pacific charged rates which included the return fare from San Francisco. The line ruthlessly raised its rates to shippers who resorted to the coastal steamships which it also owned. When Harris Newmark, H. W. Hellman, and others attempted to fight by chartering a tramp steamer, the Southern Pacific reduced rates on selected items, expressing readiness to lose a million dollars to break such competition. Newmark and Hellman's fellow shippers deserted them, and were compelled finally to make peace by permitting the railroad to buy out their contract with the steamer; thus ended "the first fight in Los Angeles against a railroad."[81]

The Chamber of Commerce continued until 1876. It strongly opposed the Archer Freight and Fares Bill, which incorporated freight rates discriminatory to southern California, and ultimately saw it defeated.[82] To insure that the Southern Pacific would include southern California among its destinations, it sent a telegram of "such classical eloquence that it poured seventy-five dollars into the coffers of the telegraph company.[83] But the first Chamber of Commerce, so largely a Jewish enterprise, was stricken by the depression of 1875 and lay dormant by the close of 1876. It was not to be reorganized until the boom days of 1886.[84]

Economic Setback and Recovery

As Los Angeles' remoteness from the rest of the country lessened, its implication in economic fluctuations had to increase. The nation-wide—in fact, worldwide—economic crisis which began in 1873 struck California in 1875. The Bank of California in San Francisco failed on August 26, 1875, and two commercial banks of Los Angeles, the Farmers and Merchants and the Temple and Workman, promptly suspended operations when a run began.[85] The former, however, offered to cash checks for less than $250 at the Hellman, Haas & Company office.

I. W. Hellman, whose reputation and wealth were mounting steadily during the Farmers and Merchants' prosperous years, happened to be visiting his native Germany when the panic struck. He immediately left for home when news reached him, and arrived in Los Angeles within a remarkably short twenty-three days. John Downey had meanwhile hurried to San Francisco and borrowed $200,000 at 1½% per month to enable full-scale banking operations to resume. Recovery was rapid and complete: the Farmers and Merchants reopened on October 1, displaying piles of gold coins in its windows, borrowed from San Francisco but repaid in one year. At the Temple and Workman Bank there was a tragic story. The two partners borrowed $310,000 from E. J. (Lucky) Baldwin, against all of their real estate and that of their friend Juan Sanchez. Yet within four months they closed permanently, driving the aged Workman to suicide and Temple and Sanchez to pauperdom.

Hellman, a strong, ambitious man, was now determined to become sole master at Farmers and Merchants. Reportedly he was angered at Downey's hasty closing of the bank. Probably he no longer needed the prestige or assets of the former governor, whose banking abilities were far inferior to his own. He quickly bought up enough additional bank stock to possess a majority interest and in July 1876 removed Downey from control. Hellman remained in unchallenged command of the Farmers and Merchants, even for the last thirty years of his life, which he spent in San Francisco at the head of the Wells Fargo-Nevada Bank.

As the founder of banking in southern California and probably the most important banker on the West Coast during his lifetime, Hellman was a man under public scrutiny. He was well aware of being a banker who was a Jew. Thus, mendacious stories circulated that Temple and Workman failed because its Jewish depositors intentionally withdrew their funds and made it topple. The Farmers and Merchants, as the businessman's bank, actually had most of the Jewish accounts already.[86] Jackson A. Graves tells of Hellman's leniency to debtors, and that he frequently waited to foreclose until just before the statute of limitations ran out. In reply to the attorney's remonstrances, the banker replied: "Graves, I have to be a better man than you are, because I am a Jew. You can do things that I cannot do. If I did them I would be criticized, while you will not be.... I have to keep that steadily in mind, in all my dealings."[87] Perhaps it was such considerations which caused Hellman to rebuke severely Louis "Chino" Phillips for assigning him Downey's notes of indebtedness. He declined to accept them: "I am not taking this action for the purpose of justifying myself in the eyes of Governor Downey (as it is immaterial to me what the Governor thinks or talks or writes about) but it is done for the person not to allow you or anybody else to be connected with me in basic matters and use this as a lever to hurt me and in addition thereto make statements entirely contrary to the facts."[88] As to the Farmers and Merchants, a statement by the state bank commissioner was published in 1878, testifying to its sound condition.[89] On another occasion, fifty prominent businessmen did likewise.[90]

The prudence and good fortune of the Farmers and Merchants Bank during the bank panic of 1875 did much to mitigate the worst effects of the depression in Los Angeles. However, there was considerable suffering among less fortified businessmen. Numerous merchants went bankrupt, liquidated, or retired from business. Merchants Myerstein and Winter sold out in 1875. "This is no humbug. We mean what we say," they warned.[91] Without a buyer for his business, Myerstein offered to sell his lease, fixtures, and goods. "Being it is impossible for me to get rid of my store, I have decided to liquidate my stock."[92] Elias Laventhal advertised in "philosophical" style:

Existence and life being so closely related to each other, it is important to struggle for an existence while we live. The question is: "How will you exist when you sell your goods at these low figures?" I pass in silence— determined, however, to bring a still greater sacrifice, having returned from the market with the most complete stock of dry goods, clothing, boots, shoes, and hats.[93]

But "existence" failed Laventhal in Los Angeles, and in 1877 he sold out and betook himself with Mendel Meyer to Tombstone, Arizona. There they opened a store catering to gold miners.[94] In 1879 Eugene Meyer and Company, which operated the City of Paris, also sold out. Meyer moved to San Francisco to begin the career as a banker which ultimately brought his son and namesake into the ownership of the *Washington Post* and a distinguished civic and banking career.[95]

As discouraged merchants quit or went into bankruptcy, new men appeared to start afresh. In 1877 J. H. Seligman established the IXL Auction, known in later years as Seligman's Bazaar.[96] Otto Rothschild opened the California Confectionery and Candy Factory and one of the city's first delicatessens. "In connection with the confectionery, a first class ladies and gents refreshment saloon," he announced, "where we keep on hand the finest brands of coffee, tea, chocolate, ice cream, as well as sandwiches, caviar, swiss cheese, ham, and all kinds of cold lunches. For the holidays, we beg to call attention to our selected stock of Christmas toys."[97] Other Jewish entrepreneurs hopefully opened apparel and food stores.[98] Phil Hirschfield sold his fancy goods, toys, and gift book shop to one Erdman, and then bought the Uphan and Ray stationery and optical goods store. A typical advertisement by Hirschfield opens with sage advice: "Persons having a tendency to weakness of sight, or those experiencing unusual fatigue of the eyes in reading or similar occupation requiring close vision, should resort to the aid of glasses—but it is important to have the right kind of glasses. Do not buy them of vendors who have no idea of optical science, but go to Hirschfield, the practical optician."[99]

Hard times sharpened the always keen competition for the consumer's dollar. Advertising space in the town's newspapers was ample, and "copy" was as lurid and eye-catching as merchants could invent, unaided by the wiles of advertising agencies. Jewish merchants, who had learned their English as young men without benefit of books and teachers, could use the language inventively as this specimen by Lewis Brothers Boot and Shoe Store suggests:

HORRIBLE

INDIANS

A WOMAN

man or child in Los Angeles could hardly be
found that has not traded in the great half
price boot and shoe store opposite the post
office. And why? Because they have

FOUND

out that we are not only the cheapest but we
have the largest stock and best variety in Los
Angeles County. Credit has long been

DEAD

and as we buy only for cash, we are enabled
to undersell any house in the boot and shoe
line in Los Angeles. Try us and you will be
convinced that we have

MURDERED

the high prices charged elsewhere.[100]

While the graphic arrangement of the Lewis advertisement parodied the grim headlines of Indian attacks, Joseph Cohn, in *La Crónica*, announced a "Gran Revolución Mercantil."[101]

The worst effects of the 1875 economic breakdown disappeared by the close of the 1870's. The outlook of the day, forcefully expressed by Isaias W. Hellman in a letter to his brother-in-law Benjamin Neugass, not only exemplifies the businessman's aggressive hopefulness but also reflects his social ethos:

I suffer once in a while from my old complaint about headaches, but it hardly hurts me more than once a day, will have to put up with it.

The business affairs I have no cause to grumble at this time, but I assure you that I have passed the last two years some very rough years. . . . and on account of a communistic feeling which has existed in this state amongst the working class the organic law of California has been radically changed whereby capitalists thought their interests endangered in consequence of which large sums of money was sent away and still larger sums invested in Government bonds or withdrawn from circulation. Real estate commenced to decline—all enterprises languished, no new ones were started and others which were started were stopped. Last fall at the regular election the republicans carried the state and the working class party, all foreigners or mostly low Irish were totally defeated since which time a more hopeful view is taken and our business prospects are again looking up. We have also had a most favorable season this winter and our agriculture prospects are better than I have ever seen them in California. I have no doubt that commencing with the year 1880, if God spares us all well, I will again be on the road of making money but I must confess that I have added little if anything since 1875 to my capital. I have not had a year since this in which I have not made $40 or $50 [thousand] net, but the shrinkage in real estate has ate it all up, apparently the tide has turned again, and I propose to make hay while the sun is shining.

In answer to your proposal to invest some money in California, I must state that I have no confidence in any other speculation except to invest money in good farming or land suitable for the raising of semi-tropical fruits and vineyards namely broad acres at low prices.

I am satisfied that lands which are now sold here from $2 [to] $5 an acre will bring $20 – $30 in five years hence. Our soil is most fertile, our climate cannot be surpassed in the world. At this particular time a good many mortgages are being foreclosed and opportunities offer themselves to purchase lands very low at forced sales. I have no objection to invest with you $25,000 in such land and let them lay for the benefit and use of our children. Kind regards to dear Sarah and the children and also to dear Sam and Bett in which my darling wife joins,

Your affectionate brother.[102]

With chastened optimism, the Jewish businessmen of Los Angeles entered the 1880's, a period which for some years fulfilled their highest hopes. Meanwhile, they had found time to look to the building of a modest but durable Jewish community.

CHAPTER 3

The Framework of Jewish Life

———————————— ✳ ————————————

LOS ANGELES merchants were the civic and political leaders of their town. Without a class of leisured or professional men or even a clergy, and with the landholding patriarchs of Mexican days bankrupted, whatever there was of public or communal life was for merchants to organize. It was almost inevitable that the Jews, belonging almost entirely to this business group, appear prominently in civic affairs. By no means inevitable was the founding of the Los Angeles Jewish community during the 1850's and 1860's with its primary institutions of synagogue, cemetery, school, and charitable society. Yet this too was done.

The Rough and Tumble of Local Politics

Jews participated freely in the vigorous politics of the day. Their status as recent immigrants to the United States did not inhibit them at all in an environment where everyone except the Indian aborigine and the conquered Spaniard was a recent arrival. Jewish issues and the term "Jew" were bandied about in political affairs, often in an attempt to manipulate Jewish sympathies for political advantage. And Jews did not fear to retaliate upon anyone who derided or attacked them as Jews.

A piquant episode recalled by Harris Newmark illuminates the combination of principle and opportunism which functioned in politics and business. In 1865 he heard that Prudent Beaudry, partner of Solomon Lazard in the Los Angeles Water Company and the largest merchandiser south of San Francisco, had boasted that he would drive every Los Angeles Jew out of business if only he could. Newmark, angered, thereupon proposed to his friend Phineas Banning, who was in the freighting business, that they enter the wholesale grocery business as partners. Newmark would supply the capital while Banning would surreptitiously cut the freight charge of $7.50 per ton for the trip from the harbor to Los Angeles. They would divide the profits. Thanks to this saving in transportation, the new combination could compete with devastating effectiveness against Beaudry and other rivals also. Within three months, O. W. Childs sold out; Beaudry quit in six, and John Jones, a Jew, capitulated. With Beaudry humbled, the partnership was dissolved and Newmark was now a wholesale grocer as H. Newmark and Company.[1]

In the state election later in 1865 the roles were changed, for Phineas Banning was advertised as an anti-Semite when he ran for the state senate as a strong pro-railroad man. Like most merchants, he was eager to make a deal to bring rails into Los Angeles. Banning hardly stood to lose personally when the town of Wilmington, which he founded and controlled, would become a railroad terminal. Rumors spread that Banning was inimical to the Jews, disguised in the assertion that no "German adopted citizen" should support him: "When Mr. Banning monopolized the transportation between San Pedro and Los Angeles, he ruled the Jewish traders with an iron hand."[2] To this accusation twenty-seven "German adopted citizens" replied at once with a statement in support of Banning's candidacy. A Banning man reportedly remarked that Los Angeles was a "Jew town and might be played out entirely," and that Wilmington would take its place.[3] In the small town, where men and their opinions were well known to each other, newspaper reports probably meant less than in larger cities. There is no evidence of Banning's hostility to Jews, nor that Jews believed this accusation of anti-Semitism. At any rate, Phineas Banning was elected state senator.

While a Jewish issue would scarcely be raised during a local election, when the electorate and its Jewish members were well aware of the personalities and of bread-and-butter issues, in the more remote and symbolic national elections such issues arose. During the two successful campaigns of Ulysses S. Grant, in 1868 and 1872, Jews throughout America were insistently reminded of his anti-Jewish General Order No. 11 of Civil War days, which excluded Jewish merchants from behind his lines. The *Semi-Weekly News* (July 3, 1868) reprinted it, adding that "a more arbitrary, tyrannical and barbarous order could not have been made by the most hardened despot." Isaac M. Wise's declararation that Jews should not vote for a man "unfit to be Chief of a Republic whose citizens claim equal justice and equal freedom," was also published for Los Angeles readers.[4] The local press, Democratic in sympathy, borrowed liberally from eastern newspapers' appeals to Jews to remember

General Order No. 11. A letter from "N. the son of H. a Levite" to the *St. Louis Times* thus also appeared in the *Semi-Weekly News* (August 18, 1868): "We were insulted by the nomination of Grant, and as he has chosen to accept, we will in duty bound as good and loyal citizens, not only for the protection of our own race, but for all other religious sects, endeavor by honorable means and determined action, to defeat Grant." The *News* published "Defence," a poem from the *Chicago Times,* which denounced Grant's "bigoted, indecent, and unwarranted attack on our Jewish citizens."[5] The local newspaper, speaking with its own voice, maintained that Grant had expelled the Jewish merchants to give a clear field to his father and partners who were trading with the Confederacy. The *Star,* for its part, reached to Evansville, Indiana, where that town's *Courier* had published a piece by an S. Meyer which concluded, "I hope there will be honest Christians enough to show next fall how they despise wrong."[6]

These polemics in the press culminated in a Democratic rally on August 22, 1868, reportedly the "largest and most enthusiastic ever held in this city." Some of the signs and placards borne by paraders manifestly appealed to the Jews: "Kick the Jews out of camp—Grant" was one, and another caricatured Grant and his aide-de-camp standing by cotton bales marked "Jews appropriate owners of the cotton." One parader carried a placard showing Grant with a keg of whiskey, saying, "Pa and I must have the cotton. I expelled the Jews beyond my lines." Six hundred persons reportedly paraded, while two thousand looked on and attended the rally; many were probably Mexicans, wondering at the gringo's politics.[7]

In evaluating the state elections as foretelling the presidential election, the *News* believed that Jews would abandon their usual radical Republican loyalty and vote Democratic out of anger at Grant: "The radical Republican portion of the Hebrew element have a *personal quarrel* with General Grant for the Insult offered their race, and while they will vote for Seymour and Blaine, many of them made it a point to carry the election for the Radical congressman. It will thus be seen that the Democracy have great reason to be joyous and hopeful."[8]

Unfortunately, there is no certainty as to the voting of Los Angeles Jews in 1868. Democratic earlier, they probably needed little encouragement to oppose the Republican candidate. Yet it appears that American Jews in general were not strongly swayed from their habitual Republicanism.[9] When Grant stood for reelection in 1872, little was made of the controversial Civil War episode. A letter from a New York newspaper was reprinted locally, repeating the familiar denunciation, and a new item was a comparison between Grant's decree and the persecution of the Jews of Roumania.[10]

While presidential elections were held amid a hue and cry over a Jewish issue, the local elections of 1868 returned two Jews, Moritz Morris and Henry Wartenberg, to the city council without remark. Moritz Morris had served on the council in 1866 but resigned in protest when that body granted $500 of public funds to Los Angeles College, a private institution.[11] J. L. Morris, his brother and partner in the clothing business and the Morris Vineyard, had already been a county supervisor and county treasurer. Harry Wartenberg was another pioneer who participated in Jewish and public affairs and often held civic office. The city council of 1869 unanimously elected Maurice Kremer its clerk. All these positions were honorable, but they were not arduous. The officials and the organs of local government in the small town were never too busy.

The year 1869 was a rocky one for the town's government, for it was out of money. Probably for this reason the council tabled even a resolution by Morris to purchase five hundred feet of hose to attach to fire hydrants.[12] In order to pay indispensable bills, the city council began to issue scrip. This procedure of doubtful legality ended in a resounding scandal when, near the year's end, it was openly hinted by Councilman Mascarel, chairman of the Finance Committee, that Henry Wartenberg, a member of his committee, and others had been feathering their own nests by manipulating scrip. An eyewitness believed "a minature earthquake could not have created greater confusion."[13] Wartenberg and Morris explained that they had negotiated the issue of scrip and then peddled it to the few merchants who would accept it rather than gold coin. I. W. Hellman, just starting as a banker, took some. The council appointed the investigating committee demanded by the impugned members, but its inquiry was disrupted by a grand jury finding that the issuance of scrip was illegal altogether. As a result, the mayor and the entire city council were placed on trial. When the jury was selected, all three Jews on the panel were challenged by the district attorney on the ground of bias, presumably in favor of fellow-Jews Morris and Wartenberg. One challenge was upheld and two dismissed. During the judicial proceedings early in 1870, the indicted city council could not conduct its affairs, and public business was suspended. The police, not being paid, stopped work; irrigation of land, which required council action, ceased. Three councilmen resigned, and the prosecutions against them were dismissed.[14] (In the special election which was called to fill their seats, Moritz Morris' brother J. L. was appointed judge of the election.) Ultimately the mayor and the indicted councilmen were exonerated.

Former governor John Downey next entered the lists with an action to reimburse buyers of the $22,000 in scrip. He was aiming at his competitor and later banking partner I. W. Hellman, who accepted the challenge and denounced Downey in the press, insisting that the purchasers of the scrip, himself included, were innocent parties who paid good cash and came to their city's relief with gold coin. The following meeting of the city council heard Moritz Morris hint broadly that some members had sold land illegally to themselves. An investigating committee was appointed over these latest charges. Ultimately the entire matter was dropped, a step which probably caused general relief, if it did not elevate civic virtue.[15]

Jews continued to seek service on the city council. In 1872 Solomon Lazard ran for council, Maurice Kremer for city tax collector, and Samuel Meyer for county supervisor, but none was elected. Kremer continued to hold the city clerkship until 1880, when he attained a councilmanic position. During his 1875 campaign for office a newspaper review of Kremer's experience showed him a resident of Los Angeles County for twenty-three years, county treasurer for three terms, county supervisor, president of the local Board of Education, and since 1869 city clerk. "In all of these varied and responsible positions, his record has been exceptional."[16] Other offices, major and minor, were also sought after by Jews. Jacob Schlesinger, postmaster in El Monte in 1871, had Jacob Weil as assistant postmaster. A few years later, L. Blum held the same office in Compton. In 1874 H. Fleishman announced his candidacy for city treasurer, while Charles Prager and Bernard Cohn filed for council seats. Both lost, but Prager became supervisor in 1877, and his brother Sam Prager served as a supervisor in 1878; Cohn was first elected to the council in 1878.[17]

Bernard Cohn (1836-1889) was a fearless stormy figure of Los Angeles politics, who became proverbial for his intimacy with the law and city affairs. He had come to Los Angeles in 1854 and clerked in the dry goods business for some years. Cohn spent thirteen years at the gold mines of Colorado, returning to Los Angeles in 1876. For a time he was a wholesale grocer in the firm which became Hellman, Haas & Company, and then became a property owner and practicing politician.[18] As businessman and politician, Cohn feared no one and did not hesitate to go to extremes in his tactics. When the chief of police was accused of irregularities, Cohn moved to dismiss him at once, but could secure no second for his motion.[19] I. W. Hellman's application for franchises for his street railroad found Cohn as his chief opponent.[20] The city had granted land to Bishop Amat in 1862, to build a Catholic college; when the bishop sold the land to Prudent Beaudry in 1878, Cohn argued that the land had to be used for a college or revert to the city. Cohn lost this fight, and his reelection contest in 1880 was hard fought. He was charged with buying votes and helping a son get city business. But Cohn knew well how to defend himself, and his unswerving, obstinate battle for civic virtue gained grudging admiration from the press. "No African in a woodpile could conceal himself so thoroughly as to escape his lynx-eyed watchfulness. . . . while we cannot say that Mr. Cohn is personally very popular, he has elements of strength that cannot be despised."[21] Such rugged obstinacy helped Cohn to be reelected in 1880 and again in 1882 and to serve for part of the time as president of the council and mayor pro tem.

For and Against and About the Jews

While Jews occupied public office, some with distinction, the Jews as a group were from time to time the subject of public discussion. An ugly event in San Bernardino in 1862 illustrates raw frontier antagonisms, but it was an unusual incident. A young man named Dick Cole entered a store owned by Wolf Cohn, a Jewish merchant. For some reason a brawl ensued, in which Cole called Cohn "a damned Jew, son of a bitch" and shot him dead. Isaac Cohn, brother of the man just murdered, thereupon drew his gun and killed Cole.[22] Threats of retaliatory violence quickly reached the ears of San Bernardino Jews. A local newspaper, far from dispelling their anxiety, sneered that "their fears are not without a reasonable cause, so far as it is applicable only to a certain class of individuals who infest the community."[23] Some Jewish merchants began preparations to leave town for a less menacing locale. Isaac Cohn, a resident of Los Angeles, was arrested for killing Cole, but the grand jury refused to indict. The whole matter quieted down.[24]

No threat ever endangered Los Angeles' early Jews. In fact, the *News*, which lost circulation and advertising as a result of its slurs during Civil War days, became quite eulogistic a few years later, perhaps to win back the patronage it had forfeited. It observed that the Jews were honorable businessmen and absolved them as a group from responsibility for the despoiling of the ranchos. They were praised for being multilingual (meaning presumably that Spanish was their second tongue), for eschewing drinking and gambling, and for their charity. The account suggested cohesion and self-discipline: "If any of their number strays into sharpness that savors of commercial fraud, he at once becomes an object of obloquy—but let any one of their class fall into pecuniary misfortune and they run to his relief as so many samaritans." It reminded local faultfinders of Jewish virtues:

The men are marked by their sobriety and the women for their chaste and decorous demeanor. You will never witness a dissection of character or any indecent curiosity about neighbor's affairs among the Jewish ladies of Los Angeles.

With one exception of vagabond and stranger, we will venture the assertion that there has not been a criminal prosecution against a Jew since the organization of the city. Mercilessly and remorselessly have confiding Californians been plucked of their substance in this city, but it is not the Jew under guise of favor and friendship who has wrested from them their fair and hereditary possessions. . . .

As a class, they have been punctilious in their commercial dealings. . . . "He is a Jew and is getting rich," and so would you if you pursued his honorable course. . . . The secret of the Jew's thrift is economy and earnest attention to his calling. Who is so ready as the Jew descendant of Jacob in our midst to respond with heartiness to every charitable appeal. It was a Sister of Charity who told us that the Jews of Los Angeles have ever met their merciful advances with encouraging words and open purses. . . . You say he doesn't build houses. "The fool builds houses, the wise occupy them." If a Jew or Gentile can attain the same comfort in a rented domicile at less expense than one of his own construction, what business is it to either Jew or Gentile? . . . And if a Jewish female repels the advances of a Gentile swain, should he berate and vilify her? . . .

The Jews are known as linguists. There is scarcely one in our town but cannot talk to you in half a dozen tongues. . . .

They are among our best citizens and the city suffers nothing in their hands. The patriarch of the race, Joseph Newmark, whose accomplished daughters have mated with our wealthiest and best citizens—who is held in higher esteem? His urbanity and purity are the delicious comment and pride of the town.

It would be well if our Gentile population would imitate his revered example. If such as he "had" the City of Los Angeles, it would be well with us.[25]

By reading between the lines, we learn the objections to the Jew. He is greedy, rich, exclusive, and his women are standoffish. At heart he is an exploiting transient, for he rents a dwelling rather than build a home. Few hearts would melt at the *News*'s admiration for the Jewish model of the "Protestant ethic" of economic dedication and success.

More frequent were "fillers" about the Jews, reprinted from many sources.[26] One story, taken from the *New York Sun,* "reported" a vast political and financial plan to regather the Jews in Palestine.[27] An assembly of Reform rabbis and of Orthodox congregations was announced, and even the funeral of Rabbi Berush Maisel in Warsaw was described in detail.[28] Moritz Morris showed a lithograph of 1,200 German Jewish soldiers at Rosh Hashanah prayers during the recent Franco-Prussian War, and it was reprinted.[29] The dedication of a Jewish club in Chicago, the benevolence of Rothschilds, the Jews of China, the supposed affinity of Celts and Jews, estimates of world Jewish population—all were deemed of interest to Los Angeles readers.[30] In 1870 H. Z. Sneersohn, a Palestinian messenger, visited town and delivered two lectures on Palestine and the Orient at $1.50 admission to both, to benefit the needy of Jerusalem. His visit with President Grant a few weeks earlier had given Sneersohn prominence.[31] The prosperity and economic vigor of New York Jewry, as described by the *New York Times* in 1870 and 1873, also became known by reprinting, and Los Angeles readers might indeed now wonder whether their Jewish neighbors in dusty, heat-scorched shops would in time resemble wealthy New York Jews.[32]

During the notorious Hilton-Seligman affair of 1877, many articles denounced Henry Hilton's exclusion of the banker Joseph Seligman from the Grand Union Hotel in Saratoga Springs. The *Herald* (June 30, 1877) observed:

There has been one continuous stream of condemnation poured upon the Order and upon the snob who issued it. . . . Religious bigotry of every kind is at a discount in the United States. It will never be possible again in this country to fan the flame of religious hate into any formidable dimensions. It remains to be seen, whether the act will not go far to wreck the superb business left by A. T. Stewart to Hilton's care.

Henry Hilton, said the *Star,* "has really made only himself a laughing stock in our own country where no man or woman can be proscribed on account of their religion or nationality."[33]

One comment suggests that "legitimate" attacks might skirt the edges of anti-Semitism. During the heated campaign of 1873, I. W. Hellman was sharply denounced as the *Star* summoned the electorate to "form a phalanx of opposition to these infamous jobbers and pawnbrokers, and put down this Hellman democracy and its accomplishments in the ugly shape of high taxation and rates of interest, that would have made the revengeful old Shylock himself, shudder."[34]

The Founding of a Jewish Community

The Jewish settlers of Los Angeles founded the basic institutions of a Jewish community during the earliest years of the city. Notwithstanding the difficulties and adversities of life in the town, their handiwork survived and ultimately flourished.

Jewish religious services were held sporadically from 1851. Upon the arrival of Joseph Newmark in 1854 they attained some degree of regularity, and possibly a congregation was established.[35] I. J. Benjamin, who visited in 1861, records a Beth El congregation which met only on the High Holidays.[36] During the same year it was reported that "the Israelites of Los Angeles organized about six months ago, a congregation under the name of Beth El, now numbering twenty or thirty members."[37] A notice in the *Star* on August 17, 1861, announced that seats at the coming High Holiday services could be reserved for $3.00. Next month a further announcement was published:

HEBREW CONGREGATION

On the 12th ult. a meeting of the Hebrew congregation was held at the residence of Messrs. Norton and Greenbaum for the purpose of electing officers for the coming year; when the following gentlemen were chosen for the respective offices indicated: President—B. Cohn, Vice-President—M. Norton, Secretary—Elias Cohn, Trustees—H. Morris, E. Greenbaum, and H. M. Cohn.[38]

The High Holiday services were held in Arcadia Block, and a certain M. Galland was brought from San Francisco to conduct them.[39]

We know, then, that a congregation was founded between 1854 and 1861, and that by the latter date it was regularly organized and elected a second slate of officers. Sometime between September 1861 and October 1862 a second congregation, B'nai B'rith, came into existence. On October 14, 1862, it too published the names of its officers for the coming year: Joseph Newmark, President; Wolf Kalisher, Vice-President; M. Behrend, Secretary; Elias Laventhal, Isidore Cohn, Louis Levy, Trustees. This was not Beth El under a new name, for all the officers were new. B'nai B'rith may well have been founded by German Jews; Beth El's leaders were mainly of Polish origin.[40] In any case, Beth El is no longer heard from; its members probably joined the newer congregation. That the recently founded congregation displaced the early one may be due to B'nai B'rith's promptness in securing a rabbi who was originally from Poland and acceptable to both groups.

Through Rabbi Henry of San Francisco's Congregation Emanuel, the leaders of the Los Angeles B'nai B'rith made contact with a well regarded young Hebrew teacher, Rabbi Abraham Wolf Edelman. He was then about thirty, a native of Warsaw, and had studied there in a Yeshiva. In 1852 he married Hannah Pesia Cohn and for a honeymoon they sailed to America. After living briefly in New York City, Paterson, and Buffalo, he moved to San Francisco. There Rabbi Henry took him under his wing and taught him further.[41]

Rabbi Edelman was to remain rabbi of Congregation B'nai B'rith for twenty-five years, participating in every phase of Jewish life and involved fully in general community affairs. In the congregation he preached on the Sabbath and Holy Days, conducted an afternoon Hebrew school, acted as circumciser, and chanted the services. For Passover he ordered the wine and matzoth from San Francisco. His activities in the community were extensive. He was Chaplain of the

Masonic Lodge in 1864, served as Worshipful Master in 1868, and in the same year was Captain of the Los Angeles Lodge Number 33, Royal Arch Masons. Playing no favorites, he was Guard of the Odd Fellows in 1867. Rabbi Edelman organized the local Gan Eden ("Paradise") Chapter of the national Kesher shel Barzel, a traditional fraternal order, in 1870, and served as an officer.[42] At Fourth of July celebrations Rabbi Edelman was sure to be called upon to deliver a prayer, which he did felicitously and at some length.[43] Upon the establishment of B'nai B'rith Lodge in 1874, he was elected its second president.[44]

Rabbi Edelman was shohet for the community. An early rising reporter once wrote with slight hyperbole, "It may not be generally known that Rabbi Edelman selects and kills every morning of his life, the beeves and mutton that are used by the Jews of this city, in accordance with certain rules. And they do say our friend, Edelman, selects mighty nice, fine bullocks."[45]

In 1870 the B'nai B'rith congregation advertised for a shohet and teacher, offering $900 per year in gold, "extras not included." Presumably the congregation did not really expect a response, because the advertisement only appeared in the local *Star*.[46] In that year also a second service was held in the home of Louis Levy for the more orthodox members of the community. Described as "Jerusalem Israelites," they were probably organized by H. Z. Sneersohn, the Palestinian messenger then in town.[47] Succoth services that year were held at the homes of Rabbi Edelman and Mr. Levy, each of whom had a Succah.[48]

The constitution of 1862 set the ritual of the congregation as that of Polish Jewry (Minhag Polen), and prayers were required to be in Hebrew. Membership was open to Jews who did not marry out of the faith; anyone who did, forfeited his membership.[49] The president and vice-president were expected "to attend synagogue at the stated time of divine service on every Sabbath and Holy Day" and to see that order and decorum were "strictly observed."[50]

The majority of the congregational members were not observant in their personal lives or soon fell away from the orthodoxy which may have accompanied them to Los Angeles.[51] Nevertheless, in June 1862 H. M. Cohn, who had been a sheep grazer with Leopold Harris, ventured to open the first kosher meat market. In addition, he opened a French restaurant next door and invited lodgers, who could receive both bed and board.[52] Although there was a considerable French population in Los Angeles as a potential clientele, this venture did not last long. Cohn soon went into a more steady business; he became a pawnbroker.[53]

If the piety of the members did not extend to eating only kosher food or suspending business on the Sabbath, on the Jewish New Year and Day of Atonement they were impeccable. They all closed their places of business, and some merchants from outlying areas moved into Los Angeles for the days.[54] An item from Wilmington in 1868 commented, "The Day of Atonement is being observed by all those of the Hebrew persuasion in this town. All their stores were closed and most of the occupants absent, enjoying the festivities of the day elsewhere. Herman Jacoby, our postmaster, is among the absentees. He is spending the day in Los Angeles."[55] Rosh Hashanah afternoon was spent in visiting, where out-of-towners renewed old acquaintances and families held pleasant reunions.[56]

With services already held regularly on the morning and evening of festivals in accordance with traditional practice,[57] and a rabbi to preside, a synagogue building was the next logical, but costly, step. After the High Holidays of 1862, the first fund-raising affair was held for the new congregation. As evidence of mutual helpfulness in a pioneer town, the committee on arrangements included several Christians. The *Star* declared:

It is intended, we believe, by this numerous and important body of our citizens, to build a suitable house for the celebration of divine services, a congregation having been organized here. We are satisfied the community will readily respond to any appeal by this body, who are always prominent in contributing for every charitable purpose without distinction of creed or country. Such liberality should be duly recognized and reciprocated.[58]

This first social affair ever undertaken by the Jewish community was a great success. Dancing was spirited and lasted until an "advanced hour." As was the custom, a late supper was served, "the viands consisting of all that luxury could supply or art suggest."[59] The ball so happily inaugurated was repeated. In 1864 it lasted until 3:30 A.M. on a week day, netting the congregation $500.[60] More than one hundred twenty ladies were present, indicating substantial non-Jewish participation.[61]

For eleven years, Congregation B'nai B'rith used public accommodations for religious services. They first worshipped upstairs in an adobe tavern, then in a succession of rented halls; on occasion, prayers were offered to the God of Justice in vacant courtrooms.[62] "The Israelites are constantly under obligation to their Christian brethren for places in which to worship," Rabbi Edelman complained,[63] and his words fell on sympathetic ears. During hard times, however, the members were satisfied merely to meet expenses. The real drive toward a building began on June 7, 8, and 9, 1869, with an elaborate concert and fair which enlisted the support of the entire community. With great effort a net of $1,170 was raised. The concert typified the musical interests of the day. It included violin and piano selections, arias from operas, songs by Mendelssohn, and the Overture to Herold's *Zampa* arranged for eight hands on two pianos and played by Mrs. Strelitz and Messrs. Heyman, Wittelshoeffer, and Van Gulpin. The concert's climax was the San Francisco Minstrels. With tickets at $1.00 and $1.50, the gross income of $490 suggests a very admirable attendance of 350 to 400 persons. As was customary, the congregation tendered the Minstrel Company a complimentary benefit in return.[64] In June 1871 the ladies gave another ball, and again in 1872.[65] By this time the men were convinced by the ladies that a building could be erected, and began to raise funds in earnest. On a trip to San Francisco, David Solomon and Elias Laventhal collected $1,000 from the merchants for the building fund.[66] The architect E. F. Keysor was engaged.[67]

On August 18, 1872, the synagogue's cornerstone was laid at 273 South Fort Street (now Broadway). I. W. Hellman, president of the congregation, in his address praised the members "who had so long battled for this one object, always full of hope, but rarely with a prospect of success, for whom no sacrifice was too great." He lauded Rabbi Edelman, "who has for nine years so ably performed all your duties as teacher, chazan, Shochet, and spiritual advisor to our society. You were always the first at any sick bed, or giving consolation to the afflicted—To you we say, well done, faithful servant of God." He reviewed the vicissitudes of the congregation, organized, he said, on July 13, 1862, with thirty-two members. Membership for a time declined and expenses considerably outweighed income:

We struggled hard to keep our organization intact, and to defray running expenses. The judicious management of the few faithful ones at that critical period saved the society from desolation.

I am happy to state that our society is at present in a flourishing condition. Our membership is constantly increasing, and we hope soon to see the time when every Hebrew residing in the County of Los Angeles, will belong to this congregation.

Unsynagogued young men troubled the leaders:

I am sorry to see that the Jewish young men, who certainly should be the first to join kindred institutions, have so far not done it. To them, I appeal —and hope they will prove by their example that the youth of Israel still reveres the ancient faith of their forebears. In examining the list of our Founders, I find that a majority still belong to our society; some have withdrawn and settled in different portions of the continent, while two have gone to that bourne from which no traveller returns.[68]

The building progressed rapidly. By October, it towered above the surrounding homes, and in December 1872 it was receiving finishing touches.[69] The newspapers regularly reported progress of this "finest church edifice" in Los Angeles.[70] By April 1873 the synagogue was open for inspection; for the dedication ceremony to come, a choir was rehearsing a collection of liturgical music.[71] Indebtedness was cleared by a method both customary and reasonably painless—an auction of seats, on August 3, 1873. The first seat sold for $500, and prices were then lowered progressively. Ten thousand dollars was raised that morning with half the seats sold.[72]

The building itself was of Gothic architecture. In front were two massive buttresses surmounted by ornamental stone, with carved spires. A five-pointed star set in a circle fronted the building. The entrance was up two flights of stairs, six feet wide, leading to massive doors of black walnut. The interior was seventy feet long, forty feet wide, and thirty feet high, and the sanctuary seated 365 persons. In the basement the high-ceilinged schoolroom ran the length of the building and was reputed the largest in Los Angeles.[73] The building's cost was estimated between a high $56,000[74] and a low $20,000.[75] A report on the churches in Los Angeles in 1880 gave the cost at $16,000.

The consecration on Friday afternoon, August 8, 1873, at 5:00 P.M., was a civic event. The city council itself proceeded as a body to the ceremony, and a large audience, many of them not Jews, attended. An awed observer found the ceremonies one of the "grandest spectacles ever witnessed in southern California." The program began with a procession carrying the Torah scrolls. Then followed:

> Presentation of the key to the synagogue to president
> Hymn, "How Goodly Are Thy Tents," by the choir
> Recitation of first two verses of Genesis, in Hebrew
>   and in English
> Dedication prayer in English
> Reading of 122nd Psalm, in English
> Song by choir, "Shma"
> 100th Psalm, in Hebrew
> 29th Psalm, in Hebrew
> Prayer for the government, in English
> Placing of Torah scrolls in Ark
> Dedication sermon, in English
> Presentation of flowers by children
> Dedication hymn by girls
> Closing hymn by choir

After an intermission, evening Sabbath services followed.

The local reporter concluded: "The Congregation of B'nai B'rith may well feel proud of their House of Worship. It is the most superior church edifice in southern California."[76] The *Los Angeles Star* (July 23, 1873) took advantage of the occasion to chastise local Christians: "The synagogue is indeed a handsome building and all are glad that it is completed. But here we fain would stop. Look at the Congregational, the Methodist North and Methodist South— their halls are rented affairs with benches! Look at the Episcopal nondescript affair! Do all these fine looking men and noble ladies— all our business people feel no contrition, no sense of shame, as they walk up to these pitiful shanties?"

At the new synagogue the annual highlight continued to be the Jewish New Year and Day of Atonement.[77] Worship took place on the New Year from seven until noon, and all day on the Day of Atonement. These services were regularly described in detail in the newspapers. Rabbi Edelman's sermons, taking about thirty minutes, were learned, didactic, and pious.[78] His English was excellent and almost without accent. Services themselves were entirely in the immemorial Hebrew, although men and women untraditionally sat together from the founding of the congregation.[79] A public Tisha b'Av (Ninth of Av) service was first held in 1874;[80] previously, this day of mournful fast probably was marked quietly in Rabbi Edelman's home or Joseph Newmark's.

Congregation B'nai B'rith's president had a good deal of authority; weddings and circumcisions in the synagogue required his written assent. The congregation could fine members for not attending services at the house of a mourner, for absence from board meetings, or for misbehaving or using unseemly language at a meeting. The rabbi did not receive special compensation for services to members, but could charge $10 to perform a wedding for a nonmember.[81] Upon erection of the synagogue, the constitution of 1862 was revised. Now, members were to buy or rent seats by class. They sold for $125, $75, or $50, and the legal deed of sale was transferable only to another member. Seat rental cost $18, $12, or $6, and a member who did not buy or rent a seat was charged $12 a year automatically. The constitution also specified that the rabbi (called the minister) was to perform all the religious ceremonies of his office, and "teach and prepare the confirmation class and perform the ceremony of confirmation once a year at the synagogue." It is noteworthy that teaching Hebrew school or acting as a shohet were unmentioned. Quite likely the confirmation ceremony was initiated in 1870 over Rabbi Edelman's objections and was then written into the constitution to insure his compliance. Although the duties of the minister were embodied in two brief paragraphs, while the duties of the *shamash* (sexton) required eight, we know of no *shamash* functioning during the incumbency of Rabbi Edelman.

During the depression which followed soon after the completion of the synagogue in 1873, the financial condition of the congregation once again deteriorated. The interest of the members, so intense during the campaign to erect a building, now became desultory. In May 1879 the indebtedness stood at $1,500, and the congregation was forced to take a one-year mortgage on the building for that amount at monthly interest of 1.25%.[82] During this period, too, B'nai B'rith was plagued by the recalcitrance of Bernard Cohn, the businessman and politician. A founder of Congregation Beth El in 1861, he was to become president of Congregation B'nai B'rith in later years. But Cohn, a stubborn and litigious man, refused to pay assessments on the grounds that they were illegally imposed. The congregation, then under the presidency of Harris Newmark, sued him for total assessments of $98, and a judgment was received. However, Cohn took the case to the superior court and obtained a reversal on the grounds that the assessment was indeed illegally and improperly applied.[83]

Los Angeles Jews could take pride in their synagogue and appreciate their rabbi, but personal religious observance was becoming attenuated. The *Herald's* remark before Passover, 1874, that "some of the Jewish families will gather together tonight in private houses and have the usual feast," implies considerable laxity.[84] By the end of the 1870's there was reportedly no longer a kosher boardinghouse in town, and the number of families who kept to the kosher diet had dwindled to an inconsequential minority.[85] The members were getting wealthier but traditional Jewish life poorer.

Charity, Fraternity, and Conviviality

Throughout the 1860's and 1870's the Hebrew Benevolent Society continued to exist side by side with the congregation, with largely overlapping membership. It met generally at the home of Rabbi Edelman. In 1862 and 1863, Samuel Prager served as president. Henry Wartenberg became president in 1866 with I. W. Hellman as secretary and the rabbi as vice-president, and they served until 1870, with M. Kremer and E. Greenbaum as trustees.[86] In December 1868 the society petitioned the city council to grant three acres of additional cemetery ground, and at length received them "near and adjoining the Hebrew Cemetery." The Hebrew Benevolent Society in return was to donate land for a proposed street.[87] Henry Wartenberg, retiring in 1870 after six years in office, reiterated the basic policies of the society. Only Israelites should be members or be buried in the cemetery, but charity knew no distinction between Jew and Gentile. Wartenberg also recommended more frequent meetings, higher dues, and limitations on the secretary's commission for collections. He also proposed that Jewish newcomers in town be required to join the society within three months on pain of exclusion from its benefits.[88] With the erection of the synagogue building, the Hebrew Benevolent Society met there following the congregational meeting. Perhaps this practice was for the convenience of out-of-town members, who could thus attend both meetings during one trip.[89]

The Ladies' Hebrew Benevolent Society, the first women's philanthropic organization in Los Angeles, was organized in 1870 at the instigation of Rosa Newmark, wife of the patriarchal Joseph Newmark. She impelled the women to add feminine tenderness to the acts of charity and of comforting mourners. Inasmuch as Mrs. John Jones, the secretary, was not Jewish, the rules of the Ladies' Society must have been elastic enough to include the spouse of a Jew. Approximately thirty women signed as charter members.[90] In order to collaborate with the men's society, three male counselors were also selected.[91] A few months after the organization's founding, a circus from San Francisco offered the ladies a complimentary benefit, asking them to name the date.[92] The delighted women suggested Friday evening, October 28, 1870. Since no more was heard about this, we can conjecture that the ladies were reminded that the Jewish Sabbath was improper for such an event. In addition to such charity and good deeds, the Ladies' Hebrew Benevolent Society also undertook to perform the rites of bereavement, attend the female dead before burial, and comfort mourners.[93] In later years, when individuals in the last stages of consumption came to Los Angeles, the society gave indispensable service.

The ladies' first project was for the victims of the great Chicago fire in 1871, when the Jews of Los Angeles were commended for their alacrity in responding to this call. When only three people—John Downey, John Jones, and a citizen from Riverside—appeared at a meeting it called to plan philanthropic effort, the *News* editorialized: "Anything more disgraceful than this, the inhabitants of Los Angeles could not be guilty of. Let her bow her head in shame."[94] The *Star* pointed out that there were twenty and not three persons at the meeting and that "our Israelite citizens, after donating liberally at their meeting, went in a body, to the place called for the meeting of the merchants, and found it closed."[95] The Hebrew Benevolent Society gave $250, and the ladies collected another $100.[96] In financing the annual Fourth of July celebrations, "one of the ladies in charge . . . informs us that she has noted a more liberal attitude among the Spanish Americans, Italian Americans, Germans, and Jews than among the descendants of the Mayflower passengers."[97]

The ladies' balls became imposing social occasions in town. In 1878 their Calico Dress Ball was "the social sensation of Los Angeles," and it was noted that "the balls of this society have been heretofore the most popular ever given in the city."[98] At the Tenth Anniversary Ball in 1880 in Turnverein Hall, spectators filled the galleries, and 250 guests were on the dance floor. The men were dressed in claw hammer coats with kids and ties. The guests included prominent Los Angelenos as well as visitors from as far away as Tucson.[99]

By 1880 the Hebrew Benevolent Society was truly venerable, having existed for twenty-five years as the pioneer institution of social welfare in Los Angeles. It had disbursed an estimated $20,000, with the highest membership at seventy-eight; in 1880 it was down to fifty-six.[100] The Hebrew Benevolent Society also held the Jewish community together by maintaining the allegiance of unsynagogued Jews. To an extent, it provided a respectable social life for the Jewish men and women who had few ways of enjoying themselves in a town just beginning to outgrow its frontier origins.

Organized social groups, so limited around 1870, expanded much by 1880. Other lodges, fraternal orders, and social organizations arose, beckoning for the time and interest of local Jews. Thus the B'nai B'rith and the Kesher shel Barzel lodges were branches of national fraternal societies, while the Alliance Israélite Universelle was part of a world organization. Another group was the avowedly nonsectarian but practically Jewish Los Angeles Social Club. Only one of these four groups existed more than a few years. None was considered to compete with the existing organizations, because their leadership was the same as the synagogue's and the Benevolent Society's.

The Kesher shel Barzel's Gan Eden ("Garden of Eden"—local boosting!) Lodge 81, founded in 1870, met biweekly. Appealing to few local orthodox Jews, it never attracted more than fifteen members and maintained a tenuous existence. With the establishment of the B'nai B'rith lodge, the organization disappeared.[101] Similarly tenuous was the existence of a Los Angeles branch of the Alliance Israélite Universelle. In August 1868 Eugene Meyer convened a meeting for the purpose of helping "emancipate all Israelites and redress the wrongs upon the race throughout the world" by means of an Alliance branch.[102] Maurice Kremer became temporary chairman and Leon Loeb temporary secretary; Solomon Lazard, Henry

Wartenberg, and H. Fleishman were to draft by-laws. The Alliance never accomplished anything worth recording, but it seems to have maintained an official existence.

What was needed was an organization of national scope with a "secret" ritual, combining humanitarianism with mutual aid and appealing to the dominant German-Jewish population of the city. This was the Independent Order B'nai B'rith, which originated in New York in 1843 and was now reaching the West Coast. On March 17, 1874, B'nai B'rith in Los Angeles was formed. I. N. Choynski, book dealer, president of District Number 4, and sharp-tongued West Coast correspondent for the *American Israelite* under the pseudonym "Maftir," came from San Francisco to oversee the occasion. The group was named Orange Lodge Number 224, and about thirty charter members joined. The Lodge elected Samuel Prager its president, and by January 1875 its membership stood at thirty-five.[103] Each member purchased an insurance policy of one thousand dollars. Next year when Choynski visited Los Angeles en route to San Bernardino to start a lodge, some Los Angelenos accompanied him and helped to install Paradise Lodge Number 237 in San Bernardino.[104]

In 1875 Rabbi Edelman, that inveterate joiner, was elected president.[105] During his administration the first discussions were held about a hospital sponsored by the Jewish community, and B'nai B'rith resolved to sponsor it.[106] It was to be three decades before a Jewish hospital existed. By 1876 the membership had risen to forty, but income and finances were precarious.[107] B'nai B'rith limped along twenty years more.

The forerunner of all social clubs in Los Angeles was organized in 1870. This was the Los Angeles Social Club, whose first officers were almost all Jewish. The president was Constant Meyer; secretary was Julius Lyon; treasurer, Joseph Coblentz; directors were Coblentz, Aaron Smith, Simon Nordlinger, and Charles Jacoby.[108] Among the other members were such figures as the Prager brothers, Solomon Lazard, the Hellmans, J. L. Morris, Leon Loeb, Sam Meyer, and Bernard Cohn. In later days of Jewish exclusion from social clubs Harris Newmark, another member, recalled that "several were organized in the early era of sympathy, tolerance and good feeling, when the individual was appreciated at his true worth and before the advent of men whose bigotry has sown intolerance and discord, and has made a mockery of both religion and professed ideals."[109] The Los Angeles Social Club's members began a round of activities.[110] A picnic was held at the Rancho Santa Anita, then owned by the H. Newmark firm, where forty members played games, strolled in the woods, hunted, or rowed on the lake, in the company of ladies. Most who went were Jewish.[111] One hundred Jewish and non-Jewish guests made the club's ball in 1876 "one of the most brilliant assemblages of youth, beauty and fashion which has ever gathered in Los Angeles."[112] Midnight dinner and seventeen dances were typical of elegant balls of the period. Depression during the later 1870's put an end to the Los Angeles Social Club.

The Jews enjoyed the social pastimes of the community. Picnics and trips to the beach or the canyons were very popular, while hunting appealed to certain Jews. The more affluent early learned to spend summers at the beach. There are indications that Jews no less than Gentiles, and their women no less than the men, made gambling their major indoor sport. I. N. Choynski ("Maftir") did not flatter the Los Angeles Jewish gentleman and his lady: "Socially, our Jews are capital fellows. They make every stranger welcome at their firesides, and if that stranger is a poker sharp, he is doubly welcome, especially with some of the ladies who are experts."[113]

The grand social occasions for the city's Jewish families were weddings, bar mitzvahs, confirmations, and the religious holidays. As families increased in affluence, weddings became more ornate, and the newspapers described them in detail. The wedding of Rachel Edelman, daughter of Rabbi Edelman, to William T. Barnett, gives a picture of the weddings of the day. It was scheduled for three o'clock in the synagogue, but guests began to arrive at noon; by three o'clock only ladies could be seated. The groom wore a black dress suit with white cravat and kids, and walked down the aisle with the mother of the bride, as was the popular custom of the day. The celebration afterwards was held in the residence of the bride's father.[114]

Bar mitzvahs could also be grand occasions. Before the synagogue was built, they were held at home. The bar mitzvah service of Louis Polaski's son was held in two rooms of his home, and the guests remained for dinner. Rabbi Edelman spoke, and "the health of the parent was many times drunk." That evening the lad's friends met and danced, and at midnight a grand collation was spread. Many gifts were given and duly described, including a gold watch, studs, books, charms, and sleeve buttons. The lad gave a talk which probably required fifteen minutes to deliver.[115] The bar mitzvah of Julius Cohn, eldest son of Bernard Cohn, was especially lavish. Luncheon was served in a special pavilion alongside his house, and speeches and toasts followed. That evening the guests again assembled at the Cohn residence and proceeded to Leck's Hall, where a grand ball and supper were prepared for one hundred guests.[116] After the synagogue was completed, services were held there followed by home luncheons. At the bar mitzvah of Rabbi Edelman's son in 1875, a reception was held on Sabbath afternoon for the entire community.[117]

During the afternoon of the Jewish New Year unmarried gentlemen customarily paid social calls. In 1876 Messrs. Lewin, Barnett, Rothschild, Winter, and Martin Lehman announced that they had paid twenty-nine calls.[118] An annual Purim Ball was given by a Purim Society. Generally the children were first treated to an entertainment of songs, dances, a tableau or play. After they left, about 10 P.M., their parents remained to celebrate.[119]

In evaluating the social life of the Jews in this period of relatively wholehearted social acceptance, one notes that where the Jews participated socially, they did so beyond their numerical proportion. Their gregariousness was directed first toward each other and then toward the rest of the community. The impulse for Jewish self-perpetuation, the distaste for increasing the existing dangers of intermarriage, the feeling of greater ease with others of similar tastes and interests and background—all indicated that Jewish social activities could not be fully homogenized into the general community. During the decade of the 1870's there was a line of social assimilation beyond which the Jews voluntarily did not go. Social exclusion was a condition which would arise in decades to come, after Los Angeles abandoned its early openness and egalitarian spirit.

Education, General and Jewish

The public school system in Los Angeles more or less began with the opening of the first schoolhouse in 1855.[120] In addition there were private schools. Thus the Sisters of Charity school, established in 1866 alongside their hospital, was one to which "many of the first families of the city, Catholic, Jewish and Protestant sent their children" recalled Boyle Workman.[121] In the middle of the 1860's, three-fifths of the town's children were still not attending any school.[122] When St. Vincent's College, a Catholic institution founded in 1855, was reorganized in 1865, one of its chief fund-raisers was Mrs. Rosa Newmark, who conducted a lucrative fair to help put the school on its feet.[123]

It is likely a considerable number of Jewish children attended the small French and the German English schools. Henry Fleishman served as secretary of the board of the German English school in 1870, and his daughter was the first to give a prayer in German at confirmation exercises in 1880.[124] From this time on, the use of German in synagogue sermons and confirmation exercises became more frequent.[125] The guests at graduation exercises of the Catholic Sisters' school included a considerable number of Jewish girls, suggesting both Jewish enrollment and close social relations with Catholic girls.

Some parents who could afford to do so sent their children away to school. Moritz Morris in 1874 took his son to San Francisco to enroll him in Benicia College.[126] Harris Newmark sent his son Maurice to Paris, where he lived with the Chief Rabbi of France, Zadok Kahn, who was a brother-in-law of Eugene Meyer. One reason for studying in France was the value of learning French, "at that time an especially valuable acquisition in Los Angeles."[127]

The majority of Jewish children, however, attended public schools, where they won a disproportionate number of prizes for excellence.[128] The public schools were no places of cloistered calm. Thus, in 1872, a Jewish boy by the name of Blumenthal accused the principal of his grammar school, Dr. T. H. Rose, of assault. Youthful Ben W. Edelman, son of the rabbi, wrote a long letter to the press, defending Rose with vigor and asserting that he may have punished Blumenthal "the way every teacher does a scholar" but that he certainly never did "throw him up to the ceiling, letting him fall to the floor."[129] The next day Isaac Benjamin, another precocious lad, joined the fray, defending the principal. "I know that the Blumenthal boy was punished very often and richly deserved it. There also appeared something about insanity. I assure you, Mr. Editor, that it is enough to make anybody crazy when compelled to deal with a set of blockheads as Dr. Rose often has had in his school."[130]

Rabbi Edelman's Jewish school had its problems, but it also boasted achievements, especially during the early years. It began as an afternoon Hebrew school which met after public school hours; we do not know how many days per week. Girls were conspicuous among the students; thus of honor students cited in 1869, eight were boys and four were girls.[131] Rabbi Edelman began in 1868 to conduct an annual public examination of his students, in catechistic form. It was held shortly before the High Holidays, with an assemblage of parents and friends. The exhibition included the spelling and reading of Hebrew, translating from Hebrew into English, and biblical history. The children were examined for such knowledge as the Hebrew months of the year, history from Creation to the destruction of the Temple, recitation of Hebrew poems, prescribed blessings over food and drink.[132]

Such accomplishments were realized against difficulties. "Rabbi Edelman labours under great disadvantage as the pupils cannot attend classes with him until their dismissal from the other schools. Hence the children come to him fatigued and worn out, and ill prepared for entering a course of severe study."[133] The school must have met with opposition from parents who preferred a Sunday school with the more glamorous confirmation ceremony which was becoming standard in Reform temples. In 1870 the first such service was held during the Shavuot services. Five girls (Celia Katz, Rachel Edelman, Sarah Solomon, Jennie Cohn, and Sarah Goldstein) were confirmed. Four boys read from the Torah scroll, but it is not clear whether they were also confirmants. The girls sang hymns, offered prayers, and during the '*Alenu* prayer placed bouquets of flowers in the Ark. They then recited the Ten Commandments and chanted the *Yigdal* hymn.[134] The confirmation one year later included two boys and one girl, and young Isaac Benjamin again read the Torah.[135] The rendition of a prayer offered by one confirmant suggests the emotional character of the rather florid ceremony. "Miss Cohn came first and the sobs choked her utterances at the Commencement. By force of will, she calmed herself sufficiently to repeat a prayer filled with emotion and earnestness which left few dry eyes in the house."[136]

By the mid-1870's the weekday Hebrew school appears to have

been reduced to a Sunday school, with Rabbi Edelman its superintendent and four parents and former students the teachers. The textbooks for the primary grades were those written by Rabbi David A. De Sola of Montreal.[137] The new turn must have disappointed Rabbi Edelman. In keeping with his own traditional background he taught his students the Hebrew language and prayers, in addition to Bible and history. Some boys learned to read from the Torah scroll. The children had pleasant memories of their hours spent with him, but the times were against him. Most of the boys were still prepared for bar mitzvah, but the emphasis shifted to the Sunday school and to confirmation for girls and for boys who wished it. By 1880 the congregation was well on the way to a type of Jewish education compatible with the Reform leanings of most of its members.

CHAPTER 4

The 1880's: Decade of Boom and Bust

Land and Business Expansion

BY THE SPRING of 1882, Isaias W. Hellman felt confident that the hard years of the late 1870's were really finished. To his brother-in-law Mayer Lehman (father of Herbert H. Lehman) he wrote of his confidence in the city's future, and of his own possibilities:

Business is very fair with us. I am making up for former losses. Los Angeles County is being filled up very rapidly with the best people from every part of the United States. Thousands of persons of wealth have come here since the Southern Pacific Railroad has been completed and have bought homes already improved or have bought land and are improving the land. Real estate has increased greatly in value and is still rising. Capital is accumulating here to such an extent that interest has come down below Eastern rates.... The Southern part of California out of its beautiful climate and the great richness of its soil, is destined to become the garden plot of the country. Nevertheless I am making all preparations to have enough ready income laid aside to change our domicile should we feel at any time like doing it. At present we are perfectly contented here, our beautiful home is the site [sic] and pride of the city. My own standing financially, socially, and politically is as good as I can desire.[1]

The Farmers and Merchants Bank, which Hellman controlled and largely owned, had netted 12% profit during the preceding two years,[2] convincing proof that Los Angeles' urban future had arrived and that investors had a wide field before them.

The eighties seemed to move in with a rush. When the decade of boom opened, Los Angeles had eleven thousand inhabitants. In that year, 1880, the Methodist University of Southern California was founded on three hundred acres of land donated by a Catholic, John Downey, a Protestant, O. W. Childs, and a Jew, I. W. Hellman. It was the first school of higher learning in southern California. One year later, the *Los Angeles Times* began publishing, and the city's business streets began to be lit by electricity—one of the first cities in the country so illuminated. In 1882 the telephone was introduced, and in 1884 the city voted Republican for the first time in history. The population almost trebled in these three years to 31,000. Then came the boom.[3]

The town was ripe to cast away forever its Mexican frontier ways and emerge as a bustling American city, and the coming of the the Santa Fe Railroad was the precipitating factor. The Southern Pacific, since 1876 the only railroad in town, was not disposed to yield its profitable monopoly equably. It fought back in a rate war which forced fares from Chicago progressively downward from $85 to $25 to $15, until the incredible day when the ticket cost $1.00. (Skeptical scholars suggest more collusion than competition.[4]) This brought a flood of eastern visitors who could now visit California and perhaps decide to stay.

Underlying the growth in population there were, of course, more deep-seated reasons than a temporary drop in transportation rates. Thus the pastoral economy supporting a large animal population and few humans shifted to an agricultural economy supporting many farmers on limited acreage. The citrus industry grew rapidly from one million orange trees in 1880 to twelve million in 1889. Wine, then the county's most important agricultural enterprise, increased from 1,300,000 gallons in 1876 to 14,000,000 gallons in 1889.

Advertising, formal and word-of-mouth, also promoted the boom. Fliers and books, pamphlets and letters, tales by returning gold-seekers of the 1850's, spread the fame of southern California. The railroad's tireless propagandizing was complemented by letters home from eager travelers. Los Angeles became the best-advertised city in the country. "Our brethren of the city and would-be state of the Angels understand how to advertise," admitted the *San José Times-Mercury* in 1885. "The average eastern mind conceives of California as a small tract of country, situated in and about Los Angeles. . . . The result shows the pecuniary value of cheek."[5]

A further stimulus to rapid growth was the search for health. The widely advertised climate of southern California led to an invasion by health seekers. To a large extent, the ill and infirm built the hotels and resorts and boardinghouses and populated the Los Angeles area.[6] Farmers and children of farmers, exhausted by the hardships of tilling the soil of the Middle West and the Central Plains, also sought the year-round sunshine and easier life. Their cultural and social habits were to alter profoundly the character of Los Angeles.

As newcomers flocked in by the tens of thousands during the early 1880's, real estate salesmen enticed them when they stepped off the trains. They were taken to visit subdivisions or town sites. Some of the places were towns like today's Glendale, Burbank, Whittier, Azusa, Monrovia, or Hollywood, but there were also Sunset, Morocco, Vernondale, Arlington Heights, Rosecrans, Meadow Park, or any of sixty-two towns which now exist only in the archives of the Hall of Records. Los Angeles seethed with loud promoters, amateur and professional. Hotels bulged with occupants; prices soared. On the streets, in private homes, at clubs, in stores, the subject of conversation was southern California land. Everybody seemed to speculate in real estate, but the real promotion came from professionals who arrived direct from recent operations in Kansas and in other cities. At the height of the fever, some persons paid as much as $500 for a place in line at a particularly "hot" development.[7] A correspondent late in 1886 found "the streets . . . so thronged with teams and pedestrians as to necessitate there being policemen, stationed at the crossings, to keep the foot passengers from being knocked down by the passing vehicles. . . . the thoroughfares are crowded with tourists, healthy and sick, rich and poor, and I suppose good and bad. . . . The whole city is a hotel: every house, with few exceptions, no matter how wealthy the occupants, has rooms to rent and rents them at astonishing figures."[8]

Excursion trains, brass bands, free lunches, full-page newspaper advertisements, and 2,000 aggressive real estate agents in one year sold $100,000,000 in real estate. Much of it was in the city. Downtown land which fetched $20 per front foot sold for $800 a few years later. Most of the buyers and sellers were not Los Angelenos.

The Jewish residents were not in the eye of the storm. No prominent real estate firms can be traced to Jewish ownership, but undoubtedly Jews bought and sold land, as did nearly everyone. I. N. Choynski ("Maftir") asserted during the height of the boom that "the fifty Jews in Los Angeles made five million dollars this year in land. Mr. Hellman, the banker, has cleared up to three million dollars in a couple of months without investing a cent."[9]

Another source insisted that Hellman made $4,000,000 by acting as adviser to a syndicate, and that he was now the richest Jew in America.[10] Hellman, Harris Newmark, and Kaspare Cohn in 1887 organized a syndicate and purchased the large Repetto Ranch for $65,000, which was then apportioned among the five purchasers. Cohn and H. Newmark struck water on their shares, subdivided the land into five-acre lots, located the town of Newmark in the center and called the settlement Montebello. The town of Newmark disappeared, but Montebello is a large and thriving city today.[11]

Bernard Cohn "purchased" from old Pio Pico for $62,000 the Pico house property, the County Bank property, and 3,700 acres in the Rancho Paso de Bartolo Viejo. This "purchase" became a celebrated court case, finally reaching the supreme court of the state. Cohn claimed that he had purchased the property; Pico claimed that Cohn had lent him the money with the property as security. Cohn eventually won on perjured testimony, and Pico, by then in his nineties, was pauperized.[12]

Probably more than any other individual I. W. Hellman brought the boom to its end. Under his conservative management the Farmers and Merchants Bank refused to allow itself to be carried away by the tempting paper profits. At the height of the boom, it announced that no money would be lent for speculative purposes, leading other banks to follow its example.[13] The real estate boom ended by April 1888. Splashy newspaper advertising dwindled to plaintive pleading. The trains, which had come full and left empty, now arrived empty and left with their cars full of emigrants. Assessment figures which had risen from $32,000,000 to $63,000,000 dropped precipitously to $20,000,000, and the population, which stood between 80,000 and 100,000 at the height of the boom, settled back to 50,000 people.

In spite of the disastrous end of the boom, much was accomplished. As the gold rush made northern California an integral part of the United States, so the boom did for southern California. It wiped out the last vestiges of the Mexican pastoral life. Where once cattle had ranged on a thousand hills, now the newcomer from the Midwest "built his trolley lines, founded his banks, and irrigated his orange groves. The boom was the final step in the process of making California truly American."[14] There were five times as many inhabitants in Los Angeles in 1890 as in 1880.

Life in Business and Politics

By the middle 1880's the Jews in Los Angeles had gone far
with their city. Many had been in business thirty or even thirty-five
years, and their firms were among the oldest and best established in
town. Their stores were attractive and prosperous looking, with
good "french plate glass" as one correspondent remarked.[15] Well-
established Jewish businessmen continued to be active. After Eugene
Meyer's City of Paris was sold out to Nathan Cahn, Leon Loeb, and
E. L. Stern in 1883, and Meyer went into banking with Lazard
Frères in San Francisco, the advertising of the City of Paris continued to be full and flamboyant. One specimen announced: "The
rumor on Wall Street has been confirmed that Messrs. Stern, Cahn,
and Loeb of the City of Paris, Los Angeles, California, are closing
out their immense stock of men's, youth's and boy's clothing, hats,
boots, and shoes, at startling low prices."[16] Well-established firms
like those of Leopold Harris, Hellman and Haas, and Eugene
Germain continued to grow in the apparel and grocery businesses.[17]
By report, "Newmark and Company, Hellman, Haas and Company
do the leading wholesale grocery business of Los Angeles. Hellman,
Stassforth, P. Hirschfield and P. Lazarus are the kings of the book and
stationery trade."[18] The importance of the Spanish-speaking clientele was reflected in the advertising by many of these merchants in
La Crónica.

Some businessmen now began to limit their previously endless
business day. One of the first attempts at self-regulation occurred
in 1885, when the shoe merchants agreed to close at 7:45 nightly
except Saturday. Any merchant in violation would pay a $50 fine.
The shoe firm of Lewis, Benjamin and Jacob took the lead in this
movement.[19] A similar attempt at self-regulation took place a few
years later when the jewelry firms, many or most of them Jewish,
voted to close at 6:00 P.M.[20]

Besides changes in older businesses, a number of important new
firms had their beginnings during this period. Henry Siegel and his
brother Nate started as Siegel the Hatter. Meyer Siegel opened a
tailor shop, then a boot and shoe store, then went into the insurance
business, joined with Magnin in 1893, and finally established Meyer
Siegel and Company. Two sons of Rabbi Edelman, Henry and Ben,
went into the tobacco business as Edelman and Company. Siegfried
Marshutz opened his optical shop. In 1887 Morris Cohn came to

work for Jacoby Brothers; a few years later, he started Morris Cohn and Company, jobbers of shoes and clothing. In 1897 he became the first textile manufacturer in the city, making overalls and shirts and installing the first power machine in town. After Lemuel Goldwater joined the firm in 1899, the business was called Cohn-Goldwater. (Eventually Fredrick Cole joined the firm as vice-president. It is now called Cole of California.) R. Cohen celebrated the opening of his popular Vienna Bakery, where he served coffee and lunch, by inviting the B'nai B'rith lodge to dinner "on the house."[21] In 1881 Asher Hamburger arrived in town from Sacramento with his two sons S. S. and M. A., and a few years later David joined them. They called their business on Main Street the People's Store, and move it to successively larger locations. In 1908 they built the famous Hamburger Building on Broadway and Ninth, which became the city's largest and most important store. Eventually it was sold to the May Brothers, who made it the first of their chain.

These and other Jewish firms composed a substantial proportion of the commerce of Los Angeles. A correspondent ironically reported that "Jews are making about as many preparations for Christmas as the Christians and why not, since they have the largest stores and the most goods? . . ."[22]

With the growth of population and business, the need for local transportation and other utilities became apparent. The first step had been taken in 1869, when Judge Widney and some associates obtained a streetcar franchise, and they put the little Spring and Sixth line into operation in 1874. These were small beginnings before 1877, when I. W. Hellman received a twenty-five-year franchise for a line down Main Street, which ultimately extended to the Agricultural Exposition Park. This was the first double-track streetcar line in Los Angeles but was soon obsolete. In 1883 Hellman and his associates established the more modern Hellman Street Railway. The acquisition of a franchise from the city council was no mere formality. Hellman's sharpest opposition came from the doughty defender of the city's interests, Councilman Bernard Cohn, whom Hellman in exasperation accused of "animus."[23] Even after the vote in Hellman's favor, Cohn asked for a reconsideration.[24] He lost, but other opposition developed to the franchise. Faced with a lawsuit from another line, Hellman defended himself: "I have been here a long time, nearly twenty-five years, and I am now in a position to benefit and improve the city, and that is my only desire in building my road. The road is so modern and well built and the work is so costly, that it will be years before it will pay anything. But I wish to accomplish something with my money. What better monument can I leave when I die?"[25]

Neither lawsuit nor other opposition stopped Hellman, who proceeded so vigorously that a local minister attacked him from the pulpit for working his men on the Christian Sabbath.[26] The road was soon completed, and cars ran every twenty minutes, as originally promised. When East Los Angeles rapidly developed, Hellman won council permission in 1885 to extend his line to this new area, against bitter opposition from the Los Angeles and Southern Pacific Railway, which was already running a track there.[27] Hellman appeared again two years later before the city council, to change his horsecar line to a double-track cable road at a cost of $700,000. Since one set of tracks already bestrode Main Street, Hellman was asking for another. At a tempestuous meeting, the Bureau of Public Works formally favored the proposed franchise.[28] One councilman then proposed that the line be taxed at 5% of gross income. Hellman unequivocally refused to accept this stipulation, saying that he was not a stranger coming to Los Angeles to make a quick profit, but an old resident. The *Los Angeles Times* editorialized that "the double track railroad is the most important single public enterprise ever projected for Los Angeles.... The city solons are expected to stand by the public interest in this matter, but let us hope that they will not haggle it to death."[29] Hellman was enfranchised and built his line.

In the same year of 1883 Herman Silver, together with J. E. Crank, successfully applied for a franchise to build a double-track cable road to Boyle Heights and out to Downey Road.[30] The road was built and then sold to a Chicago syndicate. Silver had come to Los Angeles from Chicago as secretary and treasurer of the California Central Railroad and later became treasurer of the Santa Fe. As a political figure who once knew Abraham Lincoln,[31] Silver would be president of the city council in the 1890's and a distinguished member of the Jewish community.

I. W. Hellman and his associates successfully operated their street railway until 1891, when they joined Henry E. Huntington to establish the Pacific Electric Railroad Company. Hellman later sold his interests to the Southern Pacific Railroad, which took over the Pacific Electric, while Huntington retained the Los Angeles Railway lines.

Like other businessmen of his time concerned with business matters which government decisions affected, Hellman was deeply connected with politics. In 1873 he allegedly boasted that he carried the County of Los Angeles in his vest pocket. The local administration was stigmatized as Hellman Democracy, and the election campaign was directed primarily at him. In 1886 Hellman briefly flirted with the tempting idea of becoming senator in a day when the United States Senate was known as the Millionaire's Club. He went to Sacramento to canvass the situation and found that his chief opponent for the Democratic nomination was George Hearst. Hellman returned, declaring: "I know that all the respectable members favored me, but there are, unfortunately, a good many 'boodlers.' When I saw that there was going to be a wrangle, I came away and left the whole thing to take care of itself. I would not buy it, and I would not scramble for it. The United States Senatorship is not essential to my happiness at all."[32] Hellman had the reputation of "the shrewdest Jew in California.... Of course, everyone knows that Mr. Hellman's name must be at the head of every project to insure its success, and that his word is as good as any man's bond; but who would suppose that the whole state knows him so well? I am told that he is charitable, but always in a quiet and unpretentious manner."[33]

Hellman did not attain elective public office, but he did have the distinction of being the first Jew to be a regent of the University of California, serving from 1881 until his death.[34]

Other Jews participated actively in the political life of the city, without I. W. Hellman's casual disdain toward the scramble. Local elections divided on party lines, and Jews fought for places on both parties' tickets. In September 1882 at the Democratic councilmanic primaries, Conrad Jacoby won in the Third Ward, while Ben W. Edelman came in sixth. Bernard Cohn ran poorly in the Fourth Ward, coming in fourth. But Cohn was not satisfied to be an "also ran." In December an independent citizens' group nominated him for mayor. Now neither a Democrat nor Republican, he was well pulled apart by both sides. The Democratic *Herald* outdid itself in invective against Cohn, deeming him an "ingrained ass, Jump Jim Crow, changing chameleon, practiced professor of political thimblerig."[35] The Republican *Times* gleefully supported the right of the Citizens Convention to nominate Cohn, and remarked smugly, "we are not making Mr. Cohn's fight, and think the Citizens Convention should have endorsed Governor Mansfield [the Republican candidate]... but since that body declined to do this, we propose to see that its selection for mayor has at least a fair show...."[36]

Jacoby, Democratic nominee for the Board of Education, had it no easier. The *Times* found a witness who heard Jacoby say that his only reason for seeking the office was the $50 monthly salary paid the secretary of the Board. Vehement denials were dismissed with the triumphant clincher, "our informant is a Democrat whose word we do not doubt."[37] Jacoby responded lustily in his own *Süd Californische Post*, calling the *Times'* editor a Know-Nothing and blackmailer, who was attacking him only because of his foreign birth.[38]

Bernard Cohn lost to the Democratic candidate and ran again in 1887 as a Democrat for city council. Now the *Times* sought to impugn his candidacy by reprinting the attacks on him by the *Herald* during the 1882 campaign.[39] According to the *Times*, Cohn "found that his claims to a station which required a certain amount of social eligibility were not thought to be overshadowing." This suggested that the tough politician, a "power of the Fourth Ward," was lacking in certain social graces—or perhaps was simply a Jew. On election day Cohn came in first, and this strong, turbulent man was for a time president of the city council. His obstinate courage led him through battle after battle, almost always to victory. Again and again he stood up in court for what he conceived to be his rights, while the records of the city council are filled with his advocacy of the interests of the electorate as he understood them. When the *Times* continued to snipe at Cohn while he was on the council, suggesting he might be involved in illicit city patronage through his son who was doing business with the city, Cohn shot off a letter concluding: "If you or your informant desire it, I will demand a proper investigation. My enemies have tried to look into the city vaults for all transactions done by me in previous years and at present and they always find that I look for the city's interest and not for personal interest."[40] Controversy around Cohn did not subside even with his death. One of the sensational lawsuits of Los Angeles' history was generated by the will he left after his death in September 1889.

Other Jews continued to interest themselves more quietly in movements of economic and civic betterment. In March of 1883 a call was issued to organize a Board of Trade.[41] Since the Chamber of Commerce's demise, there had been no business association in the bustling community. Thirty leading businessmen met in the Produce Exchange rooms, where the chairman, Eugene Meyer, told of the important advantages which the late Chamber of Commerce had secured. Two Jews were among the Board of Trade's officers: Abe Haas was vice-president and Harris Newmark was a director. On the By-Laws Committee were Meyer and Eugene Germain, and fifteen substantial Jewish firms were charter members.[42] This Board of Trade functioned until 1906, when it consolidated with the wholesale Board of Trade. The Chamber of Commerce was meanwhile reestablished in 1888. Under the vigorous leadership of Charles Dwight Willard, it played a leading role making Los Angeles one of the most publicized and advertised cities in the United States. When the cornerstone of the Chamber's building was laid in 1902, it rested upon the site of Harris Newmark's former home, adjacent to the synagogue; the chairman of the building committee was M. J. Newmark.[43]

At the height of the boom of 1888 another civic pillar, the Associated Charities, was set in place. The large influx of immigrants, many of them ill or indigent, prompted the formation of this association, which could investigate the merits of claimants. The leading forces in the Associated Charities movement were the churches and the existing charitable organizations, and the moving spirit was Rabbi Emanuel Schreiber, under whose chairmanship several individuals met on January 19, 1888.[44] Schreiber explained that this new group would not overlap existing charities but would protect the community from imposture and reduce vagrancy and duplication by investigating all applications for relief. He volunteered one hour of his time every day.[45] In March 1888, a circular was issued:

Far from interfering with existing charities, the Associated Charities intend to strengthen, to aid and to support the noble hands of the disinterested and tireless workers in the cause of humanity in our midst. The non-sectarian, the undenominational and cosmopolitan character of the organization is bound to enlist for it the broadminded men and women whose heart beats warm for suffering humanity, regardless of creed, sect, nationality, race and politics. Dr. Schreiber, Rabbi of the Jewish community, has kindly volunteered his services from the start free of charge. Dr. Schreiber, registrar, has a temporary office in the Caledonian club rooms, 17 West First Street, Evening Express Building.[46]

Rabbi Schreiber left town soon afterwards, the boom broke, and the Associated Charities subsided into prolonged quiescence. Three "firsts," the Library Association of the 1850's, the Chamber of Commerce, and the Associated Charities, were thus spearheaded by Jews, failed, and were resurrected at a more propitious time.

The Social Spectrum

During the hectic 1880's, the public life of the small Jewish community greatly increased as several organizations were founded, destined to long and active lives. The third decade of Congregation B'nai B'rith's history featured a decisive shift of its religious orientation. The gradual procéss of displacing Jews from the central position they had held in the life of Los Angeles since it became an American town also began during the 1880's, but was barely noticed at the time.

Jews continued to hold a place in Los Angeles' miniature clubland. Not until a later date did their welcome disappear at many of the social and recreational clubs in the city. In January 1882, when the Los Angeles Athletic Club's first building was dedicated at a much publicized, brilliant affair, there was extensive Jewish participation.[47] The California Club, founded in 1887 for men of means, from its inception stood at a high social level. Its initiation fee was an unheard-of $100, and monthly dues were $5; membership was restricted to one hundred and fifty. Of the first 125 members, at least twelve were Jews.[48] Years later the California Club excluded Jews.

The formal social clubs added a veneer of elegance to local social life, but informal parties and receptions were the major social activity. A popular practice was surprise parties, whereby people would descend unexpectedly upon those they wished to honor. It was for the host to show that he could rise to the occasion.[49] From all available evidence, the social amusements of Jewish young people were mostly among themselves. Thus during the Los Angeles Social Club's heyday in the 1870's the Jewish girls seemed to attend only those affairs where the males were predominantly Jewish. The custom of summers at the seashore was popular. Many prosperous Jews built summer homes for themselves at Santa Monica, Catalina, and Wilmington. Others spent the summer months in San Francisco. The number summering at the shore became so considerable that Congregation B'nai B'rith in time transferred its summer Friday evening services to Ocean Park.

Music and art became popular, not only as lessons for the young but also for their parents. The three Jewish music teachers in the city had a numerous clientele. The leading families studied with "Professor" Loeb; other teachers were Miss Israel, a violinist, and a Mr. Brenner, who played the piano. Many women took painting lessons.

When the French representatives to the Yorktown Centennial in 1881 visited Los Angeles, they were entertained by the French colony. Its head was Eugene Meyer, who served for years as consular agent for France in Los Angeles. Upon his removal to San Francisco, Leon Loeb replaced him for fifteen years. M. J. Newmark, wishing to live in France for a time, applied for and received a consular position in that country. Germanic interests were also promoted by Jews. When a group of distinguished Germans, headed by Eduard Lasker, visited Los Angeles, the welcoming committee of Rabbi Edelman, I. W. Hellman, H. Newmark, M. Morris, and C. Jacoby was exclusively Jewish; the rabbi, a native of Warsaw, was the "honorary" German among them.[50]

There was another end to the Jewish social spectrum in Los Angeles, which was shunned by the prosperous and respectable. These were the evidently few Jews in shady business, or those whose personal life or conduct brought them afoul of the law. Although the incidence of Jews in crime was small, cases came to court involving pawnbrokers and secondhand furniture dealers. Bernard Solomon, a pawnbroker, was accused of being a "fence" for stolen goods.[51] One of the witnesses for the prosecution was a fellow pawnbroker, L. B. Cohn, who shortly was to be involved in serious cases of his own. Solomon was described in the newspapers as an "Israelite but not without guile."[52] The courts found him guilty. Under the euphonious headline "Levy in Limbo" another pawnbroker named M. Levy, described as an "English Jew with a hard face," was indicted for receiving stolen goods. "It is a well known fact," said the *Times* reporter, "that he could put his hand on every thief in the city if he were so disposed."[53] Yet another pawnbroker, Louis Levy, engaged in a fist fight with the city license inspector over delinquent taxes. The newspaper reported that Levy "wiped the floor" with the unpopular official, who departed "a sadder if not a wiser man."[54] Levy suffered no legal consequences.

A case that occupied the courts for years was that of an arsonist, Robert Levine. He was convicted in 1889 and sentenced to twenty-five years for setting fire to his saloon beneath the United States Hotel. The case was ultimately appealed to the Supreme Court and the sentence upheld.[55] The local demimonde included one Louis Silverstein, an opium addict, and his sister, Maude Silverstein, the town prostitute.[56] Another Jewish man, Sam Levy, was called by the newspapers an "opium fiend."[57] The offspring of an intermarriage between Jew and Mexican was Louis Laventhal. In the marriage records of 1868, there is a Joseph Laventhal who married Andrea Lopez; the boy Louis was a product of this union. Newspapers called him a "half breed Mexican Jew."[58] After a number of delinquencies, he finally was convicted of a particularly brutal murder. Another Laventhal, Brulio, accused of grand larceny in 1895, could be a brother.

Jews also came to court during the 1880's in cases which reflect the varieties of life and business in Los Angeles. Samuel Prager and Martin Wise were tried for violating the Sunday closing law.[59] A pawnbroker, Isaac Isaacson, was charged with exacting usurious interest, but the case was dismissed when he proved that he had only charged fifty cents for repairing the plaintiff's watch.[60] The supreme court heard in 1883 the case of a Jewish man who adopted the child of a Mexican couple, born after its parents were divorced. Upon the death of the adopted father, his brother, Michael Newman, applied for letters of administration. This was resisted by the natural mother. Newman argued that the divorce was never valid and therefore the adoption was not legal, not having the consent of the natural father. Therefore the child was in no sense a son of his brother Bernard, and not entitled to the estate. Moreover, even if the adoption were legal, the natural mother would be entitled to nothing because an adoptive child does not succeed to the estate of an adoptive parent. The judge, however, ruled the divorce and adoption valid, and that the child should inherit the estate of his adopted father. The mother was therefore granted letters of administration.[61]

Another unusual petition was that of Sophia Levy, to be allowed to engage in business on her own account. As she explained, her husband was afflicted with a chronic liver ailment which had the peculiar effect of making him reckless in money matters. "She wished things fixed so that she can control the purse strings."[62]

A Functioning Jewish Community

As the gradual displacement of the Jews from civic prominence began, lodge leadership also noticeably shifted away from them, although some continued to serve as leaders. Rabbi Edelman, perennial "lodger," was elected Chief Councilor of the International Order of Chosen Friends, Orange Council. Sam Prager was Grand Sword Bearer at the Grand Lodge of the Masonic Order in San Francisco in 1883. S. G. Marshutz, newly arrived in Los Angeles and destined to play an important role in the community, was elected Grand Representative to the Grand Lodge of California of the German Order of the Sons of Hermann. A number of Jews were active in the Knights of Pythias.

One coordinate of slow Jewish exclusion was heightened activity in Jewish organizational and congregational circles. The Hebrew Benevolent Society, with little to do for permanent Jewish residents, began to feel the burden of the indigent sick trickling into Los Angeles. However, its major effort during this decade was for the Johnstown flood survivors in 1889, when Harris Newmark collected $1,000.[63] Most actual charity came from the Ladies' Hebrew Benevolent Society, who cared for the sick coming into town, nourished them, and arranged to bury those who died.[64] It was in this period that the first serious talk of a Jewish hospital was heard.[65] A Hebrew Hospital Association was formed and a committee appointed to draft a constitution, but the precipitous end of the boom prevented any action.

The B'nai B'rith lodge during this period attained a twin. By 1883 the age of the members and their relative affluence led younger and less prosperous Jews to form a second lodge called the Semi-Tropic. Its leadership included some children of the founding members together with relative newcomers. The president was M. A. Hamburger, the vice-president was Ben W. Edelman, Samuel Cohn was secretary, and A. Elsasser served as treasurer. They began with thirty-six

California Registered Historical Landmark of the first Jewish site in Los Angeles, located in Chavez Ravine. Los Angeles City Hall looms in background. (Rothschild Photo.)

Minutes of the first meeting of the Common Council of Los Angeles, held on July 3, 1850. The minutes were recorded in Spanish, as were most official documents in the first two decades of the city's municipal operation. The signatures of the seven Council members, including that of Morris L. Goodman, appear at the bottom of the document. (Courtesy of Mayor Sam Yorty.)

Main St. near Temple St., showing stores of Solomon Lazard and H. W. Hellman, 1866.

Downey's Old Block, showing stores of Harris and Jacoby (successors to H. W. Hellman), Maurice Kremer, and Solomon Lazard, about 1875.

Joseph Newmark, first lay Rabbi of Los Angeles Jewry, pictured in 1881 (four generations). Left to right: Mr. Newmark, Rose Loeb, Estelle Newmark Loeb, Sarah Newmark Newmark (Mrs. Harris Newmark).

Rabbi Abraham W. Edelman, first Rabbi in Los Angeles, and his family, 1886. On porch, left to right: William T. Barnett, Mrs. William T. Barnett, Ben Edelman, Abraham M. Edelman, Etta Jacoby, Herman Jacoby, David W. Edelman, Rabbi Abraham W. Edelman, Mrs. Abraham W. Edelman, Nathan Jacoby, Mrs. Herman Jacoby. Children: Leo Barnett and Lyela Edelman. Far right: Henry W. Edelman.

Joseph P. Newmark, founder of the Hebrew Benevolent Society, at his home, taken June 24, 1854.

Solomon Lazard, pioneer merchant, member of the City Council for many years beginning in 1854.

Mrs. Virginia Katz, secretary of the Hebrew Ladies' Benevolent Society from its inception in 1870, and for over fifty years.

Mrs. Wolf Kalisher, first president of the Hebrew Ladies' Benevolent Society, taken in 1870.

Isaias W. Hellman, founder of banking in Southern California and leader in the Jewish community.

Mr. & Mrs. Maurice Kremer at their golden wedding anniversary in 1906, near the close of a long civic career.

Judge Harry A. Hollzer (1880-1946), first president of the Los Angeles Jewish Community Council.

Ben R. Meyer, first president of the Federation of Jewish Welfare Organizations 1913-1915.

Ungraded school near Laurel Canyon and Sunset Blvd., 1884. Jeanette Lazard, teacher, with children of various ages. She married Louis Lewin in 1885.

The first building of Kaspare Cohn Hospital (later Cedars-Sinai Medical Center), 1902.

Library of Jewish Alliance, first Jewish Community Center.

Jewish "high society" at the Concordia Club picnic, circa 1900.

The dedication of the Jewish Orphan Home (today Vista del Mar), 1912.

Laying the cornerstone of the Wilshire Boulevard Temple, 1928. Front row, left to right: Rabbi Maxwell Dubin, Marco Newmark, Rabbi Edgar F. Magnin, Dr. David Edelman (Pres.), George Mosbacher (Bldg. Chmn.), Mrs. James W. Hellman, James W. Hellman, and Mrs. Florine Wolstein.

B'nai B'rith Congregation (now Wilshire Boulevard Temple) 218 S. Broadway, 1873. The first Jewish building in Los Angeles. (Historical Collections, Security Pacific Bank.)

members.[66] B'nai B'rith lodges and other groups observed the centennial birthday of Moses Montefiore in 1884 as widely as was done everywhere else. The congregation held services in honor of the Anglo-Jewish patriarch, followed by a meeting sponsored by B'nai B'rith.[67] When Rabbi Edelman attempted to found a congregation a few years later, an appropriate name was Moses Montefiore Congregation.

Beginning sometime in 1885, there was discussion about a Young Men's Hebrew Association similar to one which had existed a few years before. With YMHA's being established in the larger cities of the country, this project also attained to greater immediacy in Los Angeles when the policy of excluding Jewish youths from the polite dances and socials of the city became evident. "The Gentiles have several societies and I often hear some of our young people complain of not having invitations to their dances and entertainment. The only way to remedy this is to organize a club and be independent of other associations."[68] Boyle Workman, who reckoned many Jews among his friends, in his reminiscences lists approximately one hundred fifty belles of the day, and one hundred sixty-five bachelors, yet not one was Jewish.[69]

Rabbi Schreiber stimulated local Jewish youth to found an organization with charitable, cultural, and social aims. The first aim was fulfilled when a young man, recently arrived from Canada, passed away and the organization took charge of the burial.[70] The cultural aim was realized when Rabbi M. S. Levy was invited from Oakland to address the new YMHA on the "Aims and Tendencies of Modern Thoughts."[71] By this time it had seventy members. Its social purpose was exemplified by a ball on Thanksgiving evening of 1888, to which 250 young people came.[72] One year later, however, the club was in decline.[73] An anniversary ball and banquet again scheduled for Thanksgiving evening was not held. The Young Men's Hebrew Association was probably another casualty of the boom's collapse.

The major concern of the organized Jewish community remained its religious affairs, focused in Congregation B'nai B'rith. However, as the congregation entered its twentieth year of existence, synagogue life had declined. Its nearly Orthodox services were sparsely attended, and it was difficult to find a minyan (prayer quorum) on Saturday mornings.[74] One Sabbath visitor found eleven gentlemen, one lady, and five little boys at the synagogue. On several consecutive Sabbaths public worship could not take place for lack of a minyan.[75] Of perhaps one hundred members, as few as thirty paid dues.[76] Rabbi Edelman was still the congregation's rabbi, teacher, shohet, and mohel at a reputed salary of $75 a month.[77]

The death of Joseph Newmark in 1881 released the dammed flood of change. This pious patriarch had first organized services in 1854 and was universally loved and respected. He was the elder member of the town's leading Jewish family, and his presence had restrained the critics of Orthodoxy and of Rabbi Edelman. But now the members insisted that changes be introduced in Los Angeles' only synagogue. On the High Holidays of 1883, Rabbi Edelman bowed to the demands of the hour and introduced a mixed choir.[78] The music whetted the congregation's appetite for more changes.[79] They wanted a shorter service and a Friday evening service with a "lecture." The Reform rabbi Elkan Cohn came from San Francisco and spoke to the congregation in 1883 in aid of the party agitating for reforms. He referred to the changes taking place in Jewish life, "and the whole tenor of his address seemed to be to encourage a liberal, enterprising spirit among his hearers.[80]

Harris Newmark was then president of the congregation. He was divided between his sentimental loyalty to Jewish tradition, to his dear friend Rabbi Edelman, to that which his uncle-father-in-law had represented, and his realization that reforms were the demand of the hour. For the prosperous acclimated Jews had long since deserted traditional observance. I. W. Hellman attended services only on the High Holy Days.[81] Kashruth was all but abandoned, with reportedly only one family maintaining a full kosher home;[82] probably it was that of Rabbi Edelman himself.

Rabbi Edelman could not fight. For twenty years he had struggled for Judaism in a community filled with good people and indifferent Jews. The High Holidays of 1884 were the last at which Congregation B'nai B'rith worshipped in the Orthodox manner. Soon after, a committee informed Rabbi Edelman that the somewhat Reform Jastrow prayer book would henceforth be used in the synagogue. The rabbi could compromise no more. A choir and a confirmation ceremony he could accept, and he had never opposed family pews. He had even allowed worshippers to take off their hats during his sermons, and would himself have an organ during worship a few years later.[83] But the rejection of the traditional prayer book stretched his principles beyond his limits. Quietly and peacefully he resigned.

The congregation advertised in the *American Israelite* on July 10, 1885, for a competent rabbi who could preach in English, officiate as reader, conduct a Sabbath school, and who knew music "because the congregation expects, in the course of time, to form a choir." The salary offered was $2,000. The reputation of Dr. Ephraim Schreiber of Denver had reached Los Angeles, and I. W. Hellman was asked to stop off during a business trip to hear the young man. He worshipped at Temple Emanuel in Denver on a stormy night and was attracted to the rabbi, whom he invited to call at his hotel. Dr. Schreiber reminisced that he had just been told by his doctor that Mrs. Schreiber must move to a place like Los Angeles for her health, so he felt Hellman's visit could only have been the hand of God.[84] Hellman invited Rabbi Schreiber to visit Los Angeles. In July 1885 he came and conducted a memorial service for General Grant and Moses Montefiore,[85] and on Saturday morning he spoke on "Monotheism and Polytheism." He made a splendid impression and was immediately engaged.

The Jastrow prayer book, an organ, and Rabbi Schreiber were introduced to the congregation on the High Holidays of 1885, but it was not an occasion that Rabbi Schreiber would remember with pleasure.[86] A stubborn core of Orthodox worshippers sided with an "intractable" cantor, who disregarded the previously agreed program of worship and gave the rabbi no opportunity to introduce English readings. Hot words were exchanged that afternoon. In addition, two members of the choir strangely took ill and had to be replaced on Yom Kippur by singers who knew no Hebrew. The pro-Reform *American Israelite* in Cincinnati was satisfied nonetheless. The wife of the minister attended the services, "which is an improvement on former times," and the pleased congregants were now "willing and proud to have their Christian friends attend services in the synagogue."[87]

Rabbi Schreiber was then about thirty-three years old. He was born in Moravia and studied in Berlin, where he received rabbinic ordination and a doctorate. He first served as rabbi in Elbring, West Prussia, and from 1879 to 1881 in Bonn, but in November 1883 he left for America. The cause of his departure from Germany was strangely put. He blamed it on anti-Semitism, which did great harm to the Jewish Reform movement, "the cause of which the learned doctor always most enthusiastically exposed." His Reform Judaism was too radical for German Jewry. Schreiber had already written an unpleasantly polemical work against the Jewish historian Heinrich Graetz (1817-1891), assailing his hostility to Reform Judaism.[88] (Early in his career, he apparently began to use the name Emanuel in place of Ephraim.)

The energetic young rabbi undertook many activities. He introduced Saturday morning services for children and experimented with the liturgy.[89] One of his most fruitful projects was a Ladies' Aid Society, which was "to raise funds for the synagogue, take responsibility for the administration of the Sunday school and to provide social activities for the congregation."[90] At a fair during its first year, the society raised no less than $3,000 for the "embellishment of the synagogue."[91] The ladies gave socials and fancy dress balls and took a keen interest in the school, where they visited regularly and served as teachers. The chairman of the Sunday School Committee was Mrs. H. W. Hellman, and the teachers in 1886 included five former confirmants of well-known families. The ladies arranged the annual Purim affair for the children and encouraged the women of the congregation to attend services.[92] Activity in Congregation B'nai B'rith became largely a feminine affair. The Ladies' Aid Society eventually declined into quietude, to be reestablished later by Rabbi Hecht as the Sisterhood.

Although strongly Reform by conviction, Rabbi Schreiber tried to be rabbi for the entire congregation. He wore a skullcap in deference to the opposition, until it was doffed at Shavuot services of 1888 and officially abolished thereafter.[93] Besides preaching English sermons, he differed from Rabbi Edelman by delivering a German sermon about once monthly. His sermons were in the prolix, florid style of the day, carefully written out, and mixed Talmudic tradition and prophetic ethics with modern literature, history, and philosophy. That on Yom Kippur of 1887, for instance, was entitled "Longfellow's Psalm of Life." On the High Holidays, Rabbi Schreiber read the services, while the choir and a new cantor did the singing. The rabbi and many of the congregation fasted the entire Yom Kippur, while the choir, now Christian except for the organist Leopold Loeb, "went out for refreshments and came back in time for the next anthem."[94] Rabbi Schreiber read from the Torah, while the *shamash*, H. Meyer, blew the shofar. Herman Silver, later to be president of the congregation, chanted the concluding *Ne'ilah* service and also preached.[95] Services at B'nai B'rith by this time closely resembled those held in the more traditional Reform temples throughout the country. In 1887 Rabbi Schreiber introduced the interesting, if unusual, custom of transferring the bar mitzvahs of the year to the High Holidays and the festivals.[96] Rosh Hashanah was now observed for one day only, which made things easier for the merchants noted more for their probity than their piety, who still habitually closed their stores on the High Holidays. The only Jewish stores that kept open were Meyberg's Crockery and the People's Store, but their number was soon augmented.

Rabbi Schreiber was popular among the Christian ministers of the town. On Thanksgiving Day 1886 he introduced interfaith services, held with the Unitarian Church.[97] At these first services Rabbi Schreiber declared that only in America could such a joint Thanksgiving be possible, while the Unitarian Dr. Fay pronounced that the true church is only that which produces the finest men and women. "Dr. Schreiber's pulpit cap may be square and flat at the top and mine may be oval and round at the top, but the people are beginning to see and feel that the form of our caps is not the foundation of God."[98] In addition, "Dr. Schreiber became the authority for the ministers of the area who often consulted him on doubtful passages in the Old Testament."[99] As mentioned above, he was instrumental in founding the Associated Charities and the Young Men's Hebrew Association. In 1888 he was president of B'nai B'rith Orange Lodge. He also taught Greek, German, and Latin at a Presbyterian college.

Notwithstanding Schreiber's activity and prestige among Christians, his honeymoon in the congregation did not outlast the first year. The High Holidays of 1886 saw opposition to his reforms still rampant.[100] The introduction of a Gentile choir must have caused some mutterings. And Rabbi Edelman came back to town after a short term in Portland, Oregon. On the High Holidays of 1886 the traditionalists of the B'nai B'rith Congregation joined him for their own services in the Masonic Hall.[101] These services were continued on the High Holidays by Rabbi Edelman for years, except for a short time in Altoona, Pennsylvania, where he served until the severity of the winter drove him back to Los Angeles. From 1890 this shaky Conservative congregation, called the Moses Montefiore Congregation, met for some years on the festivals and High Holidays. This group, alienated by Congregation B'nai B'rith's adoption of Reform Judaism, kept up a tenuous existence as traditionalists.

Meanwhile, attendance at B'nai B'rith's Reform services dropped off. Now the sermon was criticized for being too long, and Rabbi Schreiber found a new interest—real estate in the citrus belt. Along with most other Jews, he dabbled in the speculation of the day. Members were undoubtedly pained by the reports of the rabbi's financial speculations and widespread tales that he had made a good profit.[102] One story reported his profits so large that he was "independent of clerical 'puts and calls.'"[103] By the end of the High Holiday season in 1888, word spread that Rabbi Schreiber was leaving, probably by mutual consent. He planted stories in the Los Angeles press describing his great success as a guest preacher before important congregations in New York, Chicago, Philadelphia, Pittsburgh, and Cincinnati, four of whom allegedly offered him positions. Modestly, however, he took a position in Little Rock, Arkansas.[104] More than thirty years later Schreiber returned to Los Angeles to serve briefly as rabbi of newly organized Temple Emanuel, the second Reform congregation in Los Angeles. His short tenure at Congregation B'nai B'rith decisively turned it towards Reform, the religious direction it unquestionably wished to pursue.

During the boom, the congregation began to be dissatisfied with its home on Fort Street. The street was becoming commercial. The clangor and tumult of nearby construction, the assurance of a quick sale with a good profit, the overflowing attendance at High Holiday and interfaith services, and the affluence of the membership, all aroused eagerness to move to the "suburbs."[105] The pioneer synagogue also seemed "an old shed," a "dismal rookery."[106] Weeds grew in front, steps were unpainted, floors uncarpeted, seats stiff, hard, and dusty, ceiling soiled, and walls stained.[107] It was completely unfitting for a prosperous Jewry in the middle of a boom. In 1887 land was purchased for $8,000 on Ninth and Hope streets, south and west of the downtown district, while the existing synagogue site was becoming more and more valuable. In 1886 the land was worth $25,000, and in 1887 the leaders reportedly turned down $70,000. With the collapse of the boom, real estate plummeted and with it the high hopes for a new building. The synagogue was finally sold for $37,000 in 1893 and a new one built during a decade of economic hardship.[108]

CHAPTER 5

The Founding Age Closes

———————————>⚬<———————————

Los Angeles after its boom of the 1880's was, in Charles Dwight Willard's phrase, "now suddenly changed from a very old city to a very young one."[1] Of the one hundred thousand people who lived in the city in 1890, more than three-quarters had not been residents as long as four years. For the next half century, ninety percent of the population had arrived within less than fifteen years. Newcomers were to be a perpetual majority. The migration of the 1890's came in large measure from the Middle West, as waves of farmers and small-towners arrived from Iowa, Kansas, and Missouri—"the merchant, the uprooted professional man, the farmer with an invalid wife."[2] They brought with them their middle western ties and their sentiments and habits, and changed the ethnic landscape of Los Angeles. The earliest Los Angelenos had not come from the United States only, but from Germany, France, Great Britain, China, and, of course, Mexico. An 1870 visitor found the sixteen thousand residents of Los Angeles County about equally divided among Americans, Europeans, and Mexicans. On account of this, "on the streets of Los Angeles are heard English, French, Spanish and German."[3] The newer immigration changed this scene, as the native white Protestant American came to typify Los Angeles society.

Jewish immigrants also reached Los Angeles, but they differed noticeably from the native Americans. During the depressed mid-1890's, a few of the East European Jews who were coming to America en masse trickled into the city, and were met with no enthusiasm by the settled Jewish community. Back in 1882, at the time of the Russian pogroms, the *American Israelite* had reported from Los Angeles that no local Jew contributed a cent for Russian Jewish refugees.[4] In 1890 it had again chided the Jewish community of Los Angeles, declaring that it was not enough only to aid each other in sickness.[5] Now a few steps were taken to assist the East European newcomers. In 1894 B'nai B'rith Congregation accepted forty-two of their children into its Sunday school. "These people live among us and we must try to raise their children so they may become American Jews."[6]

The "Gay Nineties" began with little gaiety for immigrants or natives, as the hangover after the boom of the 1880's merged into the nationwide depression of 1893. In that unhappy year four Los Angeles banks closed, and the city experienced its first serious unemployment. Among the businesses forced to the wall was the famous City of Paris, which in 1893 was sold off to its creditors.

The city's foremost banker, a rock of strength in earlier crises, was no longer living in Los Angeles. After thirty years' residence Isaias W. Hellman had moved to San Francisco in 1890 to take over the Nevada Bank, which was undergoing reorganization. But he retained his financial and proprietary interest in the Farmers and Merchants Bank and remained the largest property owner in town. When the panic struck Los Angeles, Hellman's reappearance in the city worked magic. Every bank except Farmers and Merchants was closed when word flew, "Hellman is back; Hellman is in town." He put $250,000 cash in the till, another $250,000 next day, and supported all the country banks in exchange relations with Farmers and Merchants. He also persuaded the Pasadena bank not to close but rather to meet with its large depositors and secure their agreement not to withdraw their deposits. Hellman later declared that if he had resided in Los Angeles, he probably would have been able to save all the banks. In view of the record, this was hardly boastful.[7]

The economic doldrums inspired Max Meyberg's inventive faculty. He persuaded the newly organized Merchants' Association that Los Angeles needed a West Coast equivalent of New Orleans' Mardi Gras—a carnival to pump enthusiasm and business into the veins of the economy. His suggestion accepted by acclamation, Meyberg was elected director-general of La Fiesta de Los Angeles. Lodges and business associations, schools and City Council, neighboring communities and railroads participated wholeheartedly in the grandiose Fiesta, which began on April 10, 1894, with a parade:

Up and down Main, Spring and Broadway, slowly moved the quaint little parade—beautifully decorated, horse-drawn drags, nearly hidden in a wealth of spring blossoms. Tallyho's draped in swaths of bright colored bunting, gay red, white and yellow mantled floats, Roman chariots garlanded with palm branches, snappy bands pouring out Sousa marches; smartly uniformed drill corps and patrols—all climaxed by the gorgeous floats smothered in flowers bearing the queen of the Fiesta and her court of ladies; cavaliers in colorful costumes and sombreros set astride groomed horses, caparisoned with silver mounted Mexican saddles. The great Chinese dragon, two hundred feet long, carried on the heads of local orientals, serpentined in and out, bringing up the rear.[8]

Succeeding days included an international parade, a children's procession, and a workingmen's parade. There also was a citrus art and flower exhibition and, for a climax, a gigantic carnival masque ball. The Fiesta was repeated in 1895 and 1896 but ceased when costs became too heavy and rowdyism soured the event.

Many Jews besides Meyberg played leading roles in the Fiesta, including Leon Loeb, M. H. Newmark (chairman of the all-important Finance Committee), A. Jacoby, H. W. Frank, John Kahn, J. S. Salkey, L. J. Fleishman, Max Goldschmidt, and many others. Jews also continued to play an important role in the Merchants' Association. In 1896 H. W. Frank was its president, Jacob Waldeck, secretary, and D. A. Hamburger and Meyberg were members of the board. The Merchants' Association later became the Merchants' and Manufacturers' Association, representing a very conservative social and economic influence in Los Angeles.

At the lower end of the economic scale, the East European arrivals of the 1890's were tending to recapitulate the economic pattern of the earlier, Germanic generation by laboriously building their own businesses. They went into the secondhand and junk businesses and opened small shops. A few secondhand clothing merchants came into the news for creating disturbances, selling lottery tickets, buying stolen goods, and similar offenses. The *Los Angeles Times* editorially reproved the Jewish secondhand dealer:

The junk shop man, as the second hand dealer is generally called, is a peculiar kind of merchant and is looked upon by the legitimate tradesman as an outsider. Junk shops were first invented by the lower class of Jews who had been given a fair chance to show what was in them and after failing two-three times, they were knocked out of the circle of respectable merchants.... When the second hand business was first started, a certain amount of honesty surrounded him ... but a new class of enterprising Americans or foreigners came in and reasoned: 'There are thousands of thieves who need a place to dispose of their ill-gotten gains.'[9]

The members of Congregation B'nai B'rith were deeply embarrassed by some of the newcomers, whose struggle to eke out an existence in a pre-industrial community during hard times forced some of them to unacceptable methods of doing business. But they were to suffer much greater embarrassments, as we shall see, when some prominent Jewish names were involved in public scandals.

Social Exclusion and Internal Snobbery

In May 1891 the Concordia Club was incorporated for the "social and mental culture" of its members. The board of directors consisted of Leon Loeb, Herman Baruch, J. F. Waldeck, Maurice H. Newmark, J. Salkey, H. W. Frank, H. Altschul, John S. Stover, and John Kahn. Over one hundred members joined at once. In rapid succession a lease was taken on the former Elks Club, billiard tables installed, and a dance sponsored. By 1894 the Concordia had its own handsome rooms in the Burbank Building on Main Street, with large ballroom, reading room, card room, and banquet hall.[10] In later years the club built its own clubhouse on Figueroa Boulevard, which became the inner sanctum of high Jewish society. Its Jewish atmosphere eventually became so rarefied that the Concordia annually sponsored for its children what was reportedly the finest Christmas party in town. The ethos of the Concordia and the other social clubs was expressed by the *Los Angeles Times*: "With the growth of Los Angeles as a metropolis, has come a demand for social clubs, as are found in all large cities. No social club will be a thorough success which accepts anyone as a member who merely dresses decently and is able to pay the dues. . . . No person should be admitted as a member of the club whom the average member would refuse to admit as a guest in his home. . . . Only such clubs as are exclusive in regard to the character of the members, can expect to be permanently prosperous."[11] This philosophy was coupled with a policy of exclusion which was to extend to all Jews except the few who had joined in the early years. It is doubtful that there would have been a Concordia Club if it were not for this policy of social exclusion.

The two B'nai B'rith lodges also continued to function feebly. Mutual benevolence was no longer a sufficient incentive to younger men. The B'nai B'rith leaders began to organize a third local lodge, and the turn of the century was to see its establishment as Lodge 487, into which the two others ultimately merged.[12]

Sons and Heirs

One of Rabbi Edelman's sons, Ben, entered the tobacco business. Another, Henry, a popular young man who received an appointment as deputy county clerk in a department of the superior court, pained his father and brought upon himself the attention of the entire community in 1889 when he and Ben were indicted for fraud in the payment of juror fees and expenses. It was charged that they had manipulated accounts to collect the money for themselves. Falsified warrants had allegedly been cashed by the pawnbroker L. B. Cohen, Edelman's cousin, who then cashed them at the county treasurer's office. The case against Ben was dropped, but Henry's dragged on through three years and three mistrials. The jury each time was hung, seemingly because the key witness, L. B. Cohen, stoutly and persistently could not remember who had sold him the fraudulent warrants. After three years of legal maneuvering and political manipulation, Henry Edelman was discharged.[13] During Ben's trial, Rabbi Edelman received the happier news that his son David had graduated from New York State Medical College third in a class of four hundred.[14] Henry Edelman next became a saloonkeeper and in 1894 was arrested as a pioneer operator of a nickel slot-machine. He refused to remove it on the grounds that having been a court clerk, he knew his rights. Henry Edelman was again taken to court, and the jury again being strangely unable to agree, he was discharged.[15]

A much more spectacular court case which sheds light on the mores of the time was the suit of Delfina Verelas de Cohn for widow's and children's rights to the estate of Bernard Cohn. Incredibly enough, the political firebrand Bernard Cohn from 1872 until his wife Esther's death in 1885 had maintained two domestic establishments and reared two families, one Jewish and one Catholic. As a respected Jewish and civic leader, he was husband to Esther and father of Julius, Casper, and Carrie. He had been president of Congregation B'nai B'rith, city councilman, president of the Hebrew Benevolent Society, and one of the leading businessmen in town. As head of the household near the Plaza, Cohn reared six children, of whom four were living—Bernardo Matathias Joseph Cohn, Miguel Daniel Cohn, Marcus Caraco Cohn, Eduardo Anstaro Cohn. He had had the children baptized in his name, discussed their rearing with the Catholic priest, and buried in the Catholic cemetery two who died. This double relationship was not kept secret. In 1876 a newspaper, the *Jolly Giant*, published an article about the two families, calling one the Chile Pepper and the other the Jew family. After Esther Cohn died in 1885, Bernard Cohn yielded to the importunities of Delfina and married her by contract; being of different religions, they could not be married in any other way. It appears, however, that Cohn subsequently instructed his coachman to steal the contract from Delfina's drawer.

When Cohn died in 1889, his will left nothing for Delfina and her four living children. Suit was filed to secure for Delfina a widow's share and for her children their share of the father's inheritance. The case preoccupied the community for a year and a half, as more than three hundred witnesses testified to the relationship between Cohn's two households. The issue turned on whether Delfina Verelas was a wife or a mistress. Those of the Spanish community called to testify almost invariably insisted that Delfina was regarded as Bernard Cohn's wife. The numerous Jewish witnesses testified that she was known as Cohn's mistress. Rabbi Edelman asserted that Bernard Cohn was an Orthodox Hebrew and rigorously observed the rules of his faith. He had officiated at Cohn's home a number of times, dealt with him, and never heard of his being married to Delfina. He had heard, however, that Cohn kept a mistress.[16] That Bernard Cohn could be respected as an Orthodox Jew and unperturbedly maintain his standing in the Jewish and general community is a revealing comment on the mixed society and double standards of the day.

Decision was rendered on October 30, 1892. Delfina Cohn was acknowledged to have received a valid contract of marriage, but since there was no assumption of marital rights and obligations after the writing of the contract in 1885, the court ruled that there was no marriage, and Delfina did not share in the estate. Three of the children, whom Bernard Cohn had acknowledged in writing as his own, were deemed to be his children for purposes of inheritance.[17]

Dissident Rabbis and a New Temple

The 1890's were quiescent years for the Jewish community. Many of the prosperous were satisfied with their membership in the Concordia Club, while the less affluent B'nai B'rith lodge lay in the doldrums. Little was heard from other societies. During the 1890's, however, new elements within local Jewry took the first steps which were to bring forth Orthodox and Conservative congregations after 1900.

In its remoteness from the centers of Jewish life, Los Angeles Jewry could not easily attract rabbis, especially properly qualified ones. Surely the character and long service of Rabbi Edelman was sheer good fortune, while Rabbi Schreiber was qualified and respectable. Luck ran out with Schreiber's successor, Rabbi Abraham Blum, who came from Galveston, Texas. Rabbi Blum had received ordination from Zadok Kahn, Chief Rabbi of France, and from the director of the French École Rabbinique, although he was not a graduate of that institution.[18] His wife, Henriquez, became principal of the Sunday school, which had 132 children. Herman W. Hellman became president of the congregation and was even prevailed upon to teach a class in the Sunday school, perhaps because his wife served as chairman of the Sunday School Committee.[19]

In 1890, soon after Rabbi Blum's arrival, Los Angeles Jewry received its only known nineteenth-century convert. The daughter of L. B. Cohen, the pawnbroker, began to keep company with a Spanish fireman, Edward Kinney. Cohen refused paternal permission for the marriage unless Kinney would embrace Judaism. Kinney agreed, and under Rabbi Blum's tutelage he renounced his Catholic faith and was converted and married. Mrs. Kinney became a soloist in the choir and her husband one of the congregation's most regular worshippers.[20]

The congregation witnessed a brief surge of enthusiasm with its new rabbi. Services on the High Holidays were well attended. The movement toward Reform was accentuated by the introduction of the cornet in place of the shofar (ram's horn). The traditional form of services on the Jewish New Year, however, was still kept.[21] By 1893, however, the congregation lay in spiritual depression to accompany the economic depression that afflicted the city. Money was so short that the organist, Leopold Loeb, and the choir had to be dismissed. Only a handful attended Sabbath services.[22] The old synagogue on Fort Street, with its cracked walls and antiquated appearance in a busy commercial street, was not conducive to worship. In 1894 it was sold.[23] A few weeks later, Jews may have been disconcerted to read in the newspaper that "services of the Four Fold Gospel Tabernacle Church would be held this Sunday morning at the old Jewish synagogue next to the City Hall."[24] That fall the congregation was recompensed for its hospitality to the Unity Church when it was invited to use the church until the new building was completed. For the next two years they were guests of the church, where they conducted Sabbath, festival, and High Holiday services.

Criticism of Rabbi Blum and insinuation about him began to fill the air. After Passover, 1895, the congregation dismissed him with a sum of money and a sheaf of testimonials. But the rabbi did not leave Los Angeles; he became a teacher of French in Los Angeles High School. A storm broke in September 1895, while Rabbi Blum was in New York. A member of the Board of Education charged that Rabbi Blum was unfit to teach and that the congregation had given him $250 to receive his resignation. Rumors floated about that he was selling watches in which were concealed "pictures of basest and vilest sort." Blum blamed the rumors on Leopold Loeb, his erstwhile organist, who was falsely trying to injure his reputation. An altercation between the men led to fisticuffs. Leading Jewish citizens revealed that the rabbi had been given notice after the High Holidays of 1893, but was granted a year to resign gracefully. When he failed to do so, he was discharged and given a purse subscribed by individual members "who were afraid of his fierce tongue." One month later, a notice appeared in the *Los Angeles Times*: "At Number 1360 South Figueroa, there will be at Dr. Blum's, a private sale of articles not reached at the auction, such as fine glassware, bric-a-brac, elegant oil paintings, onyx clock and candelabra, to be sold today, between the hours of ten and five P.M." The rabbi was obviously of artistic temperament.[25]

Congregational Realignments

In the midst of the furor over Rabbi Blum, Rabbi Moses G. Solomon quietly moved into town, engaged on probation until after the High Holidays. A native of Germany, he was the first graduate of

Hebrew Union College, the Reform rabbinical school, to occupy a position in Los Angeles.[26] Solomon came at an opportune time. The congregation determined to erect a new building, and the cornerstone was laid on March 15, 1896. A. M. Edelman was the architect. The synagogue, which was long regarded as the finest church edifice in Los Angeles, was of red brick with twin towers and pomegranate domes, characteristic of "mosaic" architecture. Its ground floor consisted of classrooms and an assembly hall; upstairs was the sanctuary, seating 600. The floor was carpeted in deep red, the pews were plush-cushioned, and the chandelier, containing sixty bulbs, was the largest in the city. Stained glass windows were presented by H. W. Hellman, Harris Newmark, Kaspare Cohn, and Mrs. J. P. Newmark. The entire cost was $40,000, a splendid sum.

The Temple was dedicated on September 5, 1896, before a capacity audience of Jews and Christians. To the deep, measured tones of the new organ playing Mendelssohn's Processional, the rabbis of Los Angeles and the officers of the congregation marched down the aisle. Rabbi Edelman now represented the Moses Montefiore Congregation, and the Reverend Alfred Arndt, the Orthodox Kehal Yisrael Congregation, which had recently been founded.

Jacob Baruch, chairman of the Building Committee, handed the key to President Herman Silver, saying: "In presenting you with this insignificant bit of metal, we cherish the hope that you will guard it for all time, and that we will all reap our reward in that Spiritual Temple not made with hands." The dedicatory prayer was given by Rabbi Solomon, and the choir responded with words from King Solomon's dedication of the First Temple. The rabbi then spoke on the theme "There is no place like home." He was followed by Silver, city councilman and popular lay preacher, who saw the new temple as reflecting the cause of humanity, erected to honor the Creator and to benefit all of mankind. "Unfortunately, quarrels are engendered about ritual and dogma," he said, "while the ship of progress is waiting for a cargo of deeds."[27] This synagogue served the Jewish community until 1928. Its sale for $500,000 provided the financial basis for the erection of the Wilshire Boulevard Temple.

Rabbi Edelman had returned once more to Los Angeles in 1890, when the Moses Montefiore Congregation was formally organized with the following officers: A. S. Joseph, S. Goldferd, I. Laser, John B. Cohn, Felix Levy, Sam Rosenblum and M. Morris.[28] It could be considered the first Conservative congregation in Los Angeles, although it did not so describe itself. Sermons were in English and liturgy in English and Hebrew; an organ played and a female choir sang.[29] Rabbi Edelman was no longer really at home in the Orthodox environment of the Polish and Russian Jews drifting into Los Angeles. For the rest of his days, except for brief engagements elsewhere, he resided and functioned in Los Angeles.[30] With his original home sold as a building site, he was financially secure the rest of his life and required no rabbinic livelihood.[31]

When Rabbi Edelman spoke on the occasion of the groundbreaking of the Reform Temple, he said in veiled criticism, "God does not need magnificent structures. Man now needs consecrated spots to inspire him and lift him to sublime heights. . . . People apply themselves to the acquirement [sic] of money and refuse to sacrifice themselves in any way to humanity." He practiced his own sermons. At his death in 1907, he left $10,000 for charity, reputedly the most bequeathed by a Jew until that time.[32]

Beginning sometime in 1892, an Orthodox congregation began to hold services in Los Angeles in East European style. In May 1894 it was incorporated as Kehal Yisrael.[33] It directors were: M. Meyer, S. Greenwald, A. Harris, J. Meyer, B. Sold, A. Lipkin, J. Strive. A year later, when they began raising funds to build a synagogue, one S. Davis offered to contribute $500 and was promptly elected president. Having thus attained office, Davis assumed some privileges and fined one member $25 for insulting the president. The congregation now wholeheartedly demanded Davis' resignation. When he refused, a fracas of words and fists broke out. A letter in the *Los Angeles Times* adds interesting, if confusing, information: "The congregation does not consist of thirteen members [as alleged], but to the number of four-five hundred families [sic].The Congregation Kehal Israel supports a rabbi [Rev. Alfred Arndt] and a Sunday School teacher; has quite a large fund for benevolent purposes, and its members are mostly citizens who are engaged in legitimate business."[34]

Rabbi Edelman held services in the Masonic Hall during 1895 and 1896, while Kehal Yisrael met in McDowell Hall. In 1897 he officiated on the first day of New Year for Kehal Yisrael at Turnverein Hall, speaking in English, while Mr. Arndt preached on the second day. We do not know what happened, but significantly Rabbi

Edelman announced his own services for Yom Kippur and Succoth at Masonic Hall with admission free.[35] Was he no longer Orthodox enough? Next year Arndt, supported by Cantor Goldstein and his choir of five Goldstein children, officiated at McDowell Hall for Kehal Yisrael.[36] A few years later Kehal Yisrael merged with yet another newly formed Conservative congregation, People's Congregation Beth-El, to form the oldest Orthodox congregation existing today, Beth Israel.

In the meantime Rabbi Solomon was unhappily finding that Congregation B'nai B'rith had become too Reform. The congregation likewise was unhappy with him and in 1897 advertised for a rabbi. When Rabbi Solomon indignantly protested, Hellman blandly wrote him that it was an old constitutional practice of the congregation to advertise annually for a rabbi. Solomon stayed only one more year. On April 14, 1899, the congregation again advertised in the *American Hebrew*:

Rabbi M. G. Solomon, having declined to send in his application for re-election at the coming election in April, thus creating a vacancy in our pulpit on October 31, 1899.

The congregation of B'nai B'rith of Los Angeles, (a reformed congregation) herewith solicits applicants. None but a thoroughly English scholar, fully qualified as a lecturer and reader, and possessing a diploma from Hebrew Union College of Cincinnati, or a well-known University in Europe, need apply. Salary, twenty-one hundred dollars per annum and perquisites. Herman W. Hellman, president, and J. W. Waldeck, secretary.

Rabbi Solomon's parting words on the High Holidays of 1899 shocked the congregants. His sweeping indictment of Reform Judaism said in part:

Why must we listen to would-be reformers who tell us what Judaism is not? They have never told us what it is.

We may eat whatever we like and wherever and whenever we like, they say. Judaism, we are told, is not an almanac to tell us when we must fast and Jehovah does not care what we eat.

We are told that Judaism is not a bulky book, nor is it a question of hats on or hats off. The reformers say that Judaism does not consist of eating unleavened bread. . . .

We need not hope and pray for the restoration of the kingdom of David, they say. We have handsomer temples than those of Solomon, and we are satisfied. . . .

The customs of our feast days have been outlived by ourselves and our children. We are told that the Bible, that book which is the foundation of Judaism, is no more readable than the text books of other religions. That the same morality is taught in all of them.

These reformers would do away with our feast days. They would have in our synagogues operatic music and dramatic discourses instead of the humility and simplicity of Judaism. They would give Jehovah a grand reception on the New Year's Day and a farewell dinner on the Day of Atonement. They would have us build kitchens and banquet halls in connection with our temples.

Is this Judaism? I answer you that it is not. If you ask me then what it is, I must reply: It is hard to tell by what name it should be called.[37]

On December 1, 1899, one more congregation was formed, the People's Synagogue Beth El, calling itself a Conservative congregation. M. G. Solomon was its rabbi.[38] At the same time Rabbi Sigmund Hecht (1849-1927) came to Los Angeles and to Congregation B'nai B'rith.

Conclusion: A Century at Its Close

The new Reform rabbi arrived at Congregation B'nai B'rith just as the nineteenth century closed. The event not only marked a milestone in the development of the city's first and, at that time, sole synagogue; taken together with the opening of a fine edifice in 1896, it also rounded out the pioneering era of Jewish life. As the twentieth century opened, Los Angeles Jews had the communal apparatus found in most cities: a synagogue, now Reform; a B'nai B'rith lodge; a Hebrew Benevolent Society and its ladies' auxiliary group; an upper-level social club. As was common, membership in the groups overlapped and leadership interlocked. Members and officers of Congregation B'nai B'rith tended to be the same in the Hebrew Benevolent Society. The B'nai B'rith lodge seems to have been a rather plebeian and young men's group. At the other end of the Jewish social spectrum, the Concordia Club was the focus of Jewish wealth. Both Concordia and the lodge contained Jews without synagogal or other Jewish associations.

One other fixture was added to the Jewish community shortly before the century closed. In January 1897 the first issue of the *B'nai B'rith Messenger* appeared. It was named in honor of the congregation which was the principal Jewish institution in the city.

The *B'nai B'rith Messenger* tended indirectly to create the community for which it unofficially spoke. The news of a community numbering little more than two thousand, and the tidings brought from the larger Jewish world far away, in addition to the newspaper's vigorous opinions, did much to overcome the feeling of remoteness and lack of involvement in greater than local affairs. The plan to publish had been opposed by prominent figures as "unnecessary" and for other reasons which can only be surmised. Once in existence, however, *B'nai B'rith Messenger* became an important source of communal self-awareness.

For Los Angeles to possess a network of functioning Jewish organizations was important. The casual ease of a small community intricately bound by family ties was sure to disappear as the number of Jews multiplied beyond the most daring promoter's imagination. Sixty years into the twentieth century over 450,000 Jews lived in the Los Angeles region, in contrast to the 2,500 found there at its beginning: an ascent for which neither Jewish history nor the astonishing annals of Los Angeles itself provides an adequate comparison. Farmland became downtown business areas, and a staid, sunny, agriculturally based city became one of the world's metropolises of commerce and manufacturing, with a surge of science and the arts. Jews participated in every phase, particularly in films, real estate and building, and commerce. From the beginning of the twentieth century until the decade of World War II, a substantial Jewish working class made a living in Los Angeles, while still later a thick stratum of Jewish professional persons added itself to the economic layers.

Not all change in the Los Angeles environment constituted improvement. Jews participated wholeheartedly in the brawling atmosphere of nineteenth-century city government, but during the twentieth century they were excluded or confined more or less to appointive, advisory, and technical positions. Jews ranked high within the dominant Anglo-Saxon minority in early Los Angeles society, but a pattern of social exclusion, noticeable during the 1880's, became complete in the twentieth century. Exceptions could be made still to include old Jewish settlers, but even their children were kept outside the fathers' clubs. A fashionable Jewish club hardly compensated.

The first Jewish generation in Los Angeles shared fully in the city's meager cultural life. They were especially prominent in German cultural effort, and a significant group of French Jews from Alsace also preserved something of French culture in Los Angeles. Very little of this remained in the twentieth century. New cultural motifs became prominent—regional exoticism, evangelical uplift, Hollywood glitter—and only in the latter did Jews figure. On the other hand, the anemic cultural quality of local nineteenth-century Judaism was enriched notably by the extensive later development of Yiddish and by the modest growth of Hebraism and traditional learning.

Los Angeles Jewry in the nineteenth century was very much a family affair, the linking of first families such as Newmark, Kremer, Cohn, Lazard, Edelman, Norton, Hellman, and a few others. Their intimacy was not a huddling together against a hostile or indifferent environment but the comradeship of men and women brought together by religion, similar European background, language, and business, and reinforced by marriage. During the twentieth century some of the leading nineteenth-century families declined in wealth and prominence, and many of their progeny drifted away from the Jewish community. Some pioneer families, however, lost no status, indeed increased it, thanks in part to their deep roots in a city of newcomers. Los Angeles, however, definitely transcended the family-size dimension of a Jewish community. The new mode was an overlapping congeries of organizations devoted to innumerable different and frequently conflicting purposes. The one synagogue before 1900 saw dozens of successors afterwards, of many philosophies and degrees of prosperity. However confused the manner, a sense of community began to evolve. Overarching families, synagogues, and organizations, it ultimately brought forth central communal bodies.

The nineteenth-century Jews of Los Angeles have been called the "cornerstone Jews," but "foundation Jews" would be a still better term. They imparted of their own dignity and self-respect to the name and repute of the Jew. They were not intellectuals or artists or scholars, but businessmen and men of affairs. Honest and inventive, and courageous also, they were charitable for all sorts of causes. The Jewish pioneers were a civilizing and energizing force, quick to join and also to lead. They established and maintained Jewish life. One may notice the hand-to-mouth character of their Jewish life, the lack of real concern for the education of the children, the weakness of Judaism in their homes. But theirs was also the steadfastness of men in a frontier environment who could easily have dissolved into the Christian majority, yet instead built a synagogue, established organizations, and voluntarily upheld their Jewish faith in a remote corner of America. The multitudes who followed their footsteps to Los Angeles in the twentieth century built upon these achievements of the nineteenth-century "foundation Jews."[39]

PART II
Twentieth Century

CHAPTER 6

From Outpost to Major Community

———————————————— ⊰⊱ ————————————————

AMONG LOS ANGELES' 102,000 residents in 1900, the 2,500 who were Jews constituted one-fourth of one percent of the 1,000,000 Jews in the United States. Twenty years later, about 20,000 Jews lived amid the "City of the Angels'" population of 576,000, giving Los Angeles Jewry some place, but still a decidedly minor one, among the 3,500,000 Jews in America. By the onset of the Great Depression in 1929 the number had gone far higher; now there were perhaps 70,000 Jews in a city of 1,238,000. Thus the Jews of Los Angeles, multipling almost thirtyfold, more than kept pace with the fourfold increase in American Jewry. The rise in Jewish inhabitants exceeded even the boom rate of increase in the city at large.[1]

Although these decades of rapid growth coincided with the years of intensive immigration from Europe to the United States, very few immigrants came directly from the ship to southern California. A high proportion of Los Angeles' arrivals consisted of the health-seeking group, unfortunate consumptives who made their way to the Pacific Coast in search of healing. The Jewish immigrant segment among the sick and invalid stirred the concern of the Jewish community, to whom they naturally turned:

We have often dwelt upon the folly of sending penniless invalids to the West. There is room in the Pacific states for people of energy who can enter into the upbuilding of this great country with vim and vigor.

But this whole country is overrun with people who have come from all parts of the world in quest of health, with little health and less means.[2]

Pleas to invalids and their families not to come resembled somewhat the urgings of Western Jews to fellow Jews in Eastern Europe not to emigrate, and their effect was not dissimilar. The trek of ailing Jews continued, and the recipient community adjusted itself.

The first surge of able-bodied East European Jews to Los Angeles seems to have taken place in 1904. The communal newspaper, while boasting early that year that "Los Angeles contains more *real* Jews in proportion to the size of the city than many other places in the Union" did not urge an increase in that proportion nor in the numbers.[3] Deprecating talk of a Jewish agricultural colony in the area as "a practical joke" but "dangerous" to print, it could "assure our esteemed contemporaries that there is very little danger of immigration to this part of the country."[4] Soon thereafter, however, it reported that "many poor Jewish people are daily arriving in this city from all parts of the world."[5] And barely eight months later, "Los Angeles is just now crowded with Jewish immigrants." It counseled against further immigration, "although the South [of California] is preferable to all other parts of the globe."[6] During the pogroms of 1906 and 1907, Los Angeles Jews were aided locally to bring their relatives to America but not necessarily to the West Coast.[7]

The local reaction to recently arrived East European Jews was fairly typical of American Jewry. It was suspected, for example, that they would depend unduly on charity. However, after early complaints of "a few unworthy ones who are quite able to engage themselves in business" rather than accept alms, the *B'nai B'rith Messenger* was soon "glad to say that the mild and meedy 'schnorrer' seems to avoid Los Angeles."[8] Exotic attire was embarrassing: "Just the other day we noticed several Russian Jewish immigrants walking the streets wearing their beaver head coverings. It was quite a novelty here in this city and their friends should remind those fellows that they are in Los Angeles and not in Siberia."[9]

How immigrants might be discouraged from crowding in cities was another dilemma to which the answer was supposedly agricultural colonization. After first belittling the possibility of a Jewish colony as "folly" and "practical jokes," the communal organ later warmed to the subject as numerous immigrants continued to arrive.[10] Now there was talk of agricultural life for them. "Many of the Jewish immigrants who arrived in the city recently are being sent out on the farms in Southern California and are said to be doing nicely."[11] If experience elsewhere in the United States is a criterion, these Russian Jews did not remain long as farm hands, isolated from fellow Jews. Reports of Jewish colonies in rural Massachusetts and a tale of refugees from Kishinev seeking soil to till in California, together with rumored plans of subsidized agricultural settlement in the Pacific Northwest, encouraged the Los Angeles people to welcome a plan devised by Chicago entrepreneurs to settle Jews on land in Fresno County.[12] Nothing came of all these plans, and the Jewish immigrants who continued to reach Los Angeles remained there. In 1913 a Jewish Colonization Society of California appeared on the local scene. It proposed to found cooperative agricultural settlements where Jews could live together, till the soil, graze flocks and, it would seem, promote manufacturing on the side. Although it arose during years of agricultural prosperity and when California was hearing much of Utopian farm colonies, nothing came of this local proposal either.[13]

While admonitions to Jewish immigrants and talk of agricultural settlement continued, Jewish immigration to Los Angeles commenced from a new source, the Industrial Removal Office in New York City. This subsidiary of the heavily endowed Baron de Hirsch Fund sought to relieve the fearful congestion on New York City's East Side by dispersing competent immigrants and their families westward to smaller cities. From its inception in 1900 until America's entry into World War I, when it suspended operations, the Industrial Removal Office aided over 76,000 persons to quit New York City and, to an extent, Boston and Philadelphia as well. Of this total, somewhat less than 5,000 moved to California, of whom perhaps 2,200 to 2,300 arrived in Los Angeles.[14] These new settlers were an increment of greatest significance for a Jewish population which, we recall, was only 2,500 in 1900. The number sent annually from the East did not reach one hundred until 1904, when 131 Jewish individuals arrived under the Industrial Removal Office's auspices. A steadily increasing proportion of California "removals" was sent to Los Angeles instead of San Francisco, especially after the San Francisco earthquake and fire of 1906. In 1910, 208 arrived—Los Angeles' first year in excess of two hundred—and the climax came in 1912, when 396 Jews reached southern California. The none too robust Hebrew Benevolent Society took responsibility for receiving the removals and helping them to settle. Summarizing its activities for 1912, the society reported: "We have had 160 applications from the Removal Office for families and single persons to be sent to Los Angeles this winter. We gave our permission to 117 and refused 43. Though we had an agreement with the Removal Office not to send sick or indigent persons, some managed to slip in."[15] As the

IRO declined after 1914, far fewer removals arrived in Los Angeles. Most of the altogether 2,200 to 2,300 persons were single men, representing dozens of trades, who usually raised part of the substantial fare by themselves and received a subsidy for the balance. Once established in his new city, the emigrant worker sent for his family, which he often left behind, occasionally receiving IRO aid for this purpose also. The immigration drawn to southern California by the Industrial Removal movement thus exceeded the official figures, for the many reunited families remained uncounted. Besides, a satisfied "removal" served as a magnet for his larger family and acquaintances. While there is no way of measuring, perhaps one to two others came to Los Angeles on account of each person "removed." The historic importance of the Industrial Removal Office's activities would be hard to overestimate.

The Industrial Removal method required that the local Jewish community assist the new arrivals, especially with jobs. Few offers were more welcome than that from Hamburger's Department Store, which offered transportation money to attract cheap experienced tailors from New York and overcome a local trade union boycott. The New York office had originally hoped that B'nai B'rith lodges would sponsor the local arrivals, but this did not occur in Los Angeles, probably because of the order's weakness before 1905 or 1906. The local Lodge No. 487 did, however, sponsor a group of Russian Jews who came from the diversionary port at Galveston. Arriving "not only penniless but almost shoeless," they were taken in hand, and homes and jobs were sought for them.[16] A mainly honorary committee of six existed to supervise IRO work in Los Angeles, at least in 1911 and thereafter: Rabbi Hecht; Albert M. Norton and George N. Black, both active in politics; Victor Harris of the *B'nai B'rith Messenger;* and E. F. Gerecht and Henry L. Klein, merchants. Relations with New York headquarters were often fractious, basically because the Los Angeles group could not always find enough jobs, and some immigrants were dissatisfied or unsatisfactory. From the East came a letter that "we are bitterly disappointed in the fizzle in which the Los Angeles cooperation has resulted." Back came a demand for money allegedly due and a complaint that the men sent were "anarchists who would not work." Matters were patched up after this eruption, and the IRO continued to send clients to the city.

While IRO immigrants continued to arrive, others also came from the East. Probably typical was the journey of Mrs. Rachel Ana Kositza, after she was told disturbing news by her child's doctor in Paterson, New Jersey, in 1912: "The doctor knew that my Gussie had pneumonia when she was a year and a half old. The doctor examined her and found that she had severe bronchitis. . . . Since he knew the entire family as a group, and knew everyone's ailments, he also knew that my brother Notke was in California. Actually, he had sent my brother Notke to California to heal his lung ailment. The doctor told me that I also must go to California now to save the child." For the alarmed father the doctor repeated the prescription. "But we had no money. I travelled to my brother Joshua in New York, that he should lend me $50. But my brother also did not have." So only $16 could be taken from poor brother Joshua. The balance came from Mr. Kositza's employer and had to be repaid week by week. With money earned by tending a mother in confinement, together with $50 which Joshua was now able to contribute (a prosperous brother living in Los Angeles refused to help), Rachel Ana Kositza soon sent for her two children and her mother. One year later her husband came.[17] Hundreds of families undertook such painfully slow and expensive emigration from the East. Within American borders it repeated the emigration trials of East European Jews in the hundreds of thousands.

A broad view of the origins of a large segment of Los Angeles Jewry may be derived from Rabbi Sigmund Hecht's 250 marriage records. Between 1904 and 1919, 32% of the brides and grooms he united had been born in Los Angeles and another 18% elsewhere on the Pacific Coast. Thus, half of this large but not entirely representative group were natives of the Far West. Of the other half, 13% were born on the East Coast, 21% between the Appalachians and the Rockies, and only the remaining 16% had been born abroad. To be sure, many of the foreign-born had lived in America since childhood. However, from mid-1916 until Rabbi Hecht retired in 1919 a sharp change is detectable: the number of native Los Angelenos and Far Westerners declined drastically to 19%, while many more (38%) came from the Middle West and Plains States, and 31% were foreign-born. The men and women married by the Reform rabbi represented the more prosperous and acculturated sector of Los Angeles Jewry. The proportion of foreign and non-California births was undoubtedly much higher among the brides and grooms presenting themselves to Orthodox rabbis.[18]

With expectancy and trepidation, Los Angeles Jews spoke after 1912 of an impending "great problem, the solution of which we must prepare to make at once." It lay "in the mind of nearly every Jewish citizen in the community, which we must face on the opening of the [Panama] Canal,"[19] permitting direct steamship connections with Europe. It was anticipated that "our co-religionists . . . will seek their new home and new opportunities in this country and a large percentage attracted by the fame of California will come here."[20] Of course, none of these expectations came to pass; the problems of 1914 and 1915 and thereafter were tragically different.

The European Jewish immigrant environment existed in Los Angeles on a more limited scale than in the East. Ties with the Old Country were weaker, and the milieu which existed in New York and Philadelphia and Chicago, not to mention smaller cities as well, hardly came into being in Los Angeles. However, in addition to the synagogues founded by recent East European arrivals, there were such typical immigrant manifestations as *landsmanshaften*. In 1908 a Hungarian-American Club was "organized by about sixty prominent Hungarian Jews of Los Angeles, for the purpose of promoting sociability and assisting those who are seeking employment." Rather unusual for a Jewish *landsleit* society, its meeting featured addresses in Magyar and the Hungarian national dance.[21] The Roumanian Aid Society was organized probably in 1913 as the "outgrowth of the discussions of a small number of leading Roumanian Jews of this city [who realized] the dire straits of some of their co-religionists and being promised the support of the local Roumanian Jewish community, felt it their duty to do what they could to aid their co-religionists." Like the rest of the local Jewish community, this group expected a large influx with the opening of the Panama Canal. Many newcomers, it was expected, would be Roumanians, "and a goodly portion of them will be our co-religionists."[22] During the hectic time of World War I, a local branch of the American Union of Roumanian Jews was set up, evidently the Roumanian Aid Society in a new garb. Besides the usual *landsmanshaft* functions, it intended to aid Jews in Roumania toward postwar emancipation and reconstruction.[23] At about the same period, a "First Jewish Polish Society" also sprang up.[24]

While the lines between the primarily European Jews and the highly acculturated older settlers were not nearly so sharp in Los Angeles as elsewhere, a pronounced cleft could readily be noticed. The two sides neither worshipped nor kept company together and did not always flatter each other. The "German" president of the Jewish Orphans' Home complained publicly that "the class of our Jewish population out of whose midst most of our applications come, gives us·very scant support."[25] An indignant reply maintained that the accused East Europeans were "naturally generous and quick to respond to every call of charity" and self-sacrificing in the aid of their people still in Russia, but said "the German Jew ... has raised a barrier of class distinction between himself and his Russian brother, and is asking for the Russian Jew's assistance in his charitable work. ... [This shows] full well the unnatural dislike of the German Jew for the Russian Jew. ... Just forget your social superiority and ask your Russian brother to join you in your charitable work as you ask your German brother, and see how quickly and generously he will respond."[26] Antipathies so strong required years to soften. Yet notwithstanding these frictions the primarily native B'nai B'rith Lodge unwaveringly opposed all moves toward immigration restriction.[27]

World War I put a temporary end to immigration from Europe. When immigration to the United States resumed afterward, the movement of immigrants from Europe to southern California was overshadowed by a far greater westward trend on the part of American Jews. While the United States was at war in 1917 and 1918, between 18,000 and 20,000 Jews dwelled in Los Angeles.[28] Five years later perhaps 900,000 persons lived in Los Angeles, and the Jewish population had climbed steeply to approximately 45,000.[29] Total immigration slowed in the later years of the 1920's; the estimated influx was 377,000 for these years, compared with 685,000 for the first half of the decade. As Los Angeles' boom reached its end around 1927, approximately 65,000 Jews dwelled in the city.[30]

The Jews who participated in southern California's "gold rush" of the 1920's differed markedly from the migrants of twenty years earlier. The health-seeking element was submerged by those going west in search of ampler opportunities and sunshine. The newer type was likely to be an acculturated European immigrant or his grown sons who had some resources and were allured by Los Angeles' economic opportunities and not indifferent to its climate. Migratory

Jews from points east came with some money not only for their sustenance but also in hopes of founding a business or for investment and speculation, usually in real estate. This immigration depended upon Jewish communal aid only in the sense that enlarged numbers required enlarged facilities.

The immigration of foreign Jews, although overshadowed, did not cease; the Industrial Removal Office no longer existed, but Jews from Europe found their way to California anyhow. Besides Los Angeles' small group of Rhodian and Turkish Sefardim who had come before World War I, a group of Palestinian Jews, victims of wartime mistreatment and hunger, found their way to the city.[31]

Monied individuals also came to Los Angeles, often to retire or to enter some other business. Thus, George Srere came as a rich man from Chicago about 1924 "failing in health. He had made a splendid reputation for himself in the paper manufacturing industry, and while in the city was engaged in the real estate business."[32] Herman C. Neuschafer, a German Jew, had been a silk manufacturer in Italy before coming to Los Angeles about 1910. "He became interested in the development of farm lands in the Antelope Valley."[33] Young lawyers like Harry A. I. Wolch moved to Los Angeles from San Francisco, as did very well-established practitioners like Walter S. Hilborn.[34] Mark Carter, the former owner of an expropriated hardware factory in Russia, achieved great success in the same business within a few years of his arrival in 1922.[35]

Obviously, few of the estimated 685,000 immigrants who streamed into Los Angeles during the first five years of the 1920's were retired or wealthy.[36] The newly organized cutters' Local 273 of the Amalgamated Clothing Workers warned eastern cutters that "only those who absolutely have to go should go out there. There is much unemployment and it is next to impossible for those who can do only section work to get a job. One has to be an all-around tailor in order to get a job there.... Los Angeles is not a great industrial center. ... The eastern factory hand is not looked for there."[37] Nevertheless, workers came, and the clothing industry developed.[38]

The character of the Jewish immigrant differed markedly from that of the non-Jewish immigrant, if one may speak of such elusive qualities. Of the Middle Westerner who formed so great a proportion of immigrants to the region, it was said that "he came in sufficient numbers to imprint upon it his own spiritual sign manual. . . . He transferred to his dream paradise all his provincial virtues and vices—his evangelical fervor with his credulity, his native shrewdness in other matters, his capacity for self-denial, his incapacity for cultivated leisure."[39] Jewish virtues and vices would sound rather dissimilar from those of the Middle Westerner. Thus it was noted that the bonds of religious tradition loosened in the move from the East to the West Coast. The new scene was dazzlingly different from New York or the "old home" in Russia. As one Yiddish poet attempted to describe his new surroundings:

Far—
From the narrow New York streets, Chicago clouds, Pittsburgh smoke—
Los Angeles!
You are intoxicated by the smell of orange blossoms, blinded by the
    towering mountains, refreshed by the straight proud palms.
Worn out.
They have built for themselves bright, sunny little cottages, decorated
    with greens, and they stroll calmly. Contented.
The light white night falls, greater desires awake.
    They live always unsatisfied.
But the streets are silent, windows—blind, doors—shut.[40]

The Jewish Neighborhood

Unlike the Gentile immigrant from the Middle West, the Jew who settled in Los Angeles did not set his imprint upon a region. Instead, he made a neighborhood distinctly Jewish and enlarged those whose Jewishness was already pronounced. At the opening of the twentieth century, there were too few Jews to form a definitely Jewish district.[41] About one-third of Los Angeles' 2,500 Jews lived downtown, forming almost one-third of that zone's inhabitants, and smaller concentrations were found in the University, Westlake, and wholesale areas. Extensive changes occurred in the succeeding twenty years, as the wholesale and University and downtown areas steadily declined as focuses of Jewish residence. Where some 30% of Jewish households dwelled in the downtown and wholesale neighborhood in 1910, that proportion declined to 3% sixteen years later. Temple Street and the area to its south, and Central Avenue, had an estimated 1,037 Jewish households in 1908, a figure which rose to 2,181 in 1914 and 3,473 in 1926. During the 1910's, Temple Street was the Jewish "Main Street," followed during the next decade by Central Avenue.

More prosperous and acculturated Jews settled westward in such areas as Wilshire, West Adams, and Hollywood. Affluent Wilshire, with about 310 Jewish households in 1914, had 2,410 in 1926. Hollywood, still sylvan in 1914, had hardly any; by 1926 there were about 3,287. West Adams rose during the same period from 143 to 1,534.

In 1923, when immigration was flowing fastest, three areas were noted for "relative massing of the Jewish population." They were the Brooklyn Avenue and Boyle Heights section,[42] the Temple Street section,[43] and the Central Avenue section.[44] As noted, the latter two vicinities were numerically stagnating, and soon began to decline. They were old for Los Angeles, where new sections were built at an astonishing rate.

The new concentration of the Jewish worker and lower middle class—which is to say the great majority of the community—lay east of downtown, across the Los Angeles River and the railroad yards, in Boyle Heights. Jews had begun to dwell in this eastern district at the turn of the century in "the old Boyle Heights [containing] the Hebrew Sheltering Home, the Talmud Torah, the Modern Social Center, the Day Nursery, the area around Breed Street synagogue." (To these could be added the Kaspare Cohn Hospital.) Hundreds of homes were rapidly erected as the estimated 1,842 Jewish households of 1920 came to exceed 10,000 ten years later. But during these boom years there sprang up a "new Boyle Heights . . . distinctly different." This was the Wabash Avenue district, north of Brooklyn Avenue. Its new inhabitants were reported "orthodox in their religious beliefs" but in their daily life were "people of modern ideas and tendencies. . . . Newcomers from the East and from Canada [and from] the Southwestern part of Los Angeles" who wished to live in a community where their neighbors, like themselves, were Orthodox Jews.[45]

To be sure, Orthodox Judaism was not the only form known to Boyle Heights, where many varieties of Judaism and Jewish expression flourished. Thus City Terrace nearby, a hill enclosure which was developing quickly at the close of the 1920's, was well known as a

Yiddish secularists' enclave.[46] On the main streets of Boyle Heights were stores where Jews bought and sold, Yiddish was freely used, and Saturdays and Jewish holidays were marked by festive appearances and many closed businesses. Such was Boyle Heights of the late 1920's and the years following, as mass immigration created a large-scale Jewish environment.

CHAPTER 7

Economic Activity: 1900-1928

————————————————— ➤✦ —————————————————

AT THE opening of the twentieth century the limited numbers of Los Angeles Jews were generously represented in the city's business life. Many of the pioneers of the 1860's were still active, controlling firms which were reckoned among the soundest in the city. Their enterprises were generally owned by families, taking in brothers and brothers-in-law, in which sons and sons-in-law followed their forebears. Rank outsiders seldom appeared among the Jewish business families who managed as well as owned their firms. Incorporation, with its possible consequences of publicity and loss of control, was evidently shunned.[1] Jews were no different in this respect from other businessmen who preferred to avoid corporate restrictions.

Such concerns as Meyberg in electrical equipment, Nordlinger in jewelry, or Marshutz in optical goods could well exemplify uncomplicated family firms. Brothers Max and Moritz Meyberg sold out their Crystal Palace in 1901; Moritz, with his cousin Eugene Meyberg, next established the Los Angeles Gas and Electric Fixture Manufacturing Company. Max joined his brother and cousin in their new firm in 1903, staying until 1919. The firm's name changed to the Meyberg Company and continued until the death of the founders, after which it was liquidated in 1935. Simon Nordlinger, veteran jeweler, passed his business on to his sons, who changed the firm name in 1904 to "S. Nordlinger, Louis S. and Sons." They stayed in the business until they sold out in 1923. S. Marshutz, an optician since 1887, established the Marshutz Optical Company in 1916. His sons Stephen and Herbert, each possessing an optometric degree, entered the business during the 1920's. Such family firms enjoyed substantial prosperity, and their owners were pillars of the general and Jewish communities.

Somewhat larger and of greater flexibility were Haas, Baruch & Company and the Germain Seed and Plant Company. The former was one of Los Angeles' first wholesale grocers, by virtue of its descent from the earlier Hellman, Haas & Company. After Herman W.

Hellman turned to banking, the brothers Jacob and Herman Baruch took his place, and the business' name duly changed. Abraham Haas, who was the president, lived in San Francisco until his death in 1921. Both Baruch brothers had died earlier, so the firm came under the control of Karl Triest and Carl Steinlein, both relatives of Haas.[2] Eugene Germain's thriving Germain Seed and Plant Company continued well past his death in 1908. His widow and son took Max Meyberg's son Manfred into their concern. The company opened a pet department and became a wholesale house as well. After Mrs. Germain's demise and Marc Germain's sale of his holding to Walter Schoenfeld, Manfred Meyberg and the new principal expanded its tree nurseries and set up bull ranches during the 1920's—a long remove from Eugene Germain's wholesale commission house of fifty years earlier.

The leading department store in town was the People's Store, owned by David and Asher Hamburger, appealing to a working-class clientele for its cheaper line of merchandise. As such, the Hamburger store was peculiarly susceptible to the trade union boycott which was called against it in November 1901 and continued for several years.[3] It survived, however, and subsequently prospered until its sale to the May Company.

All these were the medium-sized Jewish enterprises of Los Angeles. The foremost Jewish families in the city's economic picture before the 1920's were Cohn, Newmark, and Hellman. Not surprisingly, they were related by blood, marriage, and in some cases both. It is probable that every family in Los Angeles' Jewish mercantile bourgeoisie was somehow related to one of them. Harris Newmark, patriarch of the community in 1900, was near the close of his storied career in the hide and wool business with his brother-in-law (and first cousin) Myer J. Newmark. But the latter's main interests lay in San Francisco, to which he returned after he sold out in 1905. A nephew, Alech Braunstein, bought out this venerable Los Angeles business and gave it his own name after the older man retired in 1906. Enterprises bearing the Newmark name continued, mostly in the grocery field. Generally, however, the name counted less than it once had in the city's commerce.

On the other hand, Harris Newmark's nephew Kaspare Cohn vastly increased his importance in the city's economy. Like his uncle, Cohn was long in the hide and wool business and had many dealings with Basque and other sheepherders. He too held their money for them, granted them lines of credit, and conducted informal banking operations with the funds entrusted to him. But Cohn was more venturesome than Harris Newmark had been. At the ripe age of seventy-five, he oversaw the conversion of his operations into the Kaspare Cohn Commercial and Savings Bank in 1914. Cohn was a very rich man: he had been an owner of the holdings which were sold to E. J. "Lucky" Baldwin, possessed much urban real estate, and was a pioneer financier of the city's utilities.[4] Kaspare Cohn's bank was run from its beginning by his two sons-in-law, Ben R. Meyer and Milton E. Getz, and its name changed soon after the founder's death to the Union Bank and Trust Company. By this time, in 1918, the bank was increasing its capital from the original $300,000 to $600,000; it had resources of $3,400,000.[5] Throughout Meyer's life-long administration, the Union Bank pursued a rigorous policy of "all banking under one roof" and stiffly conservative lending.[6]

In the city's economic life the name of Hellman was still the most potent of all Los Angeles Jews. The redoubtable Isaias W. Hellman, eldest of the family, resided in San Francisco from 1891 until his death in 1920, aged seventy-seven.[7] His brother Herman W. Hellman (1843-1906) remained in Los Angeles to the end of his life. I. W. Hellman remained president of the Farmers and Merchants National Bank of Los Angeles, and I. W. Hellman, Jr., was one of its four vice-presidents. The youngest brother, James W. Hellman (1861-1940), was unrelated to his brother's business. Brothers Isaias and Herman did not enjoy fraternal concord; Herman did not leave his wholesale grocery for the cashiership of the Farmers and Merchants until his elder brother removed to San Francisco. Although Herman Hellman was vice-president, a director, and local manager of the bank, the controlling interest still resided with Isaias. Herman severed all these connections in a family rupture in 1903, evidently over his brother's handling of a large embezzlement by a relative of the family, and transferred his interests to the Merchants National Bank. His fortunes advanced without interruption. When he died three years later, the younger brother was an officer or director of twelve banks in the region, leaving an estate of $2,551,000.[8]

The Farmers and Merchants under Isaias W. Hellman forged ahead, spurning mergers and branch banking. Its rock-like con-servatism made it a southern California paragon of stability and safety, for in addition to its decidedly nonspeculative lending policies the Hellman bank kept on hand a high proportion of cash, particularly in the days before Federal Reserve. Partly on this account, it slowly declined from its first place among Los Angeles' banks. The Farmers and Merchants was overtaken in 1905 by two other banks, and by 1915 it stood fifth—a rank which it more or less kept for years. In 1915 approximately $42,900,000 of the city's total banking resources of $225,742,000 were in Hellman banks in Los Angeles, aside from still larger holdings in San Francisco.

I. W. Hellman did not confine his interests to the Farmers and Merchants, for he was a large-scale landowner and a founder, president, or director of numerous other banks and public utilities. He and his son both died in 1920, and the interests of his branch of the family were thereafter concentrated in San Francisco. Herman Hellman's sons Marco and Irving Hellman were major Los Angeles bankers of the 1920's. After a series of mergers and purchases, they emerged as the controlling figures in the Merchants National Trust and Savings Bank. In sharp contrast to the comfortable simplicity of the father's and uncle's mode of life, this second generation lived lavishly. Marco and Irving Hellman were leading clubmen, sportsmen, and horsemen.

These were Hellman rather than "Jewish" banks. While there were three Jewish directors of nine in 1900, the number increased only to four of twenty-eight in 1920, and remained at that level thereafter. None of the officers was a Jew. It does not appear that Jewish entrepreneurs made a point of seeking the services of the Farmers and Merchants; they may have tended to do so at the banking enterprises of Marco and Irving Hellman.[9] "Great Bank Founded by Hellman Attains Zenith of Achievement" trumpeted the Jewish newspaper in 1928, as the Merchants National Bank opened new headquarters on Spring Street for its 36 branches with $150,000,000 in assets.[10] Behind the scenes, Marco and Irving Hellman were arranging to sell their holdings to the Bank of America chain.

The well-established Jewish businessmen of Los Angeles do not seem to have subscribed to a business ethos different from that of their day. Business operations untrammeled by government, and thrift, punctuality, and payment of one hundred cents to the dollar ranked near the top of their scale of values. During Los Angeles' long years as an anti-trade-union citadel, most Jewish members of the mercantile and manufacturing class adhered to that platform. One, David A. Hamburger, proprietor of the large People's Store, was an organizer of the Employers' Association, formed to fight trade-unionism.[11] On the other hand, a number of Jewish employers, notably manufacturers of work clothes, withstood severe pressure and retained contracts with trade unions.[12] In the garment trade, where both employers and workers were usually Jews, the nationwide influences toward unionism in that industry had to combat vigorous and long-lived opposition in southern California.

Jewish Work and Wages

Far from the seats of economic power, most Jewish families of Los Angeles strove to make their living. From all appearances, their occupations did not differ greatly from the usual pursuits of American Jews. They were shopkeepers, workingmen, artisans, or clerks, and a few followed professions. Peddling was not prominent, probably because the city's environs were too vast and sparsely populated for the man with a pack or wagon.[13] But if Los Angeles Jewish trades more or less resembled those of other American cities, Los Angeles resembled no other city in America. Attractive climate and aggressive confidence in the future had to compensate for the scarcity of water, absence of hinterland, and remoteness from natural resources. Its wage-earning class was remarkably small, and was paid substandard wages.[14] Still, several standard Jewish trades were represented in the city at the beginning of the twentieth century. One of them, cigar making, was a unionized trade which gradually waned, owing to competition from mechanized cigar making and tobacco trusts. By the 1920's there were very few Jewish cigar makers.[15]

Jewish workers were mainly makers of garments for local consumption. The number of tailors steadily increased, partly owing to their heavy representation among health-seeking immigrants to Los Angeles, but their industry itself was small.[16] Los Angeles of 1900 had nearly no place in the nationwide industry. In 1923 a mere 1.6% of women's clothing jobs in the United States and 0.6% of men's were located in the Los Angeles area, but these proportions rose significantly by 1929 to 2.9% and 1%, respectively.[17] Such a firm as Tepper-Knewbow typified the rise of this mainly Jewish industry "from a single small shop ten years ago" in 1919 to $3,000,000 in sales and

1,500 to 2,000 employees. Starting at $70,000 in sales through local stores during its first year, Tepper-Knewbow's business multiplied and sold to no less than 300 stores.[18] A high number of these few thousand workers, especially the men, were Jews. A tailor's wages in Los Angeles, however, stood approximately 25% lower than in the rest of the country.[19] Most manufacturing was "inside"— fully executed on the manufacturer's premises rather than given to contractors' "outside" shops. In the men's clothing industry, "there are no factories making [ready-made] stock. There are two or three shops employing from twenty-five to thirty-five people each. The rest of the workers are employed in shops of five or less. All work done in Los Angeles comes from store orders."[20]

The city's Jewish tailors were organized first in a local of the International Ladies' Garment Workers Union, founded in 1900. A branch of the skilled Journeymen Tailors' Union already existed, and a few years afterward the United Garment Workers came upon the scene for men's tailors. The ILGWU reported a moderately effective Local 52 with 150 members in 1916. Four years later there were three locals, but their power in the trade was a poor likeness of the strength of this union in the East.[21] Notwithstanding strikes during the tumultuous labor years of 1911-1913 and 1918-1919, only in the manufacture of work clothes did the unions really control the labor situation. Above all, pressure for the open shop was aided by the constant immigration of garment workers from the East who disregarded trade-union warnings and appeals and came to southern California. During the 1920's the Jewish unions briefly took the offensive. The new local of the Amalgamated Clothing Workers struck in 1921 against the discharge of a union shop chairman at one firm, and "compromised" the matter by "direct negotiation."[22] Two years later, with the membership risen from 100 to 700, a general strike for union recognition was called. The union reported that "the Los Angeles labor movement and the liberals ... gave much valuable aid in the fight against the employers. On the other hand, the police authorities and the Department of Justice did their utmost to render the enemies of labor all possible aid." The local's business manager was harassed with a "suspicion of criminal syndicalism" charge. Nevertheless, the strike was won within three days, which included the time needed for arbitration proceedings. Its terms provided a 10% wage increase, time-and-a-half for overtime, and improved working conditions.[23] That the settlement was confirmed only by a "verbal understanding" with ten firms and fourteen contractors, and had an "indefinite" date of expiration, suggests inadequate union strength.[24] The agreement soon fell by the wayside.

Four years later the Amalgamated Clothing Workers again planned to augment its "skeleton organization" and renew its organizing efforts.[25] The ILGWU was meanwhile racked by troubles with the Communist-managed Trade Union Unity League in its midst. It cannot be said that unionism in the garment industry successfully breached the southern California bastion of the open shop.[26]

In addition to these major occupations, trades catering specifically to Jews employed hundreds more Jewish workers. In one of these, baking, a union local of Jewish bakers held its own against severe adversity. These hard-working craftsmen's demands had a more traditional quality than the industrialized garment workers' and included Sabbath observance and Jewish holiday pay on the job. In their organization and demands, Jewish butchers resembled the bakers.[27]

The Booming Twenties

Los Angeles was the boom city in America of the 1920's. The city's economic growth was startling. The figure of 266,000 employed workers of 1920 increased to 724,000 in 1930, and in the same span of time the value of the city's product jumped from $278,000,000 (and $418,000,000 for Los Angeles County) to $757,000,000 (and $1,319,000,000 for Los Angeles County), far outdistancing the old rival, San Francisco. Credit expanded as bank debits multiplied from $3,766,000,000 in 1919 to $14,621,000,000 ten years later; an active Curb Exchange was established. Sales made in downtown Los Angeles department stores ascended from $41,970,000 in 1919 to $106,900,000 in 1929. The most extraordinary developments took place in real estate, both business and residential, in oil, and in the films. Mostly on account of the vast new population to be clothed, apparel with a value of $53,000,000 was produced in 1929.[28]

Jews shared broadly in these developments, although few could be found among the foremost business leaders of the city, with the exception of the Hellman bankers. It was claimed, however, apparently with justification, that "many of the larger builders are Jewish and some of the most representative construction work which has been done in this city has been of Jewish inception, financing, or ownership."[29] The outstanding oilmen and real estate promoters were not Jews, nor even the magnates of the large department stores, contrary to experience in many other cities. But the film industry, for so long the symbol of Los Angeles, was largely built by Jewish entrepreneurs. (It is considered separately below.) As we have seen, the clothing industry was extensively Jewish not only in entrepreneurship but also—in contrast to the films—in its working force. Such a kindred field of consumption goods as furniture included several Jewish manufacturers; one was the Los Angeles Period Furniture Company, which employed 193 persons in 1928.[30] Catering to recreational tastes, the Ben Platt Music Company, which also sold appliances of all types, climbed steadily upward. In 1928 it incorporated and immediately sold $1,000,000 worth of stock. The firm then had eighteen stores in the city.[31]

Jewish immigration to southern California during the early decades of the twentieth century established a substantial Jewish working class in Los Angeles. In 1900 few gainfully occupied Jews in Los Angeles were other than businessmen, from large wholesale merchants down to petty shopkeepers. Twenty years later the economic structure of the Jewish community had become quite variegated. To judge from a sampling of the *City Directory*,[32] perhaps 5% were members of professions, mostly teachers and lawyers, and only 3% were peddlers. Of "manufacturers and proprietors" and shopkeepers, there were 22%, mostly under the latter heading. The largest segment of Jewish labor, about 40% of the sample, could be found at white-collar work—clerks, managers, stenographers, insurance men, bookkeepers, accountants. Artisans and workers accounted for 30%. To be sure, many of these categories are by no means sharply definable: a "baker" could be an employed or an employing baker, while a tailor might work in someone's shop or operate his own. Jewish shopkeepers generally sold foodstuffs, or were clothiers of some sort. The manufacturers usually made garments, cabinets, and cigars. But alongside the Jewish tailors and bakers and grocers there were many Jews making a living in less common ways—antique stores, bartending, music, writing, and more.

During the boom decade of the 1920's several proportions changed in Jewish occupational distribution. Workers and artisans, after dipping to 25% in the 1926 sampling, rose to 33% in 1929—the highest at any time. The white-collar class rose without setback; from 40%

in 1920 it reached 46% in 1926 and 53% in 1929. Difficult to explain, however, is the decline of the manufacturers and shopkeepers to 19% in 1926 and a mere 5% in 1929. Perhaps the inflow of workers and the growth of white-collar labor was so great that they proportionately overbore the storekeeping and manufacturing group in Los Angeles Jewry. The latter group also suffered from the termination of the boom about 1926, when some of them probably went out of business. Again, the increase in salesmen from about 10% to 17% late in the decade may suggest the fate of many shopkeepers.[33] Professionals similarly fell from their 5% of 1920 to 3% in 1929 and were now exceeded by peddlers, who stood at 5%. The only clear trend in Jewish vocational distribution during the hectic 1920's is the great increase in clerical, managerial, and sales occupations. There were comparatively stable proportions of workers and artisans and a minor movement in peddling. Manufacturing, proprietorship, and the professions shifted about in a not easily explicable manner. The decline in manufacturing employment, however, parallels in exaggerated fashion a similar decline in Los Angeles at large. Immigrants were not always workers but rather sought business and white-collar occupations.[34]

Los Angeles did not always glow with opportunity to the employed worker, and its political and social atmosphere inhibited his trade-unionism. However, for the investor or entrepreneur it seemed the land of promise. Mark Carter, a newly arrived immigrant from Russia having money to open a business, or David Epstein, bankrupt in his Ohio store, almost instinctively turned to southern California.[35] Jews already residing in the city no less eagerly sought their fortune in the booming atmosphere of the 1920's. Prosperity and improved labor conditions in the Jewish trades back east combined to send a type of emigrant during the post-World War I decade rather different from the ill and impoverished Jewish worker of earlier years.

Real estate was the beloved investment for Los Angelenos. Almost anyone in town could recall how acres of farm and vineyard or even wasteland had become residential and commercial districts with startling speed. Newcomers with an eye on business chances also caught the contagion, sensing that land values would multiply.[36] Innumerable Jews invested their savings in parcels of land, sometimes to build but more often to await expectantly its rapid appreciation. With buildings in the early 1920's rising at a great rate, there was indeed good reason to expect continued ascent in land values. But the peak of 1923 was followed by a sharp downturn, to be succeeded by only moderate prosperity rather than unlimited boom. Land was still being bought for speculative purposes by the economically experienced and by unsophisticated plungers until the 1929 debacle.[37]

The discovery of oil on Signal Hill furnished an opening for the most irresponsible speculation. There could be no certainty where oil would be found, and charlatanic or fake assurances were all too readily accepted by citizens who witnessed tens of millions of gallons (and dollars) flowing from the new-found pools. The lurid outcome was the Julian oil promotion, which defrauded investors of millions of dollars by an altogether spurious scheme. To finance planned mergers, the small company issued enormous amounts of watered stock. Stock pools were formed to drive up the price of the nearly valueless securities, and prominent business and financial figures lent money to the Julian Corporation at usurious rates. The crash in May 1927 brought a loss estimated between $100,000,000 and $200,000,000. Although many of these ruined investors were Jews, far more notorious was the prominence of Jews among the culprits. The episode harmed the city by the theft of millions in private funds which might have been productively invested, and struck a damaging blow at the good repute of investment in Los Angeles which later had serious consequences. As to the Jewish group, it scarcely benefited from the prominence of Jewish names in the Julian oil scandal.[38]

During the 1920's there was much economic mobility, not only in the occupational shifts described above. Many were the grocers who owned houses, and tailors who bought up land when they could. But neither the city nor its Jews were prepared for the economic collapse which struck Los Angeles even harder than the rest of America at the end of the 1920's.

Films

There never was a business like film business, and in the world's eye it made Los Angeles unlike any other city.[39] When Jesse Lasky (1881-1957) rented a barn at Selma and Vine streets in sylvan Hollywood in 1912, and was joined by Samuel Goldfish—Goldwyn after 1916—(1882—) and Cecil B. DeMille (1880-1956) to make

The Squaw Man, films already had fifteen turbulent years of public exhibition.

For a considerable time Thomas A. Edison did not take his invention of the moving picture camera seriously, nor did theatrical men. The new camera product merely provided one more item on a vaudeville bill: a filmed fire, robbery, amour, or practical joke supplemented the comedians and singers on the stage. It also supplied proletarian entertainment at "peep shows" and nickelodeons. On Fourteenth Street in New York City, the northern limit of the Lower East Side packed with Jewish immigrants, the first "store shows" started. These soundless ten-minute reels appealed to the common people, especially when ignorance of English shut them off from most American entertainment. The "scores of ambitious young Jews" who showed these films were not very different from their patrons. "They were quick to see the possibilities of the penny arcade and living pictures on the screen. Those who had money enough joined with partners in the purchase of arcades; those who lacked capital became ticket-sellers, machine operators, ushers, anything in the show-shops to learn the business; and soon they were operating shows of their own."[40]

But the patent holders and early makers of films determined that one reel of ten minutes' length was the most the public would come to see. Their Motion Picture Patents Company, a trust which pooled the basic American film patents, attempted and briefly succeeded in holding film makers to this "businesslike" policy. Jews like William Selig, Sigmund Lubin, "Bronco Billy" Anderson (originally Max Aronson, the first film cowboy), ranking among the "Pilgrim Fathers" of the industry, were prominent in this attempt to impose responsibility and control at the price of retarding film's development as a medium of art and entertainment. But even generous indulgence in lawsuits and strong-arm methods by the "trust" failed to hold back the expansion. The sometime "store-show" merchants and their audiences panted for six-reel features in newly-built, luxurious theaters. Visible as were Jewish names among the begetters of the film industry, the predominance of Jews in its subsequent boom became spectacular (a usage they coined):

Marcus Loew, a small fur merchant, bought a penny arcade; then a small theatre, and another.... Adolph Zukor, another modest trader in furs, put his savings, amounting to a few thousand dollars, into a partnership in

arcade and parlor enterprises. A little later he became an associate of
Marcus Loew, and presently embarked on operations of his own. William
Fox, a garment worker on the East Side, was one of the several partners
in a picture show which prospered, and Fox left the garment factory to
become an exhibitor himself.[41]

During this first decade of the twentieth century Louis Mayer,
who had come from Russia with his parents to the Canadian Mari-
time Provinces and briefly followed his father into the junk business,
began to exhibit films at an unprepossessing hall in Northampton,
Massachusetts. Carl Laemmle summarily quit his clothing business
in Wisconsin; Samuel Goldfish tired of selling gloves; Lewis J.
Selznick gave up the jewelry trade in New York. All were lured by
the fantasy of films and the reality of a business whose volume was
increasing by $25,000,000 annually.[42] Men like these and the pro-
letarian audiences they instinctively understood were nearly beneath
the notice of the patent holders and their lawyers and respectable
royalty-paying exhibitors and manufacturers. While Jews could be
found on both sides of the struggle between the "independents"
and the "trust," having entered the business primarily as venturesome owners of elaborate theaters hungry for features, more of them
stood among the "independents." The meek-mannered Adolph
Zukor (1873–) dreamed of making films the vehicle of "famous
players in famous plays," but a "trust" magnate curtly "predicted
that he would 'soon be back making button-holes.' "[43] The Motion
Picture Patents Company trust unflinchingly insisted that the public
would be interested only in one-reel films about ten minutes in
length.

Films began to be made by the very exhibitors who clamored for
more and longer films and fought the "trust" to make them. Adventurous showmen and restless creators sought and found a refuge in
southern California to make their feature films furtively. As the law
closed in and rough-and-ready tactics constantly menaced them,
they found Hollywood's mellow, sunny weather as much an attraction as its proximity to Mexico. The development of films, at first
centered in the New York City area, from 1912 shifted to Hollywood. The pictures produced in the Hollywood refuge, with their
lower production costs, combined with the incredibly growing audiences for "famous players in famous plays," doomed the "trust." By

1914 the independents and feature films had won the day, and the Motion Picture Patents Company virtually dissolved.

Before 1915 the Jewish contribution to the film industry lay primarily in creating the audiences and in proving that the public insatiably desired elaborate films and would pay more to see them. Selznick, Goldwyn, and Lasky did not invent the screen's basic technology, but they envisioned the possibilities and invested in them before others did. Jews were especially prominent in developing that key to the rapid showing of pictures, the exchange. Somewhat like the jobber, the exchange accepted the product of the studios and duplicated and rented it among dependent theaters. Entrepreneurs of film distribution like Louis Mayer in New England founded film exchanges. Regional film exchanges pressed the producers to supply the ever-growing number of theaters with a dependable supply of films. From the film exchanges came the decisive step in organizing the industry as one by one the distributors, a large majority of whom were Jews, secured facilities in the new film center at Hollywood. Here, too, Adolph Zukor took the lead. After many of the solitary nocturnal strolls to which he was addicted, he determined to have his own production company. Paramount Pictures was born of his intention in 1914, and he took complete control in 1916. Zukor based his power on a massive grouping of stars and his control of production facilities, and he enforced it by the bitterly contested method of block booking. Between 1915 and 1917 numerous distribution firms acquired production facilities in Hollywood.[44] By 1919 it was estimated that there were 15,000 theaters in America, which showed films for a revenue of some $800,000,000.[45]

While Hollywood dazzled, the masters of the industry remained in New York. There they secured the indispensable financing, beginning with Kuhn, Loeb and Company's flotation of a $10,000,000 issue of Zukor's preferred stock in 1919. Hollywood, formerly the drowsy suburb, within ten years of the production of *The Squaw Man* became a fantastic pleasure dome, the symbol of all that was peculiar and exotic about films. After 1920 the activities of the stars and supporting players of films were extravagantly chronicled in innumerable pulp magazines. Very few of them were Jews. One actress, however, was Carmel Myers, daughter of Rabbi Isidore Myers of Los Angeles, who ascended to minor stardom.[46]

By 1925 Hollywood was firmly fixed in the world's imagination. The Jewish producer became a renowned personage about whom stories and local folklore gathered. But if the brothers Cohn of Columbia Pictures and the Warner brothers swashbuckled, Jesse Lasky was not so colorful, and the most potent of all, Adolph Zukor, was quite diffident. As a group the producers were extremely sensitive to public opinion and strongly desired to be known as "American" and not "Jewish" producers. Long after trade unions and the ways of corporate organization penetrated their studio strongholds, the heads of production still regarded the studios and those who worked there almost as personal chattels. Hollywood's Jewish associations were not regarded as proper to acknowledge in quite the same way as, for example, ready-made clothing. The creation of the two industries was not utterly dissimilar. Both in clothing and motion pictures Jewish entrepreneurs, starting from a mass distribution base, created mass production industries for garments and entertainment. With daring and finesse, they organized innumerable individual skills (of sewing or photographing) for the vast market of voiceless consumers. The outcome of the film men's efforts was slowly but definitely recognized as a new art form—a true innovation in modern culture.

Beneath the top layer of producers, whose backgrounds and vagaries interested large portions of the American public, came a large and relatively anonymous cross section of Hollywood's technicians. These were the men who cranked the cameras, built and painted the scenery, arranged the lighting, spliced the freshly made celluloid prints, costumed and made up the actors; few Jews could be found in these skilled manual operations. There were also casting offices for the studios, as well as press agents and actors' agents, who sought to manufacture fame and find roles for their clients. Here were many Jews, as also among the batteries of lawyers who restrained and organized the frequently wayward impulses of the film companies and producers they served.

Less than fifteen years after the first film was made under its sunshine, Hollywood attained a seeming fixity. For most of this time the leading executives lived not in Hollywood but in New York and paid regal visits to their studios. The men they hired to manage the studios from day to day were also largely Jewish, as were perhaps half the "assistant producers," "production supervisors," and similar important underlings. The most dazzling example was Irving Thalberg (1898-1936), the clerk from a Brooklyn high school who managed Carl Laemmle's Universal Studio when his contemporaries were graduating from college. His later career was no less astonishing.[47]

An abyss lay between Hollywood's and Los Angeles' kind of life. The world of the diligent lawyer, worker, or businessman was far removed from the realm of celluloid fantasy. Hardly any film magnates during early years took a role in the affairs of the Jewish or general community. Partly they felt themselves visitors. Isolation from the general community, the condition during the early years of Hollywood film making, became a rule which the industry showed little interest in breaking down.[48]

CHAPTER 8

In Local Society and Culture: 1900-1928

WHILE THEY were optimistically entering a variety of business enterprises, Los Angeles Jews also were finding free acceptance into Los Angeles culture and society while maintaining their own social and cultural ties until the 1920's. During these halcyon years they did not enter the stream of civic and social life by virtue of face-saving gestures of tolerance on the part of a none-too-tolerant majority. Jews were sought and accepted as individuals, so that a Jew in a Los Angeles social club, in politics, or in the arts had to represent no one but himself. Nor was political activity by Jews part of the group's activity. Ethnic politics barely existed in Los Angeles; the Jews did not figure as a bloc on their own nor belong, as elsewhere, to a German ethnic body. Aside from the Mexicans, who were virtually outsiders, the city was overwhelmingly white, Protestant, and generally Anglo-Saxon, with some French and German elements.[1]

Social anti-Semitism was rising throughout America during the last years of the nineteenth and the early decades of the twentieth century.[2] Its supposed absence in the Southwest, in contrast to its prevalence in the East, was regarded as a happy sign of California's "exceptionalism." As of 1905 it could be said that "never has Los Angeles contained stubborn hotel proprietors who would distinguish the Jews and Gentiles, as in some cities. Los Angeles is too up-to-date for such miserable folly."[3] Such events as Protestant and Catholic participation in the dedication of the Sinai Temple were hopefully thought to indicate "the trend of the times. Narrowness and bigotry are being broken down."[4] This sanguine view persisted into the 1920's, but in .those later years such interreligious cordiality was likelier to be hailed as a blow against old prejudices than as evidence of a sure new trend.

Limitations in Politics

Until the boom of the 1920's, Jews were to be found widely in Los Angeles politics as well as nonpartisan public service. As the twentieth century opened, Herman Silver, a Republican, ran for mayor after four years as president of the city council and suffered defeat. He served the next two years on the Water Commission and then left active politics. To judge from the *B'nai B'rith Messenger,* Jewish sympathies lay with Silver during the 1900 election. The Jewish newspaper backed him, praising his opposition to a "wide-open town" for vice and liquor. In addition to asserting Silver's integrity and honesty, the *Messenger* reported that he was "said to be a 'Lamdun'—that is a good Hebrew scholar."[5] Silver's defeat may have had far-reaching importance by fixing the new extent of Jewish participation in politics. Jews no longer appeared as municipal candidates. In 1908 it was noted that since 1900 "not a single Jewish candidate was put up by either of the dominant parties. Is it an unwritten law . . . or is it the apathy of our people to put up a suitable candidate?"[6] Next year this second alternative was ruled out: "When it comes to an elective office we stand about as much a show as a poor man to become an officer in a fashionable congregation."[7] Yet the role of Jews in party politics and in nonpartisan appointive positions remained considerable. During these years of bitter politics, when the issue of trade-unionism ended with the tragic bombing of the *Los Angeles Times* building in 1910 by the brothers McNamara, and the Progressive onslaught against the Southern Pacific Railroad's political domination convulsed California politics, Jewish chairmen presided over the parties' campaigns in Los Angeles. The Republican head was George N. Black, a leading B'nai B'rith figure. For the Democrats, young Albert M. Norton headed the County Central Committee, and the respected physician Dr. David Edelman was head of the City Committee. A rapidly rising figure was Meyer Lissner (1871-1930), chairman of the Lincoln Roosevelt Good Government Executive Committee, the organizational dynamo of the Progressive movement which swept Hiram Johnson into the governorship in 1910.[8] Lissner earned the implacable enmity of the regular Republicans' trumpet, Harrison Gray Otis (1938-1918), publisher of the *Los Angeles Times.* In attacking all Progressives, Otis denounced "Three Ball Lissnerski" who acted "true to the traditions and precepts of his race."[9] Moreover, "Lissner was cartooned as a dirty, ill-kept pawnbroker rubbing his hands in greed and muttering 'chent by chent.' "[10] Notwithstanding Otis' blatant show of anti-Semitism, it does not appear that the Jewish group went over to the camp of his Progressive foes. The Good Government group was derisively dubbed the "Goo-Goos" in the *B'nai B'rith Messenger,* which also defended the regular Republican Mayor Harper against the Progressives' successful campaign to recall him as a grafter.[11]

Jewish sympathies continued to be divided among the parties. On one point, however, respectable Jewish opinion agreed: "There is absolutely no excuse in this country for the formation of Jewish political clubs."[12] Nevertheless, such groups sprang up regularly, to disappear after serving their temporary purpose. There was an Independent Hebrew Political Club in 1902, a Jewish Republican Club in 1904, Los Angeles Hebrew Club in 1910, another Jewish Republican Club in 1914, and undoubtedly many more.[13] Each "formation of a sectarian society for political purposes" called for the "denouncing of any such attempt on the part of any Jew as un-Jewish, un-American, unwise and fruitful of danger."[14] Practically, "Jewish Political Clubs are fakes . . . promulgated for fund raising purposes," said Albert Norton, himself a politician.[15] Politicians saw advantage in encouraging a bloc of votes they might control, and some Jews saw that political service could gain material rewards. Jews joined these groups out of personal ambition or undiscriminating friendliness.[16]

Although Jews could no longer be found on the municipal ballot, they were prominent not only as political managers but in non-partisan civic affairs. The Board of Library Commissioners counted no less than four Jews among its members, including Rabbi Sigmund Hecht (1902-1906), George N. Black (1904-1906), Siegfried Marshutz (1905-1909), and Henry M. Newmark (1906-1917). To Marshutz' ingenuity the city owed the financing of its sumptuous new public library. After the voters had defeated a proposal for a bond issue which would have raised taxes, Marshutz persuaded his board and the city fathers that they could pay off a bond issue with the rent the library was then paying, and the taxpayers would be let alone.[17]

Akin to the interests of Library Commissioners were those of the Board of Education. Herman W. Frank, clothier and president of the Merchants' and Manufacturers' Association from 1896 to 1899, began an eleven-year tenure on the Board of Education in 1904, serving as its president from 1911 until 1915. Jewish ladies, Mrs. Benjamin Goldman and Mrs. Jules Kauffman, served on the city's Social Service Commission, the former from 1915 to 1919 and the latter from 1917 to 1923. Mrs. Therese Levy served for thirteen years from 1926. Mrs. Kauffman was also a member of the Municipal Art Department for six years, beginning in 1929; one of her predecessors was Sid Grauman, of cinema fame, who served from 1925 to 1927.

Law and its enforcement consistently had Jewish representatives. William W. Barman served as deputy city attorney for eight years from 1914, while Isidor W. Birnbaum was a member of the civilian Police Commission during the 1920's. The first Jew in a judicial position in the twentieth century was Bertin A. Weyl, Sr., who sat on the superior court from 1921 to 1923. Los Angeles' leading Jewish jurist, however, was Harry A. Hollzer, who sat on the superior court from 1924 until his federal judicial appointment in 1931.

Jewish interest and participation in Los Angeles politics apparently declined after World War I. Perhaps because "the business of America was business" nowhere more than in Los Angeles, political interest was thoroughly subsidiary. In addition, the free participation of earlier years was considerably pinched. Jewish appointments of the 1920's were to responsible but less prominent positions, such as the Metropolitan Water District or the Water and Power Commission. They were few, however.

Cultural Life: Participation and Creation

Openness at the beginning of the twentieth century, gradually limited by the avowed and tacit restraints of the 1920's, was the case with Jewish participation in the cultural and social life of their city. To be sure, the culture of southern California was not of a character hospitable to extensive Jewish involvement. It has been rather uncharitably described circa 1912:

Southern California, still the hygienic and Protestant 'American Mediterranean' of the pre-Hollywood Era, looked askance at corrupt, Bohemian San Francisco. For a long time it had been making strenuous efforts to create a unique culture. The result was perhaps the country's most eloquent lesson in the dilemmas of regionalism. So far, Southern California higher culture was a bizarre and unbelievably innocent mixture of Mission Days and Chautauquas, fiestas and Ebell Clubs, false exoticism and genuine uplift.[18]

More generously, California culture around the turn of the twentieth century has been represented as a "fusion" of traditional

Anglo-American literature and the Spanish, pastoral, frontier past of the state.[19] Idyllicizing of the region's past was notable, as a cult of the bygone Spanish period was tirelessly fostered by several writers, figures in local gentility, and tourist agents. California's north, not its south, was the home of a school of realists, beginning earlier with Ambrose Bierce and reaching full flower with Frank Norris and Jack London.[20] In these developments Jews played little if any role. They were firmly allied with genteel culture, exemplified in such Los Angeles institutions as the women's Friday Morning Club. Of the 1,500 ladies who in 1917 belonged to this association for cultural advancement and social betterment, about eighty were Jews. Two, Mrs. Jules Kauffman and Mrs. Bertha Hirsch Baruch, were among its officers. Mrs. Kauffman, herself of Alsatian Jewish stock, was also active with a number of her French Jewish compatriots in the local branch of L'Alliance Française for the promotion of French culture.[21] Mrs. Baruch was a practiced lecturer on social problems and for several years contributed a column on "Practical Ethics" to the *Los Angeles Sunday Times Magazine*. Much in the style of the day, she had been a kindergartener, social worker, and an advanced student of philosophy.[22] Akin to these women's cultural and social service societies was the Council of Jewish Women, which combined efforts for Jewish immigrant youth with lectures on Judaism and social problems.

During these days, cultural activity was a women's responsibility.[23] Few men, Jews or Gentiles, asserted intellectual interests. One who did in his own way was Harris Newmark (1834-1916), who began to write his autobiography in the twilight of his years. The old merchant and philanthropist employed Dr. James P. Worden as researcher to quarry material, particularly from the daily press. Yet having come to Los Angeles in 1853 as a youthful immigrant, Newmark had himself witnessed at close quarters practically the entire history of the city and had participated conspicuously in its economic development. The book appeared just after his death, bearing the title *Sixty Years in Southern California 1853-1913*. The voluminous work exceeded 600 pages, all in a matter-of-fact, impersonal, unornamented style. Newmark's is the preeminent nineteenth-century southern California memoir, a source of first importance for the history of the region, and one of the great American Jewish autobiographies.[24] With unfeignable naturalness,

Newmark mixed the history of the city with the annals of his congregation, and the development of Los Angeles' trade and commerce
with the life of the Jewish community. Harris Newmark's son Marco
(1878-1959) pursued his career as a merchant in quieter circumstances. During the 1910's and 1920's he began the amateur but
skillful narration of episodes from southern California's early history,
with particular attention to the Jewish community.[25]

The cultural life of the "average" Jew differed little from that of
his Gentile neighbor. Until the World War I years, most popular
entertainment in Los Angeles was in theaters. The Orpheum's programs were especially attractive to Jews, for it was "well filled each
week with Jewish patrons."[26] The city bothered little at first with
the entertainment revolution being made in nondescript Hollywood
lots and sheds, nor did the Jewish community particularly notice
that many of the "revolutionaries" were Jews. When Los Angeles
suddenly became world-famous for films, a procession of real and
dubious artists came to seek their fortune. Out of this stream of
talent such groups as B'nai B'rith, synagogue Sisterhoods, and the
Young Men's Hebrew Association sponsored lecturers, musical performers, and occasionally dancers. The days of homemade entertainment were past by the 1920's.

Away from the main currents of the city's cultural life, small
circles pursued the venerated ideals of Jewish learning. Very few
kept up the ancient discipline of Talmudic study. Probably there
were private students, but there was no continuous Talmud study
class (*Hevra Shass* or its cognates). On the other hand, newer cultural trends had numerous adherents, ideologically linked with
Zionism, Socialism, and the revived Hebrew and Yiddish tongues.
During his tenure at Beth Israel between 1914 and 1920, Rabbi
Isaac Werne, an Orthodox modernist with a German doctorate, also
presided over Los Angeles' small circle of Hebraists.[27] Rabbi Werne
applied his learning to the stand-by of synagogue study, the ethical
treatises of the Mishnah (*Pirkei Abot*). "His method combines
sound Biblical and Talmudical erudition with modern Jewish
science . . . besides the basic Rabbinical lore, philology, comparative
grammar, history. . . . All these elements blended . . . suit the old
fastidious Talmudic scholars as well as the young man trained in the
modern schools."[28] Here and there a learned layman appeared,
notably Louis G. Reynolds (1870-1937), a Russian immigrant physi-

cian and polyglot with extensive classical Jewish learning. The local Hebraists' branch of the Histadruth Ivrith, the Hebrew language and culture federation, was a small group.

Distinctly Jewish cultural expression in Los Angeles reached its highest development in Yiddish, which flourished from the second decade of the twentieth century. For thousands of Jewish immigrants it was a native tongue, but to many Yiddish also represented a Jewish cultural ideal associated with the varieties of Jewish socialism and secularism. A substantial organization, the Arbeiter Ring (Workmen's Circle), gave Yiddish culture moral and financial backing, besides the fraternal benefits it dispensed to members. Socialist Zionists in the Jewish National Workers Alliance (today's Farband) also had Yiddishist sympathies. Yiddish readers had the long-lived local edition of New York's *Jewish Daily Forward*, beginning in 1910. In 1922 Dr. C. Wortsmann commenced publication of the *California Jewish Voice*, which Sam Gach took over in 1931. Its originally all-Yiddish content was gradually diminished to one page. During 1925 two ambitious literary journals began and ended: *Marov* and *Zunland*. Their hopes for a deep-rooted Yiddish cultural environment in southern California remained unfulfilled.

A group of Yiddish writers in Los Angeles produced a significant corpus of literature.[29] Characteristic, perhaps, of their beginnings was the brief life of W. Lossman, who died in Los Angeles early in 1918, aged thirty-two. Of Russian birth, he came to America in 1906 and contracted tuberculosis a few years later. The rest of Lossman's life alternated between his family home in Chicago and health-seeking journeys to Denver and Los Angeles, where he settled in 1914. His posthumous *Troymen un Fantazies* [Dreams and fantasies] is typical of much of the Yiddish literature produced in California: the individual work, whether prose or poetry, is very brief, and its character as fantasy is often explicity stated. Writers seem bewitched by the drastic contrast between southern California and their earlier homes. Brevity also marks the prose and poetry: not the long span of creative contemplation but the flash of insight was the Los Angeles writer's métier.[30] During the 1920's Lune Mattes (1897-1929), another victim of the "white plague," also wrote in this mode. He published two volumes of brief verse, *Der Vayser Prints fun der Vayser Flug* [The white prince of the white river] in 1927, and *Studio* in 1928.[31] The presence of an active Yiddish stage may have stimulated him, like other authors, to write such plays as *A Yiddishe Tragedye* "of Jewish life in America" in five acts. Maurice Roger published in 1927 his three-act play of Jewish suffering during World War I in Eastern Europe, entitled *Der Gayst fun der Tsayt* [The spirit of the time]. During the 1920's, such books appeared as S. Miller's (1895-1958) *Bleter Faln* [Falling leaves], a collection of fine short stories, some set in the American West; Israel Osman's (1887-1951) *Dos Bukh fun Nisyonos* [Book of experiences; Hebrew edition, *Sefer ha Nisyonot,* 1949], mostly legendary stories recalled from childhood; Joseph Katzenogy, *Kvaytlakh* [Embroiderings], a variety of sketches; and the "little monologues" of B. Batshelis to his wife, called by the fond epithet *Shmeltsekhe.* The foremost Yiddish writer in the city was the poet Henry (Hayyim) Rosenblatt (1878-1956), whose book of poems *Bloye Flamen* [Blue flames] appeared in 1925.[32]

Yiddish cultural life was heavily political, shot through with the strife of the 1920's between sympathizers and opponents of Soviet Russia.[33] Embittered feelings between the factions were expressed in such incidents as the uproarious scenes when Abraham Reisen (1875-1950), America's leading Yiddish poet, spurned the hospitality of political opponents at his fiftieth birthday celebration, or when the vigorous anti-Bolshevik Raphael Abramovich was so furiously heckled that only police intervention permitted him to speak.[34] To be sure, these incidents represented an extreme. From rival headquarters, the factions established their own musical clubs and separate Yiddish amateur or semiprofessional theatrical troupes. Even the poets and authors were divided. Side by side with its undesirable features, factionalism also had the effect of multiplying cultural media for the Yiddish public. It generated interest and excitement, if not all of it could be called wholesome.

As the center of film drama, Los Angeles attracted individual actors as well as troupes to seek their fortune. The players of the historic Habimah company who did not make their way to a home in Palestine went on to California. Two of its leaders, Benjamin Zemach and Raiken Ben-Ari, ultimately settled in Los Angeles many years later. Notwithstanding a year's stay and some vague words, however, Habimah failed to perpetuate itself in California. No troupe fared any better, although many Yiddish plays and players, some of high artistic merit, were shown to Los Angeles Jews.[35]

Compared with the vibrancy of the Yiddish cultural sphere, little could be reported of the general cultural life of Los Angeles Jews. Neither scholars nor serious writers in English resided in the city. Synagogues, B'nai B'rith, ladies' groups, and Zionist societies heard lecturers, frequently upon themes not of specifically Jewish provenance. Many of the lectures were apologetic refutations of current anti-Semitic charges: Jewish "contributions" to America and to civilization. Jewish ethical excellence and Jewish patriotism were staple topics throughout American Jewry. Besides the lecture platform, the principal cultural medium was the *B'nai B'rith Messenger,* by the 1920's a well-established organ. However, the communal weekly by then was losing most of its editorial individuality and tended simply to print publicity releases and "boost" indiscriminately. Nevertheless, the *B'nai B'rith Messenger* was substantial, of dignified appearance, and possessed special meaning as Los Angeles Jewry's channel of connection with America and world Jewry and the audible voice of the Jews within the city during a period of increasing stress.

Status Less Secure

Before World War I, questions of Jewish status focused on incidents like the designation of a miscreant in the press as a "Russian Jew," a practice which the local B'nai B'rith lodge combated with rather slight success.[36] The *Los Angeles Times'* reporting of Jewish events also gave offense because it "invariably portrays the proceedings in a humorous manner and flavoring, or near ridicule."[37] Yet Hyman S. Ravven, an emigrant to Los Angeles of one week's residence, happily related the "healthful impression" made upon him after frequently hearing "open expression of anti-Semitic feeling" during his nine years in Boston: "I am rejoiced to note, therefore, the absence of this unworthy feeling in this city."[38] Incidents seemed to increase, however. There was much open refusal to hire Jews.[39] In the name of high culture, the Friday Morning Club's administration insisted that of three available plays by Shakespeare, *The Merchant of Venice* be subsidized for school performance. Brushing aside angry protests by prominent Jewish clubwomen, the prestigious ladies' club sponsored a visiting troupe to play Shakespeare's problematical masterpiece to youngsters. A petition against the play signed by many Jews was also refused by school authorities. To be sure, not all Jewish opinion objected;

some regarded Shylock as the Bard's protest against injustice, portraying the harm it causes to man and society. The cause célèbre seems to have made the Jewish members of the ranking Los Angeles women's club sensitive to their standing. In this intricate combination of feminine factions, municipal politics, and cultural projects, a Jewish issue was injected which disturbed the hitherto unquestioned status of the upper-class Los Angeles Jewish woman in the social circles of the city.[40] Early in 1918, offended Jewish women threatened to resign unless their club rescinded its *fait accompli* of presenting *The Merchant of Venice*.[41]

From time to time Jews were irritated by fundamentalist Christian detractions. The master evangelist Billy Sunday used Jesus' strictures against the Pharisees to assail the good name of contemporary Jews.[42] Of a piece with Sunday's attack were the implications of Mrs. West Stevenson's *Pilgrimage Play* depicting the last days and death of Jesus, produced by local volunteers. On this occasion, Rabbi Isidore Myers was invited by the Pilgrimage Club to give his answer to "Who Crucified Jesus?" His endeavors to tone down the anti-Jewish features of the *Pilgrimage Play* were successful.[43]

Such incidents, which were never altogether absent from Los Angeles, seemed to give the tone after 1920. The end of World War I inaugurated a period of anti-Semitism in America which was felt in many spheres of life. Such phases as the lurid accusations in Henry Ford's *International Jew*, the tide of exclusion from social clubs and private universities, and the invidious quota by national origins in the Immigration Act of 1924, shocked and disturbed Jews.[44] Los Angeles was still remote from the full pressures upon Jews in the East and Middle West. Yet discrimination by colleges and medical schools against Jewish applicants became well known in the city, and Jewish businessmen found themselves unable to gain entry into the clubs which had once been open to them. "Little by little the various clubs of Southern California have been closing their doors to the Jew." Unknown in previous years, prejudice was by 1920 "gradually encroaching upon the confines of even this broad and splendid community." On account of this, members of old Los Angeles families, children and descendants of earlier settlers who had been freely accepted into local society, now spoke of "a Jewish country club, the membership of which should be both cosmopolitan and select."[45] During the 1920's, in Los Angeles as elsewhere, social prejudice against Jews penetrated all social strata. The Jewish film makers kept to their Hollywood enclave, maintained most of their personal and business connections in New York, and were thus little troubled by Jewish exclusion from downtown business society.

Prominent Jews did not quite understand what was under way. Thus, Louis M. Cole (1870-1931), a leader in the business community and civic life, seems to have thought that the use of Yiddish by Jews was estranging them from other Americans and, apparently, that this stirred up anti-Semitism. He confided his fears to Louis Marshall, but the leader of American Jewry warmly defended the language and its speakers.[46] What effect if any Marshall's reply had upon Cole's "evident alarm" is not known. A source of internal tension was the touchy matter of licenses during the Prohibition years for "sacramental" wine. The phenomenon of pseudo-congregations employing pseudo-rabbis to make wine for bootlegging purposes angered the Jewish community. It was disturbing to hear that " 'If you want to drink booze, you'll have to join the Hebrew church,' is coming to be a rather common expression."[47] Alongside disclaimers from responsible Jewish sources, sentiment was expressed in Reform circles that disgrace could be avoided by informing the government that Judaism regarded fermented wine as altogether unnecessary for religious purposes. A tone of anger between Reform and Orthodox appears in discussions of the problem in Los Angeles, as elsewhere.[48] By 1923 or thereabouts, the issuance of licenses was under control and the matter died down.

The first decades of the century marked the first retrogression in the status of the Jew in Los Angeles. Even in the case of Jewish families settled since pioneer days, he came to be regarded as a person apart. The 1920's, years of booming economy, were bitter years for those who recalled that the old days were also the good days.

Within Jewish Society 1900-1928

Jewish society had its inner concerns and pleasures, even while access to the wider community remained open. The development of Jewish youth in Los Angeles became a Jewish communal concern rather than solely a parental matter early in the twentieth century. As elsewhere, the arrival of immigrants stirred fears among American Jews that their children would fall prey to undesirable or even criminal influences. Not only might individuals suffer tragedy, but the Jews as a group would then be cast into disrepute.

Jewish efforts to aid children and youth, which began in eastern metropolises during the 1880's, were first undertaken in Los Angeles in July 1907. Three ladies of the National Council of Jewish Women, which made this work its specialty,[49] were the pioneers— Mrs. Jules Kauffman, Mrs. J. Y. Baruh (Rabbi Hecht's daughter), and Mrs. Berthold Baruch. At 738 Turner Street they opened the Mendelssohn Settlement Home for girls who needed shelter and support. Named after the German Jewish philosopher who originated in the eighteenth-century ghetto, the short-lived project was the progenitor of the later Hamburger Home for Working Girls. Soon after, in 1911, the three ladies undertook a more ambitious step by opening the Educational Alliance on Temple Street to provide generally for the "moral education and social welfare of the Jewish immigrant."[50]

In 1915 the Educational Alliance renamed itself the Jewish Alliance and took over a frame building at 610½ Temple Street. These modest premises teemed with activity while Temple Street remained a Jewish neighborhood, and they later carried on as the headquarters of the Federation of Jewish Charities. Youngsters who came with their friends to play, youths developing their skill in crafts or dramatics, mothers learning improved methods of child rearing, somehow all fitted into one large and one small room. Most of all, the Educational Alliance was a place to meet and play and socialize off the streets and out of cramped little houses. The cultural and charitable organizations of the new Jewish arrivals also held their meetings in the house on Temple Street. Yet the atmosphere of charity and settlement house hung heavy over the place, even though the Jews it served were more accustomed to American ways than the immigrants back east.

As young people grew older, they sought their measure of independence. One group again organized the Young Men's Hebrew Association about 1915 and even secured a charter of incorporation.[51] Although they could not secure a place of their own, they stayed out of 610½ Temple Street. A Young Women's Hebrew Association also existed, which drew nearly 250 young women onto its rolls before it gave up about 1923. The officers of the YMHA could not fathom why the community would not endow them with a home. Comparing the paltriness of their position with the generosity of the support for the Young Men's Christian Association (an expedient much used for demanding better Jewish support), they wondered whether "we Jews are not interested in Jewish welfare of our boys, young men and adults. . . . There is evidently something awry in our system, our Jewish body politic."[52] Perhaps the givers were more habituated to charity donations than to broad communal purposes.

The classic tension between European immigrants and their children existed even in Los Angeles, although the great majority of the adults had spent years elsewhere before coming to California. More than one father felt bewildered: "I'm a father and am trying to set good ideals. As soon as the boy leaves home the influences tend to tear those down, so what can I do? We have a religious atmosphere in our home, but outside there are anti-religious tendencies even."[53]

Social workers also worried over the suddenly arrived age of automobiles and films, both easily available to youth: "Nearly every Jewish home has a car, even among the poorer people, where they have second-hand Fords, but these tend to separate the children from their parents. And there is the movie which also creates a disrespect for parental authority. The Jewish parent is very much up against it from every angle of contrast."[54]

Although by no means "nearly every Jewish home"[55] possessed an automobile, Los Angeles Jewish youth in a boom city joined their peers in discarding European and earlier American restraints on personal conduct. Nevertheless, they too felt the need for some place of meeting under the aegis of the Jewish community. By the 1920's, as Temple Street and Central Avenue were emptying of Jews and Boyle Heights was filling, it was time for the Educational Alliance to change addresses. After prodding by professional observers of local needs from the Bureau of Jewish Social Research in New York City, the Modern Social Center opened in 1924. It was the city's first Jewish "community center" of the type which were then replacing the older settlement houses. Jacob M. Alkow, a young Zionist and Jewish educator, was director, and paid and volunteer workers served with him. The Modern Social Center was a three-story frame building, housing several dozen clubs of youngsters and adults who filled its meeting rooms, gynasium-auditorium, and outdoor playground. Three years after its opening, about 500 persons regularly used the premises.[56] The Young Men's Hebrew Association, whose 150 members had stayed out of the Educational Alliance on Temple Street, now entered the Modern Social Center and became absorbed in it.

Much of the impetus for the Center came from circles interested in modern Hebraic education under communal auspices. The Talmud Torah was housed there until the Center entered a new building in 1930. Not far from the Modern Social Center, near the City Terrace enclave, the Menorah Center arose—an institution closer to the hearts of traditional and Zionist Jews. Its core was a Talmud Torah, of which the Menorah's director, Moses Tolchinsky, was also principal. The institution reflected the sharp ideological cleavage in such neighborhoods as City Terrace between traditional and religious Jews and those under left-wing secularist influence; in fact, the Menorah Center was brought into existence partly to counter the attractions of a Communist center for Jewish youth. The Menorah's Hebrew school and Sabbath synagogue were surrounded by a gymnasium, clubrooms, crafts, and so forth. The building with a large dome, atop a hill, later added a swimming pool and playground.

Outside the doors of established institutions, Los Angeles Jews found social life and entertainment among themselves. Young people of the day desired each other's company for dances, beach parties, discussions, and outings to mountain fastnesses, and an informal network of clubs and societies served the purpose. Their peculiar significance in Los Angeles was expressed in the words of the Golden West Social Club's leaders: "[It] has for its scope the promotion of sociability and friendship among the Jewish young element of this city. It also appeals to those who come here from different parts of the country, as they can find an institution wherein they may become acquainted among the young element and avoid going around to public places seeking friends, and from practical experience [we know that] they find a place which is no credit to our faith."[57]

The "undesirable places" were doubtless the public poolrooms and dance halls, populated by the local demimonde; they were frequented, of course, not only by Jews, nor owned solely by them.[58]

The Jolly Bachelors, who crossed the scene from about 1914 to 1919, are a passable specimen of a social club of their day. In 1914 "in spite of the inclement weather, over 600 of the younger set were in attendance" at its seasonal ball.[59] Another group, the Sinai Literary and Social Society, was organized about 1910. It called upon younger people "desiring a literary and socially [sic] good time, [to] make haste now to join this society which holds the reputation of being one of the largest and finest of its kind in Southern California."[60] The Young Zionists Association, founded in 1903, likewise combined "Social Literary" meetings and amusements with devotion to the Zionist program.[61] Before mass-produced entertainment swept aside amateur effort, the youthful memberships themselves provided many a "long, interesting, jolly program." Thus, one evening after each YMHA officer spoke of his duties with due solemnity and pledged assistance to the war effort (it was January 1918), the members heard from their ranks a pianist, a singer, a humorous dialogue and, following refreshments, a "song monologue," a "humorous selection," and a recitation of Kipling's "Gunga Din."[62] The "Social and Literary Forum" offered "a real April Fool Party" with dancing and entertainment, followed next meeting by a speaker on "Progress and Ancient Judaism."[63]

Before the 1920's the Jewish press had the social, sporting, and mildly educational activities of several dozen young Jewish groups to announce. They were constantly dissolving and new ones were being organized as cliques of friends and acquaintances entered adult life and preoccupations fully. The activities of these evanescent groups were of little intrinsic significance, but they served the function of creating a Jewish sphere for the maritally ripe.

The only one of these social groups connected with a syngagogue seems to have been that in Temple Sinai. The Young Men's Hebrew Association, which complained of communal neglect, did secure clubrooms for a time at the B'nai B'rith Temple.[64] In those years, however, the Reform congregation had a stable social milieu, so that youth groups were unnecessary. In a sense, the smallness of the Jewish community made a communal center superfluous, convenient as it might have been. But matters changed when the great Los Angeles boom erupted after the first World War. Then "the stranger in our city who found it hard to get acquainted with other young Jewish people" must have had many comrades in loneliness who, like him, appealed for a " 'Friendly Jewish Club' that would hold a helping hand to such a stranger."[65]

During the 1920's a wide range of Jewish social clubs weekly announced parties, dances, games, athletics. There were Greek-letter fraternities and sororities—not, however, connected with any college; Jokers, Jesters, Jolly Comrades, Ramblers—names intimating adolescent members; branches of adult organizations, like Junior Hadassah and Junior Council [of Jewish Women] Buds; ladies' auxiliaries of local and national charitable institutions.[66] Young people's sporting clubs were extremely popular, and a Jewish athletic league existed during the 1920's, that glamorous age of American sport. The *B'nai B'rith Messenger* conducted a febrile weekly column, "Our Own Sports," encouraging Jewish athletes and verbally vindicating their prowess against competitors. Distinction in athletics was urged not only for its own sake, but to dissipate anti-Semitic views that Jews were "cowards," "weaklings" who avoided bodily exertion on playing fields and personal danger in patriotic war. Hence, it was especially regretted that Los Angeles Jewish sporting clubs played mainly each other: "Clannish? Is it possible? But if it isn't fear, egotism, or clannishness, what in the name of all that's wonderful is keeping our boys from outside competition?"[67] Men like the college football star Benny Friedman were accorded almost demigod status during the 1920's, as the achievements of Jewish athletes gave assurance to some of true "Americanism."

In the desire of Jews to meet with Jews on a comradely, religiously neutral basis lay a major function of B'nai B'rith Los Angeles Lodge No. 487, founded in 1899. It soon absorbed two minor B'nai B'rith groups which had existed earlier, the Orange Lodge and the Semi-Tropic Lodge, with aging membership. Lodge No. 487, like its predecessors, also began as an association for bonhomie and benevo-lence. However, when B'nai B'rith abandoned cash benefits and turned its attention to charitable work and defense against anti-Semitism, all lodges were freed of a constant preoccupation. In its early days, the Los Angeles lodge yielded happily to "the Bohe-mian side of human nature. . . . It used to be the custom after lodge hours to adjourn to the old Al Levy café and there, in one of the upstairs banquet rooms, assemble in a carefree bunch around a festive board replete with steins of bèer, the atmosphere redolent with the odor of tobacco."[68] Cards and cigars joined convivially with beer in a masculine paradise. The editor of the Jewish newspaper had only praise for "card playing for pleasure and pastime," and brushed aside opposition to it even after Friday evening synagogue attendance as "much talk and nothing in it."[69] The brethren of the lodge took in good humor a letter from their rabbinic member, Isidore Myers, greeting those "who had gathered to discuss subjects of an eatological, drinkological, smokological, jokeological, and sociological character."[70] All was jovial in Lodge 487, but attendance dropped: once, in 1902, as low as three. The now desperate group appealed for recruits at a source disregarded by B'nai B'rith elsewhere, by seeking out recent Russian immigrants at the Olive Street synagogue. An assemblage heard the humanitarian efforts and social amenities of the order lauded, and from this point the lodge began to climb in numbers and force with hardly a backward step.[71] There were 172 members in 1905 and 365 in 1910; the 500 mark was passed in 1913, and the close of World War I showed 1,000 men enrolled. With 2,000 "sons of the covenant" in 1924, the Los Angeles lodge was the largest anywhere.[72]

So great an expansion suggested that a deep need was met by the fraternal order. Jews new to Los Angeles found in B'nai B'rith a Jewish nest where they could readily satisfy a desire to associate with other Jews, which was all the keener because many lacked local family ties. If traditional Judaism weakened in the movement to the West Coast, the desire for Jewish companionship probably became stronger. The neutral, unphilosophical environment of B'nai B'rith, resting upon humanitarian service and Jewish self-defense, attracted its thousands. The lodge was also a place where Jewish lawyers, insurance brokers, accountants, and dentists could find clients. B'nai B'rith became the representative Jewish organization in Los Angeles, rejoicing in its ability to mobilize Jewish energies for Jewish and civic effort.

The main Los Angeles lodge was born at the time the order undertook to sponsor Roumanian Jewish immigrants in 1900-1902, and it shared in this effort. From 1906, the lodge made the local Jewish Orphan Asylum a project specifically its own. Some officers expressed a broader, almost ideological conception of their order's function. George N. Black, a West Coast leader, maintained that it "comes nearer than any other organization now in existence to being the logical spokesman for the common aspirations of the people of Israel."[73] M. Salzman floridly insisted that, although the peregrinations of the wandering Jew ended forever in Los Angeles, something was needed still: "As a Nation, though he has his laws, his sense of society and his religion, he has no flag around which to rally, save one, *The Independent Order of B'nai B'rith.* . . . this great national, international world compassing Order . . . exerts its organized strength to guard in this great land and elsewhere your civic and religious liberty."[74] The lodge felt committed officially to an unequivocally Jewish membership, and publicly questioned whether a Ben B'rith might be connected with the Christian Science movement.[75] An occasion for the Jewish self-protection implied by Black and Salzman arose one year later, in 1910, when the Los Angeles lodge took up "A Serious Question": "Should steps be taken to put a stop to the ridicule of the Jew by a certain morning paper in this city?" Without dissent, it was affirmed that "in this city it is unquestioned that the B'nai B'rith lodge represents the entire Jewish community."[76] So far as any organization justifiably laid claim to representing Jewish interest, B'nai B'rith could. There were no rivals. While B'nai B'rith was not the only Jewish fraternal body, in Los Angeles it far outshadowed such others as B'rith Abraham or all-Jewish lodges of nonsectarian orders like the Western Star and the Odd Fellows.[77]

The order acquired lodge rooms in 1909, encumbered by a $6,000 mortgage, but—a point never lost on enterprising citizens—"situated on property that is rapidly enhancing in value."[78] However, the brethren paid little attention to repeated invitations to make this their social center. After the first decade of growth and enterprise, the lodge's *élan* rather declined until the 1920's.[79] Not many joined, nor were significant projects initiated.

Alongside the fraternal orders arose such groups as the Jewish Professional Men's Club, which came on the scene about 1913 and maintained itself for many years. Its forty members in 1915 were all "Jewish men who are in active practice of the accepted professions, physicians, lawyers, civil engineers, electrical engineers, dentists and architects."[80] The Jewish Professional Men's Club dined regularly together, when they heard and entertained legal, scientific, and scholarly speakers of note. The Club and its postprandial practices have continued for many years.

At the pinnacle of Los Angeles Jewish society until the 1920's were the hundred members of the Concordia Club, in whose sumptuous quarters Jewish gentlemen of the city whiled away their leisure hours. Here matrons entertained out-of-town guests, and in the gilded atmosphere their children's nuptials and family celebrations took place. Like its Gentile counterparts, the Concordia Club staged genteel debuts for its young ladies at an elaborate annual ball. In the religiously rarefied atmosphere, Christmas was a major social event, and a handsome tree adorned the celebrations of the season. Withal, not only Gentile exclusion but also a real desire to keep one another's company perpetuated the Concordia. However, during the 1920's it became old-fashioned, a perilous position in fashionable society.[81] Its place at the top was lost to the new Hillcrest Country Club, which offered golf and outdoor recreation to its members at a site beyond the then settled part of Los Angeles.[82]

For the Jewish social elite of Los Angeles, pastimes varied from the formal ball to euchre and whist parties or card parties to raise charity money and amuse visiting friends. Jews were leaders in organizing horse shows and providing such necessities of equitation as bridle paths. The Bridle Path Association, which laid out paths along Sunset Boulevard in Beverly Hills and the canyons, had as its leaders the brothers Marco and Irving Hellman. The Hollywood Polo and Riding Club invited "many Jewish riders who have found that the glad hand is not extended to them everywhere." Professing that "the more Jewish members, the merrier," this club's roster had a majority of Jews, a condition it considered "something different, something grand."[83] Horse breeding and its style of life were a species of "status symbol" of the 1920's.

From the youthful societies and modest lodges through the gilded amenities of the Concordia, the most characteristic form of Jewish association was a social or fraternal bond. Los Angeles Jews perhaps had more desire to associate socially than they could give reasons for.

CHAPTER 9

Religious Growth and Adaptation

DURING THE early decades of the twentieth century, Jewish religious life in Los Angeles continued its even tenor. New congregations and religious preferences appeared upon the scene, and new religious leadership arrived in the city. There was one congregation in Los Angeles in 1900 and another was founded in that year; twenty years later ten existed. Los Angeles' great boom of the 1920's, however, brought multiplicity and confusion of congregations, and an instability of group and personal religious orientations quite out of the ordinary for American Jews. During that decade the number of known congregations ascended beyond thirty, with undoubtedly many more little-known conventicles.[1] The picture in 1929 was thus not too coherent.

Concern for the present and especially the future of Judaism was a note constantly sounded. That in religious life "Los Angeles is by no means worse off than any other place" was cold comfort; likewise, that the city "is up to date in the Temple line, and while they are not filled to 'overflowing,' we are not all asleep." Crowded synagogues during the High Holiday season, the climax of the religious year, "proved that Judaism is very much alive yet, despite that many had already sounded its death knell." The sense of concern, as always, focused upon young people and their "lack of serious interest in their religion" and failure to attend the synagogues.[2] The spirit of the times or the failure of elders properly to rear their children alternately bore the blame.

With the religious scene in Los Angeles divided between stern puritanical standards and nearly utopian religious liberalism, Jewish sympathies tended strongly toward the lenient course. Said Rabbi Hecht shortly after his arrival: "The time is upon us when we must work for the cause of an enlightened religion, that shall beneficially affect our young and our old, our men and our women, and re-act with equal beneficence upon our whole life."[3] Mrs. Isidore Myers, the wife of another rabbi, was more explicit. In an early idealization of southern California, she delighted that immigrants of all types to "the Southland" find "all the bolts and barriers removed. . . . they feel the warm grasp of real brotherhood." She hailed the arriving Shriners' work of brotherly love, which she found ultimately derived from Judaism: "May the day dawn in our time, when the tenderest hope that the heart of our people has cherished for so many thousands of years will be realized, that all mankind will become one great Fraternal Order of Universal Brotherhood."[4] From sunlit Jewish cosmopolitan brotherhood it was but a step to the same ideal without Jewish separateness. Such views were not often heard openly, but Jewish fiction and publicistic writing were shot through with it. The feminine leader Mrs. Bertha Hirsch Baruch indirectly expressed the mood in reprobating overeagerness for "tolerance" at any price:

Unfortunately we are suffering from a simple case of Jewish timidity or fright. . . . It is said they have no right to be different from their neighbors in the land of their adoption. . . . If Judaism is to endure as a religion of life we can not sacrifice our distinctively Jewish beliefs and customs for mere expediency to eradicate prejudice. Progress says it must disappear. Let us be hopeful and optimistic that there will be a speedy awakening of public conscience.[5]

In this view, which was widespread among cultured Jews and Christians, spiritual and material progress were correlated, and religion, including the reformed and liberalized Jewish religion, furnished prophecy and inspiration. Judaism would benefit in turn from the progress of the age; in Rabbi Hecht's words:

For, while it is true that vice, corruption, immorality, greed, hatred and persecution, with their concomitant general unrest, have disported themselves in this as in other countries of the earth, among Jews as among non-Jews, there has been a vigorous and successful campaign instituted by those spiritual forces that make for purity, honesty, efficiency and brotherliness, resulting in an ever growing sense of security and liberty. The voice of Justice has been heard; Peace has fluttered her wings; Right has triumphed over Might, and the redemption of mankind from the fetters of error and ignorance has been raised and advanced by several notches.
Nor has Judaism escaped the benefits of this progressive tendency.[6]

The movement to assimilate, based on diffuse doctrines of cosmopolitanism or an imminent millenium, was pursued by some acculturated Jews of the city. At the other pole was the growing community of traditional Jews, more at home in the Yiddish language and its ways of thought than in English. In their circles religious Orthodoxy was renewed in Los Angeles and Conservative Judaism established. Lacking the firm institutional structure so gradually developed by earlier Los Angeles Jews, the religious scene among the traditionalist newcomers included numerous "mushroom" and irregular congregations, rabbinic pretenders, and other signs of instability. By 1900 several minyanim (prayer quorums) met in rented quarters during the High Holidays; in that season of 1906 it was noted that "several . . . small communities of worshipers will hold forth in improvised halls."[7] Unconnected, usually self-ordained rabbis and entrepreneurial, unsynagogued cantors promoted services at halls in the Jewish district. The homes of the Elks and Turners did duty, and sumptuous cinemas served later on. These "mushroom" synagogues, conducted for private profit and extensively advertised, were severely arraigned by the established congregations and others concerned with Jewish communal dignity. To be sure, they had defenders who would not fault the sanctity of a temporary synagogue no matter what its previous use or who the promoters were.[8] With unaffiliated Jews streaming into the city, the desire to worship, if only on a transient basis, exceeded the available accommodations. It was odd but quite explicable to announce at the outset of the boom of the 1920's: "A new Congregation is to be started before Rosh Hashono. . . . A Rabbi, great preacher, a cantor and excellent choir are secured. Those interested may correspond with . . . They are particularly requested to express their opinion as to the section of the city promising the best prospects for such a congregation. . . . No dues will be asked of people who cannot afford to pay."[9]

Just as arriving rabbis sought to found congregations, so did displaced rabbis establish institutions of their own. Rabbi Isidore Myers, after his departure from Sinai Temple, established the "People's Synagogue" about 1912 and there were other instances.[10]

Reform Judaism

Towering over these laborious beginnings stood Temple B'nai B'rith in unchallenged ascendancy among the congregations of Los Angeles. Its fifteen-year transition from Orthodoxy to Reform, marked by many waverings and tensions, reached a conclusion with the arrival of Rabbi Sigmund Hecht late in 1899 and the full adoption of Reform Judaism under his direction. Originally from Hungary and educated in Vienna, he had come to the United States in 1868, aged nineteen. His first ministry, in Montgomery, Alabama, began in 1876 and was followed by eleven years in Milwaukee, which terminated with his departure for Los Angeles. Hecht had received a Doctorate of Divinity from the University of Alabama for an elementary post-biblical textbook history of the Jews. His interests lay heavily in the personal ethic and social righteousness of contemporary American religious liberalism, expounded from biblical and occasionally rabbinic sources. Sigmund Hecht was slight of stature, solemn, and dignified: the Temple had had so much of unstable ministers in fifteen years that it must have welcomed this solid, conscientious, middle-aged man. It had courted Hecht in Milwaukee for many months to make him its rabbi. For twenty years, until his retirement in 1919 at the age of seventy, Sigmund Hecht appeared before the Jewish and general community as the authoritative spokesman of Judaism. What he presented was not vivid or intense but was rather clear and sober, well in accord, as Hecht devoutly desired it to be, with the thinking of the generous, broad-minded bourgeois of the time.[11]

B'nai B'rith's rabbi installed definitively Reform worship based on the standardized Union Prayer Book. The organ, a mixed choir of Gentiles with instrumental music, bare heads, one day of holiday observance, English as the basic language of the liturgy, the centrality of the sermon and of the rabbi as leader in worship, the hushed atmosphere: all marked B'nai B'rith as a Reform Temple. The congregation thirsted to hear a persuasive, lucid exposition of the Reform Judaism they had adopted. Rabbi Hecht's first years provided this, too.

As he presented Judaism, its theology (usually denoted slightingly as "creeds" and "dogmas") was virtually shared by all men of good will. Religion gave man the power to transcend his earthly limitations, while Judaism offered the greatest expression for the divine powers latent in man. Still, Judaism was only for Jews, since Christians had a noble religion to inspire them. With "Diversity of Creed, Unity of Deed the Keynote of True Religion," moral and ethical conduct mattered most, regardless of what source it issued from.

Hecht advocated "an ideal religion, a religion that shall be worthy of its name, a religion that shall unite, not separate the children of the Common Father, a religion that shall flower into the recognition of man's rights and man's duties, a religion finally whose fruit is to be peace on earth, good will to men, and acts of righteousness, of love and light and truth." This was "Common Sense Religion,"[12] towards which the world was inexorably progressing with Israel in the vanguard. The justification and meaning of separate Jewish existence lay in the obligation of the "Priest People" to diffuse their teachings as a "light to the nations" ever since Sinaitic and prophetic revelation. Because Jewish distinctness therefore had to be maintained, Rabbi Hecht would perform no intermarriage.[13]

In 1914, when Hecht was sixty-five years old, the congregation gave their aging rabbi a younger assistant. A twenty-five-year-old native Californian serving in Stockton was engaged as associate rabbi at a salary of $2,500: such was the entry upon the Los Angeles scene of Rabbi Edgar Fogel Magnin.[14] The scion of a prosperous San Francisco mercantile family, Rabbi Magnin had attended Hebrew Union College and returned to California for his rabbinic service. The young colleague differed greatly from Rabbi Hecht in bearing: his speech in and out of the pulpit and his personal manner were forthright and direct. During the 1920's he gradually became the spokesman for Judaism in quarters where it was seldom heard of. The radio, Kiwanis Club, and Hollywood Bowl were platforms for the vigorous, outspoken Rabbi Magnin. His reputation soon extended far beyond Los Angeles.

Judaism as expounded by Rabbi Magnin did not have much theological cutting edge. It was viewed as that tradition, drastically but necessarily amended, whose power and truth inspired all men to conduct good lives and erect the good society. Rabbis ought to lead in this greatest of enterprises, and Rabbi Magnin personally furnished an exemplar of meaningful civic endeavor. The most notable chapters of his rabbinic service were written after the crisis of 1929 and the onset of depression.

When Rabbi Hecht arrived, Temple B'nai B'rith had "about 95" members. One year later there were 168, and growth thenceforward was steady to 329 in 1917-1918.[15] Probably the outstanding personage within the Temple's life was Dr. David Wolf Edelman (1862-1933), son of old Rabbi Edelman, a physician, and president of the congregation from 1910 until his death.[16] Edelman was not only a "lay" leader or an adminstrator. He also filled the pulpit during the rabbis' absence or illness, and sometimes bluntly addressed the membership on their religious duties. In 1908 Congregation B'nai B'rith rectified the curious arrangement whereby members who paid dues at a lower rate did not possess equal rights nor regular seats in the Temple. Equality, once established in 1908,[17] was followed by efforts to raise the dues voluntarily. In 1911 all but 135 of the Temple's 282 members paid the minimal $18 yearly, enjoying the same privileges as those who assessed themselves $30 to $100 yearly.[18]

Early in the 1920's, Temple B'nai B'rith decided to quit its antiquated and now dowdy building at Ninth and Hope streets in an area long since abandoned by its members, and to rear an edifice on a lot in the midst of Wilshire Boulevard. The new structure took its place as one of the most notable buildings in Los Angeles and one of the classic American synagogues.[19]

Twentieth-century Temple B'nai B'rith developed a network of auxiliary groups. Besides the adults' Temple Union there was a Literary Section promoting cultural and social purposes for young people. Another group, the Jewish Endeavorers, was "a society with a membership of about sixty . . . the object of which is to make better Jews of its members." Its semimonthly meetings opened with prayer, heard a talk by Rabbi Hecht on a religious topic, and concluded with a "pleasing literary or musical program rendered by the talent of the numerous members." The inspiration of Christian Endeavor societies was apparent.[20] A young people's Temple Forum for debate and discussion appeared late in 1912.[21] After the Ladies' Aid Society, dating back to the 1880's, dissolved in 1911, the Temple Union Sewing Circle took its place.[22] Foremost among the Temple's auxiliaries during these years was, of course, its Sisterhood. ·

Worship in the Los Angeles Reform Temple resembled that of many American Reform houses of worship.

The services at the Temple are always characterized by decorum and dignity, towards which the attendants always willingly and cheerfully contribute, and it is safe to predict that with the emphasis put upon the solemnity of the services on the high festivals, emphasis in prayer, song and sermon, their effects will be felt long after the last sounds shall have died away. . . . though the prayers are largely in the vernacular, and though the people worshipping there have discarded many of the prayers of the old MACHZOR, together with certain forms and customs, yet are the worshippers there JEWS, and the prayers and orisons and sermons strictly and intensely Jewish.[23]

Perhaps typical for its decade is the account of a visitor in May 1908. He found 118 persons at Friday evening services, of whom he estimated one-third were not congregants or not Jews. Forty-eight came, like himself, to recite Kaddish for the dead. Among the thirty or so remaining were the rabbi's family and the officers, so that barely one-tenth of Temple B'nai B'rith's 230 families attended as a matter of course.[24] The synagogue filled only on the High Holidays and on Passover and Shavuoth (confirmation day). Poor attendance was evidently a favorite subject for discussion; there was much of urging and cajoling to attend services, and of suggestions to improve the condition. On the other hand, radical proposals to transfer the Sabbath to Sunday were firmly rejected. Whether attendance was better or worse than at Christian churches was a source of cold comfort or distressful reflection, respectively.[25]

Traditional Religion Reorganizes

The congregational nuclei outside Temple B'nai B'rith which existed during the 1890's united at last in 1900. There had been a Moses Montefiore Hebrew Congregation, a People's Synagogue Beth El, and Kahal Israel (or Kehal Yisrael), and perhaps other groups unrecorded. All consisted of Russian and Polish Jews, besides a few native Jews out of accord with Reform Judaism. Old Rabbi Edelman was a kind of informal minister to them. They all fused to form Kehal Adath Beth Israel ("Assembled Community of the House of Israel"), which held its first services at Forester's Hall on or about Passover, 1900. Later that year a lot was purchased on Olive Street, near most of the members' homes. During 1901 while building was underway on Olive Street, Beth Israel worshipped in Lincoln Hall at 130½ Spring Street.[26] On April 13, 1902, the synagogue was dedicated, "thereby consummating the struggles and prayers and hopes for a number of years for a suitable temple for the worship of the universal God." In addition to Cantor A.

Arndt, Rabbi Hecht spoke and prayed, and a long list of musical offerings poured forth. A visiting rabbi from San Francisco, Isidore Myers, made his first local appearance on the program. Thus was consecrated for worship the structure known to two generations as the "Olive Street shul." From the outset it was an Orthodox congregation which long retained its character as an immigrant synagogue, consciously preserving the Judaism remembered from Eastern Europe. Rabbi Isidore Myers recalled these deep feelings at the dedication: "Many of you remember when you left the old country your father said, 'May you remain a true and loyal Jew.' You will never forget these words."[27]

A. Arndt, a Los Angeleno from the 1890's, served as cantor and teacher in the heder attached to the synagogue until the fall of 1907, when he was succeeded by M. A. Alter. B. Leve served for a relatively lengthy period thereafter, until 1913;[28] an S. Rosen is mentioned as having been elected cantor, but it does not appear that he actually served.[29] To find a rabbi was more complicated. True to its nature as an immigrant synagogue, Beth Israel had none before 1915. In 1902 there had been a flare-up over the proposed election of a rabbi, caused by a question as to the candidate's possession of valid rabbinic ordination. The majority clearly desired a full-fledged Orthodox Talmudist rather than a teacher or officiant.[30] Late in 1904 or early in 1905 another attempt was made with the election of Isidore Myers, then of San Francisco. In March 1905 he had not yet assumed the post; in any case, he resigned by the following summer and soon cast his lot with the Congregation Sinai.[31]

At last, in 1914, Beth Israel brought to the city Rabbi Isaac Werne, aged thirty-seven, a native of Slonim, Lithuania. Their new leader had a rare combination of orthodox rabbinic qualifications and a doctorate from the University of Königsberg.[32] Werne had written for Zionist journals and served as a rabbi in Chicago before coming to Los Angeles for a six-year stay. He fulfilled the customary duties of an Orthodox rabbi, with homilies on the Sabbath and classes at other times during the week, and by responding to Jewish legal questions as needed. Rabbi Werne was also the mainstay of the Hebrew culturists until he and his family left for Dallas in 1920. He was to return during the 1930's.[33]

Early in 1904, less than four years after the foundation of Beth Israel, it was "rumored that another synagogue is to go up in this city. On this question we may say that Los Angeles is supplied with two—the reform temple and the orthodox—which we believe is quite sufficient for the present."[34] In disregard of this editorial frown, the first service of the new Congregation Sinai was held on December 14, 1906, at a nicely decorated B'nai B'rith hall. Unlike the beginnings of most religious bodies, its origin was not cloudy or improvised. Rabbi Myers was on hand to speak on "Sinai," and Cantor M. Katz reportedly dazzled the assemblage even without the announced choir.[35] Three years were spent in rented halls while the Willing Workers and the young people and adults conducted bazaars, whist parties, celebrations, and direct appeals for money. A lot was finally bought on 12th and Valencia streets. On June 13, 1909, the cornerstone was laid, and the formal dedication took place on September 5 of that year.[36] At the cornerstone ceremony, the principal speakers were leading local Jews and Christians, including Rabbi Hecht, Mayor George Alexander, and the Rev. Baker P. Lee. The new temple had "weathered oak furnishings and tinting in blending shades in brown and blue, with splendid art glass and windows and magnificent pipe organ." The program at the dedication included versifications of the Hebrew prayers composed for that occasion by the poetasting Rabbi Myers. He characterized the religious outlook of Congregation Sinai: "This congregation stands for Conservative, that is, Rabbinical Judaism. It has not sprung up in opposition to any other existing congregation. It stands for definite lines."[37] Conservative Judaism as developed at Sinai meant moderate changes in public worship. An organ played; the rabbi not only preached at late Friday evening and Sabbath morning services but conducted the prayers; such ceremonies as confirmation were introduced. Its cantor competed with that of Beth Israel; the feeling for liturgical chant reached deeper than theological interests. The language at Sinai was English, while that at Beth Israel was primarily Yiddish. Aesthetic satisfaction, a pleasant atmosphere, and attractiveness to youth were important elements in the congregational psyche. All in all, Conservative Judaism at Sinai was distinctly for acculturated Jews and their children, aiming to accommodate traditional Judaism to their general environment. Its intellectual basis was barely visible.

Isidore Myers, a native of Australia who had arrived in the United States around the turn of the century, was about fifty years old when he came to Sinai.[38] He remained six years, and then turned his hand to a People's Synagogue of his own. Rabbi Rudolph Farber replaced him for a tenure of three years, the latter part troubled by ill health. Then Rabbi David Liknaitz came in 1915, to depart in 1918. His reasons for leaving illuminate the lack of religious clarity at Sinai:

This synagogue, like many of its kind, has had a very conglomerate ritual. I found three books in use, namely: Friday evening Minhag Jastrow [a semi-Reform prayer book of the 1870's], Sabbath morning the old siddur, with all its defects and none of its merits, and on Rosh Hashonah and Yom Kippur, the old Machzor. With the consent of the ritual committee, which by the way was presided over by a scholarly and God-fearing gentleman, we introduced English reading and hymns in our services. Not wishing to change the Siddur in the morning, we supplemented with English psalms which, although primarily for the younger folks, proved to be very welcome to the older people also. On the High Holidays the difficulties were still greater. At the request of the Board I compiled a booklet of devotions which proved to be very useful on those great days.[39]

The internal opposition to change was too great to overcome: "Unfortunately, this congregation, like others of its kind, has a membership that is negative, allowing all business to be managed by a few self-appointed men."[40]

Whatever their shortcomings, the number of Sinai members rose sharply. At the beginning of 1911 there were 102 and at the end of 1912, 203. Hopeful talk circulated that the three-year-old building would soon be outgrown.[41]

Congregation Sinai held Sabbath and holiday services as well as weekday afternoon worship. Its auxiliaries included Willing Workers and several groups of young people, besides the Religious School which met three times weekly.[42] During the hiatuses between rabbis, talented laymen were well qualified to preside in the pulpit. Thus, the scholarly physician Louis G. Reynolds could preach quite effectively. In 1918 Rabbi Liknaitz' successor, Rabbi

Moses Rosenthal, arrived for a four-year tenure. He was the first link between the Conservative Jewish outpost in California and the Jewish Theological Seminary, where he had been ordained. Of more traditional convictions than his predecessor, Rabbi Rosenthal served the congregation while it was contemplating a larger, more sumptuous home at Fourth and Hampshire.

As Beth Israel and Congregation Sinai held their predominance among the traditional synagogues, other congregations sprang up, especially during the booming 1920's. Unlike most eastern congregations of immigrant origin, new groups were not based on a common European home town. Los Angeles Jews from Eastern Europe had made too many stops en route to organize upon a *landsleit* basis. Most congregations were founded, simply enough, by neighborhood. They were prone to characterize themselves as "modern orthodox," like Shaaray Tefila,[43] or "traditional," or "in conservative form," like Rodef Sholom.[44] Such descriptions, they hoped, would attract younger people as well as older orthodox. Outright Orthodox congregations also arose, the most important of which was Congregation Talmud Torah. This began in 1905 as a society to support a Jewish afternoon school for children. By 1912 it left its quarters on Rose Street for a large, attractive synagogue on Breed Street. Like its nearby Olive Street contemporary, the "Breed Street shul" became a Jewish neighborhood fixture for many years to come.[45] As old as these East Side institutions was Agudath Achim Anshe Sfard, founded about 1903 and housed at 21st Street and Central Avenue.[46] Newer neighborhoods like West Jefferson or the southwest (whose contemporary meaning was lower Vermont Avenue) also built their houses of worship. Pasadena Jews succeeded three times in founding congregations, in 1907, 1909, and 1920.[47]

After World War I, attempts were made in many cities to consolidate the existing Orthodox congregations. The United Hebrew Orthodox Congregations, with Rabbi Werne designated its "Chief Rabbi," was established in Los Angeles. Ten synagogues belonged.[48] In the following year of 1921, a Beth Din of Los Angeles was founded. Its first session, spent in examining the qualifications of shohtim, showed that kashruth was the principal concern of the congregational union and its affiliated rabbinic tribunal.[49] However, it had far less than the strength it needed to supervise aggressive economic interests effectively.

Reform Judaism also grew when Temple Emanuel was founded as the second Reform temple in Los Angeles. David Liknaitz, its first rabbi, recently of Sinai, was succeeded for a spell by the elderly Rabbi Emanuel Schreiber, who had served B'nai B'rith Temple long before. Then in 1921 the Reform temple, still worshipping in a Masonic Hall, brought to Los Angeles the young Ernest R. Trattner and secured Rabbi Magnin to install him. Trattner was twenty-four years old, with a "boy wonder" reputation. He had eloquence, presence, some erudition, but no rabbinic degree. Besides, he was a writer of quite exceptional gifts. All these talents were put to full use during a lengthy and checkered career, all of which was spent in Los Angeles. Rabbi Trattner was also a writer in the spirit of liberal, exuberantly optimistic, antitraditional religion. His first book, *Unravelling the Book of Books,* was a vigorous, somewhat breathless account of critical biblical scholarship, all of whose conclusions he enthusiastically accepted. It was quite contemptuous of precritical biblical study.[50] Rabbi Trattner continued with *The Autobiography of God,* published only one year later. Here, God tells how mankind is painfully progressing to a higher, purer idea of Himself, as advocated by liberal religionists. There was nothing remarkable, except that this stiffly anti-anthropomorphic message was delivered by God in the first person.[51] After his book on the Bible in 1929 and one "by" God in 1930, Trattner next wrote on Jesus, from the chimerical "Jewish point of view."[52] He urged a rehabilitation of the Christian Messiah in the spirit of Joseph Klausner's recent *Jesus of Nazareth*: that his spiritual greatness be recognized and that he be accorded a significant place in Judaism. As Christians were becoming more liberal. Trattner urged, Jews were drawing to a kinder view of Jesus.

Trattner's books were informed, if not scholarly. Taken together, they represent Reform Judaism extended to a universalizing, syncretistic extreme. There is no record that they personally influenced in Los Angeles anyone but their author's devoted following. The decade following their appearance hardly lent itself to the mood cheerfully taken by Rabbi Trattner.

Gropings in Jewish Education

At the turn of the twentieth century, Jewish education in Los Angeles was weak and little regarded. It was conducted by the congregations and remained under their aegis, with few exceptions, for many years. Aside from private tutoring given by old Rabbi Edelman and one or two others, the sole institution where the rudiments of Judaism were taught was Temple B'nai B'rith's Sunday school. It had 75 children in attendance upon Rabbi Hecht's arrival in 1899 and, to judge from the unstable condition of the temple itself, there was little of academic substance. Elementary education in the city generally was behind the standard of other large cities, while high school education was still for the few.[53]

During the first decade of the twentieth century several types of Jewish schooling grew up. Under Rabbi Hecht's direction the Sunday school of the Reform temple grew to 106 children in 1910, apparently in five classes. Its weekly routine followed a pattern:

Our Sunday School sessions are regularly opened with prayer and singing, after which the members of each class in rotation recite selected Bible verses, the meaning of which is brought out before the whole school, and an original essay, read by one of the pupils, appointed for each Sunday, concludes the opening exercises. The pupils are then dismissed from the assembly hall into their respective classrooms, and remain in charge of their teachers until re-assembled at the close of the morning hour, and dismissed to their respective homes.[54]

Much of the time was spent on preparation for performances and public examinations. There was a Purim show, a graduation program, and formal examinations of each grade; for the graduating class there was a rather elaborate confirmation ceremony. Among its purposes, the Sunday school aimed to "inculcate into the minds of the young the lessons of practical religion, and charity is one of the foremost doctrines of Judaism. And the little one were apt pupils," for they brought generous offerings for (on that occasion) the Alliance Israélite Universelle.[55]

The Sunday classes studied Bible, history, and bits of Hebrew for liturgical purposes. The fifteen-year-old boys and girls preparing for their confirmation pursued similar studies more seriously. "The Bible Class conducted by Dr. Hecht has finished the study of the prophets Hosea and Micah as well as some selected Psalms. The discussion of current topics affecting Jews and Judaism . . . has proved both interesting and helpful."[56] It was said with some diffidence that "whatever the future may prove in their case, whether they will apply in their life the lessons which they have learned, or neglect them, so much is certain that at the time of the confirmation the children have a fair knowledge of Judaism and its requirements."[57]

In 1909 the congregation erected a school wing for the Temple, permitting the Sunday school's growth from 106 students in 1910 to 408 in 1920. Although instruction was intended primarily for children of Temple members, somewhat grudging permission existed for outsiders' children to be educated there.[58] In addition to the regular Sunday sessions, an optional hour of Hebrew language instruction and a junior Sabbath service were held. Rabbi Hecht, as superintendent of the Sunday school, appraised the educational efforts as "far, far from being satisfactory." The reasons were ascribed to "a little indifference on the part of the home, a little incompetency on the part of the teacher, and the little interest toward this branch on the part of the congregational authorities. . . . when neither love nor money is strong enough to secure the necessary teaching force, it is easy to understand that and why so little is being accomplished."[59] Plain-spoken Dr. Edelman, president of the congregation, also reflected in 1912 upon educational realities: "My appeal of a year ago, relative to a more earnest support of the Sabbath services for children, has also fallen upon barren soil. I trust that violin, French, and dancing lessons will wait that one hour a week while religion endeavors to teach the children God and morality. . . . Doctor Hecht has informed me that the congregation of little ones each Saturday morning has never been very formidable."[60]

The Temple's Sunday school fairly represented its educational species. However, the newer elements in the Jewish community were accustomed to more intensive study and ceremonial observance, while the modernists among them brought the Hebraic revival and Zionist hopes to transform the old-fashioned classroom. New types of schooling began to appear. True, A. Arndt, the religious functionary, was conducting a "Hebrew Free School" which moved early in 1900 to 605½ East First Street—"more thickly settled with

Jewish people."[61] Undoubtedly this was a heder, the one-room schoolhouse where the rudiments of the Hebrew prayer book and religious law were rather badly inculcated. Not long after, however, there was word of "the Jewish school under the management of Rabbi Myers . . . attended by many children residing all over the city, and whose parents are anxious that they attend regularly."[62] This was the beginning of Sinai Temple's school, which had distinct Sunday school and Hebrew school departments. Although Sinai maintained that "knowledge of Hebrew strengthens the Jewish consciousness in our children and it assumes added importance because it is again a living language," all but 62 of its 204 children in 1914 were enrolled in Sunday classes only.[63] Beth Israel, the Olive Street synagogue, evidently developed its Orthodox Talmud Torah from Arndt's heder beginnings. Another school of significance was maintained by Congregation Talmud Torah on Breed Street, which proposed to teach "every Jewish child, male or female, not only the tenets of Judaism but its history as well. Many of our pupils have proved the good results of our work in this that they have learned not to be ashamed of their race and nationality."[64]

B'nai B'rith Temple itself established in 1912 a short-lived daily Hebrew school in the poorer Jewish district. The Temple blamed its quick demise on the "act of influence" of a few parents "who hoped to control the management" and said that "children were induced to remain away," and the school shut down.[65] Probably there was conflict between the sponsors' plans and the expectations of parents who were far from Reform Judaism. When Congregation Agudas Achim at Central Avenue and 21st Street opened its Talmud Torah, it used "scare" tactics to draw support: "The missionary's headquarters is situated in that location . . . many of them have already been attracted by the missionaries, and it is our duty to attract them to their own religious school before it is too late."[66] (Neither there nor elsewhere were the rather obtrusive Christian missions influential.) The last educational genre to develop was the Yiddish school—professedly radical in its politics and secular in its Judaism.[67] When the teacher Israel Osman arrived in Los Angeles in 1914, he found three Talmud Torahs, one Sunday school, and one Yiddish school.[68] Probably there were others—private hadarim and transient congregational schoolrooms.

All the new schools were influenced by Hebraism and Zionism, the newer Jewish ideals. Parents, however, generally demanded that their children possess mechanical facility in Hebrew, if only for bar mitzvah and Kaddish purposes. The teaching of the language "has by some been considered a waste of time . . . children of American birth should not be burdened with the study of a dead language."[69] It was therefore a matter of pride and publicity that "Hebrew can be taught to children born and growing up in this land of the free."[70] Miss S. R. Glazer, a Palestinian, taught her class "the modern Hebrew that makes it so easy for children to learn."[71] The Orthodox Talmud Torah of Boyle Heights offered its sixty children "a Hebrew education such as would satisfy the religious and nationalist Jews." The curriculum included Bible, Hebrew, and Jewish history. Rabbi Werne, of Beth Israel, himself a Hebraic modernist, reported *B'nai B'rith Messenger* (November 2, 1917), "visits school every Thursday, examines the children and gives the program for the coming week." The annual public examination included "Hebrew reading, writing, spelling, speaking, translation of Chumosh [Pentateuch], grammar and fluent reading of the prayer book. The pupils showed a remarkable store of knowledge."[72]

B'nai B'rith Temple during the 1920's instructed 400 children in its kindergarten, primary, high school, and confirmation classes, and employed the services of Rabbi Maxwell Dubin to direct these educational efforts. "The aim is to teach Jewish history and tradition with a view to correlating ancient and modern Judaism, and arousing the youthful mind relative to things Jewish; not only religious subjects but Jewish culture and literature and art."[73] Students in the highest grade were taught about the Jewish community and Jewish movements. As to Zionism, a touchy matter in Reform Judaism, "the attitude is taken that Judaism is a religion and Palestine a refuge for oppressed Jews of the world."[74]

In 1923 Jewish education in Los Angeles extended to approximately 1,500 children at a given time, perhaps one-third of Jewish elementary school children in the city. About half attended Sunday schools, mainly at B'nai B'rith Temple. One of the largest of the afternoon schools was the Breed Street Talmud Torah, with 100 boys and ten girls; six others were smaller. The most substantial and best housed was the Yiddish Folk School on Soto Street, with 130 children. It was estimated that the Jewish schools altogether employed eleven weekday teachers and twenty-nine Sunday teachers and spent about $17,000 yearly on their entire effort. They were quite uncoordinated, lacking pedagogic or curricular standards, and very ill-housed. No support yet came from Jewish communal sources, where Jewish education was still regarded as a solely parental and synagogal interest, or as the child of ideological groups.[75]

The teaching corps was not very impressive. Many of the Sunday school teachers were described as "only fairly competent. . . . do not possess a Jewish soul . . . whether through their own fault or not, they are inclined to be without Jewish feeling or sentiment." Since most of them were young volunteers, it was thought a considerable improvement when public school teachers, slightly trained by the rabbi, were paid to teach on Sundays.[76] Most of the teachers in the weekday schools were also employed in other occupations, especially synagogal ones. While they had "soul" and "feeling," and not a little learning in many cases, they were not very effective pedagogues: the gap between them and their pupils was too great. The more professional teachers established a local group of the Hebrew Teachers Union (Agudath Hamorim), which complained that "very frequently schools accept teachers who are unworthy of the position of Hebrew educator."[77] But some few devoted teachers fired the imaginations of their children. Such teachers as A. M. Tonnis and Israel Osman developed cadres of students devoted to the ideals of Hebraic (or Yiddish) cultural modernism and Zionism.

The general picture was disheartening throughout the first three decades of the twentieth century. With slight exaggeration, a distinguished visiting educator told the community that "Jewish education in Los Angeles is practically nonexistent. . . . Los Angeles is not on the Jewish educational map in this country. With as many Jews as you say there are in this city, a greater effort could be made."[78] Even in its nonreligious sector, Jewish education focused upon the training needed for bar mitzvah or confirmation. It was rather barren rote study, irrelevant to the higher interests of adolescence or maturity. As in far larger American Jewish communities of the time, it was not possible in Los Angeles to learn Hebrew really well nor to study comprehensively the history of philosophy or classic texts of the Jews. The congregations did poorly what almost no one else did at all.

CHAPTER 10

Philanthropy

AT THE OPENING of the twentieth century the Jews of Los Angeles maintained the charities typical of most American Jewish communities. There was a Hebrew Benevolent Society, organized in 1854, with some of its founders still on hand. Originally a mutual aid and burial society, its members' ascent to prosperity made it a philanthropy which doled out between $1,000 and $3,000 per annum. Alongside the Hebrew Benevolent Society was the Ladies' Hebrew Benevolent Society, providing services like food and medicine. Temple B'nai B'rith's women founded the Temple Union Sewing Circle, collecting material to sew into garments and distribute to the poor. A few years later the Fruit and Flower Mission, consisting of Jewish girls, gave out baskets of provisions weekly to needy Jews.

At the turn of the century, recalled Victor Harris, the Hebrew Benevolent Society's secretary:

The office of the H.B.S. . . . was in the old DuCommon Block, corner North Main and Commercial Streets. It occupied one room and at a rental of $5.00 a month. Besides the regulation desk and a few chairs, I found a big, round basket full of old shoes, an old trunk, in another corner, and a large map of the old Home of Peace Cemetery, adorning one of the walls. The applicants for relief had to wait their turn in the hallway, the cynosure of passers-by, and often the line stretched to the street below.[1]

The officers who had to hear and adjudge the applicants' merits hardly vied for the honor of election. Harris recalled that he first entered upon the secretaryship by wandering into the annual meeting as a new, unknown member. All eyes presently turned to him for the onerous job. (He could not have demurred too vigorously, for he served many terms in the office.)[2] After Harris there were very few new faces even though the Germanness of the Hebrew Benevolent Society became less pronounced: "While most of the income is from our coreligionists who were born and raised in Germany, the management is in the hands of other nationalities, the present Board of Officers consisting of 3 Russians, 3 Austrians, and 1 German."[3] The society counted 211 members at the opening of the century, and ten years later there were 213.[4] It sought to put away its funerary beginnings. "At the present time [1909] we have done away with religious services [i.e., conducting funerals] and we are trying to do away with the burial part of it. We want to confine ourselves strictly to the charitable and benevolent part."[5] Some idea may be gained of this charity from the 850 cases accepted during the economically depressed year of 1914. The society supported 27 regular pensioners, aided 115 single men and 88 new family cases, and afforded temporary shelter to 39 single men. In 267 cases it furnished shoes and clothing. Workers sent by the Industrial Removal Office in New York to establish themselves in a new city numbered 87.[6] All in all, it was routine giving of goods and cash, punctuated by complaints against the difficulties caused by impoverished consumptives from the East.

The city and the Jewish community felt themselves beset by these pitiable victims of infectious slums and sweatshops. While it is not clear how many Jews came among the tubercular health seekers, there were evidently hundreds. Stricken Jewish tailors left home and sometimes took their families to find healing in the sunshine of southern California. "From one of the Railroad stations, the poor consumptive hies to a lonely dark room in an illy [sic] ventilated cheap lodging house, where he remains until his scanty means are exhausted. . . . The next recourse is to the Hebrew Benevolent Society to be furnished with transportation home or supported here."[7] To judge from the rather small amounts the HBS devoted to return fare, not many returned to their native place. The society declared: "Our means are not sufficient to supply the demands of the needy, the sick and the homeless in our midst—not counting the new ones that are sent here [by Eastern charities] or come on their own account. And they continue to come, no matter how many circular letters we send out, warning them not to come. When they get here, it means that we will have to take care of them, or send them back to New York, Chicago, or St. Louis, Philadelphia and other large cities in the East."[8]

Yet some within the Hebrew Benevolent Society were saying that a Jewish haven should be established for consumptives. Two were founded in Denver, Los Angeles' rival as a refuge for "lungers," in 1900 and 1904, and drew countrywide support. But early in 1902 the Los Angeles leaders were still "contending that the founding of a free hospital for consumptives here will be tantamount to an invitation" to masses of victims.[9] Subsequent developments had pleasant irony. Jacob Schlesinger, president of the HBS and principal advocate of the consumptives' home, won over the contrary-minded Kaspare Cohn, perhaps the richest Jew in town. When Cohn gave his large home on Carroll Avenue, the Kaspare Cohn Hospital Association to relieve consumptives came into existence on July 11, 1902. Soon, however, Cohn's former neighbors, objecting to tubercular patients next door, persuaded the city council to prohibit institutional treatment of the disease within the city. Kaspare Cohn's house had to be put to other medical purposes, and Schlesinger was back where he had started. Now a new subsidiary, the Hebrew Consumptive Relief Association, was founded in 1906.[10] By an agreement with the Barlow Sanitarium, it was permitted to erect cottages on Sanitarium grounds and support the two Jewish patients inhabiting each one. Four years later, there were two cottages and four patients, each costing $7 weekly.[11] The association also made similar arrangements with three other institutions and with the County Hospital.[12]

The Hebrew Benevolent Society moved forward by establishing a Free Loan Fund in 1911, thanks to the determination of Rabbi Hecht. He had $3,000 when he assumed office as treasurer of the fund. If the fund resembled those in other Jewish communities, then the average loan would have been about $25, with perhaps $50 available for a small business. From the first, the loan fund was a "success story." It later became the Hebrew Loan and Housing Association, presumably lending money for house building during post-World War I prosperity.[13]

The New Philanthropy, 1909-1914

About 1909, new currents began to transform Jewish charity as recently arrived Jews were beginning to adapt their inbred ideas of *zedakah* to the new environment. The new Jewish philanthropy of East European background was less inclined to depend upon arrangements with general charities for the care of Jews. It was deeply concerned that the Jewish sick and orphans and other clients have a Jewish environment: kosher food, religious service, Yiddish speech where necessary, and the intangibles of being in the company of fellow Jews. Although they were organized during California's Progressive era of efficiency and nonpartisanship, the newer Jewish charities raised their funds by rather clamorous appeals instead of genteel private solicitation. Not only was there an immemorial Jewish habit of furnishing endless opportunities to perform the sacred precept of almsgiving; few givers could give as much as one dollar at a time, and they had to be solicited often. The recently arrived segment of the Jewish community supported many charitable groups which had such purposes as burial, Jewish education, Passover relief, and endowment of brides. Of these charities, a few were to become major communal enterprises with the years. This newer philosophy and the means by which it raised money are exemplified in the Jewish Consumptive Relief Association, which established a full-fledged tuberculosis sanitarium at Duarte. Another institution, the Hebrew Sheltering and Home for the Aged, began as a temporary asylum for the homeless and the down-and-out and soon became a haven for the aged, providing the atmosphere and amenities familiar to East European Jews.

Not all innovation came from European immigrant circles. A fertile source was B'nai B'rith, which in 1910 founded the Jewish Orphans' Home. Nor were the old charities by any means barren of achievement during the years from 1909 to 1914. They founded the Federation of Jewish Charities in 1912, emulating a movement widespread in American Jewish charity, and that unexpected child, the Kaspare Cohn Hospital, was converted into a Jewish general hospital.[14]

The Sheltering Home was at first "an Hachosas Orchim, temporary shelter, where the stranger and wayfarer may find temporary accommodation until he finds employment."[15] It was organized in 1911, and acquired a twelve-room house for its twenty to twenty-five daily clients.[16] The Tifereth Israel Synagogue took a special interest.[17] Soon the managers were considering a larger "home for the homeless, *and aged* Hebrews [authors' italics] where they may be comfortable, happy, well cared for during their declining years."[18] With 1,500 cases assisted during 1914, the Hebrew Sheltering Society, by employing "monster mass meetings" and picnics, paid down $4,000 of the $10,000 price for the Glass estate on South Boyle Avenue. Several elderly men were installed within.[19]

The grounds were developed, a synagogue was added, and the Home's functions as a temporary shelter were overshadowed. Still, in 1919, 600 strangers stayed from three to ten days. With a membership exceeding 500 and an active ladies' group, the Home in less than a decade became a communal fixture, attracting wealthy patronage.[20]

More ambitious and controversial was the new conception of the amelioration of tuberculosis. By 1910 the Hebrew Consumptive Relief Association was well along in its collaboration with the Barlow and other sanitariums.[21] On September 28, 1912, the new Southern California Jewish Consumptive Relief Association came into being. About forty persons attended the founding meeting, "a large number" of whom were physicians. B. Cohn became president; he later became executive director and was the driving force. Two fully equipped beds and $278 were the first donations. The association proposed to establish a tuberculosis sanitarium not only for Los Angeles Jews but for Jewish consumptives who might come from anywhere in the country. The Hebrew Consumptive Relief Association was appalled. Its president observed that "all over the United States they are trying to localize the care of consumptives and let the localities take care of their own sick. It will be very hard to get outside support. . . . We ought not to induce the sick to come here. . . . I am afraid that the people behind the new institution are treading on dangerous ground. . . . My advice is to localize this institution and attend to whatever cases may come along and not ask for outside support. Let us combine all our effort to this purpose."[22]

B'nai B'rith in the city did agree to a Jewish sanitarium, but only for local sufferers.[23] JCRA President B. Cohn insisted that "the idea of a sanitarium is not the creation of one mind or one person. The need was felt throughout the community and a movement was therefore started simultaneously in many different localities and for divergent classes."[24] Ten acres were bought on the outskirts of the city at the Duarte site which was to become famous, and notwithstanding the lack of water, telephone, or electricity, six incipient consumptives were installed at once in tent houses.[25] On December 13, 1914, several hundred people rode a "Sanitarium Special" on the Santa Fe Railroad to visit the fifteen patients at Duarte and attend the dedication.

When the guests stepped out from the cars, they saw before them, the new rising little "Town of Hope," known to you as the Sanitarium. The Ladies' Tents, the platform built especially for the occasion, and all other cottages and buildings were decorated with American and Jewish flags. The Mogen-David covered with American flags, on the top of all buildings. What a beautiful idea! What a great combination from the Jewish standpoint, for when and where had Judaism enjoyed greater liberty and opportunity than was accorded to them under this flag.[26]

Against the enthusiasm which the JCRA engendered, the staid Hebrew Consumptive Relief Association deplored in vain. It admitted fourteen patients to its cottages during 1914 and reiterated a philosophy of local responsibility: "Our community is not rich enough to support a national institution for the care of consumptives, and it will take many years before we are able to support one, and so let us strive to take care of the local cases and not attract more from the East by raising false hopes."[27]

Exactly as feared by the old-line communal leaders, the JCRA proceeded to seek nationwide support. Already in 1914, $1,400 in dues came from outside the city to $2,200 in local payments.[28] By 1917, $8,402 was contributed from Los Angeles and donations of $21,755 came from elsewhere.[29] The apparatus in New York and Philadelphia promoted mass meetings, picnics, and theater benefits for the Duarte Sanitarium, competing with campaigns for the two Jewish tubercular sanitariums at Denver. But a price was paid for this overexpansion. By 1917 and 1918 the JCRA exploded with incidents of exorbitant commissions levied by out-of-town solicitors and extravagant promotions at a loss. Many directors resigned, including influential figures from New York's East Side, and the JCRA's affairs were put "through the wringer."[30] Humorously but truthfully, the JCRA divided Los Angeles Jewry into factions of Members, Friends, Enemies, and Neutrals.[31] Notwithstanding all this, a campus for the tubercular was gradually arising at Duarte, complete with lounges, library, and synagogue. The idea of a nationwide tuberculosis sanitarium in Los Angeles, and its vigorous methods of promotion, remained for some time a fighting subject. The "City of Hope," as the Duarte sanitarium came to be called, was in fact the only nationwide Jewish institution based in Los Angeles, drawing most of its leadership from southern California.[32]

Other institutions were making their way meanwhile in a more harmonious atmosphere, notably the Orphan Asylum, beloved child of the B'nai B'rith lodge. Already in 1906 the men of No. 487 were considering the plight of orphaned or neglected children, many from the families of impoverished tubercular health-seekers. "Some little ones were in the hands of the Salvation Army, others found in poor conditions on the streets, there to roam for themselves, others were in the Los Angeles Orphans' Home, an excellent non-sectarian institution, where the children received as good care as we can give them, but where they were removed from all Jewish influence."[33] Several unfit Jewish homes for children were conducted by private individuals.[34] With the help of Oscar Lawler, United States District Attorney, a B'nai B'rith group incorporated on October 3, 1908, as the Jewish Orphans' Home of Southern California. Compared with the usual struggles of beginning charities, this was a "success story" from the outset. Substantial funds flowed in from the lodge and also from prominent families. The first children entered a rented house on January 4, 1909; one year later, two houses were required to accommodate 51 boys and girls.[35] The Jewish Orphans' Home narrowly averted a major tragedy when the home burned to the ground on August 1, 1910, without death or injury.[36] The accident probably speeded the erection of the planned new home, especially after the old pioneer Harris Newmark gave $10,000 and 16 acres in Montebello for the Harris and Sarah Newmark Park.[37] However, the site was shifted to Huntington Park to gain access to city utilities. On Thanksgiving Day, 1912, President Siegfried Marshutz presided over the dedication of the $75,000 home, and the 74 children took occupancy in June 1913.[38] Economic prosperity and unified, energetic leadership had "made" the Jewish Orphans' Home in less than five years. In later years it evolved into Vista Del Mar Child Care agency of Los Angeles Jewry.

The orphans' institutional routine was kindly but exacting:

When at 6 A.M. the bell sounds forth its morning greetings, the house becomes lively. All the children leave their beds, dress and wash cleanly. Another salute of the bell 30 minutes later calls them to breakfast. Some of the older children have to wait at the tables. When they have finished their meals every one attends to his duties. By eight they are done and make ready for school. Then they file in to march off. None must be overlooked but everyone looked over. If one is not "comme il faut," that means to stay back and be properly adjusted.[39]

The rest of the day was governed by a similar routine. Jewish education and worship were provided under a director, Sigmund Frey, who had been for many years a Reform rabbi. On the other hand, the diet was not kosher. To the Jewish community, the children had the old-fashioned aspect of wards of the community—individuals regularly contributed food or a treat in honor of a family event, and donated clothing and shoes, and were invited to visit weekly. The children would recite Kaddish for someone's departed relatives or for a benefactor. It was recognized that home care was far better than an institution, but the Orphans' Home residents lacked any home or had parents who could not bring them up.

At the same time that the Orphans' Home and the Duarte site of the JCRA and the shelter for the aged were being developed, the Kaspare Cohn Hospital was turning into a general hospital. Unable to serve its original purpose of ministering to the tubercular, the new hospital adapted itself to general medical, surgical, and obstetric care, for which the Cohn home on Carroll Avenue hardly suited. It admitted 125 new cases in 1907 and 166 in 1908, few of whom paid anything. Dr. Sarah Vasen was superintendent and resident physician and supervised three nurses, a cook, and a janitor. Donations of food, clothing, and English and Yiddish newspapers were regularly received.[40] Doctors David W. Edelman, Adolph Tyroler, and E. M. Lazard constituted the medical staff, with approximately twenty-five patients to attend at any given time. Patients stayed about sixteen days.[41] The Kaspare Cohn directors planned a building on Stephenson Avenue in Boyle Heights, just beyond the city limits, where the hospital would not only be suitably housed and equipped, but could resume its original objective of treating consumptives. The economic downturn of 1907-1908 slowed fund raising, but from 1909 the pace was rapid. On Thanksgiving Day, 1909, the cornerstone was laid, and on June 19, 1910, the new structure was dedicated.[42] The remaining $13,000 debt was cleared mainly by a donation of $5,300 from Kaspare Cohn himself.[43] The hospital now sought to outgrow its charity beginnings and to attract the sick who could pay. Dr. Edelman exhorted:

... those of you who know of a patient with means who needs care, medical or surgical, not to recommend him to seek the advice of this or that physician whom he has never seen, heard of and does not know, and to go to some other hospital of the city which does not need him—only to come knocking at the portals of this institution when his money is gone and the other doctor and the other hospital look for pay and look in vain. . . . talk this institution up to those who need hospital care and have the means to pay for good service, so that the small amount of profit made from them may help take care of some other sick fellow who hasn't a cent.[44]

By 1915, $2,500 was received in fees, and the Kaspare Cohn Hospital slowly lost its standing as a charity hospital exclusively. As related below, it ultimately became the Cedars of Lebanon Hospital.

With new philanthropies springing up, the idea of federating them began to seem natural and necessary. In 1909 Rabbi Hecht surveyed the scene to point a moral: "We have now an Orphans' Home, a hospital for the sick poor, a society for the relief of consumptives, a Ladies' Benevolent Society, a Fruit and Flower Mission, several Ladies' Auxiliaries, a nucleus for settlement work, and a number of other philanthropic and semiphilanthropic organizations in this city alone. Besides these we contribute to several kindred organizations in the different parts of the country." Nevertheless, he added, "we do not achieve as much by way of permanent results as other cities do," largely because "we are scattering our resources instead of concentrating them; and *Federation* is the desideratum."[45] The rabbi had been instrumental in founding the federation in Milwaukee during the 1890's, and his role was also catalytic in Los Angeles. A federation of Jewish charitable bodies meant a united appeal, followed by distribution among the constituents of funds raised. Each institution would not need to raise its own money, and contributors would be spared separate appeals. In time, there would be communal coordination and planing. It was just then the heyday of American and Californian Progressivism, and President Theodore Roosevelt's and Governor Hiram Johnson's ideals of governmental coordination and efficiency and economy appealed strongly to the social classes which supported Jewish charities. To apply these bywords of Progressivism in Jewish life seemed reasonable and necessary.[46]

Rabbi Hecht had first suggested a charity federation in 1906 without recorded results, and his repeated appeal in 1909 only produced a false start.[47] Institutional loyalties were stronger than a communal conception, and there was no assurance that one general appeal would produce more than individual institutions' solicitation by their enthusiasts. The federation movement started definitively in 1911, strongly encouraged by the pulpit appearance at B'nai B'rith Temple of a notable visitor, Federal Circuit Judge Julian W. Mack.[48] The new Federation of Jewish Charities began with éclat. Its first board of directors was elected on December 23, 1911, and the first executive committee meeting took place on January 12, 1912. Six men attended. Ben R. Meyer, president, a banker and son-in-law of Kaspare Cohn, was interested especially in the hospital bearing that name. The old rabbi's son, Dr. D. W. Edelman, was president of the Reform temple, to which all present belonged, and medical leader of the hospital. Louis M. Cole was a food wholesaler, civic leader, and a Hellman son-in-law. M. N. Newmark and Isaac Norton, each of a pioneer family, were primarily connected with the old Hebrew Benevolent Society, while S. G. Marshutz, a B'nai B'rith lodge man, held dearest the Jewish Orphans' Home.[49] No six men were more representative of the established Jewish community. From an office in the Chamber of Commerce building the Federation began to solicit energetically. Soon it secured 800 pledges—a promising start—and Rabbi Hecht proudly claimed that Federation had become a household word.[50] The impetus slowed, however, for three years later the Federation of Jewish Charities received no more than 742 contributions. Of the nearly $42,000 it disbursed in 1915, $18,000 went to the Orphans' Home, $15,000 to the Hospital, and $5,650 to the two benevolent societies, which were then about to merge.[51] Both the JCRA and the Hebrew Sheltering Home for the Aged were absent, as were also the whole penumbra of immigrant groups. The Federation was conspicuously an institution of the older acculturated Jewish community.

World War I and After

A six years' flowering of new institutions demarcates the most significant period in the first century of Los Angeles Jewish philanthropy. Between 1909 and 1915, five major institutions were founded or transformed, and the transition from charity aid to systematic welfare was clearly discernible. Philanthropy became a central rather than peripheral interest of the Jewish community. The effort focused upon local needs, with occasional collections and small Federation subsidies to a few national institutions. However, one result of World War I in Los Angeles, as in other American Jewish communities, was to set overseas relief in a central position.

Mass rally at the Hollywood Bowl, June 11, 1967, at the close of the Six Days War. (Rothschild Photo.)

Mendel Silberberg, left, Chairman of the Community Relations Committee, receives a citation in 1958 from Charles Brown, a president of the Jewish Community Council. (Rothschild Photo.)

Rabbi Jacob Kohn (1881-1968), of Sinai Temple. (Jules Porter Photographers.)

Rabbi Edgar F. Magnin, Wilshire Boulevard Temple.

The Jewish Community Building of the Jewish Federation-Council, erected in 1951 at 590 N. Vermont, which provides headquarters for more than forty agencies and services.

Hillel Hebrew Academy, the largest Jewish Orthodox day school in Los Angeles with Nursery School through Junior High, accents the current trend in intensive formal Jewish and secular education. (Bernard M. Cohn, Photography.)

Wilshire Boulevard Temple (Congregation B'nai B'rith) today.

Sinai Temple, leading congregation of Conservative Judaism. (Rothschild Photo.)

Steve Broidy, left, first president of the merged Jewish Federation-Council of Greater Los Angeles, and Walter S. Hilborn, Chairman of the Merger Committee, 1959.

Los Angeles Jews had been active on occasion for world Jewish aid. During the Russian pogroms and revolutions from 1904 to 1907, they raised tens of thousands under the impact of appeals from the recognized national leader Jacob H. Schiff.[52] A Jewish Women's Foreign Relief Association gave loans to help local Russian Jews remove their relatives from Russia and "to give moral support to all worthy Russian refugees."[53] The Association later concentrated on immigrant aid, especially settlement houses.[54] Aside from minor efforts for Balkan Jewry, little more was done for overseas Jews before 1914.

When World War I broke out, the segment of the community which was close to its East European origins became extremely active. During the High Holidays in the early autumn of 1914, the synagogues of Los Angeles were filled with pleas on behalf of suffering European and Palestinian Jewry. The B'nai B'rith lodge also took up relief work.[55] Besides the activities of small groups, a representative Jewish War Sufferers Relief Society existed in the city, remitting the funds it received to the newly founded American Jewish Joint Distribution Committee in New York. The Jewish upper class was drawn into the effort by a visit from the brothers Nathan and Oscar Straus. At the meeting held on March 7, 1915, an appeal by the much-loved philanthropist Nathan Straus raised $2,200 on the spot.[56] War relief became the principal charity of the Jewish community and was carried on with previously unknown zeal and emotion. Besides vigorous appeals among the affluent, street collections and "tag days" stirred the residents of more modest Jewish neighborhoods. A continuous round of collections was led by the five hundred dues-paying members of the Jewish War Sufferers Relief Society. It conducted picnics and benefit shows and constantly received contributions made in the traditional manner from such events as circumcisions, bar mitzvot, synagogue offerings, marriages, and so forth. The balls and celebrations of numerous Jewish societies likewise raised funds for the European Jewish victims.[57] These campaigns drew some of their passion from worried families, unable to send remittances to relatives cut off by hostilities. By the opening of 1917, the local orthodox synagogues had raised $3,200 through appeals at services alone.[58]

When Jewish Sufferers' Day was proclaimed by President Wilson for January 27, 1916, an unparalleled campaign was initiated, again under the imposing leadership of Jacob H. Schiff. During the year of 1916, Los Angeles Jews contributed altogether $40,000 as conditions abroad grew more desperate.[59] The close of the war in 1918 brought a tapering of interest in overseas charity, more or less concurring with America's withdrawal of interest in foreign affairs. In 1920 a full-scale Jewish War Relief campaign was organized, paralleling other war relief efforts, and a Jewish War Relief Week was proclaimed by Governor William D. Stephens; the Sponsoring Committee was a premier list of Jews and Christians. Yet this postwar drive closed with but $150,000 collected of the $275,000 quota.[60] Beneath the surface there were sharp differences regarding the allocation of the money between the Joint Distribution Committee and the Yiddish-laborite People's Relief.[61] Jewish contributions also poured in for such overseas charities as the Vienna Relief, as they had throughout the years of war.[62] In the Joint Distribution Committee's campaign for war orphans, Los Angeles was asked to "adopt" 300 of the 35,000 Jewish child victims of the war's ravages. Another campaign early in 1922 hoped for greater success than in 1920, but it fell during a brief period of depression.[63] Except for 1926 and 1927 campaigns which combined European and Palestinian aid in a United Jewish Appeal, Jewish overseas aid languished in Los Angeles during the 1920's. After six or seven years of concentration upon the needs of world Jewry, philanthropic interests were again turned inward.[64] The Federation of Jewish Charities sharply reduced its efforts, however. During World War I, the united War Chest was successfully established to support all local philanthropy, and included the Jewish institutions. It was renamed the Community Chest after the war. The Federation gave up its fund-raising activities to the Chest, and became solely a planning and budgeting body.

Expansion During the Twenties

The Los Angeles boom of the 1920's was more notable for the expansion of existing philanthropies than for the genesis of new ones. "Uncle George" Mosbacher (1852-1944), a retired merchant who had come as a boy from Germany, began nine years' signal service as president of the Federation of Jewish Charities in 1922. (In the last ten years of his old age he was to head the Wilshire Boulevard Temple.) In 1923, the Federation brought William R.

Blumenthal from San Francisco as its first full-time superintendent. They began plans for large-scale development of Jewish social service in the city. A Million Dollar Fund for large-scale capital construction was initiated by Blumenthal and continued by his successor, Boris D. Bogen. After I. Irving Lipsitch succeeded Bogen in 1925, the fund aimed to collect $200,000 for the Orphans' Home, $30,000 for the combined Talmud Torah and Social Center, and the remainder in order to erect a new Kaspare Cohn Hospital. Of this unprecedented amount, $800,000 was pledged and $735,000 collected within five years. In May 1930 the hospital, renamed Cedars of Lebanon after the legendary curative of the Bible, opened its doors. It cost $1,650,000 to erect, of which only $250,000 was still owed.[65] Within one generation, the frame house of Kaspare Cohn, intended as a last stop for consumptives, had thus become one of the foremost hospitals on the West Coast.

Rather more modest efforts were undertaken in social service. The Jewish Aid Society, the merged benevolent societies of earlier days, slowly transformed its efforts from almsgiving into case work among troubled families and individuals.[66] A constructive venture by volunteers was the Jewish Big Brothers, "an organization of men, each of whom is pledged to assume responsibility in a social way for some boy, between the ages of 10 and 18 years" in the manner of an older brother, "helping him along in the way of pleasures, advice and companionship."[67] Besides treats and picknicking, the Big Brothers collaborated with the services of the Jewish Aid Society.

In addition to the well-established Kaspare Cohn Hospital, a modest facility opened in 1920 under the aegis of the Bikur Cholim [sick aid] Society. This was the Mount Sinai Home for Incurables, which started during an influenza epidemic. During the 1920's it succeeded in establishing a frame building sheltering nine chronic patients in its eight rooms. By 1930 it was known as the Mount Sinai Home for Chronic Invalids and housed fifty persons.[68]

The Million Dollar Fund marked the peak of Los Angeles Jewish philanthropy during the 1920's. Inventiveness in methods and institutions was less in evidence than in pre-World War I years. The challenges of depression and permanent overseas emergency during the 1930's were to require new men and ideas.

CHAPTER 11

The Broadened Horizon of Wartime

————————————————— ➤◄ —————————————————

WHEN WORLD WAR I broke out in 1914, Los Angeles was occupied like the rest of America with its normal activities of peace. A minor depression was visiting the city, and economic energies had slowed. However, the Panama Canal, just opened, was expected to bring a broad stream of immigration direct from Europe. Californians wholeheartedly shared the American sentiment of neutrality toward the European conflict, particularly because of their closer concern with Far Eastern questions.

To Jews, the war literally reached home. Thousands of Los Angeles Jews had been born in Russian and Polish towns which were now battlefields, where parents and brothers and sisters lived in terror and starvation. One of the strongest emotions during the period was the passionate desire to help and save beleaguered brethren. As we shall see, this simple human concern of Los Angeles Jews, and of American Jewry in general, had far-reaching effects in broadening the Jewish community's interests and stirring thought and emotion about Jewish destinies on a world scale.

At the war's beginning, Victor Harris of the *B'nai B'rith Messenger* expressed what were probably widespread feelings. Rejecting the reasons offered by S. G. Marshutz for Jews to favor German arms, Harris maintained that "the Jew has received but little from the majority of European countries, in spite of what he has contributed to them." They were all more or less infected with anti-Semitism, and none deserved particular favor. Jewish feelings thus combined with American isolationism to produce an attitude of righteous neutrality. "Americans have an interest in the war only insofar as it will lend itself to forward the cause of universal peace and at the same time develop the countries of Europe, as far as government is concerned."[1] Rabbi Sigmund Hecht drew a moral somewhat at cross-purposes with that of Harris. He plaintively noted that Jews were being improperly bracketed with other nationalities rather than with Catholics and Protestants. Such an error begot a lamentable misunderstanding: "We often read of the sad comments journalists make in their daily publications concerning the abnormality of Jew fighting Jew, and of Jew killing Jew. When such a lament is raised in Jewish publications by Jewish writers, as is quite often the case, I wonder at the inconsistency. . . . That is no more justified matter of regret that the Jew of France should fight and kill the Jew of the German army than that the Catholic of Austria should fight and kill the Catholic of France."[2] One may wonder how many Jews maintained such conscientious equanimity.

As the European conflict became prolonged, Jewish thinking broadened beyond the tasks of rescue and relief. Great changes could be expected in Eastern Europe which might at last bring peace and justice to Jewry in the Czar's dominions and in Roumania, while Turkish participation in the war opened exciting possibilities for realizing the Zionist program in Palestine. With the other major Jewish communities in the world engrossed in the conflict, the Jews in neutral America, numbering over 3,000,000 souls, assumed novel responsibilities. Even remote Los Angeles was affected by world-wide political storms as Jewish groups, especially the Zionists, became more active than ever before. During 1915, Los Angeles Jewry heard a scholarly visitor, Horace M. Kallen (1881–), the University of Wisconsin philosopher and Zionist, connect the future of war-racked European Jewry with the prospects of Zionism.[3] Not long after, Rabbi Stephen S. Wise came to the city. In two well-prepared meetings, one at Congregation B'nai B'rith and the other a public luncheon, the famed Reform rabbi portrayed to a representative audience the current sufferings of Palestinian Jewry under the Turks and the future glory of a reborn homeland.[4] With the World War one year old, an ambitious plan for an American Jewish Congress also began to be spoken of in Los Angeles. Originating with Zionists who distrusted the tepid imagination of the established American Jewish leadership, the movement demanded a "congress" of American Jewish delegates, to be named at nationwide elections, which would enunciate the needs of Jews in the postwar world.[5]

The war-propelled Congress movement in Los Angeles coincided with a deepening of communal sentiment among the city's Jews. Not only Zionists spoke tirelessly of the Jewish group as a community, larger than the sum of its institutions. The Federation of Jewish Philanthropies, founded in 1912, a body far from Zionism, appealed to the entire Jewish community for support. Rabbi Farber of Sinai Temple energetically fostered the idea of an organized kehillah ("community"), and partly at his initiative the Agudas Kehillah began a short life span in 1912.[6] The *B'nai B'rith Messenger,* which in 1904 had found it "a puzzle . . . why more Jewish institutions are not established in this city," ten years later asserted "without fear of contradiction that the community has more charitable societies and institutions relatively, than any other city in the world."[7] This increase in the number of communal bodies stimulated the sense of Los Angeles Jewry as a community.[8]

Zionist Upsurge

The Zionist movement, which first appeared in Los Angeles at the beginning of the century, came to the fore during World War I, especially because of its communal outlook and concern with the collective unity of world Jewry. Even before a Zionist organization appeared, the *B'nai B'rith Messenger* called for it to arise and "take hold of those interests for the general welfare of Judaism which they better than others can handle." Zionist groups were needed to teach the Hebrew language to young and old and to promote vigorously the study of Jewish history—in the place, obviously, of the uninspired routine at the city's only established congregation.[9] The communal newspaper printed articles by Christians lavishly praising Zionism as the fulfillment of biblical prophecy and the salvation of suffering Jewry.[10] Two Zionist societies apparently arose during 1902, the Young Zionist Association and the Ahabath Zion Society, but on rather shaky bases.[11] Both were devoted mainly to raising funds for the new Palestinian institutions and purchasing shares in the Jewish Colonial Trust. There were a good many lectures by Rabbi Isidore Myers in early years, and later on by intellectual younger men like Harry Fram, Al Horowitz, and Morris Kaufman. After several active years the Young Zionists declined to a low estate around 1910. By now they were men with families and had run a cycle of effort; the Jewish state was remote.[12] After reorganization and a new charter, however, the Young Zionists began to resume their old place, while the Ahabath Zion, composed of approximately eighty older people, continued at a less exciting pace. Its members did once hear a debate on "Zionism vs. Socialism" covering two consecutive meetings, between their Dr. Louis G. Reynolds

and L. Levin. The debate was unrecorded, but there is little doubt
that it resembled the controversies around this theme which were
common in those years.[13]

By 1912 there were four Zionist societies in Los Angeles: two
named Ahabath Zion, the Young Zionists, and the Sons of Zion.[14]
They spent their efforts in fund raising for the growing Palestinian
institutions, for land purchase by the Jewish National Fund, and in
selling the shekel for elections to the Zionist congresses held in
Europe. Most of the synagogues hospitably permitted the Zionists
to meet in their quarters, but except for Rabbi Myers, rabbis were
not prominent in Los Angeles Zionism. Adherents of the Zionist left
wing also settled in Los Angeles. In 1912 a Yiddish-speaking "National Radical Club" was organized of Poale Zion (Palestine-
oriented socialist Zionists), Socialist Territorialists (i.e., not necessarily Palestine), nationalist Bundists (ethnically oriented socialist
laborites). But razor-sharp ideological dialectics divided the intellectual Yiddishist "National Radicals" among themselves. They soon
went their separate ways, leaving Poale Zion to organize distinctly.[15]

The conception of Zion held in Los Angeles, as in America generally, was primarily philanthropic. All were Zionists who sought
a home in Palestine for suffering Jews. There are European lands,
they said, "where our co-religionists are driven as a pest. . . . And in
prayers alone, we cannot relieve their misery. It is by material help
that our High Holiday prayers can be answered and that help lies
in the accomplishment of Zionism's aim, a home for our persecuted
brethren."[16] A Zionist writer mildly took Rabbi Myers to task for
insisting that the coming Jewish state had to be religious. Dividing
Zionists between the "national and political" and the "ceremonial or
Orthodox," the editor found them united on the moral laws of the
Torah. The new Palestine "must be a country where the Jewish
morals will be upheld and wherein Judaism shall have as its backbone, The Torah, the greatest of all teachers of morality and equality
of mankind."[17] But the traditional religious life was no longer to be
binding in Palestine. A thoughtful member, Morris Kaufman, took
the drastic step of detaching the movement for a Jewish homeland
from Jewish moral and religious traditions and from beliefs in Jewish uniqueness and chosenness as well. Judaism is nothing other
than the national culture of the Jews, and simply requires as its
basis a national territory like that of any other nation: "Americanism

concedes to every nation what it claims for itself: the right to live its own national life. In this respect, the Hebrew nationalists claim the sympathy of all American citizens, Jews and Gentiles." Kaufman's combination of Ahad Ha-Am's cultural nationalism and Wilsonian national self-determination had small attraction in Los Angeles. There Zionism meant basically a refuge for suffering Jews and, to some, an attempt to strengthen Judaism against erosion from assimilation.[18]

Old Jewish settlers in Los Angeles were generally hostile or indifferent to Zionism. However, Rabbi Hecht, their spokesman on matters Jewish, considerably lessened the hostility of his Milwaukee days in the 1890's; in 1914 he avowed himself sympathetic but "absolutely neutral" on Zionism.[19] On the other hand, the local B'nai B'rith was reportedly more pro-Zionist than the order as a whole.[20] Old Rabbi Edelman appears to have sympathized, while his son, the physician and influential local figure, was also favorably inclined. The Los Angeles fascination with land development brought about the first non-Zionist investment in Palestine. A local branch of Hoachoosa Palestine Land Development was organized in 1913, promoting a plan for the purchase of seventeen-acre cultivated plots at $1,500, payable in ten years. An optimistic report was dispatched to the Berlin headquarters of the World Zionist Organization: "The Zionists of California are very active. A Hoachooza Corp. has been started. . . . $1500 has already been subscribed & we expect to double the amount in the near future. The Shekel collection amounts to double the amount of last year. A Hebrew speaking society with a membership of 20 has been started and for the Yemenites $200 has been collected."[21] Land schemes were meat and drink for many Los Angelenos, who helped the company to make a promising start.[22] The most promising non-Zionist step was taken through the intervention of the city's famed winter visitor, Nathan Straus, who had visited Palestine several times and made large donations. In May 1914 the Nathan Straus Palestine Advancement Society was founded, to "contribute and assist institutions whose purposes are the advancement of Jewish people in Palestine."[23] With Marco R. Newmark as the society's first president and Louis M. Cole his successor, aid to Jewish Palestine became an interest of the Jewish elite of Los Angeles years before similar developments occurred in other cities. The Nathan

Straus Palestine Advancement Society at first proposed to help the country's new educational and agricultural institutions. However, the World War forced it to turn to simple relief, and the Society contributed a truly modest $1,000 for Palestinian Jewry during the twelve months ending in November 1917.[24] Non-Zionist interest in the Jewish homeland had still not advanced very far.

American Jewry in the War

These movements toward community organization, a Jewish Congress, and Zionism approached their climax as America drew near to entering World War I. For Jews especially, growing sympathy for the Allied cause had been inhibited by the Western Allies' connection with the Russian regime. The fall of Czarism in March 1917 aroused universal satisfaction, which Los Angeles Jews displayed at an enthusiastic mass meeting.[25] Now the way was conscientiously clearer for entry into the war. Opposition to the declaration of war on Germany on April 6, 1917, seems to have been more muted than in many other parts of the country, as demonstrative patriotism became the order of the day. However, five months after entry into the war a Jewish mass meeting was announced, linked with the anti-war People's Council of America. The Jewish speaker was to be be the Socialist attorney and Zionist Chaim Shapiro, discussing "the attitude of the radical Jew toward the People's Council."[26] Obviously, prowar sentiment was not universal, but it does not appear that the meeting was actually held. Federal prosecution soon terminated the People's Council.[27] To the great majority of Jews, of course, their country was at war and had to be supported.

Soon the Jewish community began to see its young men leave for military service. The Jolly Bachelors Club spoke as lightheartedly of the induction of its members as of its customary social affairs; if this was in part bravado, it was also ignorance of what war meant.[28] More and more, young Jewish men joined their fellow townsmen in military camps en route to French battlefields. By the end of 1917, combat participants already had stories to tell. The Sinai Young People's Society held an "extraordinarily interesting" meeting listening to the narrative of Corporal Harry Borax, recently returned from France. He "gave a vivid description of the horrors of the war, and his many encounters with the 'Fritzies' on 'No Man's Land.' In conclusion he gave us a few witty sayings and songs."[29]

The Jews who remained at home participated earnestly in "home front" endeavors. The B'nai B'rith lodge, for example, ran an entertainment to buy a Red Cross ambulance. With the use of the Masonic auditorium donated, a capacity audience was regaled by such performers as Leopold Godowsky, Ernestine Schumann-Heink, and Ruth St. Denis, and provided the ambulance.[30] A Jewish auxiliary to the Red Cross was established by the local branch of the National Council of Jewish Women. Entertainment, the packaging of food and amenities, knitting, and other Red Cross service was undertaken with an intensity unknown in the records of the Jewish or general community. The local Jewish women's organizations combined once to organize a street fete in the Jewish neighborhood for the Red Cross. For soldiers on leave, the Jewish Institute on Franklin Street held constant open house.[31]

During 1918 a number of Jewish youth were attracted to enlist in the Jewish Legion and fight in the British Army to capture Palestine; this would meet their American military obligations as well. Local Zionists organized a Jewish Legion Committee, and Governor Stephens came to the send-off for the recruits. Those who went abroad joined the British campaign to conquer the Near East from the Turks, and the imminent British entry into Palestine opened thrilling possibilities that the country might be given to the Jews.[32]

Far from diminishing interest in Jewish needs, American participation in the war greatly enhanced it. The world to be made safe for democracy had to recognize the rights of Jews, especially in Eastern Europe and Palestine, and the Jewish Congress movement succeeded partly as a result of these feelings. Early in 1917, twenty-eight organizations and congregations established the Jewish Congress Executive Committee, with Marco R. Newmark as chairman. On April 29, 1917, a Jewish Congress Conference at B'nai B'rith Hall appointed four men (Newmark, Maurice Salzman, George Mosbacher, and Aaron Shapiro) to convene a nominating convention which was to place four men on the ballot, who would be voted on by the Jewish community. Fifty-three organizations named four prominent figures: two physicians, Dr. Leo Blass and Dr. David W. Edelman, and two attorneys, Maurice Salzman and Aaron Shapiro.[33] Edelman and Salzman belonged to the more "English" segment of the community, while Blass and Shapiro were more at home with the Yiddish group. All candidates were more or less Zionist, so that the issues were not sharply divisive, and the poll became a measure of popularity and renown as four candidates electioneered mildly at meetings and in print. The extent of the balloting was a disappointment. Barely three thousand appeared at the polls on June 10, 1917, paid the ten-cent tax, and voted as follows: Edelman, 1,024; Blass, 919; Salzman, 518; Shapiro, 407. Thus the physicians were chosen over the lawyers.[34] The actual meeting of the American Jewish Congress was postponed until the war's end. When it met in Philadelphia in December 1918, the Jewish situation had changed drastically.[35]

Great Britain's Balfour Declaration on Palestine was welcomed in Los Angeles as everywhere else. The Zionists first marked the occasion at a Hanukkah celebration, and then in Clune's Auditorium on January 27, 1918, at the "crowning success of all Jewish affairs in the West," attended by thousands. Before the multitude the veteran Rabbi Myers expressed the theme: America and her British ally, linked by common ideals of justice and democracy first taught by the Jewish prophets, had done for the Jews what they were fighting to achieve for mankind. The Reverend William E. Blackstone, who had organized a proto-Zionist petition to President Benjamin Harrison in 1890, was one of the speakers. Hundreds of schoolchildren came and were treated to a picture show afterwards. Another peak of enthusiasm was touched in 1920, when an estimated ten thousand Jews (and three thousand automobiles) made their way to Exposition Park to celebrate the first anniversary of the British Mandate.[36]

The close of the war in November 1918, however, marked a sharp revulsion from nearly Messianic hopes. This reaction coincided with America's withdrawal of interest from foreign affairs. Bloody pogroms swept Eastern Europe, while in Palestine unexpected problems began to arise. After the 1917-1919 period the Zionist organizations declined in interest and membership, as the various Zionist clubs became the Los Angeles District of the reorganized Zionist Organization of America. The labor Zionists were separately grouped in Poale Zion, while the orthodox had the Mizrachi Organization. Most important, the ladies' Hadassah grew rapidly to importance after its founding in 1916 and first public meeting in October 1917.[37] The Nathan Straus Palestine Advancement Society's non-Zionist philanthropic aid was not spectacular; monies raised did not exceed $2,000 in any year. Gradually, however, B'nai B'rith resumed its earlier interest by participation in such projects as the Jewish National Fund and its "Golden Book," resolutions of sympathy and the like. Notables like Rabbi Edgar F. Magnin, Dr. David W. Edelman, and Marco Newmark, who were favorable to Zionism, were joined by such figures as Dr. George Saylin and Dr. Louis Reynolds (both physicians), Theodore Strimling, and Aaron Riche. Others were merely indifferent; active anti-Zionism did not exist until the 1940's.[38]

The solemn last act of World War I for Los Angeles fell in June 1921. Forty Los Angelenos who fell in France were returned for burial. Three of them were Jews, Morris Lynchik, Henry L. Schwartz, and Harry Tarson, and they were buried with dignified public ceremonies.[39] The memory of war was also laid to rest as southern California turned to boom times for eight feverish years.

CHAPTER 12

The Trials of Depression

THE CITY's boom of the 1920's subsided by 1927 and was followed by a period of slower growth. The real estate market also declined, as an increasing proportion of residential and particularly business rentals had no takers. These were trends specific to the local economy, which in the perspective of today's economics might have been corrected by increased spending in the starved public sector. When the economic cataclysm of 1929 came, it struck Los Angeles promptly and hard, and required a recovery which was not complete until World War II. The crash was nationwide and worldwide in its scope, with the Los Angeles economy one of the hardest hit in America. The county's 1930 population of 2,208,000 rose only to 2,785,000 in 1940, the smallest proportionate increase in its history. The number of persons employed had already fallen steeply when the 1930 census counted 723,824, and it dropped further before rebounding to 1,036,984 in 1940. The excesses of real estate promotion exacted a harsh price as thousands of lots zoned and bought speculatively for business development stood forlorn, often in default of taxes, tying up their owners' capital.[1]

The most serious human problem brought forth by the depression was that of the unemployed, in addition to workers who could secure no more than part-time employment. Wage earners out of work were 7.7% of "all gainful workers" in April 1930, about the same as other large cities. By January 1931, however, the percentage was 16.9%, slightly higher than the 15.3% of other large American cities, and 4.6% above San Francisco. Although these figures somewhat declined later in the 1930's, the census of 1940 still showed the Los Angeles unemployment rate at 14.5% of the "civilian labor force."[2]

During the earlier years of depression there was extensive reliance upon local and private rather than federal aid to the unemployed, and Los Angeles also employed such methods. A central job registry, self-help cooperatives, and relief by private charities carried on to

1932, but with constantly decreasing resources. In addition to its resident unemployed, Los Angeles in depression attracted immigrants as it had in prosperity. As 1932 closed, local relief resources were almost exhausted and radical agitation among the unemployed was disturbing the sound citizens of the city. With the coming of the New Deal, federal funds became available and work relief was given on an unprecedented scale. However, unemployment remained social dynamite, as its victims vigorously demanded improvement in their treatment by the public authorities.[3]

The Jew occupied a place among the masses of men without work. The *B'nai B'rith Messenger* complained that "the Jewish employee, in times of distress, is the first to feel the brunt of unemployment."[4] Doubtful as that may be, it made little difference in view of the rapidity of the economic collapse in southern California. For the first time, the Jewish community had to concern itself with a great throng of able-bodied persons desiring work but unable to find it. Early reports of distress came from Jewish carpenters, who lost their jobs as building and repair activities were postponed or canceled. A "group of two hundred Jewish carpenters cannot find work, or to put it in milder terms, sixty per cent of the Jewish carpenters belonging to this group have been out of employment . . . for many, many months." Jews were solicited to employ them, assured that although they were union men these carpenters were "neither radicals nor communists" but good citizens and good Jews.[5] Alfred Cane, director of the local B'nai B'rith Placement Bureau, calling for "better cooperation between [Jewish] employer and employee," deplored discrimination by some Jewish employers in addition to "the prejudice against us of the gentile firm. . . . We should face our employment situation as a people and solve our problems within the group."[6] A Jewish employment bureau was founded to aid "the flood of unemployed. . . . Federation officers told of the hundreds of unemployed who came to them looking for work."[7] The *B'nai B'rith Messenger* offered free space for "Jobs Wanted" advertisements.[8] But these earnest efforts could do little against the increasing number of Jewish unemployed—or more exactly, the decreasing number of jobs. In Los Angeles, as elsewhere, proud slogans that "Jews take care of their own" had to be discarded as Jewish distress merged into the general distress of a region and nation.

Claims of improvement were made, in the spirit of President

Hoover's ill-starred prediction that prosperity was "just around the corner." Thus, the Jewish communal newspaper carried a column of hopeful counsel on the stock market and business trends. Even the Case Committee of the Jewish Social Service Bureau, intimate with the bitterest details of hardship, was beguiled during 1932 by a successful week of job placement into imagining "a steady upward trend in obtaining jobs, which presages a return to normal conditions."[9]

Not only the Jewish wage earner was hit hard by the economic collapse. Many Jewish entrepreneurs suffered severe losses or lost their businesses altogether. In perhaps the most extreme case, the Los Angeles branch of the Hellmans, the famous pioneer banking family, were virtually wiped out. A. P. Giannini had bought out their entire bank holdings in 1928 and paid in securities which were held in escrow. Renegotiated in 1929, the agreement still exchanged the Merchants National Bank with its twenty-six branches for stock of Giannini's Transamerica holding corporation. With their securities locked in escrow, Marco and Irving Hellman could only watch helplessly as their fortune was wiped out by the precipitous decline of the stock market.[10] The fall of the Hellmans was the most dramatic, but thousands of lesser folk suffered shattered hopes or hovered close to destitution as their jobs or their customers melted away.

If Jewish unemployment stood at the level of the city as a whole, then in 1937 perhaps 6,500 to 7,000 were out of work or on emergency work programs, and 1,600 to 1,700 could find only part-time work.[11] Many cases undoubtedly resembled Mr. and Mrs. W., a couple with three young children. "Mr. W. is working as a presser irregularly, averaging $3.50 per week. Family is unable to manage and requests supplemental assistance."[12] A grant of $27 for one month was made.

In Los Angeles "supplemental assistance" meant monies the Jewish Social Service Bureau granted in addition to the cruelly stringent budgets which were the standard for county welfare payments. The Jewish group's method of supplementing public aid rather than attempting to shoulder the entire burden is well illustrated by the case of a "divorced woman with two children, a son, twenty, and a daughter, seventeen. . . . The BCW [Board of County Welfare] has refused to accept the case on the basis that the son aged twenty earns $36 a month. Since this is an unemployment case and $36 equals the BCW budget they will give no relief. According to JSSB budget the total amount is $39.22 plus warehouse orders [for food supplies]. . . . It was moved and carried that for a period of one month JSSB supplement the budget."[13]

Less stern and more flexible than public welfare, the Jewish community found innumerable ways to assist individuals. Frequently there were temporary rent payments to avoid eviction or foreclosure before a job was found, or until a son graduated from college and could contribute to support the family. The JSSB had a Self-Support Fund which extended such aid as helping an unemployed chiropodist reestablish himself in an office. County welfare provided for a destitute peddler but not for feeding the horse whose labors might again provide him a living.[14] Many were the cases relieved because they could not in some way meet the county's harsh residence requirements. A growing group during the 1930's were refugees from Nazi Germany, all of whose welfare needs had to come from the Jewish community. In addition to cash grants, the five case workers who spent long days in Boyle Heights dispensed ten thousand quarts of milk monthly, at the rate of one quart per child daily.[15] Thus, three to four hundred children were protected against malnutrition.

Less impoverished than the relief cases but as crippled in self-esteem was the businessman. Such a firm as Sun Realty, headed by Isidore Eisner, with which a conservative banker like Ben R. Meyer of Union Bank invested his fortune, was ruined. Real estate investors were, if anything, harder hit than stock speculators, since their land required tax and mortgage payments, which many paid in the vain hope of an early recovery.

Just as in better times, migration to Los Angeles continued, although in reduced numbers. During the years of deepest depression from 1930 through 1934, "only" 268,000 immigrants arrived in Los Angeles County, and that figure increased to 332,000 during the improved five-year period which followed.[16] Data on Jewish movement to Los Angeles is lacking, but the Jewish population of approximately 70,000 in 1930 rose to 130,000 in 1941. If the local ratio between natural increase and increase from migration holds for Jews also, it would appear that at least 40,000 Jews arrived from many cities throughout North America. Thus the Rochester, New

York Club of California, organized in 1932, counted 200 members five years later, but that smaller Jewish community hardly sent so many to Los Angeles within five years.[17]

A small portion of this Jewish immigration had deep moral significance. These were the German and Austrian Jewish refugees, of whom no more than 2,500 lived in the city late in 1939. Three years later, it was "estimated that between 1500 and 2000 families with an average of three to the family" lived in Los Angeles.[18] Their lot was a hard one, for in addition to the trials of making a living within a new culture they usually had to adjust themselves to a lower social status. In their quest of livelihood, many began to make petit point bags and other novel products.[19] By 1942, the refugees' economic position was becoming more favorable:

Scores of artists, musicians, writers, actors, etc. are gainfully employed. A handful of former physicians were able to complete their internship and are now practicing. Approximately 10% of the emigres in this community operate their own businesses. . . . About 100 newcomers are employed as domestics of various types. Then there are the sales persons, clerks, bookkeepers, and other clerical workers. The other group of emigres are working in factories, in buildings as maintenance workers, and are employed as craftsmen.[20]

Within the Jewish Social Service Bureau an Emigre Service Committee was set up, long and devotedly headed by Ludwig Schiff. The German Jewish refugee was a responsibility of the Jewish community, for neither law nor sentiment would permit him on public welfare.

Brightened Outlook

In the middle of the 1930's times began to improve. Manufacturing, particularly of apparel and aircraft, increased considerably.[21] Trade-unionism enjoyed a hard-fought resurgence. In the changed social climate the International Ladies' Garment Workers Union and the Amalgamated Clothing Workers succeeded in reestablishing themselves, while the Bakery Workers, the United Hat, Cap and Millinery Workers, and the Fur Workers also struggled through to recognition. The Ladies' Garment Workers, torn by a virtual civil war with its local pro-Communist elements, had a mainly Mexican clientele of unorganized dressmakers scattered among 175 small firms in the downtown garment district. Cutters, pressers, and cloakmakers were already organized. Late in 1933 several hundred of these Spanish-speaking dressmakers struck effectively behind the leadership of this historically Jewish (and somewhat Italian) union. The strike was settled by arbitration, one of the arbitrators being Rabbi Isadore Isaacson of Hollywood. The men's clothing trade, better organized, numbered at least 860 highly skilled men. A long and victorious strike by the Amalgamated Clothing Workers against Kurtzman Brothers in 1933 effectively demonstrated its strength.

Strikes in Los Angeles were peculiarly susceptible to violence and legal harassment, inspired by the virulent anti-unionism in local business circles and the bitterness of labor's reaction. The notorious "Red Squad" of Police Captain John B. Hynes played a prominent, provocative role. On one occasion William Shainak, the Ladies' Garment Workers organizer, complained that he had been arrested on a pretext and was then lodged in one cell with a police informer who cajoled him in Yiddish.[22]

By 1935 the Los Angeles locals of the Ladies' Garment Workers, which had been nearly extinct five years earlier, reported 2,460 members and contractual agreements with 112 local manufacturers. The cloak workers, a group mainly of Jewish men, was the most completely organized branch of the industry, while the cotton dress and undergarment line, employing mostly non-Jewish women, was vigorously organized only in that year. Los Angeles' millinery workers, however, proved unable to sustain their early success of 1934;[23] in this trade both employers and union leaders were generally Jews, while the workers were a more varied group.

The Amalgamated Clothing Workers further strengthened its position in 1935 with favorable contracts. Clothing workers, so high a proportion of whom were Jews, were among the first to turn to advantage the New Deal friendliness to union labor, and the economic upturn, in order to crack the open shop in Los Angeles. After 1936 strikes were conducted mostly against willful anti-union holdouts rather than disrupting the trade as a whole. The Fur Workers, another union under Communist dominance with heavily Jewish membership, also broke through the anti-union barriers in its trade. Of a different order were the misadventures of the Heirshberg Rye Bakery, a Boyle Heights firm baking a type of bread relished by Jews. After accepting the Blue Eagle of the National Recovery Administration with its labor provisos, Heirshberg repudiated the agreement, thereby incurring a boycott. Refusing to surrender its Blue Eagle, the firm won the curious distinction of being perhaps the first Los Angeles business to have the NRA emblem taken away.[24] Three years later, in 1936, Heirshberg underwent a nine-week strike before a union member bought it out and signed with Local 453 of the Bakers' Union. The Jewish bakers' union pay scale was distinctly higher than that of non-Jewish union men. A first hand earned $52.52 for a forty-hour week, compared with the $42.00 of a foreman in other union bakeries.[25]

During a few years of the 1930's, trade unions whose leadership and membership were all or mostly Jewish thus advanced dramatically, as did the Los Angeles labor movement as a whole. By the time of World War II and the rapid growth which it brought to the garment trade in southern California, the apparel makers were as strongly unionized as any workers in the region.[26]

Occupational Mobility

Less visible than the trade-union revival but perhaps more significant in the long run was the changing economic stratification of Los Angeles Jewry, away from laboring and artisan employment and toward professional and technical occupations. Thus, the 3% of Los Angeles Jews who were professionals in 1932 rose by 1940 to 11.2%, as the proportion of workers, laborers, and artisans sagged from 28% in the former year to 24% in the latter.[27]

Not much data is available regarding Jewish professionals, including physicians, lawyers, accountants, teachers, social workers, and others. Of physicians, the only profession for whose welfare the Jewish community felt somewhat responsible, there were some 440 in 1938. Their professional focus was the Cedars of Lebanon Hospital, not only for its medical excellence but also because of the anti-Semitism rife in their profession. Los Angeles' Jewish hospital was the place where more by far of the city's Jewish doctors were affiliated than anywhere else, particularly on the out-patient staff.[28] Other professions concerned with health showed considerable Jewish representation: there were some 261 pharmacists, 233 dentists, 200 social workers, 94 nurses, 20 chiropractors, and 9 osteopaths.[29] To these figures it seems reasonable to add at least 1,000 to 1,500 lawyers, teachers, and accountants, not to mention hundreds of artists and writers employed in the Hollywood film studios. Jewish spokesmen warned young Jews to avoid "overcrowded professions," emphasizing that prospects were far from encouraging. Symptomatic of the times was the subject of a planned (but apparently not held) debate by college students before the local B'nai B'rith upon the proposition, "Resolved that Jewish leaders dissuade Jewish students from entering the crowded professions with special reference to law, medicine, and teaching."[30] Indifferent to rhetoric, beneath the tribulations of the 1930's a strong current was running towards the professions.

Political Opening

The travail of depression finally shook the established political habits of Los Angeles. For some years after the crash of 1929, the old ways changed little. Revelations of political corruption merely hastened the election of a flashy "reform" mayor, Frank B. Shaw, whose personal corruption was deepened by a measure of viciousness. Alongside Shaw was Buron Fitts, a flamboyant district attorney. During the local political wars and scandals in the 1930's, Jews were found both among the fighters for municipal virtue, headed by the Minute Man organization, and among those who benefited from the lucrative favors which Shaw's administration had in its power to give.[31] Even during the hectic days of the New Deal, politics in Los Angeles was generally conceived in old-fashioned terms of righteousness versus corruption rather than in a framework of social policies and goals. The veteran liberal Oswald Garrison Villard, visiting "one of the loveliest spots in the world," observed: "People live so comfortably and easily here that one can appreciate why Los Angeles has been and still is one of the most reactionary of cities. Even in these times there is a general air of well-being, however great the individual distress and insecurity within those little homes. . . . there is a stirring here. . . . But the mass of the people, here as elsewhere, is quiet, patient, and resigned."[32]

Throughout the 1930's, Jews remained partly outside municipal politics. Groups or individuals not belonging to white Protestantdom were little recognized in the city's political life. Running a Jewish candidate for elective office was an unrealistic thought in Los Angeles of the 1920's and 1930's, even though appointive office was by no means rare. When that came, it was usually to the bench:

Los Angeles had a string of Jewish jurists, some of whom achieved judicial eminence.[33] Owing in part to the tacit limitations upon their participation in city affairs, Los Angeles Jews were prominent at Sacramento during the administration of Governor Culbert L. Olson. Under this first liberal state regime since Progressive days, Isaac Pacht, a lawyer and former judge, served as a member and then as chairman of the State Board of Prison Directors. He spearheaded the movement to reform California's debased penal system and earned outstanding success in modernizing and humanizing the state's prisons and reformatories. Dr. Aaron J. Rosanoff, a psychiatrist, served as Director of Institutions. His department pioneered in research and early treatment of mental illnesses, while reforming correctional institutions for the young. Stanley Mosk as Governor Olson's executive secretary, and Ben Rosenthal, Democratic floor leader in the Assembly, fought hard in the bitter political struggles of the day.[34] On the state political scene Jews could play roles which were virtually denied to them under the constricted political horizons of their own city.

Although political recognition had importance, most Jews were far more anxious about their employment and security than their opportunities for public office. Enthusiastic Jewish support for the New Deal of the 1930's is well attested, in Los Angeles as elsewhere. However, the city's emphatic Republican past continued to be well represented among Jews, mainly those more affluent and longer settled. One, Mendel B. Silberberg, a leading lawyer and American Legionnaire, was a major figure in that party. The perusal of an evenly divided group declaring for the presidential candidates in 1940 tends to show that the more recently arrived Jews generally favored Roosevelt; earlier settlers seemed to prefer Willkie.[35] In Hollywood many of the most successful Jewish (and non-Jewish) producers and directors were pro-New Deal, not only because of their personal convictions but because the New Deal policies increased mass purchasing power and encouraged cheap movie admissions. Hollywood was almost unscathed by the depression.

The Fad of Communism

During the depression the disappointed lawyer or teacher, idealistic social worker, or battered workingman was baffled by the seeming impotence of American society to fulfill its promise and opportunity. Many were enticed by the shallow but glittering utopia of Communism, with its assured explanation and solutions for depressions or anti-Semitism. The attraction of Communism was enhanced by the chaotic politics of southern California, where no coherent, left-of-center political focus existed. To its earnest followers, Communism seemed not a scheme to subvert democracy but rather a way to achieve it by radical means, with Soviet Russia the shining model.

Many of the first Communists in southern California were Jews, but they and their successors alienated themselves from their people.[36] A peculiarity of Communist activity in the region was the endeavor in the film studios, especially among screen writers, where many also were Jews. No Communist propaganda was smuggled into films, but the Hollywood Anti-Nazi League, to which many celebrities belonged, was taken over by adherents of the "party line" unknown to most of its members. In fact, the Communists were distinguished for their diligence and success in founding "front" organizations. A few Jewish names appeared unfailingly on the stationery of such bodies. Notwithstanding the articulate Communist contempt for Judaism, there were pro-Communist activities here and there within the Jewish community. Thus, the local branch of the American Jewish Congress adhered all too frequently to the turns and twists of the "party line." (It was finally expelled by the national organization.) During the "Popular Front" years from 1935 to 1939, some employees of Jewish Community Centers were noticeably attracted by the dash and inventiveness of the "party line" for the young. In some instances their programming reflected these sympathies.[37]

The most faithful followers could be found among Yiddish-speaking groups, where considerable pro-Communism had been entrenched since the 1920's. By dint of extensive literary and propagandistic activity, and thanks to the isolation of these constituents from the mainstream of political and cultural life, the Yiddish-speaking following remained in large part faithful well into the 1940's.[38]

The Hitler-Stalin pact of August 1939 staggered fellow-travelers and party members, especially because so much had been made of Russia's anti-Nazi leadership. Many, however, still held true and joined a demonstration on City Hall steps against the "imperialist blood bath" on May 8, 1940.[39] The mass murder of Polish Jewry, a Nazi army in Paris, German bombs over London could not alter this definition of World War II; that was done by the invading Wehrmacht treading upon Russian soil one year later.

Jewish Homes and Neighborhoods

Jews of many political convictions and economic levels continued to live near each other. During the depression era Jewish residence in Los Angeles reached its maximum concentration in Jewish neighborhoods, where not only was there a high proportion of Jews, but the neighborhood possessed a distinctive physiognomy. To speak of the Boyle Heights section: "In 1908 there were just two Jewish families in this district; they now number 60,000 [actually less] . . . . ten synagogues, nine attractive hotels, two theatres, lodge rooms, apartment houses built in Spanish style, bungalow courts . . . kosher restaurants, an Old People's Home as fine as an expensive hotel . . . a kosher slaughter-house."[40] The thousands of Jews who dwelled there inhaled Jewishness in its stores, clubrooms, and synagogues, from the Yiddish extensively heard and the warmth of political debate. Over 10,000 Jewish households stood in Boyle Heights in 1929, and more than 14,000 nine years later. In a hilly, not too accessible section not far away was the Jewish enclave of City Terrace. This was a more prosperous group, mostly homeowners, in an area which nearly doubled its Jewish households between 1935 and 1938 to 2,200.[41] Other neighborhoods of Los Angeles had substantial Jewish settlements, although none so large and concentrated as that in Boyle Heights. After its residential boom during the 1920's, Hollywood's Jewish and general population again moved ahead during the later 1930's. The nearly 3,000 Jewish households of 1935 ascended to 6,200 in 1938. During the same short three years the central Wilshire and the Wilshire-Pico districts sharply increased, the former from 3,800 to 7,200 and the latter from 1,300 to 3,100. The rapid increases and shifts in concentration following six earlier years of comparative immobility suggest that better times were bringing back the days of rapid neighborhood change and that many Jewish residents were "making up" for earlier, unavoidable delays in moving. On the other hand, Jewish households in West Adams declined slightly, from 4,700 to 4,500. Older areas which had seen their heyday during the 1920's or before, now nearly vanished as focuses of Jewish settlement.[42] Thus the Central area, where over 2,000 Jewish households could be found in 1923, receded to some 778 in 1929, notwithstanding vast population increases in general. Perhaps on account of belt-tightening during the depression, this poor neighborhood underwent a mild resurgence to 1,500 in 1935; but it virtually disappeared by 1940, when little over 100 Jewish households could be found. The Westlake–Temple Street neighborhood, a focal district during the World War I period, increased in Jewish households but below the proportion to the city at large. The neighborhood's numbers fluctuated between 2,000 and 3,000 during the 1930's.

Thus a demographic scanning of Los Angeles Jewry during the depression decade shows Boyle Heights and nearby City Terrace as the center of Jewish settlement, where nearly one-third of Los Angeles Jews lived, but with a slow diminution. Wilshire and West Pico became focal, while Hollywood nearly kept pace with the general population increase. It was calculated in 1941 that in three areas roughly identical with Boyle Heights–City Terrace, Central Wilshire and West Pico–Wilshire, and Hollywood, 94,700 Jews resided. The first area held an estimated 35,900, while in Hollywood there were supposed to be 18,700. Beverly-Wilshire and the West Central area, more than covering Central Wilshire and Wilshire–West Pico, held 40,100.[43]

Regardless of their degree of acculturation, Jews generally wished to dwell together. Even where Yiddish was little heard or seen and Hebrew "kosher" or other lettering not widespread, certain shopping streets were unmistakably Jewish. The famous promenade street, Hollywood Boulevard, had several Jewish eating places to attract the throngs of tourists on that street. Some proof of Jewish residential concentration may be their "isolation," defined as "the ratio of their average percentage in the populations of neighborhoods where they live to their percentages in the total population of an area." On a scale from one (homogeneous distribution throughout a given area) to twenty (total isolation from other groups), "Russians," mostly Jews but including a Russian sectarian group in Boyle Heights, scored 5.84. They were thus more concentrated than Los Angeles Mexicans (4.63), less than the Orientals (7.32), and far below the ghettoized Negroes (17.81). Jewish concentration contrasted drastically with native whites, Canadians, or Germans, all of whom stood close to the "one" of homogeneous distribution.[44] For many, Jewish life must have meant living close to other Jews.

Disturbed Security

Some part of Jewish residential concentration may be due to a sense of external menace. At no time during the harsh years of depression, reform, and slow recovery were Jewish rights openly attacked in any reputable quarter. No significant public figure or major party spoke against Jews. Even the future state senator and anti-Communist and anti-Semitic opportunist of the 1940's, Jack B. Tenney, was still a liberal official of the musicians' union, extensively associating with Jews. Despite this façade of safety, Los Angeles Jews were nervous and insecure, as was American Jewry. The alarming ascent of anti-Semitism on the world scene, preeminently in Nazi Germany, demanded that its every form, including some having a local pedigree, be regarded with urgency. The first thoughts turned obviously to the local Nazis, few but noisy and brazen. Their main service to their masters during these years was as a funnel for the Western distribution of Nazi propaganda, which was far more artful and dangerous than they. To be sure, neither the Nazis nor the like-minded Silver Shirts were the main menace in Los Angeles. That lay in anti-Semitism of the "respectable" variety, such as the Ku Klux Klan groups in Glendale and Inglewood which functioned by "gentlemen's agreements" to exclude Jews from home ownership and social groups in their neighborhoods. Many areas were closed tight to Jews by means of restrictive covenants (agreements among owners not to sell to Jews or other "undesirables") and other devices.

By the 1930's such major civic bodies as the Chamber of Commerce—which had had Jewish founders and officers—maintained an unspoken but recognized policy of keeping out Jews. Elite social and business clubs behaved similarly. Some made self-righteous exceptions for a few old-time Jewish members, but one of those resigned anyhow when his son was denied admittance. From these citadels of exclusiveness emanated the attitudes of dislike and contempt. The economically powerful Jewish magnates in Hollywood might have broken through some of these barriers, had they not preferred to remain within their own enclave.

To genteel anti-Semitism and crude Nazism were joined some of the uglier aspects of Protestant Fundamentalism. A belief that the Jew caused depression and war came all too readily to those who had accepted Christian myths about the Jewish "Antichrist" in their crudest form. Radio listeners in Los Angeles of the 1930's could hear this type of preachment from the Reverend Martin Luther Thomas. During the two years before Pearl Harbor, G. Ellison Phelps was an isolationist radio speaker who also traded on such conceptions. Myths about Jews could be found in such places as police records and probate reports, where a Jewish defendant might exhibit "typical tricks of his race in attempting to turn a deal wherever he can."[45] It was no less significant and of greater practical importance, however, that Jews were not a minority victimized by the police or in the courts. Perhaps this was true partly because there were numerous Jewish lawyers and judges.

No aspect of anti-Semitism troubled Jews more than discrimination in employment. It was the openest of secrets that jobs in banks, insurance, retail trade, and business offices were generally shut to Jews, except for the few who might be employed (but not promoted) as window dressing. A Jewish lawyer had few illusions about a job in all but a few non-Jewish firms, while, as we have seen, most Los Angeles hospitals excluded the Jewish physician and thus his patients also. Even qualified teachers who were Jews found great difficulty in securing employment in southern California's schools.[46] Thus, the upper-class Jew was often kept at arm's length by Gentile groups of his own social standing; young Jews had to think hard about seeking entry to professions which might exclude them from facilities and rewards; in an age of unemployment, job-seeking Jews had to bear the burden of restricted opportunities; all had to worry over the sharp, overt manifestations of anti-Semitism which made for realization that a deep stratum of latent anti-Semitism existed.

During the 1930's a hesitant start was made in the struggle against this ancient phenomenon, mainly by the two tactics of detection and good will. The Jewish Community Committee (later the Community Relations Committee), established in 1933, employed private investigators to learn and publicly expose what local Nazi cohorts were planning. At another level, "good will" efforts were strongly stressed. Radio broadcasts by friendly Gentiles, particularly Protestant clergy, and by such Jews such as Rabbi Edgar F.

Magnin, stressed the contributions of Jews to civilization, and the un-American character of group prejudice. Notwithstanding much seriousness, the techniques were too superficial and rudimentary to cope with deeply rooted fears and hatred. The cloud of anti-Semitism hung over the Jewish community throughout the depression years.

CHAPTER 13

The Community Weakened and Rejuvenated: 1929-1941

——————————————————➤:◀——————————————————

THE COMMUNAL LIFE of Los Angeles Jewry was stricken by the depression of the 1930's no less than the economic status of individual Jews. The thousands who lost jobs or struggled desperately to hold what they had could devote little time and less money to the development of institutions or to cultural enrichment. Jewish institutions suffered severely as their support dropped away and limited funds had to be devoted to relief. The advocacy of radical social change, a hallmark of the decade, took place largely outside the Jewish community, and during the trying years conventional Jewish interests appeared inconsequential to a large proportion of the Jewish population. Nevertheless, the restlessness during the 1930's with the established order and its leaders produced momentous consequences in Jewish outlook and in the interests of the Jewish community.

During the early 1930's communal paralysis seemed to pervade the scene as institutions withered and individuals withdrew. When times improved later in the 1930's, new energies began to flow, a central communal apparatus was erected, and local response to overseas Jewish problems became vigorous. New organizations sprang up on the Jewish scene and old ones were revitalized; funds could more readily be raised, and new leaders assumed the direction of affairs as World War II approached.

Many features of the Jewish religious scene in Los Angeles were strongly reminiscent of parallel conditions among the Protestant churches. Large, established institutions functioned among unaffiliated little houses of worship, while trained and ordained rabbis had the competition of numerous ill-qualified rabbinic pretenders. It was thus by no means simple even to estimate the number of congregations in Los Angeles. The United States Census of Religious Bodies, conducted in 1936, found 42 Jewish congregations in Los Angeles which claimed no less than 82,000 "members," meaning Jews dwelling in their area.[1] Yet five years later, after full use of the best local data, communal enumerators "were able to locate 32 synagogues instead of the 42 which was the total number reported by the Government as being in existence in 1936. The chances are that our local data was incomplete . . . but since 1936 it is quite likely that quite a number of new synagogues have been established and the number may now be somewhere in the 50's."[2]

Similarly, the local rabbinic association was composed of recognized rabbis, but they were outnumbered by unqualified men whom the association did not admit. The rabbinic pretenders did not all deceive their congregations: some congregations upon electing a rabbi considered that they had thereby conferred the rabbinic title upon the man they chose.

Of unrecognized congregations, many were the private property of a "rabbi" who conducted its affairs and adapted the services to the "customers'" demand as would any other businessman. The advertising of synagogue facilities for the High Holidays on billboards and in streetcar signs was common practice; in addition, there were the customary notices in Jewish newspapers. Thus, one aspiring house of worship announced the schedules for separate "Orthodox" and "Reform" services to be held within its walls on the same holiday. In another instance, the "First Reform Congregation of American Israelites," ministered to by "Dr. H. Cerf Strauss, Rabbi," invited all to High Holiday services at its quarters in the First Unitarian Church.[3] Its assurance that no charge was made for seats could hardly have been taken too seriously by those who decided to attend.

The large number of irregular and proprietary synagogues tends to show that many Jews participated in worship only on the High Holidays and on the few holidays when the customary *"yizkor"* prayer memorialized near relatives. Such behavior was typical in American Jewry. The "Jewishness" of many neighborhoods exceeded their formal Judaism, as typified in a religious sense by public eating places purveying "Jewish" or "kosher style" foods yet not adhering to the stringent rules of kosher diet.

The proprietary and unrecognized houses of worship served their own circles for better or worse, but broader communal interests could come only from responsible synagogues owned by membership corporations. In 1941 nineteen of perhaps fifty synagogues existing in Los Angeles reported a total seating capacity of 9,147, with no more than 2,713 paid-up members. Although this was hardly half the probable number of synagogues, all the major institutions were included, so that the great majority of seats and members were accounted for.[4] One local reason for the small membership was that new settlers were slow to regard Los Angeles as home and join one of its synagogues. They felt themselves still affiliated with a congregation "back home" in New York City or Chicago. The cost of membership, especially during hard times, and personal lack of identification with Jewish religious life are also obvious reasons. No statistics exist for synagogue attendance, but this was below membership and seating capacity, notwithstanding the prevalence in Orthodox synagogues of unaffiliated but regular worshippers.

As in the past, the Wilshire Boulevard Temple ranked first among Los Angeles' Jewish houses of worship in age, prestige, stability, and affluence. This Reform bastion weathered the depression with comparative ease, while Sinai Temple, the principal Conservative congregation, hovered close to bankruptcy. Only the personal help of some leading personalities saved Sinai Temple. The Wilshire congregation had 900 members and 2,000 seats, while the younger Conservative body claimed 350 members for its 1,217 seats.[5] Among the Orthodox, two sizable synagogues, the "Olive Street shul" (Beth Israel) and the "Breed Street shul" (Congregation Talmud Torah) did not have large memberships but drew considerable attendance at services from the large reservoir of traditional Jews in their neighborhood. A fairly large semi-Orthodox congregation was Beth Jacob in West Adams, where N. I. Addleson, an English immigrant, was rabbi during the 1930's. As new Los Angeles areas developed, synagogues were founded. Thus the first Jewish worship in Westwood, near the UCLA campus, took place in 1938 at temporary quarters in a sorority house. Some five hundred Jewish families then lived in the district.[6]

To the outside world, Rabbi Edgar F. Magnin was rabbi par excellence, just as the Temple on Wilshire Boulevard represented Judaism to non-Jews. The depression period was Rabbi Magnin's mid-career. As in earlier years, he combined ministerial responsibilities to the large congregation (in long-time collaboration with Rabbi Maxwell H. Dubin) with an extensive program of speaking before the non-Jewish community, in person and over the radio. Other Reform figures included Ernest R. Trattner (1897-1965), a gifted writer and magnetic speaker, whose talents were not balanced by stability in his congregational positions. Jacob Sonderling (1878-1965) was a remarkable figure. He had been the rabbi of an important Reform Temple in Hamburg before emigrating to America in 1923, and occupied several pulpits in the East before arriving in Los Angeles in 1935. Here Rabbi Sonderling founded the Society for Jewish Culture, humanistic in its religious tendency and experimental in its worship, in the Fairfax area. With a considerable membership of German refugees, it tried "dramatic lectures" and "dramatic interpretations" in worship, and announced "conservative reform" Yom Kippur services but with "many innovations and changes."[7] Another rabbi who followed a way of his own was Herman Lissauer, to whom the forum over which he presided at Temple Beth El in Hollywood became an all-embracing interest. After leading the congregation close to Reform Judaism, Lissauer resigned and presently ceased using his rabbinic title. He conducted the Modern Forum, which became a stimulating local lecture series where prominent persons discussed issues of the day.

Rabbi Mayer Winkler also rather ostentatiously quit Sinai Temple in 1929 and founded his own Community Temple, which broadcast regularly on his "Synagogue of the Air." Sinai installed in his place Rabbi Jacob Kohn (1881-1968), who had for many years held a Manhattan pulpit. A soft-spoken rabbi of theological originality and liberal political views, Rabbi Kohn pursued his scholarly studies with no milieu to encourage him. Not many understood the abstractions he would employ in his sermons, but he was held in great personal esteem.[8]

In 1930 Rabbi Isaac Werne returned to Los Angeles after a nine-year sojourn in Columbus, Ohio. He resumed his position at Beth Israel and as the leading Orthodox rabbi until his death in 1942. The incumbent at the "Breed Street shul" for some years was Rabbi Solomon M. Neches (1893-1957), a Palestinian, Hebraist, and possessor of a large personal library. Rabbi Osher Zilberstein followed him from 1935 in a lengthy and communally important career. From the Boyle Heights congregation Rabbi Neches moved to the Beverly-Fairfax neighborhood, where he founded the Western Jewish Institute. Although there were rather flashy academic trappings—Rabbi Neches was styled Dean, and academic gowns were worn at occasions—the Institute was actually a center of night classes for young people and public lectures and addresses.[9]

The Orthodox rabbis of Los Angeles maintained a Va'ad Harabbonim (Rabbinical Council), and their congregations were connected with each other in an Agudas Hakehillos (Associated Congregations). The group wielded little authority, since the Orthodox scene particularly suffered from unattached or entrepreneurial rabbis and disinterested congregations. The two bodies' main task, the supervision of kosher provisions, lay beyond their capacities.

It cannot be said that the religious sector of Los Angeles Jewry contained very much spiritual or intellectual power. Jewish religious traditions seemed unable to attract or hold the loyalty of younger people. Partly on account of emergency needs during depression, there was an undue taint of commercialism in many of the synagogues. However, the depression years were basically not a religious age in Los Angeles nor in American life.[10]

Jewish Educational Decline

The weakness of Jewish study at all levels was also apparent during the 1930's in Jewish education. The promising beginnings of communal aid for the Jewish schools vanished with the onset of depression. Congregations also decreased support to their own schools and many fell far in arrears to teachers. Even attempts to maintain records of schools and enrollment were not made, at least until the Bureau of Jewish Education was founded in 1936. At that time the *Census of Religious Bodies* reported that seventeen local congregations had 2,319 pupils, mostly in Sunday schools.[11] Besides these congregations' schools, several of the Yiddish type were conducted by the Workmen's Circle and the Labor Zionist Farband. The main Hebrew school was the Menorah Center's while the West Adams Community Center also housed a traditional Hebrew school. During these unhappy years two developments began whose importance was increasingly felt. Under the auspices of the newly organized Los Angeles Jewish Community Council a Bureau of Jewish Education was established to publicize Jewish education, provide extracurricular services, and grant subsidies. It made a promising beginning with Rabbi Bernard Cohen as its first executive director. By 1941 it had granted some $24,000 to thirteen non-congregational schools, which was approximately 38% of their total budgets. One recipient was the Los Angeles Jewish Academy, founded in 1935, which pioneered the Jewish day schools that were in time to assume importance. The Academy enrolled 127 children in 1941. An estimate for that year added the 1,200 to 1,300 Jewish children at schools associated with the Bureau of Jewish Education to. an estimated 3,700 in the congregational schools, and found that perhaps 5,000 Jewish children were receiving some Jewish schooling. This was approximately one-third of Jewish children of elementary school age.

Public attitudes toward the Jewish educational effort varied. The large school at the Menorah Center was an essential part of the institution. However, the school housed at the Soto-Michigan Center was regarded with skepticism by at least some of the Center's board. The founding of the Bureau of Jewish Education was intrinsically and financially important, for it demonstrated the recognition of education as a responsibility of the entire Jewish community.[12]

The Content of Jewishness

Outside the Hollywood enclave, Jews participated with no great luster in the tame and derivative cultural life of Los Angeles in the years between 1928 and 1941. Southern California was not yet the scientific and literary elysium it became in the 1950's; the literary genres of the 1920's and 1930's, with their fervent Westernism, hardly gave room for recently arrived Jews to make any appreciable contribution. The film industry tended to scoop in the gifted if they could write (scenarios) or paint (scenery) or compose or play music (on sound tracks); the city saw no more of them. A few Jews appeared in the formal cultural enterprises of the city, such as its orchestra and its art museum, but these were decorative associations. Jewish painters and sculptors were as rare as scholars, scientists, and writers. A few were journalists. The Southern Branch of the University of California, as the University of California at Los Angeles was still known, for years boasted one recognizable Jewish academic, the geophysicist Joseph Kaplan. Like financial capital, the cultural capital of Los Angeles was still imported from the East and somewhat less from San Francisco—which, however, had practically nothing to offer to Jewish culture.

Tens of thousands of Jews also maintained a distinctive Jewish cultural milieu which resembled those to be found in New York, Chicago, Detroit, Philadelphia, and other eastern cities. Jewish cultural zeal did not lessen in the southern California sunshine, even in as typical a matter as using the public library's riches. In the judgment of the head librarian of the city's system: "Although there are no exact figures concerning the Jewish participation, our library has always felt that the Jewish people read more than any other racial group in the community. They also read on the whole a very high level of non-fiction. There is a Yiddish circulation of approximately 2,000. Much of the circulation of music is also due to the interest of Jewish borrowers."[13] There were already Jewish bibliophiles and art collectors, and some joined in the quest for a cultured "southern California way of life."

Besides Jewish participation in the general cultural life of the city there was also a cultural sphere entirely their own, encompassing both historic religious forms and modern Jewish ideologies. The weakness of traditional Judaism was illustrated by the feebleness of classic Jewish learning even in the rabbinate. The creative activity conducted in Los Angeles lay not in these fields but in Yiddish, where politics and culture were inextricably intertwined. A flow of writing continued to come from the pens of Los Angeles' Yiddish writers.[14] The Yiddishists also established a Yiddish club at 1348 Douglas Street about 1929. Besides a series of lectures and café nights for members, they had far-reaching hopes of creating an autonomous Yiddish culture in southern California. There would be a Yiddish library and theater and even a Yiddish "university," which would engage a corps of lecturers who would cumulatively offer a coherent course of Jewish study.[15] Nothing so grandiose was realized. More within the Yiddishists' capacities was such an event as a cheerful Jewish Culture Week in the spring of 1935, conducted by a Jewish Culture Club affiliated with the Workmen's Circle. It featured nightly celebrations of Jewish Music, Living Newspapers, Yiddish Folklore, May Day, Ladies' Night, Children's Evening, and a Rosenblatt Jubilee Evening for the leading local Yiddish poet. Yet the sponsors still felt discouraged: "Our cultural life is poor and limited. Disregarding that our cultural values have greatly advanced in the past few decades; disregarding that our cultural work has spread and that our literature has developed; the Jewish masses stand aside and alienated from all these achievements and our cultural life is poor and pale."[16]

With good Yiddish lectures and concerts well attended, one may perhaps wonder at the Yiddishists' dissatisfaction with their rather substantial achievement. Their social ideals, however, did not permit them to accept a disparity between "high" and "mass" Jewish culture. Moreover, they were well aware of the ceaseless seepage from their ranks by linguistic Anglicization.

Compared with the extensive Yiddish environment, Zionism in Los Angeles was comparatively weak. The Labor Zionists competed effectively with anti-Zionists for the Yiddish group's adherence. The religious Mizrachi Zionists were rather feeble, however, and were almost coextensive with the Orthodox synagogues and their leadership. The Zionist Organization of America (ZOA) was at low ebb in 1933, with three groups and perhaps fifty members. Thanks to emergencies abroad and the slow return of better times, an aggressive leadership (including Dr. George Saylin, Dr. Louis G. Reynolds, Rabbi Jacob Kohn, Gustave Goldstein, and Aaron Riche) succeeded in reaching almost 2,000 members at the close of the decade.[17] However, neither the ZOA nor the larger Hadassah pursued cultural or educational objectives with the energy they successfully devoted to fund raising and, later, to political endeavors.

Thus a Jewish cultural milieu in English barely existed. The Reform Temples were unmindful, while at the more traditional Conservative Temple Sinai, Rabbi Jacob Kohn (who arrived in 1931) pursued his theological scholarship in solitude. A printed sermon or a story from Jewish lore was the characteristic cultural expression found in the English Jewish newspapers of the city.

The principal gathering places for the majority of Jews not rooted in religion and the synagogal environment were the Jewish Centers of Los Angeles. In the years between 1929 and 1941 the conception of these Centers as "Americanization" philanthropic institutions, although admittedly outdated, was not yet replaced by newly articulated principles or objectives.

Uncertainty as to its Jewish character marked the Jewish Center movement. According to its Articles of Incorporation of 1932, the aim was "to foster and develop the highest ideals of American citizenship and Jewish culture," by serving "residents of the city of Los Angeles." By 1938 the Center spoke of serving "the Jewish community of Los Angeles." In the Boyle Heights and West Adams of the 1930's, the fact of Jewishness could be assumed. The problems as seen were vocational choice for the young, employment for the mature, and Jewish access to general society. The Centers were then Jewish in membership but less so in interest.

In 1929 its director left the Modern Social Center, and soon afterward the Community Chest found the institution unsatisfactory. Gradually the Center converted itself into a professionally organized institution; in 1934 its home at Michigan and Soto was refurbished and enlarged to include a gymnasium-auditorium and an outdoor playground. The house at Michigan and Soto was torn down in 1938 and a new building went up on its site. The clientele was mainly youngsters: over two-thirds were under eighteen years of age, and most others were not much older.[18] Similar in ambition to Boyle Heights's community center was that in the more attractive Jewish district of West Adams. It opened next to the Beth Jacob Synagogue in 1937 in as unsuitable a building as could be found. Even its officials reckoned it "not a suitable place for children to play in. The stairs are in a dangerous condition, the doors, windows and railings and many salient portions of the building are in a shameful state."[19]

Anxiety over unemployed or defeatist youth gave the prevention of juvenile delinquency a curious prominence among the Centers' purposes. Perhaps it was easier to raise funds by emphasizing the peril of delinquency among young Jews. There were, to be sure, forthright and well-founded admonitions to well-meaning organizers from local leaders: "I feel you are mistaken and are proceeding along the wrong line of action, as there is no Jewish delinquency among the children or adults in the West Adams district, and there never has been any and it doesn't look like there will be any."[20]

The Menorah Center, "their confidential corner" to many who lived in its City Terrace bailiwick, arose not from settlement beginnings but from an expanded Talmud Torah. Built by a grant from the trust of Clement Kaufman, it had a club program aimed to supplement the formal education of the Talmud Torah. The Menorah Center's domed structure on a hilltop, whose drab interior belied its impressive exterior, was a meeting place for many social and athletic youth clubs. Formal education at Menorah was assisted by New Deal funds, for the Works Progress Administration and the Emergency Educational Program sent nine teachers several times weekly to teach elementary and advanced English, Americanization (meaning preparation for naturalization tests), history and civics, vocal and instrumental music, contemporary Jewish history, physical education for men and women, child care, home visitation, cooking, food chemistry, and nutrition.[21] About 860 Jewish adults made their way weekly to the Menorah Center for these courses. In their classes the grown pupils "feel . . . rather members of a social club where they may discuss freely the problems of life, spending their leisure time profitably as a citizen of a community and at the same time having recreation and a certain degree of relaxation from the every day task of earning a livelihood."[22] Whether or not he was aware that these classes perpetuated an immemorial Jewish tradition of study as the highest form of recreation, even for working people, the government supervisor emphatically considered "the work that is being accomplished as of the greatest importance in the way of education and rehabilitation of adults that is at present carried on in the City of Los Angeles." It was a "splendid success that is being realized among the Jewish people of this [City Terrace] section."[23] In contrast to the youthful predominance at Soto-Michigan, some 30% of the membership (1,359 at the end of our period) was over twenty-one years old."[24] The Menorah Center, unsupported before the 1940's by the Community Chest or the Federation of Jewish Welfare Organizations because of the absence of social work professionalism, furnished a considerable part of the articulate Jewishness of Boyle Heights and City Terrace.

The Jewish quality of Boyle Heights was still on display in its streets during the 1930's: stores retailing Jewish foods, books, and religious articles, Jewish candy stores and cafés, theaters exhibiting Yiddish films. Some sights, quite natural to residents, seemed exotic to visitors:

One of the leading enterprises of the place is marriage—marriage brokers, wedding specialists, circumcision surgeons. This is the sign that fronts a handsome private house:

PARADISE WEDDING PARLOR
Rabbi Cantor Aaron Lipitz

Specialist surgeon mohel and marriages performed. Accepts weddings at home as well as outside. Speeches in English and Jewish.[25]

These were the outward appearances which bespoke the internal cohesion of Los Angeles Jewry.

Defining A Community

Los Angeles Jewry entered the period of depression with a community leadership based upon philanthropic activity which did not, however, bear the responsibility of actually raising money. The characteristic quality of this leadership at the close of the 1920's was a respected position in the wider community and some wealth, much more than positive identification with Jewish affairs. Perhaps owing to the fluidity and newness of the economic structure, leadership based on long-established wealth was rare. Rather it fell to those having entree to the legal and political network, who "knew people." Men like Lester W. Roth, Harry Hollzer, Benjamin Scheinman, and Mendel B. Silberberg reached prominence as the successors to the leadership of the Newmarks and Hellmans and their relatives. The leaders generally belonged to B'nai B'rith Temple (later Wilshire Boulevard Temple) and were prominent in the Federation of Jewish Philanthropies; the B'nai B'rith lodge was their organization, although the older leaders figured less prominently in its affairs after it became a mass organization. As the conduit for bringing new personages to the foreground of Jewish communal affairs, Los Angeles Lodge No. 487 outdistanced the synagogues and the Zionists. Los Angeles Jewry's representative figures of the 1930's were raised in B'nai B'rith of the 1910's and 1920's.

By assuming that the common bond of Jews was the impulse of charity, it was widely supposed that the Federation of Jewish Welfare Organizations was the fitting expression of the unity of Los Angeles Jews. The leading Jews of the city had founded it in 1912, and those who joined the Federation's ranks followed their outlook. Thus in April 1929 a group led by Lester Roth selected five hundred men for invitations to contribute $25 each to the Federation's Amalgamation Deficit Appeal and thus earn recognition as a member of the "Five Hundred Club"—Los Angeles Jewry's "Aristocracy of Service." The Federation of Jewish Welfare Organizations received money for its twelve local constituents from the Los Angeles Community Chest and disbursed them. It was to coordinate and plan and, unofficially, lobby for the twelve Jewish recipients. Jewish receipts fluctuated with Chest income. Thus, instead of the promised $356,000 of an anticipated Chest income of $3,200,000 during the twelvemonth following November 1, 1928, only $275,000 reached

the Jewish Federation because the Chest raised but $2,725,000.
When the central agency's income next declined to approximately
$2,688,000, the Jewish body had to accept a corresponding cut in
its share. Short $7,000 a month and interest on the Cedars of Leb-
anon debt, they again faced a serious curtailment of their work.[26]
So long as the Community Chest raised the money, Jewish needs
could not be realistically integrated by the Jewish group into the
welfare picture of the city as a whole.

The Community Chest did permit the Federation to conduct one
appeal yearly in the form of soliciting members. A contribution of
$4 entitled a person to select three beneficiary institutions upon
which to bestow his membership; for $10 one could be counted a
member of every Federation beneficiary![27] This preposterous arrangement raised little money and denigrated the meaning of
membership. Since the Community Chest failed to grant capital
funds, the Jewish community had to harness, if it could, private
generosity for this all-important purpose. Aside from the inadequa-
cies of the Federation–Community Chest connection, the Jewish
partner had the fundamental limitation of serving local charitable
needs exclusively, tacitly assuming that calls from Jewry overseas
were occasional.

The 1930's were a time of Jewish communal trial and change.
Some of the established leadership lost their wealth, and all suffered from the general questioning of earlier values and spokesmen.
Moreover, they were unprepared in mind and pocketbook for new
challenges which emanated from overseas. The limited outlook and
diminished prestige of local leaders helped a newer group to ease
into the driver's seat. The expanded Jewish communal structure
began tentatively with the organization of the United Jewish Welfare Fund in 1929. It proposed to combine appeals for European
Jewry and Palestine, previously in the United Jewish Appeal (an
earlier organization distinct from the later UJA), with local Jewish
needs which the Federation did not support. The Federation of
Jewish Welfare Organizations itself sponsored the new Fund. A
committee whose chairman was Lester W. Roth and which included
representatives of the Jewish Educational Association, B'nai B'rith,
and the United Palestine Appeal, meeting at the Federation Office,
"unanimously felt that the United Jewish Welfare Fund should

be organized to gather in May, 1929 and annually thereafter, a sum of money which shall make possible an adequate contribution by the Jewish community of Los Angeles toward the support of those Jewish causes and movements which are international, national, or regional in character and which cannot procure contributions from the Community Chest."[28]

The phrase "causes and movements" and the absence of terms like "needy" and "distressed" were suggestive of Jewish philanthropy's newer approaches. The goal remained unchanged from the United Jewish Appeal's $200,000 in 1928, when "owing to economic stress" it could be no higher.[29] After complaints against the "apparent indifference of representative men and women in the community," pressure was openly applied to the trustees of the Federation to work harder. The United Jewish Welfare Fund's first campaign showed $106,000 pledged, and $93,000 collected by the close of 1929.[30] In the cheerless year of 1930 the directors repeatedly postponed the drive and finally disbanded, not to reconstitute until December 1934. By then another body of major potentialities existed, the United Jewish Community, founded in 1933.

Myth-making upon the United Jewish Community's origins seems to have begun early. In the early days of the Nazi regime in Germany, a local newspaper reportedly requested I. Irving Lipsitch, executive director of the Federation, to describe Jewish opinion on Nazism. He could give only his own (not that there were two Jewish views, upon that subject at least), and observed to Marco Newmark that a body of Los Angeles Jews seemed desirable for such representative purposes. Eight men were convened, with Rabbi Edgar F. Magnin as chairman and Lipsitch as secretary.[31]

Like the UJWF, the United Jewish Community was founded by the Federation leadership, which intended to mold the newer elements in the Jewish community more or less under its patronage and direction. Rather curious was the Federation's endorsement of the nomenclature "United Jewish Community"—a term virtually anathema to the older Jewish leadership elsewhere. Judge Harry Hollzer was president. Succeeding the deceased I. I. Lipsitch, Charles I. Schottland served as professional director both of the new institution and the Federation. The United Jewish Community's mainly internal focus drew it to matters like kashruth, youth organization, and Jewish education. It sought to enforce inner discipline and thus prevent periodic scandals over kashruth. It desired to eliminate streetcar and billboard advertising of High Holiday services, especially by "mushroom" synagogues. By the time of the United Jewish Community's fourth annual meeting in November 1936, ninety-two Jewish organizations, congregations, and societies in Los Angeles were sending delegates to augment the numerous members at large on the UJC Board.[32] There were close relations with the United Jewish Welfare Fund, for both bodies had similar origins and interlocked leadership.

A third entity, the Jewish Community Committee, also appeared upon the scene in 1933 for external purposes. It was a basically self-appointed body of Jewish notables, disturbed by the anti-Semitic pressure in the city and especially its links with Germany's new Nazi regime. A Jewish public relations body in the film capital, many of whose members stood high in the industry, tended also to speak for Jews to the writers and producers of films where Jewish subjects and the treatment of Jewish types were concerned. The Jewish Community Committee's lifelong chairman was Mendel B. Silberberg (1887-1965), who had wide-ranging personal, political, and professional connections. Its relations with national Jewish organizations devoted to the same field later became an occasional source of jurisdictional friction, but the Community Relations Committee (as it was later renamed) emerged with local primacy.

This triad of the United Jewish Community for internal matters, the United Jewish Welfare Fund for foreign and some local philanthropy, and the Jewish Community Committee for defense energetically pursued their challenging fields of work, outdoing their progenitor, the Federation of Jewish Welfare Organizations. Many men were prominent in all three groups. Lester Roth, Isaac Pacht, Harry Hollzer, Walter S. Hilborn, Mendel B. Silberberg, J. J. Lieberman, David Blumberg, Mrs. Bertha Sieroty, Alexander Brick, Herman Bachrack, and Aaron Riche appear with constancy in these formative years of the contemporary Jewish community. Nearly all were lawyers. The prominence of the bar in contrast to business may in part be explained by the weakness of merchants and manufacturers after their crushing depression experience, in addition to the Jewish community's special need for men associated with general civic life and experienced in problems of structure and polity. All these bodies were unadorned by rabbis, except for the place reserved everywhere for Rabbi Magnin and (somewhat less) Rabbi Jacob Kohn of Sinai Temple. At the United Jewish Community's annual meeting in 1936 Rabbi Kohn, whose convictions particularly interested him in communal democracy, regretted the absence of the rabbinate from that body, whereupon "Judge Hollzer stated that we were waiting a message from the rabbinate on the subject of unity. Rabbi Neches stated that he had no complaints."[33] The community had a lay leadership, particularly because of the concentration upon defense, philanthropy, and self-discipline.

In the summer of 1937 Joseph P. Loeb, of pioneer stock and one of the city's leading lawyers, presented the report and resolution of a survey committee "to widen the activities and the scope of the organization . . . to incorporate . . . under the name of the Los Angeles Jewish Conference."[34] On August 10, 1937, the United Jewish Community incorporated as the Los Angeles Jewish Council and four months later amplified its name to the Los Angeles Jewish Community Council. A momentous further result of these negotiations was the merger of the United Jewish Welfare Fund into the new body. Sixty-one Los Angeles Jewish notables signed the Articles of Incorporation.[35] The Jewish Community Council stated as its main purposes:

To promulgate and promote studies, plans and programs whereby social service problems and community needs and the relief and welfare work incidental thereto may be thoroughly understood, efficiently and economically dealt with, and adequately met. . . .

To co-ordinate and harmonize the activities [of Jewish organizations] and in particular [to] foster, develop and co-ordinate all phases of Jewish social service, relief, welfare, educational, recreational and community life.

To achieve these ends, the Articles concluded, centralized appeals for funds were to be conducted.

Among the most interesting Articles were those which transformed the old United Jewish Community into a more representative body and provided for allocating the funds raised by its new constituent, the United Jewish Welfare Fund. Like those of its predecessor, the Jewish Community Council's constituents were Jewish organizations, not individual Jews. A constituent could be "any organization, institution or agency having Jewish community services . . . not organized for pecuniary profit . . . and not having political or purely social purposes or objectives."[36] Such a group could apply after one year's existence for the status of institutional member. Once admitted, it sent three "representative members" to sit on the Jewish Community Council. The Council could itself co-opt one member at large for each fifteen representative members, thereby allowing institutionally unaffiliated notables to sit on the Council.[37] The Council, which began its career with over one hundred organizations, was to elect a board of forty-nine directors by ballot.[38] They would serve staggered terms of three years each and generally control the affairs of the Jewish Community Council. In addition to its annual meeting, the Council held plenary meetings twice yearly.

The uniquely important Allocations Committee "shall act fairly and impartially and shall not be appointed to the Committee as representatives of a particular group, cause or agency." Even the budget of the Jewish Community Council itself was subject to the Allocations Committee's hearings and requests for specific information.[39] Although the JCC Board of Directors had final voice over the findings and recommendations of its most potent committee, the Allocations Committee's reports were never rejected and rarely even modified. The Jewish Community Committee's functions of defense and public relations were considered unsuited for regular scrutiny or criticism. Hence it remained outside the new communal frame until 1941, when it entered and took the name of Community Relations Committee. However, its self-appointed membership (now formally ratified by the Board of the JCC) remained unaltered, and its budget was uniquely spared the rigors of close examination by the Allocations Committee.

Many other American Jewish communities founded central bodies during the 1930's, but in none was the Jewish Community Council of Los Angeles exceeded in the power it gathered. The social fluidity of Los Angeles and the ineffectiveness of its previous Jewish leadership had opened wide the opportunities for newer elements to take control. Above all, unprecedented and soul-stirring calls for overseas aid lay entirely within the province of the new leaders, together with many Los Angeles Jewish institutions which had never before received communal aid. The new communal structure had the additional advantage of starting on an upswing. The United

Jewish Welfare Fund secured only 1,800 individual pledges in the first campaign after its revival in 1934,[40] but the number multiplied to 9,900 in 1938. Intensification of Jewish distress abroad was the underlying reason for the increase, while improving conditions at home made the rise possible. No less encouraging, the 92 affiliated organizations of 1937 increased, at the close of 1941, to 156 of approximately 350 functioning and eligible Jewish organizations in the city.[41] Los Angeles Jewry by then possessed the central institutions which it required for the unforeseen future.

CHAPTER 14

Soaring Population and Economic Expansion

———————————— ✖ ————————————

Cross-Country Movement

WHEN WORLD WAR II ended, 150,000 Jews were estimated to live in the 449 square miles of the city of Los Angeles, about 20,000 more than had been there when the war began.[1] A reasonably well-informed estimate one year later gave 168,000: a great surge was beginning.[2] In 1948 a competent local study concluded "that the Jewish population of greater Los Angeles is already approximately one-fourth of a million and that our rate of growth is in excess of two thousand a month."[3] The Jewish increase went hand in hand with that of the city and the much larger Los Angeles County as a whole; in this larger sphere, the 2,285,000 of 1940 mounted to 4,151,687 in 1950. With new residents arriving at the rate of 16,000 a month in the late 1940's, Jews—at any rate for some brief period —formed one-eighth of total immigration.

Southern California reportedly sighed with relief at the end of the war, as masses of outsiders who had worked in its war industries packed and left the state. With all of its nearly centennial experience of westward immigrants, it was unprepared for and surprised by the vast inflow, which far exceeded the exodus of war workers.[4] Jewish communal leaders, however, were less surprised. During the closing months of World War II, Judge Harry A. Hollzer, as president of the Jewish Community Council, had openly predicted "a new and larger influx of Jewish families in our midst."[5] With movement in full tide, Charles Brown spoke dramatically but with discernment from the same platform as Judge Hollzer:

We in the Los Angeles Jewish community are living in a frontier which is as dramatic in its way as the original pioneer town of Los Angeles which was the goal of the first movement of Americans westward.

Jews are trekking westward to Los Angeles in one of the greatest waves of migration in Jewish history. Each day the urban centers of the East lose their Jewish citizens to the attractions of our climate and resources. Jewish people are coming from Chicago, Philadelphia, Boston, Pittsburgh, Detroit, Omaha and a hundred other places.[6]

The American Jews on the move from points east did not differ in many respects from the non-Jewish masses who moved with them. The summary of Carey McWilliams, a perspicacious native, is generally apposite for Christians as well as Jews:

California's migrants . . . represent a selection rather than a cross-section of the American population. Many of them are veterans; perhaps 250,000 veterans have settled in Los Angeles alone since the end of the war. They are young people, active, in their best working years; 45 per cent, for example, are between 15 and 34 years of age. On the whole, they are much younger than the resident population. . . . the war migrants show a higher proportion of college graduates than is to be found in California. The number of high school graduates, among the migrants, is considerably higher than the average in the states from which the migrants have come. Three-fourths of them come from points west of the Mississippi River.[7]

In 1951, 44.5% of Jewish households in Los Angeles were estimated to have resided in southern California only since 1940, and half of these had come in the first three years after the war. In other words, between 1945 and 1948 a net estimate of 66,000 Jews moved across the continent to Los Angeles. Since the overwhelming majority of American Jews lived east of the Mississippi, and approximately 40% in the New York City region, the more westerly geographic origin of the Christian trekkers could not be duplicated among the Jews. Yet the Middle West, particularly Chicago, contributed disproportionately to Los Angeles' newer Jewish population: perhaps as high as 38% of Los Angeles Jewry in 1951, compared with 36% of New England and Middle Atlantic origin, were born there.[8] Since the Northeast and Middle Atlantic had five times as many Jews as the Middle West, the inroads of Jewish emigration were felt far more heavily in the Jewish communities of the Middle West. Thus, the virtual failure of the Jewish community in the metropolitan area of Cleveland to increase its numbers after the 1930's was blamed primarily upon "the unmeasured but impressive outmigration to the West and Southwest after the war with little compensating in-migration." In the same community, one-third of a Temple confirmation class of 1937 resided in California when they reached their years of maturity.[9] Undoubtedly, similar statistical stories may be told of Jewish communities in other cities in the Great Lakes area, including Canada.

In 1951 the Jewish Community Council produced "A Report on the Jewish Population of Los Angeles" under the professional direction of Fred Massarik, summing up and greatly advancing what was known about the booming community.[10] It was closely estimated that there were 104,098 Jewish households in Los Angeles, with an average size of 3.03 persons. To the 315,227 individuals thus calculated could be added approximately 8,000 more in Santa Monica, 4,500 in Long Beach, and 1,800 in Pasadena. The total approximated 330,000 Jews in the metropolitan area and County of Los Angeles. In contrast to the composition of the 130,000 Jews found by Kohs in 1941, the newer element was considerably younger; while every age grouping increased greatly, that of young people almost trebled.[11]

Most of the Jewish and non-Jewish postwar arrivals had never seen Los Angeles and knew very little about it before wartime military service brought them to southern California, frequently en route to or from the Pacific Theater of Operations. Many recalled the impression made by balmy midwinter temperature which thawed soldiers inured to the frost and blizzards of continental climate. However superficially, they also observed the plentiful opportunities in Los Angeles' boom. When they resumed civilian life and began to raise a family, they resolved to settle in the Land of Promise.[12] In 1948 Los Angeles thus had 715,000 veterans, more than any city in America. Westbound Jewish migrants were not exclusively young, ambitious, and without means. To southern California also came the traditional migration of the elderly in quest of easier living during their declining years. After World War II, however, they were a smaller proportion of immigrants.[13] Little noticed but of importance was the migration of the well-to-do, who combined a luxurious style of "Southern California living" with excellent returns on their new investments in local land, construction, and business.

For some years after their arrival, immigrants clung in one or another way to their home town. "Home town" and "home state" societies formed part of plebeian society in Los Angeles. The Iowa Society's immense annual picnic attracted a reported 80,000 persons

—not all of whom, to be sure, were actually born in that state. In 1949 new Los Angeles Jews kept up at least two dozen "neo-landsman-shaften" based upon city of origin; assuredly there were twice that many of these evanescent groups. They bore titles like the "Milwau-kee Jewish Social Club of Los Angeles" or the "Jewish Friendship Club" of Omaha or Minneapolis or elsewhere. That middle western places predominated among Jewish home town societies may only mean a closer feeling among emigrants from smaller communities of 20,000 to 30,000 Jews than from the more impersonal vastness of Philadelphia or Boston, not to mention New York City. Friendship and hospitality to newcomers and genial recollection of "the old days back home" gave these groups a role in the social accommo-dation of southern California's new residents. They barely played a role in the Jewish community.[14]

The weekly Anglo-Jewish press in the home town also kept up connections for the many who subscribed or received secondhand copies, while the "neo-landsmanshaft" in turn reported news from southern California. The *American Jewish World* of Minneapolis sold 300 to 400 copies weekly in Los Angeles, while the *Jewish News* of Detroit rose by about a dozen yearly from its 105 Los Angeles subscribers in 1952. The *Intermountain Jewish News* of Denver also had a significant number of subscribers beyond the Continental Divide. Such numbers suggest a steady migration of Jews from these and other cities: "Normally, people ... continue their sub-scription to their home town Jewish publication anywhere from four to ten years after moving to Los Angeles and vicinity, until they become so immersed in their new environment and activities that they lose interest in the personalities of their place of origin."[15]

The foundation of new Jewish neighborhoods within the Los Angeles area was closely linked with the arrival of immigrants from distant places. Thus, in "tiny" Compton "a half dozen alert, young Jewish parents were eager to develop some form of Jewish com-munal life. They planned a get-together for all Jews and expected perhaps fifty persons to attend. To their utter amazement, two hundred and fifty people overflowed the Salvation Army Hall which had been secured for the meeting."[16]

In Westchester, in the far south of the city, where fields were planted to lima beans and seventeen scattered houses stood in 1941, 30,000 people dwelled in 1948. The remarkably homogeneous settlement of parents of young children began as a Jewish community with its small congregation using the Baptist church.[17]

Refugee Settlers

For none of these migrants from the United States and Canada did the Jewish community assume direct responsibility. Far different was the case of immigrants from overseas, survivors of unbelievable barbarities. The Jewish community, in common with American Jewry, felt that it owed them assistance in settling and establishing themselves. Moreover, California's strict laws concerning immigrants on public relief placed deportation from the United States for indigent refugees well within the realm of possibility. Actually, no such case ever occurred, thanks to the cooperation of sympathetic county officials with the Jewish community's Emigre Service Committee. The latter, a coordinating body working with many other Jewish agencies and financed by the United Jewish Welfare Fund, continued to have as its indefatigably devoted chairman Ludwig Schiff, a native Los Angeleno.

During the decade following the conclusion of World War II, Los Angeles Jewry's recognized spokesmen agreed to guarantee by affidavit 643 Jewish families, of whom 567 actually came to the city.[18] Thanks to geography, Los Angeles for a time received a disproportionate number of the Jewish refugee group from Shanghai. In assuming communal responsibility for an immigrant refugee family, the presence in the city of family which could help was a factor which weighed with the Emigre Service Committee. The record of a reasonably typical case, comprising a refugee couple and their daughter, with the husband having a brother in Los Angeles, may illustrate:

[The brother] can pay part of transportation and will assume maintenance responsibility. He is also willing to house the child, but will need assistance in finding housing for Mr. & Mrs. S. . . . The Committee was of the opinion that the affiant [brother] should be notified that we will help with the housing problem but will not assume any responsibility for the family. The affiant's income is said to be $450 per month. AUTHORIZATION GRANTED.[19]

The failure of an affiant to keep his pledge owing to death, financial reverses, or ordinary irresponsibility threw an added burden on the community. It was out of the question to abandon such refugees to their fate, and "the matter could not be made public."[20]

The number of "accepted" cases was few compared with "unauthorized or non-resettled cases" and "floaters."[21] While the community guaranteed 591 cases to 1954, or perhaps 1,500 to 1,800 individuals, Los Angeles reportedly accrued 10,000 Jewish refugees by 1953.[22] In the midst of reportedly the most severe housing shortage in the United States and a keen search for jobs by an immense throng of returned soldiers, an effort to find homes and employment for refugees had to be most discreetly conducted. "When housing in relation to the emigres was discussed publicly, there were some bitter reactions from the general community since they felt that newcomers were being given more consideration than American citizens."[23] The same danger affected public solicitation of jobs, many of which were quietly found in the garment industry.[24] Among the thousands who had come by 1949, five hundred "still unemployed, aimlessly pounding the sidewalks" for a time presented a sad problem.[25] As it cost $170 monthly to maintain an immigrant family, unemployment was expensive to the Jewish community, not to mention depressing for the immigrant. Immigrants psychologically maimed or physically crippled by the horrors they had undergone were a tragic but small minority. The great majority cherished an almost bitter determination to "make up" for the years lost in the machinery of murder and oppression. The immigrants organized their 1939 Club or the Association of American Jews of Polish Descent in 1952, and combined social pleasures with harsh memories and aid to their fellows.[26] It was not rodomontade to assert in 1953 that in the near future people would "marvel that this community has absorbed some 10,000 new Americans without fanfare."[27] They too formed an element in the huge population growth of Los Angeles.

Economic Expansion

The immigrants to Los Angeles after World War II, allured though they were by the climate, sought first of all to advance their fortunes. Los Angeles' history had combined dizzying booms with shattering busts, more or less in succession, but its economic history after 1945 exhibited a steady expansion far transcending anything before, yet untouched by any major setback. The flow of immigration (and World War II) raised the number of jobs in Los Angeles to 2,615,496 in 1960 and increased the bank deposits in the city from $3,297,772,000 in 1945 to $9,130,527,000 in 1958; the value of Los Angeles' manufactured product ascended from $2,021,513,000 in 1947 to $7,080,593,000 in 1958, and the residents of Los Angeles County who had earned median incomes of $3,669 in the former year could compare this figure with $7,066 in 1960, virtually the highest in the country.[28]

Jews obviously had a role in these developments. They shared generously in the prosperity of their city, both as contributors of skill and capital and recipients of the abundant fruits. Many phases of their economic activity were connected with that pace-setter for Los Angeles' growth, the construction industry. Long-range Jewish occupational trends differed quite little, however, from those in other American cities.

Jewish incomes ascended measurably. Unemployment, which still reached perhaps 10% among Jews in 1940, not to mention some 3% more employed on public works, remained only a grievous memory.[29] By 1950 a mere 1.7% of the Jewish members of the labor force had no work, and the mild recession late in the 1950's did no more than raise that rate to 1.8%.[30] While Jewish unemployment sank nearly out of sight, Jewish income levels rose to a point where Los Angeles Jews were in receipt of incomes considerably above the general level of the Los Angeles area. The median income of employed men over twenty-five stood at $2,879 in 1950, while that of the average Jewish head of household attained $5,077 two years later in a very rough estimate.[31] Eight years later, in 1959, the median income of Los Angeles Jewish households far outstripped the 16% price rise of the intervening years to reach $6,465, or $1,244 more than the average urban American family of 1956.[32] Within the Jewish group sharp variations existed, with neighborhoods symptomatic of the main lines of division. The Beverly Hills median exceeded $10,000 in 1951, while that of South Boyle Heights was reported at one-fifth that figure; several other older areas heavily inhabited by Jews stood beneath $4,000 median annual income in 1950.[33] By 1959 some 45% of the Jewish household heads of Los Angeles had incomes exceeding $7,000 annually, compared with the 28% of American urban families who had attained this level by 1956.[34] Despite the roughness of the Jewish calculations compared with the precision of United States Census Bureau data, the contrast is too large and consistent to be rationalized away.

While Jewish incomes rose and unemployment virtually disappeared except for the elderly and the foreign immigrant enclaves, extensive occupational shifts were under way. The class of Jewish "proprietors, managers, and officials," mainly the shopkeepers, was exceedingly large as the depression era closed. Many of the "clerical, sales, and kindred" individuals of 1940 stepped up during that perilous but prosperous decade to the dignity of "proprietors, managers, and officials." Notwithstanding the decline of small trade and business throughout the country and the much-noted tendencies to large businesses and corporations, the proportion of Jews on wages and salary declined throughout the 1940's relative to those working on their own account or employing others. In simple terms, they ceased to work for an employer and went into business for themselves. By 1950 the self-employed in trade and commerce among Los Angeles Jews probably outnumbered those in that category working for others.[35] Among employed Jewish males in 1951 the ratio of the two groups was approximately 7 to 5.[36] A thoughtful observer reported in 1949: "Los Angeles as an area of economic opportunity, it seems to me, is peculiarly suited to the Jewish entrepreneur. It is an area of small businesses and concentrated in the soft goods field. The enterprising Jewish businessman could find here in Los Angeles an economic area in which he could start small and make quicker progress."[37]

The combined number of Jewish "craftsmen, foremen, and kindred," and "operatives and kindred," remained at a steady proportion, so far as data hint. The places of those who "migrated" from these categories during the 1940's may have been taken by other Jews who arrived in Los Angeles; many of the job-seeking unemployed of 1940 went to work in the succeeding years as skilled employees. In the course of the two decades which began in 1940, their proportion among employed Jewish heads of households shrank from 22% to 16%—a slow slippage.[38] Meanwhile, the category of "labor" among Jews receded steadily to the vanishing point.

The "proprietors, managers, and officials" who increased so greatly during the 1940's declined during the 1950's in proportion to the great expansion of "professional and semiprofessional" workers. Where the business group rose from some 29% in a community of 130,000 (1940) to 35% in a community of 300,000 (1950), at the close of the 1950's the proportion declined to about 30% in a community numbering 391,000 Jews. Indeed, between 1940 and 1959 every category of Jewish occupation in Los Angeles declined proportionately with the triumphant rise of the professional and semiprofessional from 11% to about 25% of employed heads of household, over twice their percentage in Los Angeles altogether. The newer the neighborhood, the higher the proportion of professionals.[39] Apparently, immediate postwar migration to Los Angeles differed from that of the 1950's in that the earlier movement attracted the actual and the would-be entrepreneur, while the professional found his way to Los Angeles during the decade following.[40]

Builders and Businessmen

The ceaseless influx of immigrants with their need for housing helped to make construction the principal industry of Los Angeles. The role of Jews in fostering the increase of dwellings in the area from approximately 1,055,000 in 1945 to 2,370,000 in 1960 is greater than that suggested by the 7% or 8% actually occupied in the construction industry. Certainly, many of the additional 7% or 8% occupied in "finance, insurance, and real estate" made their livelihood from construction. Jewish promoters, many with a background in law or accountancy, undertook to buy, subdivide, construct, and sell land and homes on vast tracts in the southern and eastern reaches of Los Angeles or in the San Fernando and San Gabriel Valleys.[41] Many stories of entrepreneurial success are contained within these figures. S. Mark Taper, an English Jew of Polish birth, brought his extensive experience of building government-subsidized houses on London subdivisions when he settled in southern California in 1939. He played a large role in this type of construction for wartime needs throughout California. After the war, he gradually turned to savings and loan banking with the fortune he had made.[42] Others, although lacking Taper's extensive experience, also made their fortunes from satisfying the unending demand for homes. Louis H. Boyar became one of the largest home developers in the United States, with over 50,000 home units built by the mid-1960's. His Lakewood Park development, which he began in 1949, had 17,000 homes, with a population today exceeding 80,000. Boyar himself was prominent in Jewish endeavors, particularly as chairman of the National Board of Governors of Israel Bonds. Lawrence Weinberg, fresh out of the Army and a student at UCLA, lacked the capital to satisfy his desire to own a launderette (automatic laundry). Instead he employed his capital of $10,000 to build four homes in the Mar Vista section. His profit was $32, but the experience was tempting enough to keep him in the business. As his next venture Weinberg bought ten acres of land in San Fernando Valley and trudged systematically from one savings and loan bank to the next, seeking credit to build during the housing hunger of 1947. He finally secured the money and erected thirty houses on the tract; now he profited about $1,000 per house. By 1950 Weinberg had built 250 homes, and in the years following he never placed less than 1,000 freshly constructed homes on the market annually, except for a highly successful three-year term as the owner of an aircraft manufacturing plant. To Lawrence Weinberg and probably to other Jewish builders, the pure entrepreneurship of construction was most appealing. Unlike the high integration of skills needed in a factory, in the construction field he could control every step of the operation without unwanted dependence on expert employees.[43]

During the later 1950's, with the satiation of the post-World War II housing famine, builders began to find the market more competitive in attracting the home buyer. Research enterprises began to appear on the scene to investigate for the prudent entrepreneur the wishes and motivations of his prospective buyers before he committed himself to blueprints. The Sanford Goodkin Research Corporation prospered by providing such novel special services.[44]

Other Jewish entrepreneurs derived their business from construction. Building supply underlay the prosperity of an older firm, the Familian Pipe and Supply Company, which remained from its beginning a business owned and operated by David Familian (1883-1946) and two of his sons, George and Isidore. From its low point in 1934 the firm had become a far-flung manufacturing and jobbing complex, reaping rich rewards for its earlier liberality in supplying new accounts during sellers' market. The Familian firm did a huge business while remaining wholly owned by the family.[45]

Another old firm scored important gains during this period. Reuben and Lester Finkelstein, long successful in the scrap metal business founded by their grandfather, realized their delayed ambition to produce steel. Their Southwest Steel Rolling Mills, supplied with scrap by the old Finkelstein Supply Corporation, grew to employ 500 men. Like the Familian firm, it was wholly owned by the family. Notwithstanding its considerable size, Southwest was small alongside the colossi of the American steel industry who were its competitors.[46] Much of the same could be said of another family firm, Harvey Aluminum, Inc., founded by Leo Harvey in 1914 as the Harvey Machinery Company. As a primary producer of aluminum and major supplier of titanium and special alloys and metals, with holdings abroad, it employed 6,000 persons and did a $146,000,000 business by the late 1960's.

Late in the 1950's it was estimated that perhaps 20% of southern California's home builders were Jews, but that their share of the market was more than twice that proportion. Only in commercial building was the proportion of Jews among builders 15% or less. Half of the builders of shopping centers were Jews—perhaps not surprisingly, in view of Jewish prominence in retail trade.[47] Jewish businessmen played a noteworthy role in developing southern California's chains of retail supermarkets. Theodore Cummings' Food Giant Markets, with 85 units, was the largest, and Joseph Goldstein's Boys Markets was second in size with 33 units. Other sizable chains were also built up by Jewish businessmen.

Other Jewish entrepreneurs specialized in the finance and mortgage field of construction. For many years the Union Bank, founded long before by Kaspare Cohn and conducted for many years by his son-in-law Ben R. Meyer, had been Los Angeles' "Jewish bank." A considerable number of its officers and directors were Jews. Small Jewish entrepreneurs banked and sought credit there in large numbers and remained customers after they became substantial businessmen. The "Jewish bank" expanded rapidly during the 1950's, entering branch and regional banking and becoming the thirtieth in size in the country.[48] Late in the 1950's a significant trend was noted as Jewish builders began to invest their substantial capital in new banks and in savings and loan associations.[49]

The Jewish builder replaced the Jewish film magnate as the entrepreneur par excellence. Just as films were no longer central to the economy of southern California, so the Jewish segment of that industry was no longer the financial pinwheel of Jewish communal effort. The importance of the builder within the Jewish community is suggested by his trade's increased proportion among the business categories of the United Jewish Welfare Fund. His contribution to funds raised rose from between 6% and 7% in 1944 to approximately 19% one decade later, and showed no sign of decrease during the later 1950's.[50]

In producing consumer goods such as garments and furniture and certain foods, Jews continued to play an important role. The clothing industry in southern California, which specialized in sportswear, was largely run by Jewish businessmen, who produced the informal "California designs" which Los Angelenos desired in their garments. They carved out a nationwide market against hard competition from New York City. In 1947 the 1,276 garment-making shops in the city employed 33,000 workers and sold much of their $145,000,000 product east of the Rockies.[51] During the decade after World War II the industry expanded considerably but without using the sub-contracting system typical of the New York City center. In 1954 there were 2,189 garment production units in the Los Angeles area which employed 55,000 persons to produce an annual product valued at $279,000,000. However, succeeding years witnessed a contraction of the industry, to judge from United States Census figures.[52] Los Angeles' garment industry remained heavily Jewish in entrepreneurship, design, and merchandising. Max Factor & Company produced a kind of "garment" which grew to a far-flung cosmetics empire. Beginning as a little cosmetics and hair goods shop in 1910, it originated make-up for films and produced important, widely imitated innovations in its field. The enterprise, with sales in excess of $100,000,000 yearly, remained under the control of the Factor family and their Firestein in-laws.

A consumer commodity of the "hard" variety, furniture, occupied numerous Jewish entrepreneurs, both as merchants and manufacturers. Finally, the food trades were furnishing livelihoods for a host of Jewish merchants and wholesalers. There were, of course, many smaller and larger Jewish groceries, bakeries, and liquor and tobacco stores.[53] Above the retail level stood wholesale houses, an example of which was the Westco firm—the West Coast Bakery Supply Company, owned by the Ziegler family. From modest beginnings during the 1930's selling supplies to individual bakeries, Westco burgeoned into the region's largest wholesale manufacturer and distributor of bakery products. Like many Jewish counterparts in other fields, Westco remained a wholly family enterprise: founded by a father, greatly expanded by sons, and gradually inherited by grandsons trained in the business. The firm's resourcefulness had to withstand the entry into the trade of national firms, through mergers and holding arrangements.[54] Jews were also very prominent as wholesalers and distributors of produce, liquor, candy, tobacco, and dairy products.

These areas of independent business had always beckoned Jews, but only after World War II was the possibility of working for banks, utilities, and large corporations taken seriously by young Jews. Earlier Jewish inclinations to eschew entry into large corporate organizations had long been reinforced by the discriminatory policies of many of these companies. In 1948 "a comparatively small number" of Jews "worked for seven large insurance companies," and about the same time Jewish bank employees were reported "very meager" in number.[55] To be sure, there was actually one large "Jewish" insurance company—the Beneficial Casualty Insurance Company, founded in 1940 by Edward D. Mitchell, Oscar Pattiz, and J. C. Earle. The firm evolved into the Beneficial Insurance Group, with Mitchell and his son Joseph N. Mitchell its principal officers. Both father and son were prominent in Jewish communal and philanthropic affairs. The economic boom and labor shortage, not to mention Jewish communal efforts, helped to open many almost closed areas. Now there was "significant evidence of progress" in bank employment, and promise of fair employment policies was reported from fields so disparate as aircraft, accounting, printing, retail automobile dealers, insurance, large law firms, and others. Sometimes there was more openness in principle than employment in practice, for such industries as steel and public utilities still showed "lack of gravitation" by Jews.[56] Notwithstanding these successes for democratic principles, from which other disadvantaged groups would also benefit, the Jewish occupational thrust continued toward the professions and independent business.

CHAPTER 15

Equal Rights and Their Diffusion

THE WAR'S END ushered in a period of hesitancy concerning the status of Los Angeles Jews. Wartime unity had made the struggle for equality and against bigotry one "in which we stand side by side with the overwhelming majority of our fellow Americans,"[1] but depression and social tension were expected once peace came. From the communal forum where the hopeful words above were spoken in 1943, a respected leader foresaw early in 1945 the possibility of renascent anti-Semitism. Were that to befall the Jewish community, it might "again have to look after the interests of Jewish aspirants for jobs when the employment market becomes less demanding and discrimination becomes serious."[2] Los Angeles Jewry tensed for an expected revival of anti-Semitism. No authoritative person expected the easy transition to peace which actually happened.

Jewish participation in the civic and public life of the city continued to remain limited, at least in comparison with some cities back east. Los Angeles had a vast civic agenda when World War II ended. The city's wartime experience showed that the most serious problem to be faced was that of relations between the strata of its population. Civic resources were perilously underdeveloped. Jews contributed beyond measure to the bodies which strove for better relations among the peoples of Los Angeles.

It seemed somewhat an issue whether Jewish energies should not be devoted more to civic purposes than to Jewish communal effort. The view was heard that Jewish organizations "are so wrapped up" that the Jews fail to take "a proper role in matters affecting the political, social and philanthropic life of the community in general." It was even argued that the Jewish community "has erected around itself a wall which insulates it and cuts it off." In disagreeing, others contended that "our Jewish community has been an effective bridge whereby the Jewish population has become integrated in and assumed leadership in the general civic and philanthropic life of our city."³ Many activities of the Jewish community had little to do directly with the broader reaches of Los Angeles society, and thousands of Jews preferred to "specialize" in such affairs. Others, however, contributed directly and invaluably to the political and social health of the city. Some prominent local Jews expressed concern in 1958 that Jews were not rapidly entering the social openings which had occurred during the preceding decade. "Jewish participation is welcome in the Philharmonic Society, the Hollywood Bowl group, and others, but ... a very few Jews have shown an interest in these groups. Furthermore, some of the Jewish people who have been drawn in have not taken a role sufficiently active to warrant their continuation as board members, etc." To a former Chicagoan, the contrast with his old home made this abstention particularly apparent.⁴ The opportunity for Jews to render this type of civic service and philanthropy had come so recently that not many were prepared for it.

While such Los Angeles Jews as Isaac Pacht, Stanley Mosk, and Ben Rosenthal reached prominence in state affairs by 1945, local politics promised little; no Jew had even run for municipal office on a major party ticket for years. However, Jews filled numerous judgeships. Following the death of Harry A. Hollzer early in 1946, Leon Yankwich was the sole Jewish incumbent on the federal bench. At the state and municipal level, Jews like Pacht, Lester Roth, David Coleman, Benjamin J. Scheinman, and Lewis Drucker served as judges. In comparison with the limited openings for Jews, even less place in municipal politics was found for the disadvantaged Mexicans, Negroes, and Orientals. Allegedly even "the favorable treatment which Jews receive in the Los Angeles press and public life [ca. 1945] comes at a price. Before elections, quiet, informal conferences between Jewish leaders and politicians are held. The politicians are not noted for liberalism; concessions are made to the Jews in return for political support of some measure that they would be inclined to oppose."⁵ Such "conferences" may be dubious, but candidates did seek out prominent Jews who supposedly could "deliver the Jewish vote."

When after the conclusion of World War II the cold war became central in American life, a fresh canard expressed the old hatred. Now "the most dangerous situation at the present time [1947] is the growth of the belief that Communism and Judaism [are] synonymous."[6] Little help came from the comment of the egregious Rabbi Benjamin Schultz before a House of Representatives Sub-Committee on Un-American Activities, that Los Angeles Jewry was not energetic enough in rooting Communism from its midst.[7] In October 1950, three months after the American intervention in Korea began to generate the highest tensions of the post–World War II period, Jewish consensus reported "an increasing tendency in recent months to associate Jews with Communism . . . experienced . . . within various organizations, such as veterans' groups, the County Medical Association and others." Admittedly its extent was difficult for Jews to measure.[8] Besides, Communism was defined so fantastically that anything new or "foreign" or unwontedly intellectual could fit, and thus add another target for anti-Semitic attack by twisted minds. Public education, vulnerable to inquisitorial questioning, fell victim. In 1951 and for years following, many attacks on education were anti-Semitic in nature, and elections to the Board of Education became the occasion of extremist attacks and bitter contests. Together with their energetic sponsorship of intercultural education concerning racial and ethnic groups, Jewish agencies had constantly to combat vigilante proposals for "citizen" screening of school textbooks to insure their freedom from "subversive" content. A rather incredible uproar was generated by the "discovery" in the schools' curriculum of materials issued by the United Nations Educational, Scientific and Cultural Organization (UNESCO). The prominence of Jewish agencies and individuals in championing educational autonomy and the teaching of world understanding subjected them to bitter attacks, not all of which were untinged by anti-Semitism.[9]

Openly anti-Semitic agitators continued, heedless of the Nazi downfall, each with his minor following. The notorious "Christian" anti-Semite Gerald L. K. Smith was active in the Los Angeles area, preferring for a time to stress his equation of "sinful" Hollywood with American Jewry. The "youthful and 'typical American'" countenances which appeared at one of his mass meetings in 1951 caused concern because they differed markedly from his weather-beaten clientele.[10] More active than the itinerant Gerald L. K. Smith was his "unofficial representative on the west coast," Wesley Swift. This glib, forceful agitator's platform was his "Anglo-Saxon Christian Congregation" and a quasi-religious group called "Great Pyramids," alongside a "Voice of Arabia." Other professional anti-Semites were just as unsavory. All more or less combined ancient anti-Semitic motifs with newer ones, equating Zionism and Communism, and the United Nations with both. In angry, noisy circles they and their few hundred followers awaited better days, which fortunately never came.

The presidential campaign of 1952 in Los Angeles was flecked with nastiness, although "references to race and religion were more subtle in most instances, and were rumored rather than openly stated."[11] During the bitterly controversial election, southern California was "flooded with rumors to the effect that Senator Nixon [candidate for vice-president] is an anti-Semite."[12] Anti-Semitism was intimately allied in southern California with some of the wild-eyed anti-Communism which flourished during the later presidency of Truman and the earlier years of Eisenhower. Under the embittered conditions of 1952 a hero of anti-Communists, like Nixon, could easily be tarred as an anti-Semite, notwithstanding knowledge to the contrary and repudiation of the charge by official Jewish sources. Fundamentalist anti-Semitism sometimes found expression in a ranting anti-Israelism. Stock tirades combined the hoary motifs of Jews and accursed Christ-killers, a perilous international element, and usurers. Thus, the "illicit" state of Israel, instrument of international Jewry, would drag America into war for the profits to be reaped by the Jews. Ostentatious concern for the Arab refugees was added, more or less as an afterthought. The Reverend James W. Fifield, Los Angeles' most conspicuous Congregationalist, sometimes played on these themes in muted tones when he preached in his huge church and to a faithful radio audience. He often denied ill intent, and reportedly he occasionally repented of his unpleasant performances. Jewish and liberal Protestant spokesmen replied to Fifield on the air, but he remained a thorn in the side of Los Angeles Jewry and liberal religionists.[13]

Notwithstanding Fifield, the struggle to found the Jewish state was generally regarded with favor locally, as it was in America generally. From the standpoint of local Jewish interests, there were touchy moments during these years. A British consul made some dubious remarks in 1947, while, at the other extreme, statements from Israel calling for mass American Jewish settlement disconcerted some.[14] The deep psychological meaning of the state of Israel for American Jews was warmly recognized: "What it does, or fails to do, will reflect upon us. Its existence and the fight to maintain itself has given Jews more self-respect and encouraged the respect for us of our non-Jewish neighbor."[15]

Jewish status was linked with the status of minority groups within Los Angeles. Alongside the 168,000 Jews in Los Angeles in 1946, an estimated 200,000 Negroes and 235,000 Mexicans, as well as 5,000 Chinese and 12,000 Japanese lived in the city.[16] Notwithstanding wide differences in status between these minorities, their leaders implicitly recognized common interests among them. The intensive organization of the Jews and their better economic position placed them at the head of the minority groups. Jews broadly aided local bodies which labored in these fields, such as the Pacific Coast Council on Intercultural Relations and the Community Relations Conference. The County Commission on Human Relations, an official body, and Mayor Fletcher Bowron's Human Relations Committee had their genesis in the example of these private organizations and in prolonged efforts by Jews and their allies.

Jewish relations with the religious denominations in Los Angeles displayed marked variations. Among the differences between the religious picture in Los Angeles and other American cities of major Jewish settlement was the prominence of fundamentalists, ensconced in independent churches. Jewish relations with them were unsatisfactory. Fundamentalists were most influenced by ancient mythology about Jews and quite resistant to the social gospel which penetrated much of American Protestantism. More pleasant were Jewish associations with the city's liberal Protestant denominations, with whom Jews frequently collaborated for common goals of social peace and improvement. Roman Catholics, in the smallest minority their faith showed in any major metropolis, were prevailingly liberal during the reign of Archbishop Cantwell. In the years following, however, the archdiocese turned its interests to internal institutional development, pursuing a line of political and social conservatism and aloofness from interreligious activity.

Similar to the varied connections between Jews and Christian denominations were the differences in relations between Jews and Los Angeles' ethnic groups. Although Jewish voices were heard no louder than others in defending the Californians of Japanese ancestry who were shut away in internment camps during World War II, relations between Japanese and Jews exhibited conspicuous warmth for years thereafter. The Nisei reportedly felt that Jews especially had befriended them with moral and material aid during the hardships of their resettlement and had helped in securing their indemnification.[17] Jewish assistance meant much at this time, for the younger Japanese generation was undergoing the difficult stages of quitting such traditional ethnic occupations as truck gardening and flowers in favor of business and the professions.

Los Angeles' 235,000 Mexicans, who formed its largest minority, dwelled among the Jews in Boyle Heights and City Terrace and slowly predominated in these areas. Notwithstanding the memory of notorious wartime race riots, good relations subsisted between these two very disparate groups. Jews led and openhandedly financed the organizations which sought to repair the damage after wartime race riots and to prevent recurrences. They also assisted the local Mexicans to organize communally and secure political recognition through the County Conference on Human Relations, the Council on Civic Unity, and other groups. As the vicinity of the Soto-Michigan Center in Boyle Heights gradually filled with Mexicans, the Jewish institution's doors opened to them and its programs reflected, however superficially, some of their interests.[18] It was the meeting ground for the Hollenbeck Youth Council, in which Negro, Jewish, and Mexican adolescents came together for frank discussion and youth activities.[19]

The ceaseless flow of Negroes out of the South reached the Far West in such dimensions that the Negro population of Los Angeles, which stood at 171,000 in 1950, grew to 461,000 in 1960.[20] Jews had Negroes as near neighbors in Boyle Heights and City Terrace in the 1940's, and during the following decade in West Adams as well. At heart, the Negroes' needs were those of the Jews immeasurably multiplied: housing, jobs and opportunities for economic advancement, and a modicum of social acceptance. Lacking a business class and residing in faded Jewish areas, they bought largely from Jewish stores and often worked for Jewish employers. In addition, many Jewish households were served by Negro domestics.

Negro bodies, including the Los Angeles branch of the National Association for the Advancement of Colored People, which sought to strengthen the Negro's rights, were aided by Jewish organizations and those heavily supported by Jews. Negroes and Jews steadily collaborated in common causes. Thus, in the agitation which began about 1950 for a local fair employment practices law, Jews were leaders in stirring labor and liberal groups into action, in countering objections, and in steering the legislation through.[21] Far more important to Negroes than to Jews was the acquisition of equal rights in the Los Angeles County Housing Authority's developments. Mainly through the efforts of the local American Jewish Committee, which visited the Housing Authority and simply cited law and public policy, the practice of segregation in public housing was abandoned. Then it was arranged for several qualified Negroes to apply for admission to previously segregated projects, in which few, if any, Jews ever dwelled.[22] Prolonged efforts by Jews, among others, also secured the admittance of the first Negro lawyer to the Los Angeles Bar Association in 1950.

As helpful as such efforts proved, several areas of Negro-Jewish friction persisted. Jewish businesses founded in areas once Jewish, and remaining to serve the Negro inhabitants, were assailed for charging unduly high prices and employing Negroes in menial jobs only. Educational efforts were needed on both sides, and on the Jewish side there could be a sharp word from influential communal sources to some Jewish offenders. Resentment of dependence on Jewish aid welled up in the claim that "the Jews come to us only when there is a mutuality of interest!"[23] Although the leadership of the Negro group, as far as it was stable, valued Jewish aid highly, there was "a small 'activist' chauvinistic clique who believe that only independent . . . [Negro] action can be productive. Further, the organized Jewish community is held in distrust and suspicion by this segment . . . and there are reports of anti-Semitic statements attributed to these leaders. . . . the anti-Jewish community . . . clique has attracted a limited following" in certain Negro organizations.[24] Yet they complained when the " 'great wealth' " of the Jews was not freely available for their cause. It was even claimed that "if the Jews would give the Negroes the money to finance their own agencies properly, there would be no other role for the Jewish community to play."[25] Jewish communal facilities, including hospitals, centers, free loan, and vocational counseling, were open to Negroes.

Mexican-Oriental-Negro-Jewish mutuality of interest placed such problems as discrimination in housing and employment in the

framework not of "Jewish interests" but of human rights. Contrary
to Jewish forebodings at the end of World War II, there was neither
a general depression nor severe anti-Jewish discrimination accom-
panying it. "When economic difficulties develop, there will be
discrimination. . . . We have been instrumental in developing a better
relationship. We have broken down certain barriers that existed."[26]
Nevertheless, areas of remorseless discrimination remained at both
the higher and humbler levels of economic opportunity. Thus, the
outlook for the aspiring Jewish physician was bleak: of two medical
schools in the city in 1948, one would take no Jews and the other
had a *numerus clausus*. Moreover, during the seven years ending
in 1949, one of 323 internships in private hospitals went to a Jew.
Residencies were particularly difficult to obtain, even in public
hospitals. Since established physicians administered these policies
in league with bigoted hospital administrators, the medical societies of Los Angeles were, predictably, anti-Semitic.[27] Under the
circumstances, the Jewish Cedars of Lebanon and Mount Sinai
hospitals had the necessary though medically irrelevant function of
providing facilities for internship and advanced training to victims
of medical anti-Semitism. The Jewish physicians who used "exqui-
site judgment" to improve matters from within had their hand at last
strengthened by Los Angeles' severe shortage of medical service.[28]

At the level of securing jobs, extensive discrimination existed during the late 1940's despite reported improvements. Thus, seven
large insurance companies excused their practices with the statement that they did not employ "too many of any one group." The
employment of Jews by banks was also very meager. Many private
(but not public) employment agencies "will not entertain applications from Jewish applicants because they cannot place them."[29]
When prodded by the Jewish Personnel Relations Bureau (a department of the Jewish Community Council) and other sources, some
discriminating firms changed, but others refused. The refusal might
be devious ("Jews would not feel at home amongst the other employees") or blunt ("I shall continue my present policy"), but the
outcome was the same.[30] Long after Los Angeles' boom years began,
there remained "a number of areas . . . from which Jews are excluded . . . particularly from the top echelon." One could point to
"whole industries, for example, petroleum refining, insurance, finance,

mining, some heavy manufacturing in which Jews either have no access at all even at the lower levels, or if they do get in they simply do not rise. . . . [Yet] things on the whole are improving."[31]

It was most embarrassing to encounter occasional Jewish employers who discriminated against Jews. Overpowering pressure might be applied to small men, but communal offices were at a loss to proceed when complaints of discriminatory practices at one of the foremost Jewish studios in Hollywood were verified. More subversive of communal efforts were the Jewish builders who violated equal housing rights. The Jewish Community Council reaffirmed a resolution condemning discrimination in both employment and housing.[32] On the other hand, the moral consistency of the campaign against the exclusion of Jews from elite social and business clubs was established by opening the Hillcrest, the elite Jewish club, to Gentiles. Although done "with the implication that other clubs which are closed to Jews might similarly act,"[33] this gesture produced no further result in a decade than that "some of the segregated non-Jewish clubs take in a few token Jewish members."[34]

This polite anti-Semitic subsurface not surprisingly brought forth occasional specimens of open, crass anti-Semitism. Thus, State Senator Jack B. Tenney, chairman of the California Senate's Fact-Finding Committee on Un-American Activities, who yearly increased his notoriety with the unfairness and irresponsibility of his procedures, turned on Jewish institutions with an attack in 1948 on "Communism" at the Jewish Center Association's Soto-Michigan Center and upon members of its staff in particular.[35] Although the charges—made without a word of inquiry or rebuttal permitted the accused—were demonstrated to be false, another example was provided of the Jew-Communist link. Highly disturbing for their source were inflammatory leaflets distributed during a college student election, caricaturing the opposing side's Jewish candidates and accusing them of "radicalism." The erection of "Americanism" versus "Jewish" radicalism worried college as well as Jewish sources.[36]

The educational problem par excellence, however, was the issue of religion in the public schools. It could reach an extreme such as occurred late in the 1950's, when a board of education in the metropolitan area which banned nativity plays and New Testament readings was subjected to anti-Semitic abuse at a Parent-Teachers

Association meeting. Hearteningly enough, 250 citizens in turn denounced these displays of anti-Semitism and prejudice.[37]

Religion in the public schools remained a matter of utmost sensitivity and nowhere approached solution. Within Jewish communal circles there was no unanimous opinion concerning the place of religion in the public schools. The released time program, which permitted school children to be dismissed an hour earlier once weekly to receive religious training, was strongly opposed. Reportedly, 1,500 Jews at most exercised this option. In 1949 the Jewish community withdrew from this program and began to consider a constitutional test, which, however, was not attempted.[38] The "annual December dilemma" also perplexed and divided Jewish opinion. All were against strongly Christian observances in the schools, but vigor of opposition tended to decline as the observance became less sectarian. Some Jews argued that Christmas observance in the schools in one or another form was unavoidable, and that the task was to make it interdenominational or "intercultural" and perhaps accept the observance of Hanukkah as sort of *quid pro quo.* The organized Jewish community looked with disfavor upon both Christmas and Hanukkah in the schools. Realizing, however, the deep cultural basis of Christmas observance, as well as the precautions taken by school administrators to respect non-Christian sensitivities, it declined to combat these school festivities outright.[39]

The proposed introduction of "moral and religious values" as a nonsectarian part of the school curriculum met with Jewish disfavor. The values themselves could not be impugned, but this inculcation would take place in an inevitably Christian environment. Nor was it expected that "moral and spiritual values" represented the last word in religious faith that its proponents desired to inculcate through the schools. Throughout the 1950's Jews stood against using Los Angeles' public schools to fulfill the moral and religious responsibilities of the homes and churches.

CHAPTER 16

Education for Life and Judaism

———————————————— ✦ ————————————————

No DIFFERENTLY from the great masses of other children in the city, Jewish youth attended the public schools of Los Angeles. They, too, underwent the difficulties of local expansion, both of teachers and school plant, and the indirect effects of the sometimes violent politics which inflamed the educational scene.[1] Jewish interests as such hardly existed in public schooling. While the Jewish community more or less actively opposed sectarian religious infringements in the public schools, it did so more on constitutional grounds than from a feeling that its young were being psychologically harmed. Minor issues like the opening of a school semester on the Jewish New Year were harmoniously resolved.

Owing to Jewish neighborhood concentrations, certain public schools inevitably were heavily Jewish. Since school policies permitted transfers from other districts, some Jewish parents, evidently anxious that their adolescent children develop Jewish friendships, employed their transfer rights quite vigorously. They also feared the situation reported among the few Jewish public school children in an outlying area, "where they are always being *taunted* because they are Jewish."[2] Other parents, preferring their children to be educated in a more mixed school environment, employed transfers in the contrary direction.[3]

The Jewish student's urge to attend college was as notable in Los Angeles as elsewhere. While Jews formed perhaps 8% of the population and probably were proportionately even fewer in the college age strata, they were rather disproportionate among Los Angeles' college students. The number of Jewish college students continued to ascend while their proportion in the student bodies declined— testimony, perhaps, to the increasing popularity of college study. In 1953, 5,800 Jews could be found among the more than 46,000 students in attendance at Los Angeles colleges and universities. At UCLA 1,800 Jewish students were enrolled, compared with 2,400 at the more vocational Los Angeles City College. The University of

Southern California, where substantial tuition had to be paid, had 900 Jewish students, a disproportionately low 8.4% compared with virtually 13% at UCLA. In addition to local colleges, an indeterminate number of Los Angeles Jewry's sons and daughters studied at other branches of the vast University of California, at Stanford, and at many other schools reaching east to the Ivy League.

The Jewish community of Los Angeles maintained the Jewish segment of the University Religious Conference at UCLA, a campus institution which contained separate but cooperative accommodations for the religious bodies. Film magnates, particularly Sol Lesser and the Warner brothers, subsidized and took a benign interest in this institution, whose founders included Judge Hollzer and Rabbi Magnin. The B'nai B'rith Hillel Foundations, which functioned within this framework as they did at most American universities, carried on its ramified program of social, cultural, and religious activities. Their best efforts did not always arouse the interest of Jewish students, but the mood of the 1950's reportedly brought changes. Now it was informally found that "the hostility toward Jewish life which once characterized the attitude of Jewish students has lessened, although it by no means has disappeared. . . . In numerous cases it has been found that students have begun to accept their Judaism but are still asking, 'Where do we go from here?'"[4] Later in the 1950's, the role of the Jewish community in assisting the establishment of a distinguished Department of Near Eastern Languages at UCLA was a step of educational importance to the university as well as to Jews.[5]

General education involved virtually all Jews but was of marginal concern to the Jewish community. Jewish education, however, fell exclusively within the Jewish province, and was widespread but superficial in Los Angeles. The great majority of Jewish adult men and women had had some exposure to Jewish education, ranging from a Reform Sunday school to a European talmudic yeshiva. Overwhelming majorities of Jews held that Jewish children "should" or "must" have Jewish education, and sponsorship of Jewish education ranked first in their estimation of Jewish communal responsibilities.[6] The reality of the Jewish schools, however, was often dissatisfying. The prevalent form of Jewish education was the Sunday school, a fine example of which was provided by the Wilshire Boulevard Temple School. Less in evidence was the weekday school, meeting on two or more days after public school; these were Hebrew schools, generally conducted in a Zionist and religious spirit, and Yiddish schools, largely secular in outlook and politically to the left. The Orthodox day school, or elementary yeshiva, gave a complete education: to this full-time private school some were "opposed in principle . . . because it was opposed to the American concept and therefore should not be supported by the community."[7]

As the number of children in the city grew, so did enrollment in the Jewish schools. However, the proportionate distribution among the types of school changed little, as may be seen from figures compiled by the Bureau of Jewish Education:

	1947	1951	1956
Sunday schools	2,815	5,631	10,618
Hebrew weekday	1,751	2,951	3,916
Yiddish weekday	742	597	203
Kindergarten Yiddish & Hebrew	337	461	282
All day	134	261	256
Released Time	1,300	abolished	abolished
Unaffiliated[8]	1,565		ca. 4,600

As the figures confirm, the two- or three-hour session on Sunday was the prevalent form of Jewish education. Most Sunday schools were conducted by Reform Temples, but Conservative and even some Orthodox synagogues maintained them. Well into the 1940's Hebrew weekday schools were maintained by neighborhood groups, principally in the older areas of the city. As Boyle Heights and City Terrace lost their Jewish residents, Hebrew weekday schools also declined. New schools in new areas were usually connected with congregations. The Conservatives, in keeping with their country-wide trend, slowly shifted from Sunday school to weekday education in their synagogues' schools.

The schools where Yiddish was taught suffered the most drastic decline, even when the addition is made of approximately six hundred youngsters in the "Progressive" (formerly International Workers Order–Jewish Peoples Fraternal Order) Jewish schools. The latter taught little Yiddish, to be sure, and no Hebrew, and had the political overtone of their parent body.[9] The establishment in 1955 of a Los Angeles Committee for Jewish Secular Education to awaken "the old enthusiasm" led to few concrete results.[10] Still, a rather substantial number of Los Angeles Jews desired Jewish education for their children in a secular spirit, although not in Yiddish. The Hebrew schools in the Jewish Centers served these "parents who want a broad cultural education for their children not identified with a particular religious ideology," and were traditional and Zionist. Their "broad generalized program [was] not provided for elsewhere."[11]

In the close environment of a Boyle Heights or a Beverly-Fairfax, Jewish education was likely to be conceived in terms of specific knowledge and articulate values to be inculcated in the Jewish young, or as an affirmation of ethnic identification. In new areas, or where Jews formed a small minority, Jewish education was sooner expected to furnish that primary "sense of belonging" which even the streets and stores could provide in denser districts. "We moved here from Cleveland last August and . . . although my husband and I have never taken an active part in Jewish organizations we feel that our daughter should be given the chance to associate with her own people in school life."[12]

Educational leaders formulated their objectives rather differently, to be sure. A Reform Sunday school emphasized as its "first aim . . . to develop within your child a growing feeling of being 'at home' in his Jewish religion." Further: "We want him to feel the meaning of being part of the Jewish people in relation to all mankind. We want him to understand the religious ideas and ideals of our Jewish heritage so that he may have a storehouse from which he may develop his own philosophy of life." This program, undoubtedly reflecting the wishes of parents as well as Reform Jewish philosophy, emphasized the pleasant, the "creative," and the group experience.[13] The Conservative aim, in opposition to the secular Jewishness of the Yiddish group and in contrast to the more humanistic and subjective religion taught at the Reform Temple, had a more traditional bent. Children were to achieve "a working knowledge of modern Hebrew, an adequate background in Jewish History, Customs, Ceremonies, and Ethics." The goal was to enable the youth "to take his place in the traditional Jewish community."[14]

These varied—at points conflicting—goals were difficult to achieve under the best circumstances. But in Los Angeles during the 1940's and 1950's they labored under the handicap of a crippling shortage of competent teachers and educators. The generation of old-style melammed schoolmasters and of learned, devoted Hebraists typified by A. M. Tonnis and Moses Tolchinsky was disappearing. Qualified successors were few; the salaries were very low and the training requirements high. Public school teachers for the Sunday schools and Israeli students for the Hebrew schools were substitutes. Moreover, Jewish education, like Jewish institutional buildings, had to cope with the rapid rise and decline of Jewish neighborhoods: "There has been a breakup of large schools in the old areas; the old active workers have been lost; the new suburban schools provide less instruction due to limited facilities, transportation problems and lack of trained personnel. The standards of tuition payment, Bar Mitzvah study and personnel selection have become low."[15]

Except for the very few who attended the all-day school, the level of Jewish education in Los Angeles left its elementary graduates far from the basic knowledge of Hebrew (or, for that matter, Yiddish) which enabled them to understand the Bible, prayer book, Talmud, or any poem or story. In 1947 the Jewish Theological Seminary established a University of Judaism as its West Coast school, with a Teachers Institute as its primary branch and with many academic activities in addition. It was Los Angeles' first institution for higher Jewish studies connecting the city with a major Jewish academic center, and it built upon earlier courses arranged by the Bureau of Jewish Education and such stalwarts as Peter M. Kahn and Dr. Nathan Saltzman. With the Hebrew classics and traditionalist religion its core, the University of Judaism aimed to embrace the whole of Jewish thought and expression in its scope. It commenced a slow growth in developing a body of teachers and a Judaic intelligentsia. Another institution was the College of Jewish Studies and the Hebrew Union College, California School, opened under Reform auspices. There, the principal emphasis was placed on teacher and rabbinic training. Quite special in character was the countryside Brandeis Camp Institute near Santa Susana in Simi Valley, the creation of its imaginative director Dr. Shlomo Bardin, where a rather secular, slightly Israeli Judaism was projected in dramatic, aesthetic terms.

The canopy which covered Jewish education in Los Angeles was the Bureau of Jewish Education, a department of the Jewish Community Council supported by the United Jewish Welfare Fund. Its main development occurred in the decade of the professional direction of Dr. Samuel Dinin, who arrived from New York in 1946, with Morris Liebman and Irwin Soref his local coadjutors. The Bureau's allocations ranged between $200,000 and $300,000, depending on Fund income and its own persuasive friends, and were distributed among necessitous schools which met the established standards. Its functions of raising curricular and pedagogic standards, and of subsidies to upgrade teachers' salaries, may have been the Bureau's most important services to the welter of poorly developed schools. The Bureau also made Jewish education more attractive by its encouragement of arts and crafts, music and dance, and city-wide assemblies and contests.[16] At the close of the period of Jewish educational development late in the 1950's, the finding of a balance between Judaism and general culture required the elevation of the impoverished intellectual standards of Jewish life; this, however, waited on the painfully slow development of lower and higher Jewish education in school and community centers.

Jewishness and the Center

More Jewish by identification than by content was the Jewish center, whose history in Los Angeles, as elsewhere, reached back to the days of immigrant aid. Samuel C. Kohs had summed up and projected forward the need for a social, cultural, and recreational center for Los Angeles Jews, but his report in 1942 had to wait out the war for realization. The Jewish Centers of Los Angeles continued their activities in the meantime. At the close of the war, the Soto-Michigan Center in Boyle Heights was still the largest but was overcrowded and "extremely noisy. There [was] a problem of membership discipline." Nearby, Menorah Center's emphasis was more educational and religious, where still "Americanization programs [were] being conducted." The converted private school which served as the Beverly-Fairfax Center and the shabby store for West Adams were also inadequate and overcrowded. During the war years, however, the Jewish Centers Association was effectively reorganized, and Meyer E. Fichman came to Los Angeles to give experienced professional direction and a revivified rationale. The JCA's main communal figure was Irvin Stalmaster, formerly a judge in Nebraska. The Association struggled on two fronts during the

1940's. It had to enforce its financial autonomy within the Federation of Jewish Welfare Organizations against various measures such as close budgetary review, surveys, and capital funds campaigns.[17] The Jewish Centers Association won "complete autonomy in all areas of policy making, membership, personnel and programming for the constituent Centers" subject only to "those general regulations applicable to all constituent agencies of the Federation."[18] The modernized Center was to "be participated in by all the community, in distinction to the Settlement House which has a program conducted by a few for other people's children."[19] As such, the JCA conferred membership not only upon Federation members so designating their contributions, and other contributors, but everyone aged eighteen or over who belonged to any Center.[20] Even the constitution of the Board moved away from the Settlement House's benevolent oligarchy.[21] The most meaningful issue was the Center's search for a definition of "Jewish." In the flush of assimilative cosmopolitanism, an openly Jewish name was by no means axiomatic. President Leslie Cramer recollected in 1949: "Five years ago there was controversy in one of the Centers as to whether or not its name should have the word 'Jewish' in it, whereas today because of the emphasis, program and approach to Centers, there would hardly give rise [sic] to such discussion." It was not enough to adopt a negative policy of disallowing social activities on religious holidays.[22] Fichman, whose signal services as executive director included those of theoretician, considered that " the objective of the Center is to strengthen self-knowledge and diminish self-hate." He exalted the institution as "an expression of faith in the vitality of democracy and the value of Jewish identification and expression."[23]

Left-wing humanitarianism, some of which possessed the self-hating overtones hinted by Fichman, declined in the Jewish centers as it did elsewhere. Thanks to the metamorphosed Jewish world—in its tragic and inspiring senses—and the changed professional thinking epitomized in the Janowsky report of 1948, the Jewish Centers sought to make distinctively Jewish many elements of their program. Jewish song, dance, art, books, the Yiddish language, and holiday observances became widely employed as "program resources." Members of the staff seriously searched out a personal Jewish commitment as the Centers sought a more Jewish orientation. After the notorious episode in which State Senator Jack B.

Tenney falsely denounced the Soto-Michigan Center and its director in 1948 for Communist tendencies, a somewhat less free-for-all policy was adopted on permission for outside speakers.[24]

Jewish Centers were built, but not without bitter disappointment for some neighborhoods. West Adams Jews, long expecting a fine building to supplant their wretched accommodations, unhappily learned publicly what many knew in their hearts—that Jews had left the area and a still larger percentage were planning soon to leave, making a $500,000 building imprudent.[25] In 1952 it was voted to maintain the strongly intercultural Soto-Michigan Center and close the religio-educational Menorah Center, over the bitter opposition of many local residents.[26] Soto-Michigan's turn, however, was not long deferred. Thus were evacuated the neighborhoods of the 1930's. The new Westside Jewish Community Center, a magnificently appointed structure, rose on Olympic Boulevard in 1954, and satellite centers arose in the San Fernando Valley, Santa Monica, and the Hollywood-Los Feliz neighborhood. Ample facilities now existed to make the Jewish Centers the focus of "informal education" and "meaningful identification" for all, particularly the youthful and the elderly.

CHAPTER 17

Religious Life

—————————————————————>∺<—————————————————————

MEASURED BY THE standards applicable to Los Angeles' great boom, religion in the city likewise "boomed." Religion, however, ultimately eludes attempts at measurement, so that Los Angeles Judaism may be "measured" only with limitations. Yet everything increased numerically: synagogues and religious functionaries doubled, buildings for worship expanded in size and number, and synagogue membership soared. Approximately 24,000 to 25,000 Los Angeles Jewish households had some synagogal affiliation in 1951, if only by their acquisition of High Holiday seating. Eight years later, the number exceeded 41,000.[1]

Like the immigrants who came before them, Easterners who settled in Los Angeles sought the new in life and environment. What was old seemed fit only for discard, so that venerable forms of Judaism impressed thousands of Los Angeles Jews as unfitting to their new home. Much of Jewish life was pervaded by the "necessity" for newness. Noticeable also in Los Angeles was a negative attitude to the demands and restrictions in Jewish tradition upon Sabbath activity, foods, and the like. The hedonistic, antipuritanical bent in southern California bore down hard on the conception of Judaism as law.

Southern California's relative isolation from the religious affairs of American Jewry ended after 1945. Where Wilshire Boulevard Temple had stood in unique splendor for Reform Judaism and Sinai Temple rather less so for Conservatism, an impressive network of synagogues was grouping around the banners of the national organizations, the Union of American Hebrew Congregations and the United Synagogue. The Orthodox congregations were the most fragmented, and their Union of Orthodox Jewish Congregations remained weak.

No less a disadvantage than Los Angeles' remoteness from the eastern and middle western focuses of American Jewry was the character of its rabbinate. The incumbents in most pulpits were indeed worthy men, but as the Jewish community advanced with blinding speed to the second largest in America, the absence of rabbis distinguished as Talmudists, scholars, theologians, writers, preachers, public spokesmen, and communal consciences became glaring. Both Rabbi Edgar F. Magnin, born in 1890, and Rabbi Jacob Kohn, born in 1881, fulfilled some of these roles in their own ways, but younger men generally did not. An external reason was that most congregations were new and needed rabbis primarily as organizers and builders. Precisely because of Los Angeles' geographic remoteness and its reputation for untraditional, unscholarly Judaism, learned and intellectual rabbis as a rule showed little interest in accepting pulpits there. Quite a few pulpits within the Jewish community were still occupied by ambitious, untrained "free lancers" who assumed the title of "rabbi." Many congregations were not affiliated with any central or even local synagogal or communal body, and some were the actual property of their "rabbi." The looseness of synagogal life in Los Angeles still resembled the situation of the city's Protestant churches, of whom less than half were affiliated with any national denomination.

At the base of Jewish religious life, even when they seemed overshadowed by institutional edifices, lay personal belief and observance. Little information can be secured on this point. However, numerous testimonies indicate that relatively observant Jews from eastern communities fell away from religious meticulousness under California sunshine. On the other hand, many Jews increased their religious interests as the community solidified and synagogue membership and Jewish education for children under synagogal auspices became widespread. A profile of ritual observance in Los Angeles of 1959 showed that the majority of Jews (64.0%) were entirely nonkosher in their diet, lit candles on Hanukkah (57.1%) but not on the Sabbath (48.8%), and regularly attended a Passover Seder somewhere (65.5%).[2] While no comparison exists with any earlier decade, synagogue attendance and membership had risen during the 1950's. Significantly fewer heads of household never went to Jewish worship, and many more attended three times yearly (presumably on the High Holidays) than in earlier years. However, the proportion of more regular attendants, who had been mainly older people, decreased from 36.7% to 31.1% of the respondents. An impression prevails of a drift away from the poles of steady synagogue-going and complete abstention, toward a middle ground of High Holiday attendance.

Judaism in all of its forms did not represent the sum of religious experience for Los Angeles Jews. An indeterminate number combined their celebration, if any, of Jewish holidays with observance of some Christian holiday, notably Christmas. A "spirited discussion" once held by a group of fairly affluent younger Jews and led by a psychiatrist, concerning "the proper attitude toward celebrating Christmas," produced only the consensus that "this could be an individual matter."

All agreed that ceremonies, beauty and family action are desirable things in the home, and many held that their fondest memories related to Christmas morning and a tree. Others felt that Chanukah candles were an adequate substitute. It was agreed that a child's reaction might depend largely on how such a thing as a Christmas tree was presented. If the religious aspects were eliminated, and if the parents could genuinely avoid hostile feelings, the children would probably enjoy a tree, particularly if most of their friends had them.[3]

Profoundly syncretistic were the funerary practices in Los Angeles, whose costliness and elaboration continued throughout our period. The embalming of bodies, "visiting hours" for viewing a corpse, floral decorations, elaborate ceremonies, and above all the underlying tendency to deny unconsciously the fact of death, reached an extreme degree in Los Angeles. Jewish mortuaries advertised extensively, using waiting benches on public streets and billboards on the highways to sell their services. In all these respects, Los Angeles copied and intensified what was widespread in American Jewish life. Nor were the synagogues themselves void of syncretism so long as ceremonies like the "consecration" of newborn infants took place within their walls.

Slogans like the widely ridiculed "The family that prays together, stays together" were naïvely used to promote Jewish faith and worship. Anxiety over a social fabric loosened by affluence probably underlay that adage of the 1950's. In contrast, Charles Brown, addressing the Jewish Community Council in 1948, put Jewish self-identification foremost among the meanings of Judaism: "I suggest that you have a minimum observance in your home: light [Sabbath] candles or have a morning prayer. But do you know that today the only contact some families have with Jewish life is when they attend services during the high holidays?"—or when Palestine, Jewish charity appeals, or publicity about anti-Semitism brought about the shock of recognition.[4]

Not only did Jewish religious identification increase, as measured by the Jewish population surveys of 1951 and 1959, but affiliations shifted among the Jewish denominations. Almost one-third of the Jews in 1951 had declined to identify themselves with Orthodox, Conservative, or Reform Judaism, but eight years later the proportion declined beneath one-quarter. Orthodoxy, none too strong outside the older generation, dropped sharply from 17.1% in 1951 to 12.6% in 1959; Reform Judaism lost very slightly. It was the Conservatives who increased startlingly from 20.5% of local Jewish households in 1951 to 35.3% in 1959, or approximately from 21,340 households in 1951 to 43,188 in 1959.[5] Yet in 1957 the Conservative congregations of the area counted no more than 7,400 families. So there was a long step indeed between the sense of denominational identification and actual affiliation.[6] The gap between self-identification as Conservative Jewish and affiliation with a Conservative synagogue existed among the Orthodox and Reform as well. Very many even identified themselves from their attendance at "mushroom" synagogues on the High Holidays, when Jews were solicited to attend services sponsored for profit by one or another promoter. The Conservatives became especially militant in combating this widespread practice, and their regional president could report with satisfaction: " 'Mushrooms' were held down to a minimum of five (from a previous high of 30) with one of the most vicious offenders taking a sound financial beating when he attempted to open services in one of the [San Fernando] Valley restaurants. . . . this worthy wound up with a total of some 120 people attending. His expenses would have necessitated about 400 to break even."[7] The participation of the Community Relations Committee of the Jewish Community Council against "mushroom" worship also was enlisted, on the grounds that commercial exploitation of religious worship dishonored the Jewish community.

The least edifying aspect of religious life was the kashruth situation, especially the trade in kosher meat. In the absence of any central or impartial responsibility, a group called the Kosher Butchers Association succeeded in dominating the kosher meat market.

Those responsible for overseeing the religious aspects of kashruth, the *mashgihim* (supervisors), were employed by those whose kashruth they were to guarantee. The Jewish Community Council at the beginning of its career had sought ineffectually to establish communal control of Jewish dietary matters, and when the Kosher Butchers Association faced court action in 1952 for restraint of trade, the communal body began another promising effort. A large Kashruth Committee of the Council sought to enroll all kosher butchers under its emblem and to install independent *mashgihim*. Jewish legal aspects were entrusted to the exclusive control of an Halacha Committee of Orthodox rabbis. Yet the opponents were neither cowed nor cooperative, and for dubious reasons attacked the entire scheme as religiously unacceptable. They brought "rabbis" from elsewhere and defiantly reestablished the old system. Within two years, the Jewish Community Council's well-wrought and costly effort came to naught. Anarchy again reigned in the abattoirs and shops as the butchers continued the arbiters of the kashruth they claimed for themselves.[8] Certainly, kashruth was not much honored in the Jewish community. While 21.9% of Los Angeles Jews kept "many or some kosher observances," only 13.7% more regarded themselves as "strictly kosher." Communal institutions and Jewish public dinners were usually not kosher.[9]

The synagogues of Los Angeles had perhaps more variety than anywhere in America. Supreme in age, social position, and prominence continued the Wilshire Boulevard Temple, to which a fourth generation of members already belonged. Its rabbi, Edgar F. Magnin, continued to be rabbi par excellence in the eyes of the Christian community. Sinai Temple's veteran of the rabbinate, Jacob Kohn, won a reputation for defense of the workingman's right to organize. Rabbi Kohn became known beyond Los Angeles for significant writings which espoused a radical theological position.[10] As he aged, Sinai Temple's membership also aged, and was unreplaced by younger people. The elderly scholar's successor in the pulpit was Rabbi Israel Chodos, a powerful orator, under whose leadership the congregation moved from its Moorish edifice at Fourth and Hampshire to an extraordinary, modernist synagogue in the fashionable far western end of Wilshire Boulevard. Rabbi Max Nussbaum's Temple Israel in Hollywood was Reform, and the rabbi became prominent by his association with well-known Jewish film figures. Of greater importance was his service as a Zionist leader in Los Angeles and later on the national scene. By general acknowledgement, the Orthodox rabbinic leadership of the city was vested in Rabbi Osher Zilberstein in matters of Jewish religious practice. His leadership, which was rooted in the older piety, contrasted with that of Rabbi Simon Dolgin, a native of Chicago, who led his Beth Jacob Congregation from West Adams to Beverly Hills, and gradually to more meticulously Orthodox practice. Such a synagogue as Beth Jacob began to exemplify a middle-class American Orthodox synagogue. The habitual connection of social ascent with departure from Orthodox and even Conservative identification lost some of its prevalence. Of other Orthodox congregations, Young Israel was a branch of its national association of Orthodox synagogues, while Shaarei Tefila was descended from Rabbi Neches' Western Jewish Institute.

Aside from the established metropolitan houses of worship, many more grew up in rapidly urbanized suburbs. One of the largest, the [San Fernando] Valley Jewish Community Center, was founded in the 1930's and inched ahead until about 1948, changing its rabbinic leadership several times. Then it burst forward, reaching 745 families in 1957 under the rabbinate of Aaron M. Wise. It also boasted a substantial Hebrew school. Somewhat similar was the early experience of Southwest B'nai Zion Temple Center, in the far south of the city on Vermont Avenue from its foundation in 1909. Just after the end of World War II, the congregation recorded

a milestone in our Temple History . . . the moving of the Temple to our lots on 79th and Western. This was imperative, not only because we did not have room at the present site for the increase of our children's activities, but also because the tremendous new increase after the war of the entire Southwest area. . . .

The added population with its proportionate share of Jewish families had veered to the west and it was more favorable for all concerned to be on our Western [Avenue] lots.[11]

During the 1950's the congregation, unable to move once more, gave away all its belongings and went out of existence. Some congregations in the San Gabriel Valley remained the isolated outposts of Judaism they were before the great boom visited Los Angeles.

A particular niche was occupied by the 1,500 families of Sefardim, approximately half of whom affiliated with Sefardic organizations. The "Sefardic Community" and its Temple Tifereth Israel merged with the Sefardic Brotherhood's Temple Israel in 1959; the small Magen David Sephardic Congregation, composed of Near Eastern Jews, remained the only other non-Ashkenazi congregation in Los Angeles.[12]

Self-recognition as a Jew, rather than religious faith and practice rooted in Judaism, remained the guiding motives of Jewish life in Los Angeles. However, some congregations made earnest efforts to acquaint their people with religious principles. Thus, one Reform Temple rather revealingly depicted its conception of Judaism as practiced:

Ceremonies in religion serve to enrich our religion emotionally. We observe religious ceremonies to give color to our holidays—to *enjoy them.* If we do not enjoy our ceremonies, then we are missing their purpose. . . .

You are missing something yourself, because by not observing meaningful ceremonies you are missing an opportunity for fun and for the enjoyment of your religion. . . .

Judaism is a religion which emphasizes life in the world, living here and now. As a Jew you should be religious in order to get much more out of life today.

At the same time, much effort went into explaining how Judaism differed from Christianity and where Reform Judaism differed from Orthodoxy. Central to the whole exposition was the parental role in explaining Judaism to the child—evidently the point at which such questions began to be taken seriously in innumerable Jewish households.[13]

Thus, immense numerical increase in Los Angeles Jewry did not find a like increase in religious commitment. However, membership in one of the city's eighty-two congregations remained the most pervasive form of Jewish association. All signs seemed to point to further increase, and a few to a deeper religion.[14]

CHAPTER 18

Community within Metropolis

THROUGHOUT THE YEARS of war and expansion, the Jewish Community Council held and strengthened its position as the voice of Los Angeles Jewry. Although some deplored its predominance as indicative of the threat of a "monolithic" community, the Council was the unquestioned spokesman of Los Angeles Jewry. To be sure, the Jewish Community Council exercised its representative function sparingly, satisfied that much of its slogan *Achdus* (unity) was implemented by the Council's substantial existence. Its severest problem, against which little headway was made during the 1950's, was to gather into its fold the multitudes of newly arrived Jews and the new neighborhoods.

Communal Polity and Policy

The Jewish Community Council followed a libertarian, politically neutral direction, carefully avoiding matters which seemed irrelevant to the Jewish group as such. Thus, the voice of Los Angeles Jewry defended civil liberties against attacks by loyalty oaths, inquisitorial investigations, or proposed legislation pretending to curb Communism. However, it declined to do battle for witnesses who frequently pleaded self-incrimination. It showed special concern for the status of minorities, and hence advocated legal prohibition of discrimination in housing and employment, as well as the teaching of harmonious social relations in the schools. On the other hand, the Council not only refused to endorse candidates for public office but declined to commit itself on such matters as legislation detrimental to organized labor, for comprehensive social reform, or on causes promoted by groups tainted with Communism. In these matters, the Jewish Community Council followed the recommendations of its Community Relations Committee. Jewish communal policy adhered to a moderate liberalism, typified by Governor Earl Warren's Republicanism in California or by the Fair Deal of President Truman. While this outlook closely resembled the general disposition of American Jewry, to maintain such a position in a city prone to political extremism was by no means simple. The years of World War II featured extensive articulation of the Council's structure, with comparatively slight growth. On the other hand, the years following, between 1945 and 1950, showed the greatest physical development. The structure of the Jewish Community Council combined representative character with the United Jewish Welfare Fund as the major activity. In 1942 the Council had 156 institutional members, personified by approximately 465 representative members.[1] In addition, there were 13 members at large: the Council was wary of exercising its legal right to increase those sitting at large. Especially during the later 1940's, institutional representation grew speedily, to 303 in 1948.[2] By 1955, 433 Jewish groups had acquired institutional membership, and they sent 1,316 men and women to represent their total constituency of 120,333 members. The number of Jewish individuals represented, however, was less than half that number. The Zionists led with their 121 groups, followed by 85 synagogues and synagogal auxiliaries, with 72 B'nai B'rith lodges and chapters ranking third.[3] The great number of representatives to the Community Council did little but attend meetings three times yearly, which inevitably resembled a mass meeting rather than a deliberative body. Service upon the board and its committees was possible: during the 1940's and 1950's between 200 and 300 persons filled these positions at any one time. To link the central body of the Jewish community with its hundreds of independent groups was the main function of the institutional representatives.

The conduct of the Jewish Community Council lay with its board of directors, who were elected by membership meetings, often accompanied by vigorous electioneering, for not more than two consecutive terms of three years. The board elected the council's officers, two including the president; (later three) vice-presidents, secretary, and treasurer (at times the latter offices had two incumbents). Aaron Riche served from the Council's inception as secretary or assistant secretary and produced a mass of detailed, carefully preserved Minutes. Federal Judge Harry A. Hollzer's tenure as president continued without interruption until his death early in 1946. Following his judicial, extremely dignified conduct of the presidency came the three-year presidency of Charles Brown, a clothing merchant of warm enthusiasm and no little vision, as his addresses to the Council testify. Without formal Jewish learning, Brown had committed all the Psalms to memory in English; he was the only man not a lawyer to occupy the presidency. His successor was Judge Isaac Pacht, followed by Mendel B. Silberberg, who had rendered his greatest service as chairman of the Community Relations Committee. Judge David Coleman succeeded Silberberg. For some years, a vice-presidency was tacitly reserved for a man from motion pictures. Harry Rapf and Jacob Karp served in these capacities, but the arrangement was later allowed to lapse.

While the Jewish Community Council adhered to a policy of political liberalism and promotion of equal rights, its Jewish policies beyond the bounds of self-defense were less developed. It was a pro-Zionist body, warmly supporting Palestinian Jewry during the epochal transformation into the state of Israel and thereafter. The place of religious belief and practice within the representative body remained vague. A consensus prevailed that "the Community Council is not a religious organization and ought not to intrude in religious matters or govern itself or its functions solely by religious standards."[4] The Council was rather reluctant to observe full kashruth in its facilities or to close its offices on all Sabbaths and Jewish holidays.[5] It favored neutral, popular Jewish cultural activity. With increasing frequency, the Council sponsored Jewish pageants, concerts, art shows, and mass cultural events, frequently of Israeli derivation.

One cannot speak of parties within the Council, but groups and interests necessarily existed. Not surprisingly, the sharpest rivalries were characteristically expressed in struggles over allocations from the United Jewish Welfare Fund. Among the competing interests, that of the Zionists was the most influential, more by force of events in the Jewish world than any other reason. Most synagogues followed the Zionist lead, and B'nai B'rith and Jewish War Veterans were usually allied with them. A contrasting group within the Jewish Community Council was composed of delegations from institutions of the Federation of Jewish Welfare Organizations; to them the mass organizational techniques so effectively utilized by the Zionists were alien. The Federation's people were interested particularly in Jewish welfare institutions, and their leaders were "local minded," unlike the more "overseas minded" Zionist Council members. Groups under Communist influence also found their way into the Jewish Community Council for several years and rather futilely occupied themselves with promoting resolutions to endorse some cherished policies. Their head and front, the Jewish People's Fraternal Order, was expelled in 1951 after lengthy quasi-judicial hearings for acts detrimental to the Council.[6] The existence of competing parties and policies required consideration and choice, as well as negotiation and compromise within the Council. At no time did a group within the Jewish Community Council refuse to accept the Council's decisions or withdraw in protest. Despite shortcomings, Council deliberations were democratic and, by thrusting forward the great issues before Jewry, had far-reaching effects in creating a Jewish communal opinion.

Seven years after its formal establishment, the Community Council's array of committees included those generic to an organization, such as Membership, Program, Plan and Scope, Nominations, By-Laws Revision, Speakers Bureau, Public Relations, and Finance, Office and Personnel.[7] The Campaign and Allocations Committees oversaw that primary activity of the Council, while Youth Organization attempted to draw younger people into the communal orbit. An Arbitration Committee embodied the desire to settle intra-communal frictions out of public view. The Bureau of Passover Relief, the Bureau on Jewish Economic Problems (i.e., discrimination in employment) and the Bureau of Jewish Education functioned in addition. The latter, together with the UJWF, became the Council's most important operation. On the eve of the merger with the Federation, additional committees (aside from old ones reorganized) included two for cultural purposes—one for the Jewish Community Library and another to award a fellowship for study in Israel. Research Service and Community Planning represented systematic efforts to look ahead.

Judge Hollzer found the Council of 1944 "as nearly democratic in structure as imperfect human beings can make it."[8] Irvin Stalmaster, a founder of the expanding Jewish Centers Association, while not dissenting, emphasized the Council's need for "inclusiveness" and the "broadening" of its work and constituency.[9] World War II had just ended when a Council committee observed that "none of us [are] satisfied with the growth and development of the Community Council in fulfilling its larger purposes outside of the Welfare

Fund."[10] The Jewish Community Council engaged professional direction capable of achieving these larger purposes. After the two years' service of Maurice J. Karpf as executive director both of the Federation and the Council, Leo Gallin replaced him at the Council in 1943 for seven memorable years. The vast expansion of the United Jewish Welfare Fund and of the Council itself were engineered by Gallin. Julius Bisno, who joined the staff in 1945, and Charles Zibbell, who came in 1946, succeeded Gallin as executive director and assistant executive director respectively, when he resigned in 1950. The Council enhanced its standing and visibility by the erection of its large building at 590 North Vermont Avenue; not only were its activities housed there, but some forty major Jewish organizations leased space in "590" also, thus giving Los Angeles a virtual Jewish community headquarters without parallel in America.

The sense of newness in southern California found expression in the thinking about Jewish life expressed by Council officers. To Charles Brown, the growth of Los Angeles Jewry represented "a challenge and an effort unequalled in American Jewish history. Here there are no vested interests, here there are no sacred cows, here there is no cold hand of the past. There is an opportunity to develop new forms of Jewish communal living geared in a realistic fashion to the actual needs of the Jewish community and creating thru [sic] the democratic process of people participating in shaping their own destiny."[11] In immediate terms, he said, the Council "represents . . . speaks and acts . . . [for] the entire organized [Jewish] community of Los Angeles," particularly "in those areas in which a great majority in a community is united." Yet it "does not interfere with the autonomy" of its constituents; indeed, "that there has been no complaint" on that score is "the highest praise that the Council can receive."[12]

While the Council, resting indirectly upon a mass membership basis, could with some justice regard itself as democratic, its massive subsidiary the United Jewish Welfare Fund, intent on attracting the "big givers," had to employ other appropriate techniques. The balance between popular democracy and large-scale philanthropic giving was not easily struck. However, the rich allegedly did not have "undue influence in Council affairs," while minority control was supposed to be prevented by an alert majority and prudent constitutional provisions.[13] The horrendous example to be avoided was

New York City, "with all its lack of unity, with all of its separateness, with all of its conflicts, with all of its failure to crystallize itself into an integrated community."[14] In presenting nominations for vacancies on the board and committees of the Jewish Community Council, the responsible Nominating Committee endeavored to maintain a balance of opinion by including representatives from such "minority" groups as labor, Yiddish, and Orthodox.

The focal character of the JCC and its bodies was reinforced rather than threatened after World War II, when the Community Relations Committee's activities were overlapped by several national Jewish organizations with offices in the city. The American Jewish Congress, the Anti-Defamation League, and the American Jewish Committee were joined by the Jewish Labor Committee and the Jewish War Veterans in aiming to enhance the status of democracy and the Jews in Los Angeles. However, the Community Relations Committee, whose co-opted members included the most prominent Jews in the city, continued to be recognized as "that organization in the community which determines policy and undertakes action in the civic defense field." While the Committee would cooperate with the national organizations, and did not imply direction or interference with them, it secured their undertaking to subject their policies on the Los Angeles scene to its direction.[15] The local primacy of the Community Relations Committee stood so well as to earn commendation four years later in the MacIver Report on the conduct of Jewish public relations and defense in the United States.[16]

Central Fund Raising and Allocating

Fund raising always predominated in the Jewish Community Council's life. The United Jewish Welfare Fund's structure underwent dangerous stress in 1942, when the Motion Picture Division insisted on controlling the disposition of the funds it had raised if dissatisfied with the formula of the Allocations Committee. Film people at that time preferred local beneficiaries, although a few years later many of them became fervently "overseas minded." A plan was presented whereby a reorganized, oligarchic Campaign Committee would not only raise but allocate the Welfare Fund, giving a "local minded" group control and practically removing the Fund from the wide spectrum of opinion in the Jewish Community Council: a result anathema to the "overseas minded" and an impairment of democratic process. A vigorous fight ensued. The plan's advocates warned especially against the danger of antagonizing the film group and perhaps losing its heavy contribution. The plan was then revised in March 1942. It established the new Campaign Committee, as demanded by the motion picture elements, but left allocations to the Jewish Community Council's Allocations Committee. These, in turn, now needed approval both by the Campaign Committee and the Board of Directors.[17] The board approved this plan over an unreconciled opposition, but the by-laws needed to execute the new departure were never submitted. Perhaps the main reason for the lapse of the whole scheme was the weakening of the cause which first begot it. In 1940 the Motion Picture Division had raised $489,389, over 56% of the $863,863 raised. However, during the 1942 campaign the Motion Picture Division produced only 26% of the $613,000 raised, and for the year following the proportion was about 31%. In 1946 the industry's $1,095,000 sank to 21% of the total raised.[18] The film industry's preponderance in Los Angeles was waning, and the changed economic picture was being felt in the Jewish community. Moreover, "Hollywood" and "downtown" thinking about allocations more and more converged as World War II continued, diminishing the pressure for special influence upon allocations.

The United Jewish Welfare Fund "made" the Jewish Community Council, and never more than during the immediate post–World War II years. Urgent needs overseas culminating in the *annus mirabilis* of 1948 raised the proceeds of the Fund from $2,705,000 in 1945 to just above $10,000,000 in 1948, and the number of contributors from 32,952 to 58,108. During these years, Jewish hearts were stirred as never before by the horrors in Europe and the bravery in Palestine. To donate to the UJWF became elevated from rather routine support of "a good cause" to a deeply emotional experience. During the feverish months around the United Nations partition decision in November 1947, the declaration of the state of Israel almost six months later, and then the state's fight against its invaders, the Welfare Fund unhesitatingly borrowed $3,000,000 against its expected income.[19] Julius Fligelman, chairman of the 1948 campaign, found that the "good people of the community understand that something very big is taking place this year." Transported by enthusiasm and concern, campaign divisions made round after round of solicitation, while many individuals pledged and paid twice and three times.[20] 1948 was the greatest year of the United Jewish Welfare Fund, when 75% of funds allocated went into the coffers of the United Jewish Appeal for overseas use. But the thrill of 1948 produced a reaction. During the years following, Welfare Fund pledges declined steadily until the nadir of $4,535,000 was reached in 1954, while demands for allocations scarcely abated. Difficult debates had to follow over distributing the shrinking amounts. Some considered that "frills or luxuries are taking away money that might be used for necessities or primary needs." To them, the issue reduced to "cultural and educational activities" versus the "people who need bread and who need a roof over their heads [who] are our primary concern." The opposite side maintained that bread and shelter could come from public facilities, "but what we don't do for Jewish culture and we don't do for our youth to make a better Jewish community won't be done by anybody."[21] Some emphasized local needs, reasoning that no others could attend to them, while all of world Jewry aided in overseas endeavors; the Federation's following especially reflected this point of view. There were crosscurrents and paradoxes in thinking about Fund allocations. Many who were deeply attached to cultural effort and successfully urged the claims of the local Bureau of Jewish Education—Zionists, Hebraists, Yiddishists—were keenly "overseas minded." Jews interested mostly in defense activities for their part gradually realized that the safety and stability of the state of Israel was of central importance to Jewish status in America.[22] Thus, lines between competing interests in UJWF allocations were never clearly drawn.

Previous experience and the balance of pressures annually produced an "allocations formula," by which money was divided between funds dispatched overseas and those retained for local and national use. As a rule, United Jewish Appeal allocations suffered more from the diminished revenues than local philanthropies. The proportion sent abroad gradually sank to 55% from its 75% peak in 1948, and fell still lower when certain special adjustments were tacked on.[23] Defense agencies jockeyed for funds from the central source, threatening, and more than once organizing, a separate Joint Defense Appeal in case of unsatisfactory allocations. The

American Jewish Congress insisted to no avail on "parity" with the other defense groups.

No attempt to set standards of eligibility for the Welfare Fund succeeded in going beyond broad generalities. Even the axiomatic requirement that local fund-raising activities not be undertaken by a beneficiary was waived on rare occasions. By and large "those [funds] . . . which have the largest general appeal," with purposes which "reflect the sentiment of the contributors," were first in line. "History has a great deal to do with it," for previous beneficiaries "have a prior claim on future allocations."[24] However, "the individual givers' intentions were not necessarily the final determining factor in allocations."[25] And the Board of Directors of the Council rejected a criterion that beneficiaries must "tend to serve the broad Jewish community rather than a particular interest," by which cultural organizations were denied allocations.[26]

The early 1950's were years of deepening worry and concern as United Jewish Welfare Fund contributions—previously the symbol par excellence of Jewish feeling and communal concern—dropped annually. New Jewish population pouring into Los Angeles somehow could not be reached, even while other appeals for national and overseas Jewish purposes seemed to thrive. "We have a moral crisis," declared Julius Bisno, Executive Secretary, early in 1954. "Do Jews have to die in order to run successful campaigns so that we can exist as a viable Jewish community?"[27]

The techniques of raising the needed monies were elaborated with great skill. The progression from "big givers" to donors of smaller amounts, and from country club to trades to neighborhoods was planned with elaborate care:

Now, one of the big factors . . . is . . . that in March we ran some very successful [stag] dinners at our two country clubs . . . and these were followed by very successful luncheons for the wives of these country club members as well as some specially selected guests. . . . In order to give "green light" to these very important country club dinners we held off having kick-off meetings in many of our Trade and Neighborhood divisions. The word has gotten out that it is no longer fashionable to cut your contribution to the Welfare Fund, and, therefore, we are getting people to either give an increase or at least hold the line.[28]

Similar reports could be rendered by Campaign Chairmen of numerous smaller drives, for at its nadir the Welfare Fund received less than half of funds for Jewish purposes in Los Angeles.

As the original causes and their ardent, self-made leaders aged and cooled, the accession of new leaders illustrated sociological doctrines of routinization and bureaucratization. The Council itself feared that the prestige and representative character of its leaders was diminishing.[29] In May 1954, "a group of 30 young Jewish business and professional men, many of them sons of prominent Jewish community leaders," was organized by the Welfare Fund. Their exclusivity was preserved by restricting membership to 125. "The average member of this group is a college graduate, age 33, living in the upper middle class section of Los Angeles."[30] Their gradual assumption of command was meant to provide a stable future for the United Jewish Welfare Fund by building a bridge between the generations.

Central Community and Suburban Surge

The intense growth of Los Angeles required strenuous efforts to incorporate newer areas into the central community. Among the scores of thousands of newcomers, most felt part of their suburb or neighborhood rather than "Los Angeles." If it failed in these new suburbs, the Jewish Community Council would slowly decay. These "rapidly growing communities with little cohesion or unity," lacking a Jewish communal leadership, had already had "experience of conflict."[31] For their part, these outlying areas felt (in 1948) that "they were 'stepchildren' in the Los Angeles Jewish community."[32] They wanted the help of the Council for Jewish education and youth services in their areas, which were heavily populated with children. Thus the three hundred members of the East Los Angeles Synagogue-Center, an area removed from the centers of Jewish residence, sought funds to complete their modest Synagogue-Center and for their weekday school and center program. However, the financing of synagogues was not undertaken by any central body, while the center and school remained ineligible because they could not meet the painfully established standards of the Bureau of Jewish Education and the Jewish Centers Association.[33] It was realized that policies originally meant to establish standards were actually militating against these standards ever being established in new

Jewish districts. Capital funds for sorely needed communal buildings also lay beyond the Welfare Fund's power to bestow, so that the new suburbs could mainly expect professional guidance from "590."

The Council rejected proposals for representation of areas as such, which had not been done in any area in the older city. It vigorously opposed small-scale Jewish Community Councils, although it wished but was financially unable to provide local centers of its own. With a San Fernando Valley Council of Jewish Organizations in existence in 1953, the ideal of Jewish communal unity seemed potentially challenged. Noting that nearly the entire increase in metropolitan Jewish population was taking place in the suburbs, the Council's Community Planning Committee finally agreed in 1956 to "local coordinating councils" in the San Fernando and San Gabriel valleys. These vast areas qualified by being "so distant geographically from the central Jewish community as to make direct liaison with central services impractical"; moreover, they possessed a "demonstrated feeling of an indigenous separate community life." While unendowed with corporate existence, the local bodies would be connected with each of the Community Council's major committees.[34]

The Jewish Community Council had indifferent success in coping with the geographical expansion of Los Angeles Jewry during the 1950's. A general slowing of its momentum during the mid-1950's and a dearth of new ideas or leaders at the center was paralleled by sporadic neighborhood developments and local synagogues which absorbed the energies of both newcomers and veterans. Confidential predictions circulated that despite the "high water mark of prestige and influence in the [Jewish] community" attained by the Council, "it appears inevitable the very magnitude of a Jewish population will result in a breakdown."[35] Only apathy and local fragmentation, not a rival body, actually endangered the Jewish Community Council.

Communal Merger

The outstanding structural development in Los Angeles Jewry during the later 1950's was the reunion of the Jewish Community Council with its progenitor, the Federation of Jewish Welfare Organizations. The tens of millions of dollars raised under its aegis, its local functions in defense, education, and culture, and its very name had elevated the Council's standing beyond anything expected when it was born in 1933 as the United Jewish Community. The Council had swum bravely with the unforeseen currents of American and Jewish history. The network of hospitals, social services, institutional homes, and community centers encompassed by the Federation of Jewish Welfare Organizations had also been enlarged during the same span of time but had had little share in the spectacular events. More to the point of merger, its financial dependence upon the Community Chest—the Federation's fiscal foundation—proved gravely inadequate, and the Federation began in 1942 to turn to the Welfare Fund for subsidy. The amounts received inevitably fluctuated, but what was intended as temporary support became a large yearly grant by the United Jewish Welfare Fund.

As old antagonisms waned between the pro-Zionist "overseas minded" Jewish Community Council, with its Jewish educational interests, and the "local minded" non-Zionist leaders of the Federation, the possibility of union was entertained. Points of contact were innumerable: some men and women were members of both boards; Federation institutions had over one hundred seats on the Council; Welfare Fund monies were basic to Federation finances. The separation and rivalry between older "German" and newer "Russian" Jews, always tenuous in Los Angeles, was much weaker and less divisive. In 1948 a Council-Federation Joint Committee presented a recommendation through its chairman, Judge Lester W. Roth, that Los Angeles Jewry should have "an integrated central organization . . . which shall have departments covering all phases of Jewish communal life. . . . [it shall be] continuously representative of all points of view and not dominated by any one point of view."[36] Sources of friction brought this recommendation to naught.

The decline of the Welfare Fund from 1948 to 1956 struck the dependent Federation hard. While it was cut less drastically than overseas allocations, social services particularly required expansion to keep pace with the multiplying Jewish population. The autumn of 1954 brought a financial crisis upon the Federation, resulting in an arrangement for more Community Chest support.[37] With common financial worries now added, each side overcame misgivings to participate in a joint merger committee which conducted tactful negotiations for several years. Power issues and personal politics had to be overcome to attain the desired result. Thus, Federation loyalists feared that Council leadership and majority vote methods might subordinate local interests to overseas need, while Council sympathizers were apprehensive of unsympathetic Jews taking power in the institutions they had erected.

The Merger Committee labored three years at its intricate task under the resourceful chairmanship of the veteran of both sides, Walter S. Hilborn. The outcome was simple: the two boards were to merge for three years without replacements for either deaths or resignations. A new board of sixty members would then gradually be constituted, staggered over three years. In its maturity, twenty of the board's sixty would be elected by the Federation's twenty agencies, and twenty more by the organizations represented in the superseded Jewish Community Council. The major novelty lay in the general suffrage for the remaining twenty directors: the 35,884 persons who had contributed $10 or more to the United Jewish Welfare Fund in 1957 would elect them by mail ballot.[38]

Los Angeles Jewry thus prepared to follow the many American Jewish communities who merged during the 1950's their older philanthropic Federations with newer Community Councils. A merger was regarded as "long overdue . . . [it] will not only bring the unity for which we have striven for so many years, but will have an invigorating effect upon every aspect of local Jewish life."[39] On May 1, 1959, the two bodies became the Jewish Federation-Council of Los Angeles. The hopes for unity and coordination were formally realized; the achievement of their full possibilities awaited the tides of time.

CHAPTER 19

Epilogue

INCREASED NUMBERS and continued prosperity, with high social and economic mobility, continued to characterize the Los Angeles Jewish population during the 1960's.

As it had during the 1940's and 1950's, Los Angeles Jewry continued to augment rapidly. Of the estimated 6,800,000 persons living in Los Angeles County in 1965, about 496,000 were Jews—24% more than the 1959 figure, constituting some 7% of the area's total population and 8% to 9% of the Jewish population of the country. The Jewish increase thus kept pace with that of the county[1] and apparently continued to come from immigration rather than natural increment. Arrivals in Los Angeles, Jewish and non-Jewish, were largely from points within the United States and Canada. The only substantial new foreign influx was of Israelis—a group much different from earlier overseas immigrants. But Jewish immigrants from Cuba, North Africa, Egypt, Roumania, and elsewhere also found their way to the metropolis.

Los Angeles Jewry came to assume its rightful prominence in the affairs of the American Jewish community, which remained focused in the New York area. Instant telephone communication, and jet air travel which sped a person from New York to Los Angeles as fast as he could travel from New York to Boston one generation earlier, enabled Jewish movements and organizations to place the southern California metropolis and its vast human and financial potential near the center of their planning.

Los Angeles Jews kept the habit of dwelling near each other, even in a city on wheels. Jewish neighborhoods rose and flourished, while others declined. The greatest advance occurred in the San Fernando Valley, where the Jewish population ascended more than 70% in six years to stand around 120,000 in 1965, surpassing the older concentrations in Beverly-Fairfax, Wilshire-Fairfax, and Hollywood with their approximately 100,000 Jewish residents. Cheviot Hills, Beverlywood, and other parts of the city to the southwest accounted for nearly 79,000, while Beverly Hills, Westwood, and Brentwood stretching west towards the ocean numbered some 53,000. Thus, over 350,000 of Los Angeles' Jews could be found in four major but far-flung areas, and within them often concentrated in particular neighborhoods. These areas preferred by Jews were among the most attractive in Los Angeles and stood as witness to Jewish economic success. Like that of Los Angelenos generally, the economic standing of the Jews steadily improved, to the point where in 1964 an estimated 42% of Jewish households could report incomes in excess of $10,000. Only 22% of Jews had earned that much in 1958, and 24.5% of all Los Angelenos in 1960. The 1964 weighted mean income of all Jewish households was $11,635, ranging from a $20,311 mean in wealthy Beverly Hills and West Los Angeles to a modest $8,360 in Wilshire-Fairfax. Beyond doubt, Los Angeles Jews as a whole prospered in their undertakings even though needy, mostly elderly, Jews were in evidence in several areas. With this general prosperity and its material benefits there was no escaping the problems that vexed urban America of the 1960's, which also were to be found in Los Angeles. Thus, the city's air was cleansed of some of its pollution and the water supply assured by feats of bringing water across the desert, but the condition of vehicular traffic and the invisibility of public transportation were probably worse than anywhere in America. Most menacing was the racial problem, arising from the economic inferiority, physical isolation, and alienation from the larger society of several hundred thousand Negroes. The disastrous, nihilistic Watts riots during the summer of 1965 shocked the city and nation, but whether any far-reaching measures would be devised to improve the Negro position and prevent further outbreaks was far from certain.

Los Angeles Jewry as a whole remained strongly allied to moderate and liberal politics. Right-wing extremists, strong enough in southern California in 1960 to elect a congressman from conservative Orange County who belonged to the John Birch Society, were shunned and feared. Jews overwhelmingly supported the Kennedy candidacy in that year and, it appears, no less decisively preferred Lyndon B. Johnson in 1964.[2] Although anti-Semitism from the Right was feared, it did not openly manifest itself. A new and disturbing phenomenon was anti-Semitism on the New Left, which included some Negroes, Arab sympathizers, and political radicals. Neither the politics of backlash nor the rise of hostility to Jews in some Negro circles impelled the Jewish community to cease battling for the equality of all races.

Jews continued to serve in a variety of state and municipal offices, some of them at long last by the grace of the electorate. Stanley Mosk, long prominent in politics and a past president of the Jewish Community Council, was elected attorney general of the state in 1958. (He subsequently was elevated to the state supreme court.) In time, Los Angeles' representation at Sacramento included one Jewish state senator and two Jewish assemblymen. The city council included three Jews among its members, and more often than not Beverly Hills elected a Jew as its mayor.

The Jewish communal structure functioned smoothly and with little agitation during the 1960's. The desirable results of merging the Jewish Community Council and the Federation of Jewish Philanthropies were visible in improved administration and unity, but no new era dawned. The most important institutional change was the merger in 1961 of the two Jewish hospitals, Cedars of Lebanon and Mount Sinai, collectively known as the Los Angeles Jewish Medical Center. Major physical expansion was to be completed in the early 1970's. Gateways, founded in 1953 as an outgrowth of the Jewish Committee for Personal Service program in state mental hospitals, became during the 1960's a full-fledged Jewish mental hospital. Few beginnings were undertaken, although the Jewish Federation-Council planned to establish a department for cultural and educational affairs to include the Bureau of Jewish Education and cultural activities. To cope with the suburban vastnesses, it opened fully staffed area offices in the Bay Cities, San Fernando Valley, San Gabriel Valley, and the southern reaches of Los Angeles County. The Jewish Community Foundation, established in 1964, sought bequests and endowment gifts which it would administer for designated purposes. The nagging problem remained the United Jewish Welfare Fund's inability to rise above its annual $6,000,000, notwithstanding the success of other Jewish campaigns in Los Angeles. In 1967 the Six Day War waged by Israel suddenly skyrocketed UJWF receipts almost to $17,000,000, and it was hoped that this would establish a new "plateau" of philanthropic giving.

The synagogue sector of the Jewish community failed to expand after the promising developments of the 1950's. The rise in affiliation and membership of that decade ceased during the 1960's as the proportion of synagogue-affiliated Jewish households declined from 34% to 27%. In absolute terms, there were perhaps 1,500 new synagogue families, but about 35,000 new Jewish households. A full 36% of Los Angeles Jews described themselves as "just Jewish" in preference to Reform (22%), Conservative (32%), or Orthodox (6%) —decreases for each denomination in proportion to total Jewish population.

The Jewish educational enterprise during the 1960's generally held to its earlier gains. There had been 16,091 children enrolled in schools affiliated with the Bureau of Jewish Education in 1956, and in 1962 there were 26,055—an increase due in part to the Wilshire Boulevard Temple's educational system, the largest in the Jewish community, becoming affiliated with the Bureau. After a slight decline during the following years, in 1967 total enrollment touched 27,439, of an estimated 92,800 Jewish children aged five to fourteen living in Los Angeles. More intensive, weekday afternoon Jewish education increased much slower than the Sunday schools; the latter taught over 58% of Jewish pupils. On the other hand, the Sunday schools, which were largely Reform and also Conservative, tended to hold their youth until confirmation at age sixteen, while the afternoon Hebrew schools lost heavily from bar mitzvah "dropouts." Day school enrollment, 526 in 1960, rose to 1,021 in 1967, while Yiddish schools stood for years at the brink of extinction.[3] The main growth in more intensive Jewish education occurred in secondary and higher studies and in yeshivot. The University of Judaism and the West Coast branches of Yeshiva University and of Hebrew Union College showed measurable increases in their enrollments and curricular offerings, which included rabbinical preparation, studies in the arts, and the training of teachers for the Jewish school system. They were leading to the creation in Los Angeles of a Jewish learned class. The Department of Near Eastern Studies at UCLA, while an integral part of the university, also contributed significantly to the increase of Jewish learning.

The recreational and informal educational activities of the Jewish Centers Association continued to develop. The San Fernando Valley, where the largest Jewish population concentration was found in the late 1960's, witnessed the gradual erection of a major new Center, which raised the total in Los Angeles to seven. Summer camping was also becoming more important.

Education and positive Jewish identification were the deepest internal problems of Los Angeles Jewry, but the greatest urgency in the later 1960's lay in the peaceful establishment of racial justice. The moral and practical impossibility of any other course was fully evident to all who could see. The 510,000 Los Angeles Jews of 1968, and American Jewry, possessed sufficient experience and vision to achieve these purposes.

Nearly one hundred thirty years after the first known Jew sojourned there, one hundred twenty years after permanent settlement began, and one hundred fifteen years from the founding of Jewish life, there could be no doubt that Jews were always part of Los Angeles. Throughout the nineteenth century they had shown no hesitancy in claiming their individual roles in the city's life. As the unspoken eloquence of Harris Newmark's memoir reveals, his fellow Jews moved without hindrance or inhibition in the hectic political and commercial life of early Los Angeles.[4] Vigorous use of freedom was habitual among American Jews all over the developing West. However, Los Angeles developed differently from such metropolises of the Middle West as Chicago, St. Louis, Milwaukee, and Cleveland—in all of which Jews were also prominent from early days. It started later, especially because the urban period did not really begin until 1865, after the disasters which hastened the end of pastoral times, and frontier days did not really end before the 1880's. Throughout these first decades of urban life, Jewish and other merchants did not confine themselves to one line of business but moved with ease among a wide variety of merchandise and business methods, later including city utilities and real estate among their interests.

The same freedom and venturesome spirit is to be seen in Jews' share in politics. There were no careers in politics before the twentieth century. During the first decades of the city, therefore, when the foundations of legality and public order were often shaky, service in the town's government was a necessity for merchants whose livelihoods depended upon the effective force of organized society. This service was not time-consuming, yet often enough it was an act of physical courage. But the businessman, as we have seen, was the founder and leader of his town, unaided and unrivaled by lawyers, clergymen, or intellectuals. Later, material benefits might be reaped by the businessmen with good political connections.

The European Jews who settled in Los Angeles were largely of the German stock which settled widely throughout the United States. There was a considerable proportion of Polish Jews, even before the great East European Jewish migration to America which commenced in the 1880's. Extensive transcontinental Jewish migration to southern California, with all its unique characteristics, also belongs within the framework of the settlement of America by European Jews. On the other hand, the nature of Gentile migration from other parts of the United States to Los Angeles affected the destinies of Los Angeles Jewry and impressed upon it a character unparalleled among the urban Jewish communities in the United States. For the masses who populated the great cities of the East and Middle West were mostly, like the Jews, European arrivals— Poles, Germans, Irish, Italians, Slovaks, and many others. As did the Jews, they spoke their own languages, formed distinct neighborhoods, maintained cultural and social ties with each other and with the old country, and tended to practice distinctive trades. The adjustment of European immigrants in all these cities was the great urban problem of the late nineteenth and early twentieth century. The radical contrast between the nationwide urban scene and that of Los Angeles after 1890 profoundly influenced the position of Jews within the burgeoning metropolis of southern California. The massive immigration to Los Angeles was not of Europeans but mainly of rural and small town people out of the Middle and Central West. These were regions marked by stormy agrarian protests against new economic forces from the 1870's until the end of the nineteenth century, and their emigrants functioned in their new southern California home as a force for the preservation of the ways of life and thought of an earlier America. At a time when other large cities were becoming heavily Catholic, Los Angeles became strongly evangelical Protestant with Fundamentalist tendencies. A new social and religious tone, moralistic and puritanical, began to pervade the city, and its overtones were not hospitable to Jews.

Around the beginning of the twentieth century, the social exclusion practiced upon Jews in the East since the 1880's also made itself conspicuous in Los Angeles. Even local politics became closed to Jewish candidates to an extent seen in few other cities. The frontier struggle to establish a livable civic environment had ended, and the spirit of common effort became a memory. Economic and social lines of division became more fixed and decisive. The "differentness" of all Jews, regardless of their religiosity or individual economic or cultural status, was unmistakable. It was also enhanced by the incomplete acculturation of the Jewish immigrants who came to the city as it was filling with Middle and Central Westerners. Los Angeles' original openness and polyglot atmosphere was superseded from the 1890's through the World War II period by a narrow, provincial era, which featured evangelical uplift, often vulgarized to "boosting," and commercialized exotic regionalism. There was little for Jews to contribute to this cultural complex. The Jewish role in the development of the film industry is immeasurable, deserving a separate study. However, it took place in the Hollywood enclave and, except for individuals, it was for a long time isolated from the life of Los Angeles and its Jews.

The internal development of the Jewish community was to a great extent shaped by these outer contours. Jewish pioneers and early settlers and their children, who had always found ready acceptance, were kept out of polite society. Jewish communal institutions, where affiliation had been altogether voluntary, became burdened by the emotions of Jewish exclusion. To the old, simple reasons for associating as Jews were added the negative motives of inability to gain entry elsewhere. Immigrant Jews of recent East European origin did not expect ready admittance, but Jews of pioneer stock must have meditated bitterly on the difference between the hospitable society of their youth or their parents' lifetime and the polite but impenetrable exclusion which was now their lot. In other words, the Jews became one of Los Angeles' "minority groups" alongside the city's Mexicans, Japanese, and Negroes, while still enjoying, to be sure, a far higher material and social status than these deprived peoples. The closest Jewish similarity was with the Japanese, who likewise possessed a rich historic culture and a well-knit community for the transmission of its heritage. The Los Angeles Jews occupied a position between the Protestant Anglo-Saxon majority and the depressed minorities. Both in outward status and Jewish viewpoints, there were extensive differences between thoroughly acculturated old-timers and recent arrivals. Thus, many of the former objected to the term "community" as a description of the Jewish group, preferring to regard their Judaism as a matter of religious affiliation and philanthropy. The latter tended more to think in comprehensive terms of a Jewish neighborhood, language, and far-ranging organizational life. Jewish community life never reached the intensity it possessed in the eastern and middle western cities. The constant "newness" of most of the city's Jews inhibited institutional stability. It was, besides, harder to gather people indoors into meetings against the alluring climate—a difficulty not found in the Northeast and Great Lakes area, where most American Jews lived. Perhaps the climate and conditions of southern California also induced an easier, more pleasure-loving disposition, carrying reluctance to meet and organize. Religious piety and intellectual ferment were markedly absent during the first half of the twentieth century, a period when they were extensively found in American Jewish life. This weakness and, it would appear, the year-round sunshine and the vast geographic dispersion also prevented weekday after-school Jewish education from attaining the extensive development which did occur in more concentrated communities of deeper piety and learning and colder weather. On the other hand, Los Angeles Jewry did organize itself quite effectively in the Jewish Community Council in 1937, after four years of experimentation. The problem of central bodies was to overcome the dispersion within "the fragmented metropolis"—this was accomplished—and to secure the affiliation of the masses of recently arrived Jews, a difficult goal which eluded more than partial realization. Jewish group solidarity in Los Angeles and throughout America (in fact, the world) was most fervent at such critical times as the aftermath of World War II, the creation of the state of Israel in 1948, and that state's Six Day War in 1967.

Vision and far-sightedness marked the conduct of Jewish community relations once its horizon advanced, after about 1940, beyond the mere rebuttal of anti-Semitic slurs and the scrutiny of the activities of anti-Semites. The peculiar genius and strength of the Jewish struggle for full political and economic equality in Los Angeles and other American Jewish communities lay in its resort to basic American principles of justice and to the Bill of Rights. Not only Jews stood to benefit, but all unjustly deprived persons gained also. Backed by effective organizing and finances, the Jewish community willingly aided the city's other minorities. Late in the 1960's, however, the Negro movement displayed tendencies which strained the long-standing cooperation between them and the Jews.

The successful settlement in Los Angeles of Jews, and their sizable contribution to every aspect of the metropolis' development, stood beyond question in the 1960's. How Jewish freedom and prosperity would fare in America's troubled society had its uncertainties. A community of 510,000 souls, exceeded in size only by New York City and Tel Aviv, seemed bound ultimately to erect monuments of scholarship and thought and art for its city and its world people.

APPENDIX I

APPENDIX I

Jewish Population		General Population		
			City	County
1850		1850	1,610	3,530
1860	100[1]	1860	4,385	11,333
1870	20 families[2]	1870	5,728	15,309
		1880	11,183	33,381
1881	"136 Jews"[3]			
		1890	50,395	101,454
1900	2,500[4]	1900	102,479	170,298
1904	3,000[5]			
1907	7,000[6]			
1910	[5,795][7]	1910	319,198	507,131
1912	10,000[8]			
1917	20,000[9]			
		1920	576,673	936,455
1923	43,000[10]			
1927	65,000[11]			
		1930	1,238,048	2,208,492
1941	130,000[12]	1940	1,504,277	2,285,643
1946	168,000[13]			
1948	260,000[14]			
		1950	1,970,358	4,151,687
1951	315,000[15]			
1959	391,000[16]			
		1960		
1967	509,000[17]			
		1968 (April)	2,829,828	7,102,897

NOTES TO APPENDIX I

[1][I. J.] Benjamin, *Three Years in America, 1859-1862*, tr. Charles Reznikoff, 2 vols., Philadelphia, 1956, Vol. II, p. 101.

[2]H. Z. Sneersohn, *Ha-Zofeh ba-Arez ha-Hadashah* (1870).

[3]*American Israelite*, July 8, 1881.

[4]Distinctive Jewish Name method; see chap. 6, note 41.

[5]*Jewish Encyclopedia*, s.v. "Los Angeles."

[6]*American Jewish Year Book, 1907-1908.*

[7]In Yiddish-speaking homes; *U.S. Census.*

[8]*AJYB, 1914-1915* (figures are given for 1912).

[9]*AJYB, 1917-1918.*

[10]Bureau of Jewish Social Research, *Jewish Population of Los Angeles, California* (mimeographed).

[11]*AJYB, 1929-1930* (figures are given for 1927).

[12]Samuel C. Kohs, "Determining the 1941 Jewish Population of Los Angeles," Part II of *Survey of Recreational and Cultural Needs of the Jewish Community of Los Angeles* (1942; mimeographed).

[13]JCC Annual Meeting, *Minutes*, October 28, 1946.

[14]Ibid., October 28, 1948.

[15]Los Angeles Jewish Community Council, *A Report on the Jewish Population of Los Angeles 1951* (mimeographed).

[16]Jewish Federation-Council of Greater Los Angeles, *A Report on the Jewish Population of Los Angeles 1959* (mimeographed).

[17]Ibid., *1967.*

APPENDIX II

ORGANIZATION CHART

JEWISH FEDERATION-COUNCIL
OF GREATER LOS ANGELES

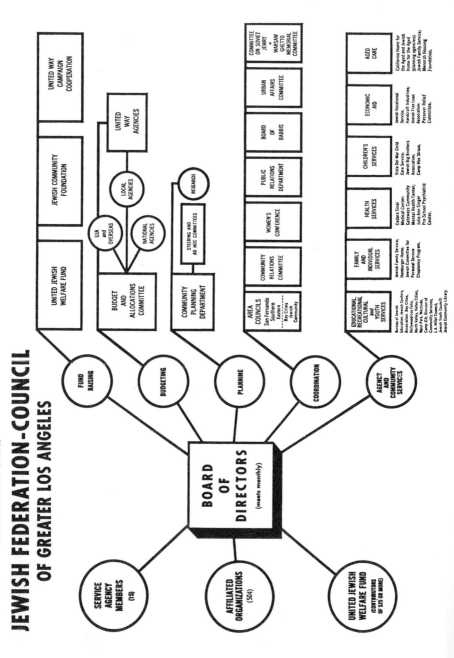

APPENDIX II

(JEWISH FEDERATION-COUNCIL)

JEWISH WELFARE FEDERATION
Presidents
Ben R. Meyer 1911-1921
George Mosbacher 1922-1931
Jay B. Jacobs 1931-1932
Marco R. Newmark 1933-1937
Milton Baruch 1937-1941
David Tannenbaum 1941-1943
Walter S. Hilborn 1944-1945
Leonard A. Chudacoff 1946-1949
Dr. George Piness 1950-1953
Mischa F. Berg 1953-1954
Ben Solnit 1954-1955
Steve Broidy 1956-1959

Executive Directors
Dora Berris 1912-1923
      (Jewish Aid Society)
William Blumenthal 1923-1924
Dr. Boris D. Bogen 1925
I. Irving Lipsitch 1925-1935
Charles Schottland 1936-1940
Dr. Maurice J. Karpf 1941-1946
Martin Ruderman 1946-1959

LOS ANGELES JEWISH COMMUNITY COUNCIL
Presidents
Judge Harry A. Hollzer 1937-1945
Charles Brown 1946-1948
Judge Isaac Pacht 1949-1951
Mendel B. Silberberg 1952
Judge David Coleman 1953-1955
Judge Stanley Mosk 1956-1957
Ike Greenberg 1958-1959

Executive Directors
I. Irving Lipsitch 1933-1937
Charles Schottland 1938-1940
Dr. Maurice J. Karpf 1941-1943
Leo Gallin 1943-1950
Julius Bisno 1950-1959

JEWISH FEDERATION-COUNCIL OF GREATER LOS ANGELES
Presidents
Steve Broidy 1959-1960
Judge Irving Hill 1960-1963
Dr. Max Wm. Bay 1964-1966
Victor M. Carter 1967-1968
Bram Goldsmith 1969-

Executive Directors
Julius Bisno and   } 1959-1965 Associate
Martin Ruderman } Executive Directors
Isidore Sobeloff 1964-1967
Alvin Bronstein 1968-

UNITED JEWISH WELFARE FUND
President
Judge Isaac Pacht............ 1935, 1936
Joseph P. Loeb 1937

General Campaign Chairman
Mendel B. Silberberg 1935
Judge Harry A. Hollzer 1936
Charles Brown 1937
Joseph P. Loeb 1938
Joseph I. Schnitzer 1939
Ben R. Meyer 1940
Rabbi Edgar F. Magnin 1941, 1942
Charles Brown 1943, 1944
Max Firestein 1945, 1946
Leonard A. Chudacoff 1947
Julius Fligelman 1948
M. F. Berg 1949
Oscar Pattiz 1950
Ben Solnit 1951
Leslie G. Cramer 1952
Mark Taper 1953
Joseph D. Shane 1954
Ike Greenberg 1955
William W. Bruck 1956
Samuel Pensick 1957
Jules Bisno 1958
Dr. Max Wm. Bay 1959
Jacob M. Stuchen 1960
Victor M. Carter 1961
Joseph N. Mitchell 1962
Steve Broidy 1963
Nathan Cramer 1964
Bram Goldsmith 1965
Albert A. Spiegel 1966, 1967
Isidore Familian 1968
David Fox 1969

Executive Secretary
J. Peckell Nathan 1935-1941

Executive Directors
Frederick A. Schreiber 1942

Frederick A. Schreiber } 1943 Due to war
Harry Shapiro } conditions, each
Bernard Gottlieb } directed the
Harry Riche } campaign for
various periods.

Leo Gallin 1944-1950
Julius Bisno 1950-1963

Campaign Director
Julius Ratner 1964

**BOARD OF RABBIS
OF SOUTHERN CALIFORNIA**
Presidents
Rabbi Edgar F. Magnin 1930-
Rabbi Jacob Kohn ....
Rabbi Abram I. Maron 1951-1952
Rabbi Jacob Pressman 1952-1953
Rabbi Alfred Wolf 1953-1954
Rabbi Morris Kaplan 1954-1955
Rabbi Aaron M. Wise 1955-1956
Rabbi Albert M. Lewis 1956-1957
Rabbi Ben Zion Bergman 1958-1959
Rabbi Julian F. Feingold 1959-1961
Rabbi William Spigelman 1961-1963
Rabbi Marvin Bornstein 1963-1965
Rabbi Samson H. Levy 1965-1967
Rabbi Jacob Levine 1967-1968
Rabbi Abraham N. Winokur ... 1968-1969

Executive Vice President
Rabbi Paul Dubin 1968-

BUREAU OF JEWISH EDUCATION
Chairmen
Herman A. Bachrack 1938-1944
Peter M. Kahn 1945-1947
Dr. Nathan S. Saltzman 1947-1949
Theodore Strimling 1949-1950
Herman A. Bachrack 1950-1951
Jacob M. Alkow 1951-1953
David S. Bassan 1953-1955
Dr. Nathan S. Saltzman 1955-1956
Cyrus Levinthal 1956-1963
Max Ponder 1963-1967
Matthew Berman 1967-1968
Albert A. Spiegel 1968-

Directors
Rabbi Bernard Cohen 1938-1943
(Educational Director)
Rabbi Rudolph Lupo 1943-1944
(Acting Director)
Dr. Samuel Dinin 1945-1956
(Executive Director)
Prof. Morris Leibman 1945-1956
(Associate Director)
Prof. Morris Leibman 1957-1964
(Executive Director)
Irwin I. Soref 1959-1964
(Associate Director)
Irwin I. Soref 1964-
(Executive Director)

**CALIFORNIA HOME FOR THE AGED
AT RESEDA**
Presidents
INDUSTRIAL CENTER 1933-1948
Isaac Grant
Samuel Raskin
Abe Newman

**CALIFORNIA HOME FOR THE AGED
AT RESEDA**
(incorporated 1948)
Norman A. Obrand 1948-1950
Harry Friedman 1951-1953
Samuel E. Willen 1954-1958
Irving H. Brott 1959-1961
Robert Silver 1962-1963
Abe Schrier 1964-1966
Hyman Getzoff 1967-

Executive Directors
Benedict L. Garon 1948-1966
Albert M. Stein 1966-

CEDARS-SINAI MEDICAL CENTER
Presidents

KASPARE COHN HOSPITAL
dedicated September 21, 1903, until
August 4, 1929, when name was changed
to

CEDARS OF LEBANON HOSPITAL
Jacob Schlesinger 1902-1903
S. S. Federman 1903-1904
Max N. Newmark 1904-1919
Ben R. Meyer 1919-1925
Lemuel Goldwater 1925-1944
Ben R. Meyer 1944-1954
George M. Thompson 1954-1957
Hart Isaacs 1957-1961

BIKUR CHOLIM SOCIETY
became *MOUNT SINAI HOSPITAL*, which
continued until 1961 (when it merged with
CEDARS OF LEBANON)

William Raab 1922-1923
H. Devore 1923-1924
M. Kaufman 1924-1928
Peter M. Kahn 1928-
Harry Blank
I. B. Benjamin
Ben Tyre
Eugene Marcus
Robert J. Gans ....(?) 1944-1951
Samuel Pensick 1951-1954
George Heltzer 1954-1957
Maurice Holman 1957-1958
Lester M. Finkelstein 1958-1960
Norman Feintech 1960-1961

294

CEDARS-SINAI MEDICAL CENTER
Presidents
Steve Broidy 1961-1964
Samuel J. Briskin 1964-1966
Steve Broidy 1966-

Executive Directors
Leo G. Rigler, M.D. 1957-1963
David Littauer, M.D. 1963-

COMMUNITY RELATIONS COMMITTEE
Chairmen
Mendel B. Silberberg 1933-1951
Isaac Pacht 1952
Mendel B. Silberberg 1953-1963
Isaac Pacht 1964-1966
Martin Gang 1967-

Executive Directors
Leon L. Lewis 1933-1946
Fred Herzberg 1946-1950
Joseph Roos 1951-

HAMBURGER HOME
Presidents
Mrs. Mamie (Henry) Klein 1918
Mrs. Florine H. (Edward)
Wolfstein 1918-1933
Mrs. Amy (Joseph) Loeb
Mrs. Jean (Irving S.) Metzler
Mrs. Lydia (Joseph C.) Lipman.. 1945-1946
Mrs. Estelle (Toscha) Seidel ... 1947-1948
Mrs. Emily (Alan) Harris 1949-1950
Mrs. Jean (Irving S.) Metzler... 1951-1952
Mrs. Adrea (Victor M.) Carter .. 1953-1954
Mrs. Louise (H. Whitney) Sall .. 1955-1956
Mrs. Marion (Ted) Lederer 1957-1958
Mrs. Jean (William S.)
Louchheim 1959-1960
Mrs. Doris (Walter N.)
Marks (Sr.) 1961-1962
Mrs. Florence (Edgar G.)
Richards 1963-1964
Mrs. Jeannette (Harold M.)
Zeigler 1965-1966
Mrs. Shirley (Basil L.) Kaufman. 1967-1968
Mrs. Selma (E. Craig)
Heringman 1969-

Superintendents
Mrs. Minnie Kahn 1918-
Mrs. Ida J. Wolfe
Mrs. Regina Benno

Executive Directors
Miss Rose Moss 1937-1957
Miss Betty Gitlin 1957-1965
Mrs. Anne H. Sax 1966-

JEWISH BIG BROTHERS ASSOCIATION—CAMP MAX STRAUS
1927 — Organized first camp.

1933 — Camp named Frederick H. Baruch
Health Camp.
1937 — Camp Max Straus established
Verdugo Hills, Glendale.

Presidents
Harry Freiberg 1915
Paul Lowenthal 1920
Lester Roth 1921
Max Hommel 1922
Sidney Irmas 1923-1924
Ernest J. Armer 1925-1926
Dr. James Steinberg 1927-1934
Hart Isaacs 1935-1940
Lawrence Frank 1941
Jerome L. Nathan 1942-1944
Leonard Chudacoff 1945-1946
Albert G. Ruben 1947-1948
Sydney Rosenberg 1949-1950
Maurice Schwarz, Jr. 1951-1954
George Miller 1955-1958
Ernest Friedman 1958-1960
Sydney Rosenberg 1961-1962
Michael Kohn 1963-1965
Robert Neiman 1966-1969

Executive Directors
Henry Straus 1915-1919
Miss Edna Schuster 1921-1945
Milton L. Goldberg 1945-

JEWISH CENTERS ASSOCIATION
Presidents
Judge Irvin Stalmaster 1943-1947
Leslie G. Cramer 1947-1949
Louis Warschaw 1949-1952
Max W. Bay 1952-1954
Jules Bisno 1954-1956
Lawrence E. Irell 1956-1959
Robert J. Felixson 1959-1962
William W. Bruck 1962-1964
Bernard Levin 1964-1966
Ralph B. Herzog 1966-1968
Jack L. Brostoff 1968-

Executive Directors
Meyer E. Fichman 1943-1954
Bertram H. Gold 1954-1967
Charles Mesnick 1967-

JEWISH COMMITTEE FOR PERSONAL SERVICE—GATEWAYS HOSPITAL
First organized as a statewide agency in 1921 by Rabbi Martin A. Mayer and I. Irving Lipsitch. Gateways Hospital organized in 1953 at its first location on Hoover Street near Temple Street; later moved in 1961 to its present location at 1891 Effie Street.

Presidents
Rabbi Edgar F. Magnin 1923-1929
Judge Isaac Pacht 1929-1935
Rabbi Edgar F. Magnin 1936-1944
Harry Graham Balter 1945-1946
Rabbi Morton A. Bauman 1947-1948
Donald E. Breyer 1949-1950
Victor M. Carter 1951-1952
George R. Olincy 1953-1954
Morton M. Silverman 1955-1957
George R. Olincy 1958-1959
Aaron Levinson 1960-1961
Sylvan S. Goldberg, M.D. 1961-1962
John Factor 1962-1963
Raymond E. Lee 1963-1966
George R. Olincy 1967-1968
Robert Silverstein 1969-

Executive Directors
Rabbi Maxwell Dubin 1923-1924
Reuben Resnick 1925-1935
Nathan Sloate 1936-1939
Louis Ziskind 1939-

JEWISH COMMUNITY LIBRARY
Chairmen
Robert Rosenson 1946-1948
Peter M. Kahn 1948-1952
Theodore Strimling 1952-1953
Ben Solnit 1953-1954
Mrs. Irwin Reiss 1954-1956
Philip Wain 1956-1959
Rabbi Morton Bauman 1959-1966
Albert A. Spiegel 1967-1968
Moshe Cohen 1969-

Professionals
Dr. Emil Bernard Cohn 1947
    (Part-time librarian)
Rabbi Rudolph Lupo 1947-1966
    (Director)
Mrs. Bluma K. Jarrick 1966-
    (Acting librarian)

JEWISH FAMILY SERVICE OF
LOS ANGELES
Created by Hebrew Benevolent Society
(org. 1854), with Jacob Elias, first presi-
dent; and Hebrew Ladies Benevolent
Society (org. 1870), first officers of which
were:
President   — Mrs. Wolf Kalisher
Vice President — Mrs. Harris Newmark
Treasurer   — Mrs. John Jones
Secretary   — Mrs. Virginia Katz
Succeeding presidents were
              — Mrs. Harris Newmark
              — Mrs. Samuel Hellman
              — Mrs. William T. Barnett
              — Mrs. Henry W. Frank

Became Jewish Aid Society of Los Angeles,
incorporated May 29, 1915. Name changed
August 1929 to Jewish Social Service Bureau; and again changed August 15, 1946
to present name — Jewish Family Service
of Los Angeles.

Presidents
Alexander Meyer 1915-1934
Isaac Norton ....   —
Milton Baruch 1934-1938
E. F. Kline 1938-1941
Frank Gunther 1941-1943
Mrs. Harry Rubel 1943-1945
Mrs. Richard Schuster 1945-1948
Eugene Frank 1948-1949
Mrs. Maurice Saeta 1949-1955
J. Edison Goldsmith 1955-1959
Mrs. Maxwell Greenberg 1959-1960
Joseph Weisman 1960-1963
Mrs. Jack Atlas 1963-1966
Morton H. Randall, M.D. 1966-1967
Hugo Zivi 1967-1969
Martin L. Kozberg 1969-

Executive Directors
Dora Berris 1918-1923
Herman Blumenthal 1923
Mrs. Meta Goldstein 1923
Mrs. Lenore Levin 1923-1930
Mrs. Emma Shencup 1930-1932
Miss Freda Mohr 1932-1966
Theodore R. Isenstadt 1966-

JEWISH FREE LOAN ASSOCIATION
Organized 1911 by Alexander Mayer and
Rabbi Sigmund Hecht.

Presidents
Rabbi Sigmund Hecht 1916-1922
Caesar Samuels 1923-1929
Jacob Steinberg 1930
Charles Brown 1930-1932
Max Goldman 1933-1947
Judge David Coleman 1948-1949
David Belinkoff 1950-1951
Irving Hill 1952-1954
Max I. Bernstein 1955-1956
Victor Menacker 1957
Hugo Zivi 1958-1960
E. P. Kurtzman 1961-1962
Samuel F. Goldman 1963
A. A. Rotberg 1964-1965
Andrew Z. Meyer 1966-1967
Morton H. Randall, M.D. 1968-

Executive Secretaries
Mrs. Lillian Gould
Herman Kretzer 1940-1943
Joseph B. Goldberg 1946-

JEWISH HOME FOR THE AGED OF LOS ANGELES

Presidents

Simon Lewis 1912-1918
Max Brown 1919
Simon Lewis 1920-1921
Abraham Horwitz 1922-1923
Charles Beaver 1924-1925
Philip Senegram 1926
Barnet Rosenburg 1927-1928
Abraham Mark 1929-1931
Jacob Farbstein 1932
Hyman Levine 1933-1934
H. Lew Zuckerman 1935-1937
Theodore Strimling 1938-1939
Samuel Tuch 1940-1941
Nathan Weisman 1942-1946
Sam Goldman 1947-1948
Sol Levine 1949-1950
Eugene M. Rosen 1951-1952
Mischa F. Berg 1953-1954
Harry B. Seelig 1955-1956
J. D. Sterling 1957-1958
Maurice Katleman 1959-1960
Judge Burnett Wolfson 1961-1962
Mischa F. Berg 1963-1965
Judge Ben Koenig 1966-1967
Harry S. Cooper 1968-

Executive Directors

Max Goldstein
Leonard Greenberg
Ysaye Hassen
William I. Boxerman 1951
Nathaniel Snyder 1952-1956
Maurice J. Ostomel 1957-

JEWISH VOCATIONAL SERVICE

Presidents

FEDERATED JEWISH EMPLOYMENT BUREAU

Edward Bastheim 1938-1940
J. A. Rosenkranz 1941-1942
Isidore Brown 1943-1944

JEWISH EMPLOYMENT & COUNSELING SERVICE

Ernest J. Armer 1945-1947
J. D. Alschuler 1948-1949
Tobias Kotzin 1950
Andrew Z. Meyer 1951-1952
Felix Juda 1953-1955
Joseph Weiss 1956-1957

JEWISH VOCATIONAL SERVICE

Robert S. Thompson 1958
Hugo Zivi 1959-1960
M. M. Maltz 1961-1962

Robert S. Thompson 1963-1964
Irwin H. Goldenberg 1965-1966
Harry Braverman 1967-

Executive Directors

H. A. Levinson 1938-1940
Irwin A. Newman 1941-1945
Dinah Connell 1946-1956
Morris Grumer 1957-

JEWISH YOUTH COUNCIL

Presidents

Lawrence E. Irell 1943-1944
Sylvia R. Zimring 1945
Fred Massarik 1946
Richard Lowe 1947-1948
Harvey Saritsky 1949-1950
George Friedman 1951
Bernard Volkman 1952
Helen Magad Volkman 1953
Janice Gordon 1954
Samuel Schiffman 1955
Sylvan Wachs 1956
Arthur Rosenthal 1957
Mike P. Shulem 1958
Melvin Cheslow 1959
Ronald Leibow 1960
Lester Leibson 1961
Donald Kaiser 1962-1963
Daniel Metlay 1964-1965
Joel Goldberg 1966-1967
Hal Kurz 1967-1968
Arnold Gross 1968-1969

Executive Directors

Miriam Horwitz 1943-1944
Charles Zibbell 1945-1947
Marvin Betnun 1948-1949
Henry Ruby 1950-1951
Ben Shreiber 1952-1953
Fred Massarik 1954-1957
Phillip Gordon 1958-1965
Rosalind Lawson 1966-

JULIA ANN SINGER PRESCHOOL PSYCHIATRIC CENTER

Jewish Mothers Alliance, organized 1913 by Mrs. Florine H. Wolfstein and Mrs. Edmund M. Lazard. In 1920, merged into the *Jewish Mothers Alliance Day Nursery,* located at Evergreen and Wabash Avenues. In 1927, moved to 244 North Breed Street, after which it became known as the *Julia Ann Singer Day Nursery,* until that location closed in 1958. Subsequently, the name was changed to *Julia Ann Singer Preschool Psychiatric Center,* located at 4734 Fountain Avenue, its present location.

Presidents

Mrs. I. Flaxman
Mrs. Bessie Meyerhoff
Mrs. Abraham (Louise)
  Muchnic 1932-1935
Mrs. Harold (Hariette)
  Blumenthal 1935-1938
Mrs. A. B. (Freda) Shore
  now Mrs. Irving Friedman .. 1938-1942
Mrs. George (Selena) Shapiro .. 1942-1945
Mrs. A. Lincoln (Rose) Desser.. 1945-1948
Mrs. Isidore (Jean) Siskin
  now Mrs. Alexander Cole .. 1948-1950
Mrs. Sidney (Bibb) Lushing ... 1950-1952
Mrs. Lionel (Helen) Stone 1952-1954
Mrs. Isaac (Beth) Olch 1954-1956
Mrs. Albert E. (Marian)
  Wollman 1956-1958
Mrs. Maurice (Marjorie)
  Schwarz 1958-1961
Mrs. Lionel (Helen) Stone 1961-1962
Mrs. Theodore (Constance)
  Zolla 1962-1963
Mrs. Maurice (Marjorie)
  Schwarz 1963-1965
Mrs. David (Frances) Matlin ... 1965-1967
Mrs. Ramon (Jeanne) Gerson .. 1967-1969
Mrs. Manuel (Ruth) Resnik 1969-

Directors

Miss Ann Sheftelman 1930-1955
Miss Ruth Waldo Rothman 1955-1958
Mrs. Louise Yum 1960-1961
Mrs. Joan Ellis 1961-

LOS ANGELES HILLEL COUNCIL
Formerly, Council of Jewish Students

Presidents

Judge Harry A. Hollzer 1940-1947
Rabbi Edgar F. Magnin 1947-1952
Isadore H. Prinzmetal 1952-1955
Mrs. Maurice Turner 1955-1958
Michael Kohn 1958-1961
Mrs. Maurice Turner 1961-1962
Jerome Schwartz 1962-1965
Mrs. Bertha Kadesh 1965-1968
John S. Biren 1969-

Executive Directors

Rabbi Bernard Harrison 1938-1948
Rabbi Jehudah M. Cohen 1948-1966
Rabbi Henry Rabin 1966-

RESEARCH SERVICE BUREAU

Chairmen

I. H. Prinzmetal 1955-1960
Jack Y. Berman 1960-1966
Max W. Bay 1967
Jack Y. Berman 1968-

Director

Fred Massarik 1954-

VISTA DEL MAR CHILD-CARE SERVICE
(JEWISH ORPHANS' HOME OF SOUTHERN CALIFORNIA)

Jewish Orphans' Home of Southern California, incorporated October 3, 1908. Opened officially January 4, 1909 with five (5) children, at 535 Mission Road, which was destroyed by fire August 1, 1910. New home dedicated November 28, 1912 at Irving and Mills Avenues in Huntington Park. In 1924, home sold, temporary quarters located at West Adams Boulevard, near Grand Avenue. March 26, 1925, occupied present site at 3200 Motor Avenue.

Presidents

Siegfried G. Marshutz 1908-1913
John Kahn 1914-1918
Joseph P. Loeb 1919-1926
Isadore Eisner 1927-1930
Irving H. Hellman 1931-1933
Mrs. E. Bastheim 1934-1936
Judge Isaac Pacht 1937-1947
Judge Benjamin Scheinman ... 1948-1950
Judge Stanley Mosk 1951-1957
Judge Ben Koenig 1958-1967
George Konheim 1968-

Superintendents

Mrs. A. Robinson
Miss Hattie Hesselberger
Rabbi (Dr.) Sigmund Frey 1909-1921
Armand Weyl 1921-1923

Executive Directors

Joseph Bonapart 1923-1966
Karl Glou 1966-

298

NOTES

List of Abbreviations

AJC–LA	American Jewish Committee Archive, Los Angeles
Am. Heb.	*American Hebrew*
Am. Isr.	*American Israelite*
BBM	*B'nai B'rith Messenger*
CRC	Community Relations Committee (of Jewish Federation-Council)
HSSCQ	*Historical Society of Southern California Quarterly*
ICOR	Organization for Jewish Colonization in Russia
JCA	Jewish Centers Association
JCC	Jewish Community Council
J. Mess.	*The Jewish Messenger*
JSSB	Jewish Social Service Bureau
UJC	United Jewish Community
UJWF	United Jewish Welfare Fund
YIVO	Institute for Jewish Research, New York City

Part i. Early Decades
CHAPTER 1. THE GOLD RUSH DAYS: 1850-1858

[1]*An Illustrated History of Los Angeles County* (Chicago, 1889), p. 61.

[2]By 1822 only 20 rancho concessions had been made (Robert Glass Cleland, *The Cattle on a Thousand Hills*, 2d ed. rev. [San Marino, 1951], p. 19); but from 1833 until American rule, more than 700 land grants were given free, comprising many millions of acres (W. W. Robinson, *Ranchos Become Cities* [Pasadena, 1939], pp. 227-234). Cleland, pp. 19-23, 26-27.

[3]Cleland, pp. 58-60.

[4]William A. Spalding, comp., *History and Reminiscences, Los Angeles City and County, California* (Los Angeles, 1931), I, 101.

[5]Hubert Howe Bancroft, *History of California* (San Francisco, 1886), IV, 276-278, and III, "Pioneer Index and Register," p. 746.

[6]Spalding, I, 121; Andrew F. Rolle, *California: A History* (New York, 1963), pp. 189-205, 228-239; William Henry Ellison, *A Self-governing Dominion: California, 1849-1860* (Berkeley, 1950), pp. 1-21.

[7]Cleland, pp. 102-110, esp. p. 103. Robert M. Fogelson, *The Fragmented Metropolis: Los Angeles, 1850-1930* (Cambridge, Mass., 1967), p. 10.

[8]*Census of the City and County of Los Angeles, California, for the Year 1850*, ed. Maurice H. and Marco R. Newmark (Los Angeles, 1929), p. 21. The census results disappeared and nothing was known of them. In 1915, a quantity of rubbish was being cleared out of an old barn and burned, near the San Fernando Mission, where Cecil B. DeMille was making a motion picture. While the bonfire was blazing, DeMille noticed a document protruding from the fire and rescued it from the flames. He showed it to Sam Behrendt, the son of a pioneering Jewish family, who procured it for the Southwest Museum. It was eventually published by the Newmark brothers.

[9]Horace Bell, *Reminiscences of a Ranger* (Santa Barbara, 1927), p. 10. Alexander Bell was the uncle of Horace Bell. Mr. and Mrs. Bell had no children of their own but were distinguished for their hospitality and kindliness. See Ana Begue de Packman, "Landmarks and Pioneers of Los Angeles in 1853," HSSCQ, XXVI (1944), 94.

[10]Newmark, *Census*, p. 42.

[11]I. J. Benjamin, *Three Years in America, 1859-1862*, trans. Charles Reznikoff (Philadelphia, 1956), II, 232.

[12]Bell, *Reminiscences*, p. 10.

[13]Morrow Mayo, *Los Angeles* (New York, 1933), pp. 35, 36.

[14]*Los Angeles Star*, Aug. 16, 1856. The Methodist, Baptist, Presbyterian, and Episcopalian preachers all closed their churches in disgust (Mayo, p. 41).

[15]*Tri-Weekly News*, Mar. 5, 1865.

[16]Bell, *Reminiscences*, p. 6.

[17]George Behrendt remembers his grandfather Kaspare, who arrived in 1851, still using the Spanish pronunciation of Los Angeles and wearing a black sombrero after fifty years. Harris Newmark recalls having spoken Spanish before he could speak English.

[18]J. J. Warner, Benjamin Hayes, and J. P. Widney, *An Historical Sketch of Los Angeles County, California* (Los Angeles, 1936, repr. of Louis Lewin's 1876 ed.), p. 104.

[19]The first Jewish advertisement of which we have record was placed in the issue of May 1, 1852 (Rudolf Glanz, *The Jews of California* [New York, 1960], p. 79).

[20]*Star,* July 26, 1856.

[21]*Star,* June 20, 1857. In 1863, Lazard went into partnership with another non-Jew, Trɪdell, in the Ville de Paris.

[22]*Southern Vineyard,* Aug. 14, 1858.

[23]Harris Newmark, *Sixty Years in Southern California 1853-1913* (New York, 1926), p. 65.

[24]*Daily News,* Jan. 12, 1870. She was the first treasurer of the Society.

[25]He died in 1876 and was buried in the Jewish cemetery (*Star,* Dec. 30, 1876).

[26]*Star,* Aug. 6, 1853, Sept. 29, 1855, Aug. 29, 1857.

[27]Newmark, *Sixty Years,* pp. 26 and 75; S. C. Davis was Jewish.

[28]Ibid., p. 75.

[29]Ibid., pp. 75-76.

[30]Ibid., p. 244.

[31]Although the majority of the shareholders were from San Francisco, a number of investors must have come from Los Angeles, because announcements to shareholders were published in the *Los Angeles Star* of Feb. 13 and Apr. 17, 1858, Jan. 15 and July 19, 1859. Charles Kohler and John Froehling were large wine and brandy distillers in Los Angeles. In 1870 they shipped from Anaheim alone 120,000 gallons, purchasing annually most of the grape crop of Anaheim farmers. Glanz, citing the *San Francisco Hebrew,* Feb. 12, 1869, considers Charles Kohler a Jew; see his *Jews of California,* p. 110.

[32]Newmark, *Sixty Years,* p. 213. In addition to Newmark's ample data, other Jewish merchants are mentioned or written up in the press: Louis Glaser (*Star,* Jan. 5 and Nov. 3, 1855, Apr. 26, 1856, Apr. 25, July 11, Aug. 15, 1867—a tale of robbery and insolvency); Abraham Schachno (*Star,* June 23, 1855); H. Goldberg, a tailor (*Star,* July 8, 1854; Mar. 1 and Apr. 19, 1856, June 13, 1857); Samuel Cohn, brother of Kaspare Cohn (*Star,* Aug. 16, 1856, Aug. 1 and Sept. 19, 1857); Simon Ferner and his wife (*Times,* Nov. 14, 1888, May 30 and Sept. 15, 1894); Louis Jaszynski (*Star,* Sept. 19, 1857, July 13, 1861); H. M. Cohn (*Star,* Jan. 7, 1860, Sept. 7, 1861, June 21 and Aug 2, 1862, Nov. 24, 1864)—he may have gone out of business in 1864 and moved to Salt Lake City—cf. Leon L. Watters, *The Pioneer Jews of Utah* (New York, 1952); Abraham Solomon (*Star,* Apr. 2, 1853); M. Calisher, also spelled Kalisher (*Star,* Aug. 24, 1854, Aug. 16, 1856, Nov. 20, 1858, June 1 and Oct. 26, 1861). The elder Joseph Newmark announced in the *Star* of Jan. 5, 1856, that he was opening a boarding house.

[33]Newmark, *Sixty Years,* pp. 290, 332.

[34]Ibid., p. 142.

[35]Full biographical details of Harris Newmark and his widespread family may be found in the 700 pages of his magnificent autobiography (see note 23 above). A professional researcher worked on his memoirs and checked the sources, so that the book is relatively free from factual error.

[36]Helen Griffen and Arthur Woodward, *Story of El Tejon* (Los Angeles, 1942), p. 109; Newmark, *Sixty Years,* p. 248.

[37]Newmark, *Sixty Years,* p. 104. Mrs. Jacob Rich is reported to be the first Jewish woman to settle in Los Angeles.

[38]Albert M. Norton, son of Isaac Norton who arrived in 1867 and who was the brother of Moses Norton, says his uncles Moses Norton and Ephraim Greenbaum arrived together in late 1851 and that the two wives came a year later by stage via

San Diego. Mr. Norton remembers his aunt Ernestine Greenbaum telling him that on the way north from San Diego they stayed at the home of a ranchero and were so impressed by the hospitality that she vowed to reciprocate. In later years she did open a hotel, the White House, which probably catered to unmarried immigrants.

[39]Newmark, *Sixty Years,* p. 177.

[40]Ibid, p. 65.

[41]The local press carried a continuous stream of such notices.

[42]*Star,* Mar. 31, Apr. 14 and 21, 1855; *Southern Californian,* Apr. 4, 1855. In 1866 the estate of Leopold Hart was admitted to probate with I. W. Hellman as administrator. There is no evidence of Hart participating in Jewish community life.

[43]The diary of this famous explorer was published in 1857 (New York) as *Incidents of Travel and Adventure in the Far West: with Col. Fremont's Last Expedition.* It was republished in 1954 with an introduction by Bertram W. Korn as *Incidents of Travel and Adventure in the Far West.*

[44]Newmark, *Sixty Years,* p. 70.

[45]Carvalho (1954 ed.), p. 316.

[46]*Southern Californian,* Aug. 10 and 31, Sept. 7, 1854; *Star,* Mar. 31, 1855.

[47]*Southern Californian,* Aug. 31, 1854.

[48]*Southern Californian,* Aug. 24, 1854.

[49]*Star,* Aug. 24, 1854.

[50]*Star,* July 8, 1854. In this interview Carvalho announces his intention of publishing his journal together with his portraits. Unfortunately the latter have disappeared.

[51]Carvalho, pp. 312-313, 315; *Star,* Sept. 21, 1854. Parts of his journal were published in the *Southern Californian,* Aug. 24 and 31, 1854.

[52]Bell, *Reminiscences,* pp. 295-296; W. Gunther Plaut, *The Jews of Minnesota: The First Seventy-five Years* (New York, 1959), pp. 23-29; Louis J. Swichkow and Lloyd P. Gartner, *The History of the Jews of Milwaukee* (Philadelphia, 1963), pp. 18-26, 58-60. This is a subject inviting detailed comparative study.

[53]Horace Bell, *On the Old West Coast* (New York, 1930), p. 105.

[54]Benjamin Ignatius Hayes, *Pioneer Notes from Diary of Judge Benjamin Hayes, 1849-1878* (Los Angeles, 1929), pp. 209, 210.

[55]William H. Brewer, *Up and Down California in 1860-64* (New Haven, 1930), p. 13.

[56]*Star,* Sept. 3, 1853.

[57]*Occident,* Apr. 1853, p. 79.

[58]*Star,* Apr. 7, 1855. An account of this episode may be found in "Anti-Jewish Sentiment in California, 1855," *American Jewish Archives,* XI, 1 (Apr. 1960), pp. 15-33.

[59]*Star,* Jan. 10, 1857.

[60]*Star,* Feb. 13, 1868.

[61]*Southern Vineyard,* Feb. 8, 1859, republished in *Occident,* Dec. 30, 1859.

[62]Ibid.

[63]*Star,* July 23, 1852.

[64]Goodman later became one of the first Jewish settlers of Anaheim, where he resumed his political career.

[65]For further biographical references see Newmark, *Sixty Years,* pp. 71-72, and J. M. Guinn, *Historical and Biographical Record of Los Angeles and Vicinity* (Chicago, 1901), p. 796. The Solomon Lazard Papers at the County Museum Library include interesting material on Lazard's incarceration in France while on a visit in 1861; he was arrested for failing to report for conscription and was released only after a great deal of diplomatic intercession.

[66]Newmark, *Sixty Years,* pp. 42-44, has an account of electioneering practices in early Los Angeles.

[67]*Star,* June 25, 1853, Dec. 19, 1857, and May 8, 1858.

[68]*Tri-Weekly News,* Mar. 25, 1865.

[69]J. Albert Wilson, *History of Los Angeles County, California* (Berkeley, 1959, repr. of Thompson & West 1880 ed.), p. 51, lists all elected city and county officials. M. Kremer is mistakenly written M. Keller.

[70]*Star,* May 5, 1855: "The following ticket was nominated by a large and enthusiastic meeting of our German citizens for city officers last night. . . ." Cf. Swichkow and Gartner, pp. 10-12, 18-23.

[71]Maurice Kremer, far outrunning his opponents, received 550 votes out of 900 cast for treasurer in 1861, while J. L. Morris, with only 238 votes, got into the city council in 1863. In that year Kremer was reelected, with 951 votes to his opponent's 730.

[72]These varied accounts must be approached with caution. All accounts of the first services in Los Angeles are taken from Marco Newmark, who wrote the "History of Wilshire Temple" on the occasion of its dedication in 1929 (*BBM,* June 7, 1929) and revised it in 1947 for the *Historical Society of Southern California Quarterly.* It is the only source, with Harris Newmark, for the religious beginnings of the local Jewish community. We know of no written account which is not taken from this source except that of I. J. Benjamin.

[73]Based on an interview with Mr. Albert M. Norton. It is not too likely that regular services of any kind were held. There might, however, have been *yortsayt* or festival services as well as Holy Day services. I. J. Benjamin wrote that the congregation met "only on New Year's and the Day of Atonement" (II, 101).

[74]Warner, Hayes, and Widney, *Historical Sketch of Los Angeles County,* p. 103, records that merchants in 1850 were Jacob Elias, M. Michaels, A. Jacoby, and Morris L. Goodman.

[75]Newmark, *Sixty Years,* p. 122. Harris Newmark lived with his uncle Joseph for a time and ultimately married one of the daughters, Sarah. His knowledge of the life of Joseph Newmark was therefore firsthand and considerable. We do not know whether he was actually ordained; if he was, he would have been the first ordained rabbi in the United States.

[76]The by-laws of the Hebrew Benevolent Society were found by accident in the Bancroft Library a few years ago. Mr. Justin G. Turner, well-known manuscript collector, had the pamphlet reprinted on the occasion of the first annual dinner meeting of the Southern California Jewish Historical Society. It was originally printed in 1855 at the *Southern Californian* newspaper offices.

[77]The number of Jews who lived in Los Angeles is purely conjectural. The proportion of Jews in Los Angeles before 1857 was very considerable in the total white population. We know the names of at least 60 male heads of families. However, we do not know how many had wives and children during this period. It would be safe to assume that during the height of the prosperity period as many as 90 Jewish men

lived in Los Angeles and the surrounding villages. Those who are known to have left the area with the collapse of the economy in 1857 included S. K. Labatt, Charles Schachno, H. Goldberg, J. J. Labatt, M. Pollack, A. B. Ephraim, M. B. Ephraim, H. Krushaar, J. Rosenblum, J. Hyman, S. Rosinski, G. Mahler, L. Rosenbach, Moritz Michael, Raphael and Israel Elias, Samuel Laubheim, Ben Schloss, Arnold Jacobi. Most had left by the time the congregation was established in 1862.

[78]*Star*, July 8, 1854; *Occident*, Sept. 1854, p. 327.

[79]*Star*, Apr. 14, 1855.

[80]*Star*, Aug. 1, 1857.

[81]*Southern Vineyard*, July 1, 1859.

[82]*Southern Vineyard*, Sept. 2, 1859.

[83]Los Angeles Welfare Council, "Outline of History of Development of Social Welfare and Related Events in Los Angeles" (1929), p. 1.

[84]Newmark, *Sixty Years*, p. 118.

[85]*Star*, Jan. 3, 1857.

[86]*Star*, July 26, 1856.

[87]*Star*, June 30, 1855.

[88]*Star*, July 26, 1856. The full study of Jewish participation in the Masonic Order in Los Angeles is still to be written.

[89]A call to the venerable secretary of the I.O.O.F. in 1960 elicited the "information" that "no Jews now or ever were active in the I.O.O.F. of Los Angeles."

[90]Kremer and Lazard, from Alsace, in 1868 were members of the French Benevolent Society and of the Alliance Israélite Universelle. In 1861, three officers of the Teutonia Society were Jews: J. Sichel, M. Kremer, and M. Schlesinger.

[91]Cleland, pp. 75-77.

[92]*Southern Vineyard*, July 1, 1859; Aug. 26, 1859, gives information about the Library Association. See also Newmark, *Sixty Years*, p. 256.

[93]Bell, *Reminiscences*, pp. 200-201.

[94]Wilson, *History of Los Angeles County*, p. 122. Samuel Prager was founding treasurer. This club was reputed the wealthiest in town, with dues as high as $20 a month.

[95]The four intermarriages were entered into by Charles Prager, Eugene Germaine, B. Solomon, and Joseph Laventhal, none of whom were active in synagogue life. The first three were well-known in the community. According to the constitution of the congregation they would not have been eligible for membership.

CHAPTER 2. DISASTER AND RECOVERY: 1860-1880

[1]Robert Glass Cleland, *The Cattle on a Thousand Hills* (San Marino, 1951), pp. 147-156, 168-180, 213-221; Robert M. Fogelson, *The Fragmented Metropolis: Los Angeles, 1850-1930* (Cambridge, Mass., 1967), pp. 15-23.

[2]W. W. Robinson, *Ranchos Become Cities* (Pasadena, 1939), p. 41; *Semi-Weekly News*, Feb. 5, 1869.

[3]*Star*, Jan. 3, 1863; Robinson, p. 209.

⁴Harris Newmark, *Sixty Years in Southern California 1853-1913* (New York, 1926), pp. 329-330; Robinson, pp. 209-210; *Star*, Jan. 9, 1864.

⁵Interview with Harris Newmark, in *Times*, Sept. 18, 1892.

⁶*Star*, Nov. 17, 1865.

⁷Horace Bell, *On the Old West Coast* (New York, 1930), p. 5.

⁸*News*, Jan. 22, 1869.

⁹*Star*, Aug. 15, 1857.

¹⁰*Star*, July 13, 1861.

¹¹*Star*, Aug. 17, 1861.

¹²*Star*, May 8, 1858, and Feb. 18, 1860.

¹³*Star*, May 23, 1864; Newmark, *Sixty Years*, p. 332.

¹⁴Newmark, *Sixty Years*, p. 290.

¹⁵*Star*, Feb. 22, 1865.

¹⁶William A. Spalding, comp., *History and Reminiscences of Los Angeles City and County, California* (1931), I, 163.

¹⁷"Mrs. Solomon Lazard, chairman, moved that $150 be expended out of the funds of the Hebrew Benevolent Society to procure nourishment for the sick and that this committee form themselves into a committee of relief to solicit contributions and to distribute the same to the indigent sick. Committee: Solomon Lazard, Julius Sichel, Maurice Kremer, Wolf Kalisher, Isidor Cohn" (*Star*, Feb. 10, 1862; see also *Star*, Feb. 14, 1863).

¹⁸*Star*, Feb. 14, 1863.

¹⁹*Star*, Mar. 7, 1863; Feb. 25, 1877.

²⁰Index Book, Civil Cases, Superior Court, in the Los Angeles County Courthouse. Most suits were to collect unpaid balances. The defendants were usually Mexicans.

²¹Newmark, *Sixty Years*, p. 379.

²²Spalding, I, 163.

²³Boyle Workman, *The City That Grew* (Los Angeles, 1935), p. 166.

²⁴*Star*, Jan. 5, 1861; Percival J. Cooney, "Southern California in Civil War Days," *Annual Publications of Historical Society of Southern California*, XIII (1924), 54-68.

²⁵*Official Records of the Civil War*, Ser. i, Vol. 50, Pt. 1, pp. 496-497.

²⁶*Murat Holstead Caucuses of 1860* (Columbus, 1860), p. 37, quoted in William Penn Moody, "Civil War and Reconstruction in California Politics" (Ph.D. diss., Univ. of Calif., Los Angeles, 1950), p. 1.

²⁷Bertram W. Korn, *American Jewry and the Civil War* (Philadelphia, 1951), pp. 29-31.

²⁸*Semi-Weekly Southern News*, Sept. 11, 1861.

²⁹Newmark, *Sixty Years*, pp. 337-338.

³⁰*Tri-Weekly News*, Apr. 22, 1865.

[31]Newmark, *Sixty Years*, p. 338. Since the early history of the Jewish community has until now been largely restricted to Newmark, whose references to the Jews during Civil War times were almost exclusively devoted to the resolutions of sympathy upon the death of Lincoln and their participation in the parade, it has been generally presumed that the Jews of Los Angeles shared the convictions of the Jews of the North.

[32]*News*, May 28, 1867.

[33]*News*, May 28, 1867.

[34]Cleland, pp. 165-177; Warren S. Thompson, *Growth and Changes in California's Population* (Los Angeles, 1955), p. 33, Table IV-1; p. 35, Table IV-2.

[35]*Tri-Weekly News*, Oct. 3, 1865.

[36]*Star*, Oct. 26, 1851.

[37]*Tri-Weekly News*, Sept. 30 and Oct. 3, 1865.

[38]Newmark, *Sixty Years*, p. 323.

[39]*Star*, Oct. 28, 1871. For earlier Jewish jurors see *News*, Apr. 15, 1865, *Star*, May 30, 1865, *Semi-Weekly News*, May 11, 1866.

[40]*Daily News*, Oct. 10, 1869.

[41]*Semi-Weekly News*, Feb. 27, 1869, Jan. 13, 1870.

[42]*Daily News*, Dec. 14, 1869.

[43]*Daily News*, Feb. 15, 1871.

[44]*San Francisco Hebrew*, June 30, 1876; Newmark, *Sixty Years*, pp. 381, 493; *Times*, Apr. 16, 1882. An apocryphal story is told that on his deathbed Lankershim called Harris Newmark and asked him to recite the *shma*, saying, "Der shma is doch shein."

[45]*City Directory*, 1875.

[46]*Star*, Apr. 9, 1870.

[47]The Harris and Frank stores are still operating. They sold out, however, to a Philadelphia firm in the 1950's.

[48]The Jacoby Brothers store eventually sold out to the May Company.

[49]*Herald*, June 5, 1874; *Star*, Jan. 3, 1873.

[50]*News*, July 17, 1870.

[51]*Herald*, Sept. 29, 1874.

[52]*Star*, Mar. 4 and 22, 1874.

[53]*La Crónica*, Sept. 4, 1875; *Herald*, Nov. 23, 1879.

[54]Mendel Meyer was in business with Hilliard Lowenstein from 1856, when he was 19. The firm dissolved in 1866. Meyer continued under the names of Mendel Meyer and "Vienna Exposition Store" until 1877. He gave concerts in the neighboring communities such as Santa Monica, Santa Ana, and Anaheim, either solo or with a troupe. He also served as musical director of the congregation's Purim parties for the children. His sale to Samuel Prager is mentioned in the *Star*, Apr. 2, 1873.

55*Herald*, Feb. 2, 1875, and May 10, 1874.

56Jewish affairs, socials, raffles, and the like were held in her front parlor; *News,* Jan. 9, 1870; *Herald*, July 30, 1874; J. Albert Wilson, *History of Los Angeles County* (Berkeley, 1959, repr. of Thompson & West 1880 ed.), p. 129.

57*Herald*, Mar. 13, 1874.

58*Star*, Dec. 18, 1871.

59*Herald*, Oct. 27 and June 14, 1874. Other fruit shippers included M. Kremer (*News*, July 6 and 30, 1869), Samuel Prager (*News*, Aug. 15, 1869), B. Katz (*News*, July 29, 1869), and Simon Levi (*Herald*, Mar. 13, 1874).

60*Herald*, Jan. 13, 1875, Apr. 18, 1865, Feb. 24, 1875. Other Jewish retailers included I. Goldsmith (*Herald*, Sept. 23, 1874), I. E. Cohn, a piano dealer and perhaps a physician later (*Herald*, July 14, 1874), the brothers Meyberg (Marco R. Newmark, "Pioneer Merchants of Los Angeles," *HSSCQ*, XXV [1943], 27, H. Newbauer and Martin Lehman (*Herald*, Mar. 9, 1874), another I. Rosenbaum (*Herald*, Jan. 9, 1875), S. Nordlinger, new in the jewelry trade (*Star*, Aug. 15, 1870).

61Newmark, *Sixty Years*, pp. 439, 474.

62L. J. Rose, Jr., *L. J. Rose of Sunnyslope* (San Marino, 1959) contains numerous references to Stern. Marco Newmark traces Stern to Los Angeles in 1849, which would make him the earliest permanent resident of Los Angeles of the Jewish faith ("Los Angeles Jewish Pioneers," typescript). *Star*, Dec. 1, 1870; Moritz Morris sold his vineyard and moved into the city; *Herald*, Apr. 16, 1874.

63*Am. Isr.*, July 28, 1882; *San Francisco Chronicle*, Dec. 18, 1879, quoted in Wilson, p. 154.

64*Star*, Aug. 8, 1868; *Daily News*, Apr. 8, 1869.

65*Star*, Oct. 1 and Dec. 8, 1864; Feb. 4, 1869; Aug. 8, 1874; June 26, 1875.

66*Herald*, Oct. 14, 1875.

67*Star*, Nov. 17, 1870.

68Newmark, *Sixty Years*, p. 510n; *Herald*, Mar. 22, 1878.

69*Star*, Apr. 15, 1865.

70Ira B. Cross, *Financing an Empire* (Chicago, 1927), II, 536-537. A valuable recent history is Robert G. Cleland and Frank B. Putnam, *Isaias W. Hellman and the Farmers and Merchants Bank* (San Marino, 1965).

71*Star*, July 18, 1868.

72*Star*, May 23, 1868.

73*Star*, Sept. 12, 1868.

74Cleland and Putnam, pp. 17-18.

75*Am. Isr.*, Dec. 10, 1886.

76Newmark, *Sixty Years*, pp. 449, 450; *Herald*, Mar. 25, 1874.

77Newmark, *Sixty Years*, pp. 482-483.

78Ibid., p. 440.

79Frank Putnam, "In Old Los Angeles—I. W. Hellman" (mimeographed pamphlet), p. 10.

80Newmark, *Sixty Years*, p. 504.

81Ibid., p. 507.

82*Herald*, Mar. 10, 1876; Newmark, *Sixty Years*, p. 489.

83Newmark, *Sixty Years*, p. 503.

84Charles Dwight Willard begins his *History of the Chamber of Commerce of Los Angeles, California* (Los Angeles, 1899) with the establishment of the Board of Trade in 1883 and proceeds to the founding of the Chamber of Commere in 1888. The first Chamber of Commerce is ignored.

85Newmark, *Sixty Years*, p. 423; *Herald*, June 19, 1874, and Jan. 1, 1875; *Star*, June 14, 1877.

86Jackson A. Graves, *My Seventy Years in California, 1857-1927* (Los Angeles, 1927), pp. 424-429.

87Quoted in Cross, II, 540.

88Hellman to Phillips, Oct. 20, 1879, Hellman Papers, Calif. Hist. Soc., San Francisco.

89*Herald*, Sept. 17, 1878.

90*Herald*, Sept. 4, 1878.

91*Herald*, Feb. 8, 1875.

92*Herald*, May 8, 1877; *La Crónica*, July 21, 1877. Other bankruptcies and liquidations are reported in *La Crónica*, July 11, Oct. 10 and 24, 1877; *Star*, Mar. 17, 1876.

93*Herald*, Mar. 20, 1874.

94*Herald*, May 1, 1877. Laventhal, who had lived in Los Angeles since 1853, returned in 1882 (*Times*, Sept. 27, 1882). Eventually he opened the firm of E. Laventhal and Co., jobbers of wines, liquors, and cigars (Marco R. Newmark, "Pioneer Merchants," *HSSCQ*, XXV [1943], 6-7).

95*Herald*, Feb. 7, 1879.

96*Herald*, Jan. 5, 1877.

97*Herald*, Jan. 4, 1877.

98Businesses opened by Jews are mentioned in *Star*, Aug. 15 and Oct. 7, 1876; *Herald*, June 2 and 29, 1877; June 1 and July 2, 1878; *La Crónica*, Jan. 24 and Oct. 24, 1877; *News*, June 17, 1879.

99*Herald*, Oct. 19, 1878.

100*Herald*, July 3, 1880.

101*La Crónica*, Sept. 4, 1875.

102Hellman to Benjamin Neugass, Hellman Papers, Calif. Hist. Soc., San Francisco. The political conditions are those of San Francisco and the North, where Dennis Kearney's Workingmen's Party had a dominant role in writing the state constitution of 1878. By this time Hellman had a statewide view, for the political agitation which disturbed him was not felt in Los Angeles. The undated letter postdates the adoption of the constitution in May 1879 and elections in November of that year; it also speaks of 1880 in the future. Its date late in November or December 1879 is certain. "Sam" and "Bett" were obviously brother and sister to Benjamin Neugass; "Bett" was Babette, Mrs. Mayer Lehman. On the family, see Allan Nevins, *Herbert H. Lehman and His Era* (New York, 1963), pp. 9, 12, 13.

CHAPTER 3. THE FRAMEWORK OF JEWISH LIFE

[1]Harris Newmark, *Sixty Years in Southern California 1853-1913* (New York, 1926), p. 342.

[2]*Tri-Weekly News,* June 17, 1865, letter to editor by C. R. Conway.

[3]*Tri-Weekly News,* Sept. 2, 1865. The *Star* was suspended between 1864 and 1868 for its anti-Union hostility, leaving only one newspaper in Los Angeles during this period.

[4]*Star,* July 4, 1868.

[5]*Semi-Weekly News,* Aug. 18, 1868.

[6]*Star,* Aug. 21 and 22, 1868.

[7]*News,* Aug. 23, 1868.

[8]*News,* Oct. 30, 1868.

[9]Bertram W. Korn, *American Jewry and the Civil War* (Philadelphia, 1951), p. 137.

[10]*Star,* July 17 and Aug. 1, 1872.

[11]*News,* Nov. 6, 1866.

[12]*News,* Oct. 23, 1869.

[13]*News,* Dec. 18, 1869.

[14]*News,* Dec. 25, 1869; Jan. 12 and 26, Feb. 2 and 25, 1870.

[15]*Star,* July 19, 1870; *News,* Aug. 19 and Sept. 9, 1870.

[16]*Anaheim Gazette,* quoted in *Herald,* Aug. 15, 1875.

[17]*Herald,* Mar. 16, 1877, Jan. 25 and Mar. 15, 1878.

[18]Dictation of B. Cohen [sic] of Los Angeles, Nov. 18, 1887, in Bancroft Library, Univ. of Calif., Berkeley.

[19]*Herald,* Mar. 15 and Nov. 18, 1878.

[20]*Times,* Sept. 5, 1882.

[21]*Herald,* Mar. 15 and Nov. 18, 1878.

[22]*Star,* Jan. 11, 1862.

[23]*Star,* Jan. 18, 1862.

[24]*Star,* Feb. 8, 1862.

[25]*News,* Jan. 22, 1869.

[26]*Star,* Jan. 28, 1860. Other examples are: the Babylonian and Palestinian Talmuds, Baron Rothschild's visit (Sept. 8, 1960), the election of a Jew as Lord Mayor of London (Nov. 11, 1865), the number of Jews in the world (Mar. 21, 1865). The *News* told of another Mortara case in Frankfurt (Aug. 8, 1865), announced the acquisition of a cemetery plot for Jews in Naples (Oct. 11, 1864), and reported that there were no Jewish beggars in New York or London because Jews take care of their own (Jan. 5, 1869).

[27]*Republican,* Aug. 3, 1867.

[28]*Star,* Nov. 20, 1869; Mar. 12 and Apr. 23, 1870.

[29]*Star,* Dec. 16, 1871.

[30]*Star,* Apr. 9, 1870.

[31]*Star,* Aug. 5 and July 22, 1870.

32*Star*, July 23, 1870; Jan. 24, 1873.

33*Star*, June 22, 1877.

34*Star*, Sept. 3 and 6, 1873.

35 Newmark, *Sixty Years*, p. 122.

36"That year the Jews organized a congregation, 'Beth El,' but they have neither *hazzan* nor teacher and assemble for religious services . . . only on New Year's and the Day of Atonement" (I. J. Benjamin, *Three Years in America, 1859-1862*, trans. Charles Reznikoff [Philadelphia, 1956], II, 101).

37*J. Mess.*, 1861.

38*Star*, Sept. 7, 1861.

39*Star*, Sept. 7, 1861. M. Galland might be A. Galland, who functioned as a rabbi in Sacramento in 1855 and served as a Torah reader in San Francisco in 1864.

40Norton and Greenbaum were both Polish, and B. Cohn, the president, was the brother-in-law of Norton. H. M. Cohn, the kosher butcher, might have been an East European.

41Joseph L. Malamut, *Southwest Jewry* (Los Angeles, 1957), II, 5. See "Reminiscences" of David W. Edelman in *BBM*, June 7, 1929. See also Newmark, *Sixty Years*, p. 314.

42Rabbi Edelman's positions in community organizations are reported in *Star*, Dec. 20, 1864; *News*, July 24, 1866; Jan. 4 and July 19, 1867; Jan. 3, 1868; Jan. 1, 1869; Aug. 2, 1870.

43*Star*, June 4, 1873; *Herald*, June 15, 1879.

44*J. Mess.*, July 30, 1875; *Herald*, July 12, 1876.

45*Star*, Feb. 25, 1877.

46*Star*, Nov. 12, 1870.

47*Hebrew*, Oct. 21, 1870, p. 4. This group may have been a temporary group functioning under the leadership of the Palestinian emissary Hayyim Zvi Sneersohn, who visited Los Angeles about this period.

48*News*, Oct. 11, 1870.

49This was widespread practice; Hyman B. Grinstein, *The Rise of the Jewish Community of New York, 1654-1860* (Philadelphia, 1945), p. 375; Louis J. Swichkow and Lloyd P. Gartner, *The History of the Jews of Milwaukee* (Philadelphia, 1963), p. 473.

50Constitution and By-laws of Congregation B'nai B'rith, adopted 1862, amended 1873.

51Typical of ritual abandonment was the description of I. M. Hellman vacationing at San Pedro, "sniffing the ocean air and catching clams for breakfast" (*Star*, June 12, 1873).

52*Star*, June 21, 1862. The *Star* (Aug. 2, 1862) helped by emphasizing that kosher meats "are perfectly healthy and free from all taint of disease."

53*Star*, Nov. 26, 1864.

54As examples of annual announcements by leading Jewish firms that they would be closed for the two days of Rosh Hashanah and one day of Yom Kippur, see *Am. Isr.*, Sept. 24, 1869; *Star*, Sept. 17, 1871; *Herald*, Sept. 30, 1875, Sept. 26, 1879, Sept. 29, 1878. In addition, the newspapers regularly mentioned that the Jewish business houses would be closed for the holidays. "Their places of business were all closed and the time devoted to religious worship" (*Tri-Weekly News*, Sept. 23, 1865).

⁵⁵*News*, Sept. 17, 1868.

⁵⁶*Star*, Sept. 20, 1876.

⁵⁷The newspapers conscientiously announced the holidays and the time of services.

⁵⁸Oct. 11, 1862.

⁵⁹*Star*, Oct. 14, 1862.

⁶⁰*Tri-Weekly News*, Dec. 31, 1864.

⁶¹*Star*, Dec. 31, 1864. In 1861, I. J. Benjamin found the town's one hundred Jews "mostly young people" (II, 101).

⁶²Newmark, *Sixty Years*, p. 314. Places of worship are mentioned in *News*, June 3 and Oct. 4, 1870; *Star*, Apr. 5, May 26, Sept. 16, 1871; Apr. 17, 1872. A letter of thanks reads: "The Congregation B'nai B'rith through their trustees would tender their many thanks to the Hon. District Judge R. M. Widney and to the Hon. County Judge Ygnacio Sepulveda for allowing the use of the court rooms to hold services during the holiday just passed. By order, M. Levy, Sec." (*Star*, Oct. 15, 1872).

⁶³*Star*, Apr. 24, 1872.

⁶⁴Cf. *Star*, June 5, 1869; *Hebrew*, June 25, 1869; *Am. Isr.*, July 16, 1869, p. 26; *News*, June 7 and 26, 1869, for story of this financial project.

⁶⁵*Star*, June 14, 1871, and Feb. 8, 1872.

⁶⁶Marco R. Newmark, "Wilshire Boulevard Temple," *BBM*, June 7, 1929, p. 167. Solomon had been a member of Beth Israel Congregation in San Francisco in 1851; perhaps he contacted former friends in the congregation.

⁶⁷*Star*, June 22, 1872.

⁶⁸*Star*, Aug. 19, 1872; the complete program of the day is found there.

⁶⁹*Star*, Aug. 19, Oct. 23, and Dec. 20, 1872. When the cornerstone was removed twenty-five years later, its contents were unfortunately decomposed.

⁷⁰*Jewish Times*, Aug. 30, 1872.

⁷¹*Star*, Apr. 15 and July 18, 1873.

⁷²*Star*, July 31 and Aug. 6, 1873.

⁷³*Star*, June 22, 1872.

⁷⁴*Star*, Aug. 23, 1873.

⁷⁵*Jewish Times*, Aug. 30, 1872; *Am. Isr.*, Sept. 6, 1872.

⁷⁶*Star*, Aug. 8, 1873.

⁷⁷"The Israelites have always observed their festivals of the Old Law, by closing houses of business and meeting for worship at designated places." (J. J. Warner, Benjamin Hayes, and J. P. Widney, *An Historical Sketch of Los Angeles County* [Los Angeles, 1876, repr. 1936], p. 89).

⁷⁸*Herald*, Apr. 21, 1875.

⁷⁹David Edelman, "Reminiscences" in *BBM*, June 7, 1929.

⁸⁰*Herald*, July 23, 1874.

⁸¹Constitution and By-Laws, B'nai B'rith Congregation, adopted 1862, revised 1874.

⁸²Request for Mortgage Approval, Jan. 16, 1885; Case 5095, Superior Court Book 13, p. 32.

⁸³Congregation B'nai B'rith versus B. Cohn, Case No. 184, Superior Court. The only known extant copy of the original Constitution was found among the records of this litigation.

[84]*Herald*, Apr. 1, 1874.

[85]*J. Mess.*, Apr. 9, 1875.

[86]It is not known how often the Hebrew Benevolent Society actually met. According to the constitution, they were to meet monthly, and special meetings were called periodically. The annual meeting was always held in July. Examples of meeting notices: *Star*, Jan. 14 and Feb. 14, 1863; Jan. 13 and June 13, 1868.

[87]Cf. *News*, Dec. 11, 1868; May 1 and 15, 1869. The first piece of land 100 feet by 50 feet had been purchased from José Sepulveda in 1854.

[88]*Star*, July 11, 1870.

[89]Leon Loeb was secretary and Simon Benjamin a trustee in 1872 (*Star*, July 8, 1872). In 1874 Samuel Meyer was president, Michael Levy was treasurer, and Moses Norton a trustee (*Herald*, Aug. 4, 1874). Bernard Cohn was a trustee in 1875 (*Star*, July 7, 1875). J. M. Rothschild was president in 1876 (*Star*, July 9, 1876). In 1877 Samuel Meyer, apparently president once again, relinquished that office to Constant Meyer (*Star*, July 4, 1877). Bernard Cohn became president in 1880 (J. Albert Wilson, *History of Los Angeles County, California* [Berkeley, 1959, repr. of Thompson & West 1880 ed.], p. 122).

[90]They included Mesdames Wolf Kalisher, John Jones, Virginia Katze, Abraham Baer, Henry Wartenberg, B. Katz, E. Greenbaum, L. Levy, S. Cohn, C. Gerson, S. Benjamin, I. Lewis, H. Newbauer, S. Norton, I. Cohen, Leopold Harris, M. Goldstein, H. Cohn, D. Solomon, Eugene Meyer, L. Lasky, A. Heller, Samuel Meyer, Louis Polaski, L. Hauch, M. Norton, William Barnett.

[91]Newmark, *Sixty Years*, p. 409.

[92]*News*, Oct. 26, 1870.

[93]*Am. Isr.*, Aug. 22, 1889.

[94]*News*, Oct. 12, 1871.

[95]*Star*, Oct. 18, 1871.

[96]Wilson, p. 110.

[97]*La Crónica*, July 4, 1877.

[98]*Herald*, Feb. 28, 1878.

[99]*Herald*, Sept. 29, 1880.

[100]Wilson, p. 122.

[101]Wilson, p. 123.

[102]*News*, Aug. 8, 1868.

[103]*Herald*, Jan. 1, 1875.

[104]*Herald*, Apr. 30, 1875.

[105]*Herald*, July 13, 1875.

[106]*J. Mess.*, July 30, 1875.

[107]*J. Mess.*, Nov. 10, 1876.

[108]Wilson, p. 123.

[109]Newmark, *Sixty Years*, p. 383.

[110]*Star*, Dec. 3, 1870.

[111]*Star*, June 22, 1872.

[112]*Star*, Jan. 1, 1876. There was a short-lived Excelsior Club in 1871, with Jewish officers (*Star*, Apr. 21, 1871).

[113]*Am. Isr.*, July 8, 1881.

[114]*Express*, Feb. 19, 1880.

[115]The text is reproduced in the *Star*, Mar. 20, 1872.

[116]*Star*, Sept. 2, 1872.

[117]*Herald*, Aug. 29, 1875.

[118]*Star*, Sept. 20, 1876.

[119]See *Herald*, Mar. 3, 1876, as an example. The synagogue had no social hall, and programs like these were held elsewhere, usually in Turnverein Hall.

[120]Newmark, *Sixty Years*, p. 105. In 1860, 288 children attended public school, and the number increased to 483 one year later (*Southern News*, Dec. 13, 1861).

[121]Boyle Workman, *The City That Grew* (Los Angeles, 1936), p. 59.

[122]In 1868, out of 3,131 children, 958 attended public schools; 508, private schools; and 1,685, no school at all; see Henry Winfred Splitter, "Education in Los Angeles: 1850-1900," *HSSCQ*, XXXIII (1951), 110.

[123]Samuel Lanner Kreider, "Volney Erskine Howard: California Pioneer," *HSSCQ*, XXXI (1949), 129.

[124]*News*, July 15, 1870.

[125]*Star*, June 15, 1872.

[126]*Herald*, May 17, 1874.

[127]Newmark, *Sixty Years*, p. 450.

[128]For example, the annual grammar school public exhibition in 1869 singled out I. Benjamin, F. H. Fleishman, H. Katz, Annie Polaski, A. Norton.

[129]*Star*, July 15, 1872.

[130]*Star*, July 16, 1872.

[131]*San Francisco Hebrew*, Oct. 1, 1869.

[132]*News*, Sept. 15, 1869.

[133]*Star*, Sept. 26, 1868.

[134]*News*, June 10, 1870.

[135]*Star*, May 27, 1871.

[136]*Star*, May 23, 1874. Eight girls and one boy were confirmed in 1876 (*Star*, May 30, 1876) and five girls and no boys in 1880 (*Express*, May 15, 1880).

[137]*J. Mess.*, July 30, 1875.

CHAPTER 4. THE 1880's: DECADE OF BOOM AND BUST

[1]Hellman to Mayer Lehman, May 6, 1882, Isaias W. Hellman Papers, Vol. II, p. 192, Calif. Hist. Soc., San Francisco.

[2]Hellman to Benjamin Neugass, Sept. 9, 1882, Hellman Papers.

[3]There is an extensive "boom" literature. See Glenn S. Dumke, *The Boom of the Eighties in Southern California* (San Marino, 1944), and Theodore S. Van Dyke, *Millionaires of a Day: An Inside History of the Great Southern California "Boom"* (New York, 1890).

[4]Dumke, pp. 24-25.

[5]Glenn Chesney Quiett, *They Built the West: An Epic of Rails and Cities* (New York, 1934), p. 275.

[6]John E. Baur, *The Health Seekers of Southern California* (San Marino, 1959), passim.

[7]John W. Caughey, *California* (New York, 1940), p. 474.

[8]*Am. Isr.*, Sept. 9, 1887.

[9]*Am. Isr.*, Aug. 26, 1887. This seems much exaggerated, particularly the tale about Hellman.

[10]*Am. Isr.*, Sept. 9, 1887.

[11]Harris Newmark, *Sixty Years in Southern California 1853-1913* (New York, 1926), p. 555.

[12]The final state supreme court decision reaffirming the decision of the lower court in favor of B. Cohn can be found in the *Times*, Feb. 12, 1891. An editorial that day in the *Times* said: "We are always averse to criticizing the decision of the legal tribunal of the country, but we cannot refrain from remarking on the apparent anomaly of a decision in favor of a defendant, one of whose principal witnesses is admittedly a perjurer." Attempts to raise funds for Pico proved abortive.

[13]Dumke, p. 267; Robert G. Cleland and Frank B. Putnam, *Isaias W. Hellman and the Farmers and Merchants Bank* (San Marino, 1965), pp. 52-54 (including quotation from *Times*, Jan. 5, 1889).

[14]Dumke, p. 276.

[15]*Am. Isr.*, Dec. 19, 1884.

[16]*Times*, Oct. 16, 1883.

[17]*Times*, Mar. 4, 1882.

[18]*Am. Isr.*, Mar. 6, 1885.

[19]*Times*, Aug. 21, 1885.

[20]*Times*, Apr. 28, 1888.

[21]Cf. Marco R. Newmark, "Pioneer Merchants of Los Angeles," *HSSCQ*, XXIV (1942) and XXV (1943); see also *Times*, Dec. 4, 1881; July 27, 1882; July 4, Dec. 14, Oct. 2, 1883; Sept. 16, 1885; July 4, 1886; Apr. 23 and 28, May 7, 1888; Nov. 17, 1889.

[22]*Am. Isr.*, Dec. 19, 1884.

[23]In a letter to the *Times*, Sept. 5, 1882.

[24]*Times*, Sept. 17, 1882.

[25]*Times*, Aug. 30, 1883. Hellman was disturbed by reports that Cohn might be appointed state bank commissioner, thus giving him some authority over the Farmers and Merchants. He worked vigorously and successfully to head him off (Hellman to R. F. del Valle, Jan. 15, 1883, and telegram, Hellman to Stephen Lacey, June 15, 1883, both in Hellman Papers, II, 307).

[26]*Times*, Aug. 30, 1883.

[27]*Times*, June 3, 1885.

[28]*Times*, Jan. 9, 1887.

[29]*Times*, Jan. 16, 1887.

[30]*Times*, Apr. 12, 1887; Newmark, *Sixty Years*, p. 594.

31Newmark, *Sixty Years,* p. 595.

32*Times,* Jan. 13, 1887.

33*Am. Isr.,* Dec. 10, 1886.

34*Times,* Mar. 10, 1883.

35*Herald,* Dec. 1, 1882.

36*Times,* Dec. 2, 1882.

37*Times,* Nov. 30, 1882.

38Quoted in *Times,* Dec. 3, 1882.

39*Herald,* Dec. 1, 1882.

40*Times,* Oct. 5 and 6, 1888.

41*Times,* Mar. 10, 1888.

42*Times,* Apr. 25, 1883.

43Newmark, *Sixty Years,* p. 625.

44*Times,* Jan. 20, 1888.

45*Times,* Feb. 17, 1888.

46*Times,* Mar. 2, 1888.

47*Times,* Jan. 26, 1882.

48*Times,* Sept. 22, 1887; Mar. 3, 1888.

49When thirty to forty young people called at the residence of Moritz Morris and announced that they wanted to give "Sig" a surprise, he proceeded to entertain them with refreshments, music, dancing, and games (*Times,* July 3, 1883). The *Star,* Apr. 18, 1863, describes a large number of men and women calling upon Mr. and Mrs. Hellman and taking them by surprise. "Refreshments were immediately provided and dancing at once commenced." The newspaper then explained the basis for such social behavior: "So agreeable a surprise coming from so large a circle of friends was a compliment of which its recipients have cause to be justly proud."

50Newmark, *Sixty Years,* pp. 539-540.

51*Times,* Mar. 10, 1888.

52*Times,* Apr. 25, 1888.

53*Times,* July 21, 1887.

54*Times,* Mar. 18, 1888.

55*Times,* July 25, 1890.

56*Times,* June 20, 1889; Sept. 7, 1890.

57*Times,* June 20, 1889.

58*Times,* Nov. 22, 1889.

59*Times,* Mar. 22 and Apr. 4, 1882.

60*Times,* Apr. 29, 1883.

61*Times,* Feb. 5 and Mar. 1, 1887.

62*Times,* June 20, 1889.

63*J. Mess.,* June 7, 1889.

64*Am. Isr.,* Aug. 22, 1889.

65*Am. Heb.,* Mar. 29, 1889.

[66]J. Mess., Aug. 17, 1883; Am. Isr., Aug. 17, 1883; Times, July 24, 1883.

[67]A program in the synagogue was followed by festivities at the Odd Fellows Hall. The major address was given by David A. Hamburger, and the mayor also spoke. The assemblage adjourned to the Turner Hall for dancing and refreshments. (La Crónica, Nov. 1, 1884; Am. Isr., Nov. 28, 1884).

[68]Am. Isr., Jan. 16, 1885.

[69]Boyle Workman, The City That Grew (Los Angeles, 1936), pp. 214-218.

[70]Am. Isr., Feb. 17, 1888.

[71]Times, Mar. 7, 1888.

[72]Times, Nov. 30, 1888.

[73]Part of the reason must have been Rabbi Schreiber's leaving. Another must have been the characters of the prime movers; both Max and Emil Harris were rough characters who went often afoul of the law and landed in court.

[74]"There are 136 Jews (families) in Los Angeles, but a minyan on Saturday is out of the question" (Am. Isr., July 8, 1881). "It is a naked truth that the audience at the synagogue has been shamefully small for months past" (Am. Isr., Sept. 5, 1884).

[75]Am. Isr., Nov. 30, 1883; July 18, 1884.

[76]Am. Isr., Nov. 30, 1883.

[77]Am. Isr., July 8, 1881.

[78]Times, Oct. 2, 1883.

[79]"We must either embrace the Reform code or else we leave our children in a bewildering darkness" (Am. Isr., Oct. 30, 1885). "The congregation is badly in need of a rabbi who has the vim and ambition to put fire and energy in the good cause" (Am. Isr., Oct. 24, 1884).

[80]Times, May 10, 1883.

[81]"The president of the congregation, I. W. Hellman, banker, visits the synagogue but once a year on Yom Kippur, and then only after banking hours" (Am. Isr., July 18, 1881).

[82]Am. Isr., Jan. 16, 1885.

[83]J. Mess., Nov. 6, 1885; "Reminiscences" of David W. Edelman, BBM, June 7, 1929.

[84]"Reminiscences of Dr. Emanuel Schreiber," BBM, June 7, 1929.

[85]Times, July 30, 1885.

[86]"Reminiscences of Dr. Emanuel Schreiber," BBM, June 7, 1929.

[87]Am. Isr., Oct. 30, 1885.

[88]A biography of Schreiber was published in the Times, Mar. 31, 1888.

[89]J. Mess., Nov. 6, 1885.

[90]Am. Isr., Oct. 30, 1885.

[91]Am. Isr., Nov. 5, 1886.

[92]Am. Isr., Jan. 14, 1887, Nov. 5, 1886, Jan. 14, 1887.

[93]"Reminiscences," BBM, June 7, 1929.

[94]Times, Sept. 16, 1888, reported that Rabbi Schreiber and the austere members of his congregation "touched not even a glass of water all day."

95*Am. Isr.*, Oct. 5, 1888.

96"A. Fleishman, I. Lowenstein and M. Meyer were bar mitzvah on the Holy Days" (*Times*, Sept. 20, 1887).

97*Am. Isr.*, Dec. 10, 1886.

98*Times*, Nov. 25, 1887.

99"Reminiscences of Dr. Emanuel Schreiber," *BBM*, June 7, 1929.

100*Am. Isr.*, Nov. 5, 1886.

101David Edelman remembers that his father's congregation was composed of "friends and old cronies" ("Reminiscences," *BBM*, June 7, 1929).

102*Am. Isr.*, Apr. 15, 1887.

103*Am. Isr.*, Oct. 28, 1887.

104*Times*, Dec. 28, 1888; *Am. Isr.*, Dec. 28, 1888.

105*Am. Isr.*, June 1, 1888; *Am. Heb.*, Aug. 16, 1889.

106*Am. Isr.*, July 4, 1889.

107*Am. Isr.*, Dec. 19, 1884; Jan. 16, 1885.

108*J. Mess.*, July 22, 1887; *Am. Isr.*, Nov. 5, 1886, and May 17, 1894.

CHAPTER 5. THE FOUNDING AGE CLOSES

1Willard, *A History of the Chamber of Commerce of Los Angeles, California* (Los Angeles, 1899), p. 336.

2Carey McWilliams, *Southern California Country* (New York, 1946) has a fine chapter on the Iowa migration and the state society movement, entitled "I'm a Stranger Here Myself," pp. 165-182.

3Ludwig Louis Salvator, *Los Angeles in the Sunny Seventies* (Los Angeles, 1929), p. 129.

4July 28, 1882.

5*Am. Isr.*, Feb. 20, 1890.

6*Am. Isr.*, Feb. 15, 1894.

7*Times*, June 29, 1893; see also Robert G. Cleland and Frank B. Putnam, *Isaias W. Hellman and the Farmers and Merchants Bank* (San Marino, 1965), pp. 58-63.

8Maynard McFie, *The Gay Nineties* (Los Angeles, 1945), p. 20.

9*Times*, May 25, 1891.

10*Times*, May 2 and 3, 1891, and Jan. 19, 1894.

11Nov. 8, 1897.

12*BBM*, Dec. 9, 1898.

13Material on the Edelman case can be found in the *Times*, Apr. 10, 11, Nov. 16, Dec. 9, 16, 21, and 23, 1890; Feb. 10, 1891; Feb. 14, Mar. 25, 29, and 31, Apr. 1, July 10, 11, 12, and 13, 1892.

14*Times*, Mar. 19, 1891.

15*Times*, June 15 and 22, 1894.

16*Times*, Jan. 8, 1892.

17For details of the trials see the *Times*, June 19, Nov. 14, 18, 19, 21, and 28, Dec. 5, 8, 10, 11, 22, 23, 24, 30, and 31, 1891; Jan. 1, 7, 8, 9, 12, and 18, Oct. 30 (verdict), 1892. An oral dictation by Cohn dated Nov. 18, 1887, is in the Bancroft Library at the Univ. of Calif., Berkeley; of course he does not refer to any of the foregoing.

18*Am. Heb.*, Feb. 23, 1894. The letter to Blum from Zadok Kahn indicated that in testimony to the ardor with which he defended the interests of Judaism, he would receive a diploma of *morenu* (our teacher) signed by the Director of the Jewish Seminary of France and the Grand Rabbi, with the seal of the Central Consistory. It would have the same value as the official diploma granted the graduates of the Jewish Seminary (École Rabbinique) of France.

19*Times*, Nov. 17, 1890.

20*Am. Isr.*, July 16, 1891.

21*Am. Isr.*, Oct. 15, 1891.

22*Am. Isr.*, Feb. 22, 1894.

23*Am. Isr.*, May 17, 1894.

24*Times*, Nov. 8 and Dec. 5, 1894.

25Newspaper material on this incident can be found in the *Times*, Aug. 30, Sept. 7, 10, 13, and 15, Oct. 11, 1895; in the *Herald* of Sept. 7, 9, and 12, 1895. Rabbi Blum subsequently became superintendent of Lebanon Hospital in New York City and was chaplain of the police force. He passed away an honored man.

26He gave his first sermon on Sept. 13, 1895, and the Holy Days began on the 18th. Full interviews were given to the *Times* on Sept. 12 and to the *Herald* on Sept. 7, 1895.

27Descriptions of the new building and of the dedication can be found in the *Times*, the *Express*, and the *Herald* of Sept. 7, 1896, and in the *American Hebrew*, Sept. 25, 1896.

28*J. Mess.*, Nov. 14, 1890.

29"There was an organ and a female choir to assist" (*Am. Isr.*, Oct. 25, 1894). David W. Edelman in his "Reminiscences" (*BBM*, June 7, 1929) substantiates this rather startling fact.

30He helped to conduct the funeral for his lifelong friend Samuel Prager on June 6 and died on July 24, 1907.

31Harris Newmark, *Sixty Years in Southern California 1853-1913* (New York, 1926), p. 314. The site of his home at the corner of Sixth and Main ultimately became the heart of the downtown district.

32Joseph L. Malamut, *Southwest Jewry* (Los Angeles, 1957), II, 6.

33*Times*, May 16, 1894.

34*Times*, Nov. 11, 1895.

35*Times*, Sept. 25 and 30, 1894.

36*BBM*, Sept. 9, 1898.

37Quoted in *BBM*, Sept. 22, 1899.

38*Am. Heb.*, Jan. 12, 1890.

39Mrs. Ana Begue de Packman in personal interview.

PART II. Twentieth Century

CHAPTER 6. FROM OUTPOST TO MAJOR COMMUNITY

[1] *The Jewish Encyclopedia*, s.v. "Los Angeles," gives 3,000 for 1904. See *American Jewish Year Book* for *1907-1908, 1918-1919, 1929-1930*, where revised figures are given; other volumes in this series merely repeat population figures from preceding years. The figure of 70,000 for 1930 is derived from the 65,000 estimate for 1927, plus natural increase and immigration.

[2] *BBM*, Nov. 30, 1900.

[3] *BBM*, Jan. 14, 1904.

[4] *BBM*, Apr. 30, 1904.

[5] *BBM*, June 30, 1904.

[6] *BBM*, Feb. 15, 1905.

[7] There were also "a lot of young men who travel all over the country, have no permanent home and do not want to work." The Hebrew Benevolent Society hoped the city would require a labor test of such irritating applicants (*BBM*, Mar. 14, 1913).

[8] *BBM*, June 30 and July 30, 1904.

[9] *BBM*, Mar. 31, 1905; the admonition was repeated on Apr. 30 and June 18 of that year.

[10] *BBM*, Apr. 30, 1904.

[11] *BBM*, Feb. 28, 1905

[12] *BBM*, July 30, 1904; Feb. 14, 1908.

[13] *BBM*, Sept. 26, 1908; see also *BBM*, Oct. 10, 1913, printing an interesting letter from the society's secretary, Isaac Pacht.

[14] On the IRO, see Samuel Joseph, *History of the Baron de Hirsch Fund* (New York, 1935), pp. 184-205. Its *Annual Reports* from 1901 through 1917 show 4,678 individuals sent from New York to California. If we had the missing figures for 1915, the total would doubtless exceed 4,800. The California and Los Angeles IRO figures are:

	California Total	Los Angeles
1901	36	123
1902	67	123 } a
1903	260	123
1904	429	131
1905	233	63
1906	403	139
1907	369	113
1908	323	149
1909	294	[168][b]
1910	301	208
1911	367	249
1912	648	396
1913	432	251
1914	281	[ ]
1915	not available	
1916	112	319 } c
1917	123	319
	4678	2309

^aExtrapolated by averaging the ratios of Los Angeles : California for 1904, 1905, 1906. They are 31%, 27%, and 34% respectively, for an average of 31% of 363 = 123.

^bInterpolated by averaging the ratios of Los Angeles : California arrivals for 1907, 1908, 1910, 1911. They are 38%, 46%, 69%, 67% respectively, for an average of 57% of 294 = 168.

^cThe same procedure has been followed as in ^a for 1911, 1912, 1913.

[15]Isaac Norton, president, at the society's annual meeting (*BBM*, Mar. 14, 1913). Presumably the figures cover only part of the year's total.

[16]*BBM*, Nov. 29, 1907.

[17]Rachel Ana Kositza, *Zikhroynes fun a Bialystoker Froy* (Los Angeles, 1964), pp. 119-120, 124, 126. Notke is a Yiddish diminutive derived from the common Hebrew compound of "Nossen Neta," as Nathan Neta was pronounced in Eastern Europe.

[18]These proportions derive from *Marriage Records Kept by Rabbi Hecht of Congregation B'nai B'rith, Los Angeles, California*, 1904-1919, Microfilm 412, American Jewish Archives. The 500 entries recorded in the 250 marriages include name, address, place of birth, parental names, data on previous marriages if any, and the (vaguely given) occupation of the groom. The number of non-Jewish partners, all of whom were converted to Judaism before their marriage, is nine, a figure too small to be significant for the present purpose. Many of the 500 lived at out-of-town addresses, suggesting the possibility of recent arrival in Los Angeles. In no case do bride and groom both have out-of-town addresses. A final observation seems worthy of mention: not more than two persons' names differed from those of their parents. Wholesale name-changing lay in the future.

[19]*BBM*, Apr. 26, 1912.

[20]"The Problem of 1915," address by Rabbi Hecht (*BBM*, Dec. 18, 1913).

[21]*BBM*, Apr. 13, 1908.

[22]*BBM*, Oct. 10, 1913.

[23]*BBM*, July 19, 1918.

[24]*BBM*, July 6, 1917.

[25]*BBM*, Feb. 25, 1910.

[26]*BBM*, Mar. 11, 1910.

[27]*BBM*, June 11, 1909.

[28]*American Jewish Year Book, 1917-1918* gives 20,000; idem, *1918-1919* gives 18,000. These figures are not much more than estimates, and perhaps not very good ones.

[29]Bureau of Jewish Social Research, "Jewish Population of Los Angeles, California," 9 pp. mimeographed, ca. 1924; in Library of Council of Jewish Federations and Welfare Funds, New York City. *The American Jewish Year Book, 1924-1925* erroneously cites the estimates as 43,000; the surveyors, however, regarded 45,000 as a "minimum estimate."

[30]*American Jewish Year Book, 1929-1930;* Jacqueline Rorabeck Kasun, *Some Social Aspects of Business Cycles in the Los Angeles Area, 1920-1950* (Los Angeles, 1954), p. 10, Table 1. However, the figure given for immigration fails to account for emigration from the city.

[31]*BBM*, July 25, 1930, reports the founding of "Agudat Erets Yisrael or Palestine Society of Los Angeles," headed by Rabbi S. M. Neches.

[32]Obituary in *BBM*, Mar. 7, 1930.

[33]Obituary in *BBM*, Jan. 6, 1928.

[34]*BBM*, Jan. 20, 1928.

[35]*BBM*, Mar. 8, 1929.

[36]Kasun, p. 10, Table 1.

[37]Amalgamated Clothing Workers of America, *Fifth Biennial Convention* (Chicago, 1922), pp. 185-186.

[38]Charles S. Goodman, *The Location of Fashion Industries: With Special Reference to the California Apparel Market*, Michigan Business Studies, Vol. X, No. 2 (Ann Arbor, 1948), Ch. 1.

[39]Lillian Ross, "The Beautiful and Dumb," *Harper's*, June 1931, p. 24.

[40]Joseph Katzenogy, *Kvaytlakh* (Los Angeles, 1925), p. 25.

[41]The estimates of Jewish neighborhood concentration have been most kindly supplied by Dr. Fred Massarik, Director of the Research Service Bureau of the Jewish Federation-Council of Greater Los Angeles. The technique employed is the standard "Distinctive Jewish Names," by which a ratio is statistically determined between the possessors of 36 distinctive Jewish family names (e.g., Cohen, Levy, Goldstein, Rosenthal, etc.) and the total number of Jews. By means of such sources as city directories, the DJN method may be projected retrospectively, as has been done here.

[42]Its rough boundaries were Whittier Boulevard, Raven Avenue, Lancaster Avenue, and Mission Road.

[43]Bounded by Sunset Boulevard, North Broadway, Fourth Street, and Douglas Street.

[44]Bounded by Naomi Street, Washington Street, Trinity Street, and South Park Avenue. These and the above boundaries are from Bureau of Jewish Social Research, "Jewish Population of Los Angeles," p. 9.

[45]*BBM*, Mar. 9, 1928.

[46]It had 112 Jewish families in 1923, 532 in 1926, 779 in 1929.

CHAPTER 7. ECONOMIC ACTIVITY: 1900-1928

[1]Much of the following data is derived from Marco R. Newmark, "Pioneer Merchants of Los Angeles," *HSSCQ*, XXIV (1942), 77-97, and XXV (1943), 5-65, and from oral recollections of Mr. Oscar Lawler.

[2]*BBM*, Jan. 15, 1909; John Steven McGroarty, *History of Los Angeles County* (Chicago and New York, 1923), p. 226; M. H. Newmark, "Jewish Builders of Southern California: Abe Haas—A Tribute," in *BBM*, Oct. 21, 1921.

[3]Grace Heilman Stimson, *Rise of the Labor Movement in Los Angeles* (Berkeley and Los Angeles, 1955), pp. 250-254, 279-281.

[4]*BBM*, July 3, 1914; McGroarty, p. 777.

[5]*BBM*, July 12, 1918.

[6]The slogan was the bank's; local businessmen have attested to the policy. See also Mark Carter, *Okay America* (Los Angeles, 1963), pp. 45-47.

[7]Robert Glass Cleland and Frank B. Putnam, *Isaias W. Hellman and the Farmers and Merchants Bank* (San Marino, 1965).

[8]Cleland and Putnam, pp. 70-72; *BBM*, Sept. 25, 1908, and Oct. 26, 1906.

⁹On the Hellmans and their banking interests, see Cleland and Putnam, pp. 70-94 and Appendixes A, B, and D; Leroy Armstrong and J. O. Denny, *Financial California: An Historical Review of the Beginnings and Progress of Banking in the State* (San Francisco, 1916), pp. 90-112; Ira B. Cross, *Financing an Empire* (Chicago, 1927), III, 222-230, 380-383, 428-434. Maurice S. Hellman, a nephew of Isaias and Herman Hellman, was long a vice-president of the Security Bank (Cross, III, 474-475).

¹⁰*BBM*, Sept. 21, 1928. A list of "Outstanding Jewish Financiers of Los Angeles" included the Hellmans, the Hamburgers, Lipman, May, A. Frank, L. B. Mayer, I. Eisner, B. R. Meyer, J. M. Schenck, R. G. Wolff, and J. Toplitzky. Few were actual financiers: thus, May and Hamburger were large retail merchants, Eisner in real estate, Mayer and Schenck in films; Toplitzky was serious tarnished in the Julian affair (see below).

¹¹Stimson, pp. 250-251.

¹²Louis B. Perry and Richard S. Perry, *A History of the Los Angeles Labor Movement, 1911-1941* (Berkeley and Los Angeles, 1963), pp. 37-38, 197, 222.

¹³Rachel Ana Kositza's husband peddled in Glendale, returning home on Friday (Kositza, *Zikhroynes fun a Bialystoker Froy* [Los Angeles, 1964], pp. 126-128).

¹⁴James Clifford Findley, "The Economic Boom of the 'Twenties in Los Angeles" (Ph.D. diss., Claremont Graduate School, 1958), pp. 247, 285-286.

¹⁵Stimson, pp. 310, 355; Perry and Perry, pp. 157-158.

¹⁶Amalgamated Clothing Workers of America, *Fifth Biennial Convention* (Chicago, 1922), pp. 185-186, and U.S. Commission on Industrial Relations, *Final Report and Testimony*, Vol. VI, 64th Cong., 1st Sess., Senate Doc. No. 415 (1916), p. 5727. See data cited below, note 22.

¹⁷Charles S. Goodman, *The Location of Fashion Industries: With Special Reference to the California Apparel Market*, Michigan Business Studies, Vol. X, No. 2 (Ann Arbor, 1948), pp. 42, 45, Tables VII, IX. Approximately 1,000 Jewish families were reportedly affected by an ILGWU strike in 1921 (*BBM*, Dec. 23, 1921).

¹⁸*BBM*, Aug. 30, 1929.

¹⁹Goodman, pp. 67-69, incl. Table XVI.

²⁰Amalgamated Clothing Workers of America, *Fifth Biennial Convention* (Chicago, 1922), pp. 185-186.

²¹International Ladies' Garment Workers Union, *Report and Proceedings, 1916*, p. 48; idem, *1920-1921*, pp. 20-21, where the claims are exaggerated.

²²Amalgamated Clothing Workers of America, *Fifth Biennial Convention* (Chicago, 1922), pp. 185, xxii.

²³Amalgamated Clothing Workers of America, *Sixth Biennial Convention* (Chicago, 1924), p. liii; the local's officers were A. Plotkin, Manager; S. Tilles, J. Golub, J. M. Berger, D. Silvers, S. Rose, D. Isaacs.

²⁴Ibid., p. lxxxii.

²⁵Amalgamated Clothing Workers of America, Report of General Executive Board, *Ninth Biennial Convention* (1930), pp. 90-91.

²⁶*Monthly Labor Review*, VII (Sept. 1918), 335; XIV (Mar. 1922), 166-167; XXII (Sept. 1925), 113; Perry and Perry, pp. 36-38, 148-151, 208-209, 221-222.

²⁷Perry and Perry, pp. 44-45, 153-154, 161, 223-224.

²⁸Findley, pp. 29, 240, 248-249, 282-283, 288, 335; other extensive data are given.

²⁹*BBM*, Jan. 4, 1929.

[30]*BBM*, Aug. 31, 1928.

[31]*BBM*, Dec. 21, 1928.

[32]This sample was drawn from the *City Directory* for the years 1920, 1923, and 1929. The technique employed was the Distinctive Jewish Names, explained above, Ch. 6, note 41. The number of persons with such names was first tabulated, and then every fourth (or fifth or sixth, as necessary) possessor was drawn, so that a sample of some 300 existed for each year. I am greatly indebted to Dr. Fred Massarik and Mrs. Ruth Gartner for their invaluable guidance and technical aid.

[33]Cf. David Epstein, *Tail of a Lion* (Los Angeles [ca. 1963]), pp. 106-110.

[34]Findley, pp. 29-30.

[35]Carter, pp. 26-28; Epstein, pp. 101-102.

[36]See, for example, Carter, pp. 28-29; Epstein, p. 110.

[37]Cf. the chart of "Real Estate Cycle in Los Angeles County," in *Southern California Report: A Study of Growth and Economic Stature*, prepared by the Research Division, Security First National Bank, Los Angeles, Jan. 1965, pp. 46-47; W. W. Robinson, "The Southern California Real Estate Boom of the Twenties," *HSSCQ*, XXIV (1942), 25-30; Findley, pp. 177, 188-189; statements by Mr. Martin B. Ruderman, Aug. 3, 1962, Mr. Leslie Cramer, Jan. 14, 1966, and Mr. Lawrence P. Frank, Jan. 19, 1966. Rachel Ana Kositza, pp. 150-151, describes the holdings of her brother, an immigrant grocer, at his death in 1929.

[38]The Jewish law firm of Loeb and Loeb successfully pressed many of the prominent Jewish lenders to make restitution of the interest they had taken. Some of these lenders testified to their regard for the firm's prestige in the Jewish community and feared some form of sanctions. A graphic, overdrawn account is Guy W. Finney, *The Great Los Angeles Bubble: A Present-Day Story of Colossal Financial Jugglery and of Penalties Paid* (Los Angeles, 1929), esp. pp. 99-100, 102, 152, 190-191; see also Findley, pp, 314-326.

[39]Three older books on earlier film history remain unsurpassed: Terry Ramsaye, *A Million and One Nights: A History of the Motion Pictures*, 2 vols. (New York, 1926; paperback reprint, 1964); Benjamin B. Hampton, *A History of the Movies* (New York, 1931); Lewis Jacobs, *The Rise of the American Film* (New York, 1939).

[40]Hampton, p. 26.

[41]Ibid.

[42]Bosley Crowther, *Hollywood Rajah: The Life and Times of Louis B. Mayer* (New York, 1960), pp. 22-66; John Drinkwater, *The Life and Adventures of Carl Laemmle* (New York, 1931), pp. 50-67.

[43]Hampton, p. 110.

[44]*Federal Trade Commission* v. *Famous Players-Lasky, et al.*, Complaint No. 835, p. 903, cited in Mae D. Huettig, *Economic Control of the Motion Picture Industry: A Study in Industrial Organization* (Philadelphia, 1944), p. 35.

[45]Hampton, pp. 199-200.

[46]Charles Donald Fox, *Famous Film Folk* (New York, 1925), s.v. Carmel Myers.

[47]Bosley Crowther, *The Lion's Share: The Story of an Entertainment Empire* (New York, 1957), pp. 74-90.

[48]Leo C. Rosten, *Hollywood: The Movie Colony, the Movie Makers* (New York, 1941), pp. 164-165.

CHAPTER 8. IN LOCAL SOCIETY AND CULTURE: 1900-1928

[1]The entries in the large compendium of J. M. Guinn, *Historical and Biographical Encyclopedia of Southern California* (Chicago, 1902) support this conclusion. The number of Jews in this listing appears unduly small, with only six entries among some 1,000 names (Leon Lehman, Emil Harris, Simon Hartman, H. W. [but not I. W.] Hellman, Lazard Kahn, Louis Phillips). Perhaps three others are also Jews.

[2]John Higham, "Social Discrimination against Jews in America, 1830-1930," *Publication of the American Jewish Historical Society*, XLVII (1957), 1-33.

[3]*BBM*, June 30, 1905.

[4]*BBM*, Sept. 10, 1909.

[5]*BBM*, Oct. 26, Nov. 16 and 30, 1900.

[6]*BBM*, Aug. 28, 1908.

[7]*BBM*, Oct. 29, 1909.

[8]*BBM*, Oct. 29, 1909; May 13, 1910. George E. Mowry, *The California Progressives* (Berkeley and Los Angeles, 1951), pp. 38-54, provides a valuable account of these turbulent years in Los Angeles' political life.

[9]Quoted in George E. Mowry, p. 125, from the *Los Angeles Times*, ca. July 27, 1910. There is no record that Lissner had changed his name; the use of "ski" apparently pandered to the "ski-ski" epithet from which the insulting "kike" was then emerging. See H. L. Mencken, *The American Language*, 4th ed. (New York, 1937), pp. 295-296, note 7, and idem, *Supplement I* (1945), pp. 613-616. (This etymology remains questionable, however.)

[10]George E. Mowry, p. 46.

[11]*BBM*, Mar. 12 and Oct. 12, 1909.

[12]*BBM*, Mar. 13, 1908.

[13]*BBM*, June 13, 1902; Oct. 15, 1904; Oct. 28, 1910; Sept. 30, 1914.

[14]*BBM*, June 13, 1902.

[15]*BBM*, May 13, 1910.

[16]On these clubs in other cities, cf. Louis J. Swichkow and Lloyd P. Gartner, *The History of the Jews of Milwaukee* (Philadelphia, 1963), pp. 150-154. For a typically emphatic rejection, see *Louis Marshall: Champion of Liberty. Selected Papers and Addresses*, ed. Charles Reznikoff (Philadelphia, 1957), II, 809-812: cf., however, I, 391-394.

[17]*Los Angeles Times*, Aug. 23, 1908, quoted in *BBM*, Sept. 10, 1908.

[18]Henry F. May, *The End of American Innocence* (New York, 1959), p. 89.

[19]Andrew F. Rolle, *California: A History* (New York, 1963), p. 416.

[20]Franklin D. Walker, *A Literary History of Southern California* (Berkeley, 1950), pp. 118-178.

[21]Materials kindly made available by Mrs. Jules Kauffman.

[22]*BBM*, Oct. 30, 1908.

[23]See the comments of Henry Steele Commager, *The American Mind: An Interpretation of American Thought and Character Since the 1880's* (New Haven, 1950), pp. 23, 424, and Morris R. Cohen, *American Thought: A Critical Sketch* (Glencoe, Ill., 1954), p. 31.

[24]The book's success prompted a second edition in 1926 and a third edition in 1930, each containing additional data, mostly biographical. Unlikely as it appears, New-

mark's closest kin among Jewish autobiographies is Samuel Gompers' two-volume *Seventy Years of Life and Labor* (New York, 1925), also large, dignified, and impersonal. Unlike Gompers, Newmark at many points has unique historical value, and the Jewish note is present throughout his book.

[25]They were printed at intervals, usually in *HSSCQ*, and some were collected in his *Jottings in Southern California History* (Los Angeles, 1955). On Marco Newmark as a historian, see Ana Begue de Packman, "In Memoriam . . . Marco Ross Newmark," *HSSCQ*, XLI (1959), 292-296. With his brother Maurice, he discovered, edited, and published in 1929 the important manuscript *Census of the City and County of Los Angeles, California, for the Year 1850*.

[26]*BBM*, Apr. 29, 1904.

[27]*BBM*, Sept. 7, 1917.

[28]*BBM*, June 21, 1918. Werne himself probably wrote the article, which concludes with an effusive letter to him from a former congregant in Chicago.

[29]Besides the Rothblatt article (below, note 33), of limited value, the Los Angeles Yiddish literary scene can be studied from two important biobibliographic encyclopedias: Zalman Reizen, *Leksikon fun der Yidisher Literatur Presse un Filologye*, 4 vols. (Vilna, 1926-29), largely superseded by the *Leksikon fun der Nayer Yidisher Literatur*, in progress, 5 vols. to date (New York, 1956–), to Hebrew letter N, containing rich bibliographies. Data about individual writers has been freely drawn from these sources.

[30]An earlier Los Angeles Yiddish imprint is the meager Russian soldier's diary of A. Kimelfeld, *Mayn Militer-Dienst in Rusland: A Tog-Bukh fun a Idishen Soldat* [My military service in Russia: diary of a Jewish soldier] (Los Angeles, 1916). A convenient check list is furnished by S. Sekuler in *Kalifornier Shriften* [California writings] (Los Angeles, 1955), pp. 67-68.

[31]Zalman Zylbercweig, ed. *Leksikon fun Yidishn Teater*, in progress, 4 vols. to date (New York and Warsaw, 1931–), Vol. II, col. 1213.

[32]Rosenblatt came to the United States in 1891 and settled in Los Angeles in 1921. His preeminence in Yiddish circles is epitomized by the two volumes in his honor upon his 60th and 70th birthdays, respectively: *H. Rosenblatt, Zekhtsig Yor* (Los Angeles, 1939), and *H. Rosenblatt, Yovel-Bukh tsu Zayn Zibetsikstn Geboyrntog* (Los Angeles, 1948). In addition to a brief biography the latter includes a comprehensive bibliography of the poet by S. Karpman (pp. 91-96).

[33]A serviceable but very tendentious review of Yiddish politico-cultural life is A: Rothblatt, "Der Entviklungs-Protses funem Idishn Yishev in Los Angeles," *Kalifornier Shriften* (Los Angeles, 1955), pp. 6-37.

[34]Rothblatt, pp. 21-22.

[35]The biographical compilation by Zalman Zylbercweig (see note 31 above) and David S. Lifson, *The Yiddish Theatre in America* (New York, 1965), give little help. Lifson is generally confined to New York, while Zylbercweig's basic work is very unwieldy. A study of the Yiddish theater in Los Angeles would be of particular interest because of its interplay with films.

[36]*Los Angeles Times,* July 8, 1915; quoted in *BBM*, July 9, 1915.

[37]*BBM*, Sept. 10, 1915.

[38]*BBM*, Mar. 10, 1916.

[39]An incident in Imperial is graphically set forth in *BBM*, Nov. 2, 1917, "Jews Not Wanted."

[40]*BBM*, Nov. 16 and 23, 1917; unidentified clippings from earlier in 1917, kindly made available by Mrs. Jules Kauffman.

[41]*BBM*, Jan. 11, 1918.

[42]*BBM*, Oct. 26, 1917, reporting "Answers to Billy Sunday" by Rabbi Isidore Myers before an overcrowded hall. The address was repeated owing to widespread interest.

[43]*BBM*, Jan. 7, 1920; Jan. 28, 1921; July 8, 1921.

[44]*Louis Marshall*, I, 244-422, documents the experience of the foremost American Jewish leader, mostly after World War I; see also John Higham, "Social Discrimination Against Jews," and his *Strangers in the Land: Patterns of American Nativism, 1860-1925* (New Brunswick, 1955), pp. 277-286.

[45]*BBM*, May 7, 1920.

[46]Marshall to Cole, May 12, 1922, in *Louis Marshall*, II, 807-809. I am indebted to Dr. Morton Rosenstock for making available Cole's letter of May 3, 1922.

[47]*BBM*, Oct. 22, 1920.

[48]*BBM*, Oct. 22, Nov. 5 and 12, 1920; cf. *Louis Marshall*, II, 933-935. The great Talmudist Louis Ginzberg issued a responsum, *Teshuvah bi-Devar Yeynot ha-Kesherim veha-Pesulim le-Mizvah* (New York, 1922), that grape juice could substitute for wine in religious ritual. Many Orthodox Jews, however, did not accept Ginzberg's finding and insisted upon fermented wine.

[49]The National Council of Jewish Women was founded in 1893, and its Southern California branch in 1909. Personal service to the poor by each member was a major aim of the organization. Their early meetings presented speakers on "Juvenile Court," New York's "Henry Street Settlement," "Immigration," and the "Problems of Working Girls" (*BBM*, July 23, 1909; for a retrospect, *BBM*, Oct. 7, 1921). In general, see Monroe Campbell and Willard Wirtz, Jr., *The First Fifty Years: The History of the National Council of Jewish Women, 1893-1943* (New York, 1943).

[50]*BBM*, Mar. 29, 1912; cf. *BBM*, June 11, 1909 and Jan. 29, 1911.

[51]*BBM*, Mar. 26, 1915.

[52]*BBM*, May 28, 1915.

[53]Emory S. Bogardus, *The City Boy and His Problems: A Survey of Boy Life in Los Angeles* (Los Angeles, 1926), p. 22. While Jews are not mentioned here, the syntax suggests Yiddish influence; note the last sentence.

[54]Ibid., p. 33.

[55]Remark of Miss Freda Mohr, Jewish Family and Children's Service.

[56]*BBM*, Dec. 28, 1928.

[57]*BBM*, Jan. 31, 1910.

[58]For a later account, see Samuel C. Kohs with Louis H. Blumenthal, "Survey of the Recreational and Cultural Needs of the Jewish Community of Los Angeles Conducted by the National Jewish Welfare Board 1942," 19 parts, separately paged, typescript (hereafter cited as Kohs Survey), Pt. XIV: Commercial Recreation. This deals with 1942. Times change, but temptations seldom do.

[59]*BBM*, Mar. 20, 1914.

[60]*BBM*, Mar. 13, 1914.

[61]*BBM*, Aug. 24, 1917.

[62]*BBM*, Jan. 11, 1918.

[63]*BBM*, Apr. 9, 1915.

[64]*BBM*, Jan. 11, 1918.

[65]*BBM*, Jan. 14, 1920.

[66]Lists of clubs and their activities are found at length in *BBM*, passim.

[67]*BBM*, June 15, 1928. These themes are at or near the surface in the *BBM's* weekly sports column. Jewish athletics in the United States developed parallel to Europe, but the auspices there were primarily Zionist and the purpose rather different.

[68]*BBM*, Oct. 12, 1906.

[69]*BBM*, Aug. 23, 1901.

[70]*BBM*, June 10, 1910.

[71]*BBM*, Oct. 12, 1900, May 30, 1902, Jan. 29, 1911.

[72]*BBM*, Aug. 5 and 26, 1921; Jan. 16, 1925.

[73]*BBM*, Mar. 12, 1909.

[74]*BBM*, Feb. 26, 1909.

[75]Marco Newmark signed the higher body's report, which denied membership to any person "directly or indirectly connected . . . or publicly professing belief" in Christian Science as a religion or in its healing powers alone. The report denying compatibility between Judaism and Christian Science was overruled on appeal as a theological question beyond the constitutional purview of the order (Independent Order of B'nai B'rith, District Grand Lodge No. 4, *Journal of Proceedings, 1912*, pp. 135-140; ibid., *1913*, pp. x-xx; *BBM*, Apr. 17, 1911). The attraction to Jews of religious movements such as Unitarianism, Universalism, Ethical Culture, and Christian Science (one may well include Zen Buddhism) in Los Angeles and elsewhere merits historical study. See now John J. Appel, "Christian Science and the Jews," *Jewish Social Studies*, XXXI (April 1969), 100-121, and "Comments" thereon by Lloyd P. Gartner and Winthrop S. Hudson, *American Jewish Historical Quarterly*, LVIII (March 1969), 323-329.

[76]*BBM*, Jan. 14, 1910.

[77]The story of Masonry appears more complex. For all the prominence of Jews in early Los Angeles Masonry, their role seems to have declined drastically. Gateway was a Jewish Masonic lodge.

[78]Mendel B. Silberberg in *BBM*, Dec. 18, 1913.

[79]*BBM*, Oct. 8, 1915.

[80]*BBM*, Oct. 8, 1915.

[81]"Maftir" column in *BBM*, Feb. 24, 1928.

[82]*BBM*, Feb. 4, 1921.

[83]*BBM*, July 13, 1928.

CHAPTER 9. RELIGIOUS GROWTH AND ADAPTATION

[1]*BBM*, Sept. 16, 1904, account of High Holiday services; *BBM* regularly listed congregations and services and published extensive advertising by synagogues during the High Holiday period.

[2]*BBM*, Sept. 16, 1904; Apr. 30, 1905; Mar. 29, 1912, editorial; Apr. 17, 1911, "Observations by a Jewish Young Lady."

[3]*Congregation B'nai B'rith Annual, 1901-1902.*

[4]*BBM*, July 23, 1909.

[5]"Recipe for an Open-Minded Bigot," *BBM*, Jan. 29, 1911.

[6]*Congregation B'nai B'rith Annual, 1911-1912*, p. 13; cf. George E. Mowry, *The California Progressives* (Berkeley and Los Angeles, 1951) on the religious outlook of that mainly urban, Protestant middle-class movement.

[7]*BBM*, Sept. 14, 1906.

[8]Letter by Rose Brockow in *BBM*, Aug. 29, 1913.

[9]*BBM*, Sept. 2, 1921.

[10]*BBM*, Aug. 30 and Sept. 27, 1912.

[11]For Hecht's earlier career, see Louis J. Swichkow and Lloyd P. Gartner, *The History of the Jews of Milwaukee* (Philadelphia, 1963), pp. 182-185 and notes. His views may be readily analyzed from his extensive statements and sermons. We are indebted to Rabbi Edgar F. Magnin for a few of these impressions and recollections of his predecessor.

[12]*BBM*, Dec. 31, 1909.

[13]*BBM*, Mar. 20, 1914, and *Congregation B'nai B'rith Annuals*, passim.

[14]*BBM*, Sept. 11, 1914; Dec. 10, 1915.

[15]*Congregation B'nai B'rith Annuals*, passim.

[16]He became a member of the Temple only after his father's death in 1907 and soon thereafter was elected a trustee. His prolonged abstention from joining was probably based on filial respect, and was so understood at the Temple.

[17]*BBM*, Oct. 30, 1908.

[18]Report of Annual Meeting in *BBM*, Oct. 27, 1911.

[19]See *BBM*, June 7, 1929.

[20]*BBM*, Apr. 30, 1909.

[21]*BBM*, Apr. 4, 1913.

[22]*BBM*, Apr. 17, 1911.

[23]*BBM*, Aug. 31, 1906.

[24]*BBM*, May 15, 1908.

[25]*BBM*, Nov. 15, 1907; Apr. 16, 1904.

[26]*BBM*, Apr. 27, Oct. 27 and Nov. 16, 1900; Mar. 29 and Oct. 30, 1901.

[27]*BBM*, Apr. 25, 1902.

[28]*BBM*, July 26, 1907, and Aug. 29, 1913.

[29]*BBM*, Oct. 22, 1905.

[30]*BBM*, May 30, 1902.

[31]*BBM*, Mar. 31, 1905; July 27, 1906; Dec. 14, 1906.

[32]His thesis on the Talmudic interpretation of a Biblical work was Isaak Wiernikowski (Werne), *Das Buch Hiob nach der Auffassung des Talmud und Midrasch*, Pt. I (Breslau, 1902); the end paper contain a *vita*. Interestingly, one of his formal "Opponenten" was "Herr Alexander Marx, cand. phil." (1878-1953), the future historian and bibliographer.

[33]Evidently his synagogue desired to retain him, for they raised his salary by $1,260 and were willing to add $1,000 more. If these figures are genuine, he must have been grossly underpaid (*BBM*, May 28, 1920).

34*BBM*, Mar. 17, 1904.

35*BBM*, Dec. 14, 1906.

36*BBM*, June 25 and Sept. 10, 1909.

37*BBM*, Sept. 10, 1909.

38Lazarus Morris Goldman, *The Jews in Victoria in the Nineteenth Century* (Melbourne, 1954), Index, s.v. "Myers, Rev. Isidore."

39*BBM*, Mar. 22, 1918.

40Ibid.

41*BBM*, Jan. 31, 1913.

42*BBM*, Oct. 5, 1917.

43*BBM*, Apr. 18, 1913.

44*BBM*, Sept. 9, 1921.

45*BBM*, Dec. 13, 1907; Sept. 27, 1912.

46*BBM*, Dec. 15, 1916; Nov. 16, 1917.

47*BBM*, Sept. 13, 1907; Apr. 30, 1909; Oct. 15, 1920.

48They were Agudath Achim, Central Avenue and 21st Street; Anshe Sefard, Temple and Custer Streets; B'nai Amunah, Moneta Avenue; Beth Israel; Hebrew Educational (a Talmud Torah group), 33rd and Central Avenue; Ezra ve-Emunah, 26th and Central; Ohave Sholom, Edendale; Poale Zedek, Santa Barbara Avenue; Shaare Zedek, Washington Street; Talmud Torah, Breed Street (*BBM*, Mar. 5, 1920).

49*BBM*, Nov. 11, 1921.

50*Unravelling the Book of Books: Being the Story of How the Puzzles of the Bible Were Solved, and Its Documents Unravelled* (New York, 1929). It was dedicated to Marco H. Hellman.

51*The Autobiography of God: An Interpretation* (New York and London, 1930).

52*As a Jew Sees Jesus* (New York and London, 1931) contains a serviceable bibliography of Jewish writing in English on Jesus. Aben Kandel, *Rabbi Burns* (New York, 1931), is a graphic, hostile caricature of a Los Angeles rabbi and was widely regarded as an attack on Trattner.

53Henry Wilfred Splitter, "Education in Los Angeles: 1850-1900," *HSSCQ*, XXXIII (1951), 101-118, 226-244, 313-330.

54*Congregation B'nai B'rith Annual, 1904-1905*, p. 10.

55*BBM*, April 24, 1903.

56*BBM*, Apr. 18, 1913.

57*BBM*, May 29, 1908.

58*BBM*, Nov. 11, 1911.

59*Congregation B'nai B'rith Annual, 1905-1906*.

60*BBM*, Nov. 15, 1912.

61*BBM*, Feb. 28, 1900.

62*BBM*, May 13, 1903.

63*BBM*, Feb. 13, 1914; cf. *BBM*, June 20, 1913.

64*BBM*, Mar. 14, 1913 and Sept. 18, 1914.

[65]*BBM*, Nov. 15, 1912.

[66]*BBM*, Sept. 10, 1917, and July 12, 1918.

[67]*Geshikhte fun der Tsiyonistisher Arbeter Bavegung in Tsofn Amerike* [History of the Zionist Labor Movement in North America] (New York, 1955), I, 269; II, 411-412.

[68]Quoted in Irwin Soref, "History of Jewish Education in Los Angeles" (M.A. thesis, Univ. of Chicago, 1949).

[69]Report of Sinai Temple Annual Meeting, *BBM*, Feb. 13, 1914.

[70]*BBM*, July 3, 1914.

[71]Report of Tifereth Israel Hebrew School, *BBM*, Jan. 29, 1911.

[72]*BBM*, Aug. 31, 1917. A 1929 examination program at the same institution concentrated on Hebrew and Pentateuch, as well as liturgical fluency. Students above the fifth grade of the school studied some prophetic books, could deliver a talk in Hebrew, and had learned some Talmud (*BBM*, Apr. 26, 1929).

[73]*BBM*, Nov. 30, 1928.

[74]*BBM*, June 7, 1929, Supplement, pp. 10-11.

[75]This information is derived from the report by the Bureau of Jewish Social Research, "Jewish Education Problem in Los Angeles" [1923], mimeographed, 7 pages plus tables; in library of Council of Jewish Federations and Welfare Funds, New York.

[76]*BBM*, Mar. 5, 1915.

[77]*BBM*, July 2, 1929.

[78]*BBM*, Aug. 16, 1929.

CHAPTER 10. PHILANTHROPY

[1]*BBM*, Jan. 2, 1914.

[2]*BBM*, Dec. 18, 1913.

[3]*BBM*, June 10, 1910.

[4]*BBM*, Jan. 25, 1901; Jan. 14, 1910.

[5]Remarks of President Isaac Norton to annual meeting, Jan. 3, 1909, in *BBM*, Jan. 15, 1909. The HBS also reduced this unwanted responsibility by selling half the ground of the old cemetery to the city for public improvements. Several years passed before all bodies were exhumed and reburied elsewhere (*BBM*, Jan. 17, 1908). Evidently satisfied with the income for charity realized from this measure, the society shortly thereafter cleared the remainder of the burial ground and paid street assessments at a total cost of $3,000 in anticipation of selling the land (*BBM*, Jan. 29, 1911).

[6]*BBM*, Jan. 22, 1915.

[7]*BBM*, May 13, 1910; Apr. 28, 1911. The consumption problem is sketched in Lee K. Frankel's paper of 1900, "Tuberculosis as Affecting Jewish Charity Organizations," in Robert Morris and Michael Freund, eds., *Trends and Issues in Jewish Social Welfare in the United States 1899-1958* (Philadelphia, 1966), pp. 78-88. Denver, not Los Angeles, was the Mecca of Jewish tuberculars, according to Frankel's discussion.

[8]*BBM*, Jan. 15, 1909.

[9]"History of the Kaspare Cohn Hospital. By the First Secretary" [Victor Harris], in *BBM*, July 23, 1909.

[10]*BBM,* Mar. 20, 1906.

[11]*BBM,* Feb. 25, 1910.

[12]*BBM,* June 10, 1910.

[13]*BBM,* Mar. 24, Sept. 29, and Nov. 11, 1911; Mar. 14, 1913. A Jewish Free Loan Society also existed from about 1903, in immigrant circles. Bureau of Jewish Social Research, New York, "General Summary and Recommendations Los Angeles Study" [ca. 1923], mimeographed, p. 1; in library of Council of Jewish Federations and Welfare Funds, New York; this report, in several parts with separate paginations, hereafter cited as "Los Angeles Study, 1923."

[14]Harry L. Lurie, *A Heritage Affirmed: The Jewish Federation Movement in America* (Philadelphia, 1961), pp. 34-58.

[15]*BBM,* Aug. 26, 1908.

[16]*BBM,* Jan. 30, 1914; the figure applies to the winter of a relatively hard year and so is probably above average.

[17]*BBM,* Sept. 10, 1915.

[18]*BBM,* Oct. 2, 1914; cf., however, *BBM,* Jan. 15, 1915, reporting the search for "a favorable site to start and erect a home for the unfortunates, those that will, no doubt, flock to the city during the coming year."

[19]*BBM,* Aug. 27, 1915.

[20]*BBM,* Nov. 24, 1916; Jan. 7, 1920; Nov. 24, 1916.

[21]*BBM,* Jan. 31, 1910.

[22]Isaac Norton, president of HCRA, in *BBM,* Mar. 14, 1913.

[23]Los Angeles Study, 1923, "Los Angeles Federation," pp. 2-3.

[24]*BBM,* Oct. 25, 1912.

[25]*BBM,* Sept. 26, 1913; Jan. 23, 1914.

[26]*BBM,* Dec. 18, 1914.

[27]*BBM,* Jan. 15, 1915.

[28]*BBM,* Dec. 18, 1914.

[29]*BBM,* Jan. 11, 1918.

[30]The YIVO Institute for Jewish Research in New York City possesses a folder of acrimonious correspondence between New York directors and the Los Angeles managers, 1918-1919; *BBM* also carried it at length—July 27, Aug. 24 and 31, Sept. 14 and 28, Nov. 9, and Dec. 7, 1917.

[31]*BBM,* Jan. 4, 1918.

[32]*BBM,* Nov. 26, 1920. On later developments, there are two informative but rather adulatory works: Mark Carter, *Okay, America* (Los Angeles, 1963), pp. 75-165, and Samuel H. Golter, *The City of Hope* (New York, 1954).

[33]From address of President S. G. Marshutz at Dedication Exercises (*BBM,* Mar. 29, 1909.

[34]*BBM,* Feb. 11, 1910.

[35]*BBM,* Jan. 15, 1909; Jan. 31, 1910.

[36]*BBM,* Aug. 12, 1910; recollections of Superintendent Frey (*BBM,* Mar. 10, 1911).

[37]*BBM,* Mar. 10, 1911.

[38]*BBM,* Nov. 29, 1912; May 31, 1913.

[39]*BBM*, Apr. 8, 1910.

[40]*BBM*, Jan. 17, 1908; Jan. 15, 1909.

[41]*BBM*, Feb. 14, 1913.

[42]*BBM*, June 24, 1910.

[43]*BBM*, Jan. 17, 1913.

[44]*BBM*, Jan. 16, 1914.

[45]*BBM*, Jan. 29, 1909.

[46]Richard Hofstadter, *The Age of Reform: From Bryan to F.D.R.* (New York, 1955), pp. 173-184, 202-212; George E. Mowry, *The California Progressives* (Berkeley and Los Angeles, 1951), pp. 86-104.

[47]*BBM*, Mar. 30, 1906; Mar. 12, 1909.

[48]*BBM*, Apr. 17, 1911; that serious discussions were then under way may be seen from the *BBM* comment on Apr. 28, 1911, that federation "cannot be consummated any too soon."

[49]"Los Angeles Study, 1923," loc. cit.

[50]*BBM*, June 14, 1912.

[51]*BBM*, Apr. 9, 1915.

[52]*BBM*, Nov. 17, 1904.

[53]*BBM*, Mar. 20, 1906.

[54]*BBM*, Feb. 15, 1907; Jan. 17, 1908, and Mar. 13, 1908.

[55]*BBM*, Oct. 23, 1914.

[56]*BBM*, Mar. 5 and 12, 1915.

[57]*BBM*, Oct. 13 and 20, and Nov. 19, 1915, printed typical lists of contributions. The Los Angeles Workmen's Circle declined to organize a branch of its People's Relief, as had been done in most other cities, on account of the effective local organization (M. J. Drosd, Secretary, W.C. Br. 248, to M. Fingerhut, New York City, Dec. 16, 1915, in People's Relief Committee Archive, Los Angeles Letter Book, at the American Jewish Historical Society).

[58]*BBM*, Feb. 9, 1917.

[59]*BBM*, Mar. 2, 1917.

[60]*BBM*, Mar. 19 and Apr. 16, 1920.

[61]There were also extensive remittances from local families to their kin in Europe. An instructive file is in the People's Relief Committee Archive Letter Book, esp. Chaim and Aaron Shapiro to B. Zuckerman, Apr. 2, 1920.

[62]*BBM*, Sept. 3, 1920.

[63]*BBM*, Sept. 16 and Nov. 18, 1921.

[64]Cf. Merle E. Curti, *American Philanthropy Abroad* (New Brunswick, 1963), pp. 264-265, 269-270, on American weariness with foreign relief.

[65]*BBM*, Aug. 23, 1923, supplement; May 9, 1930, supplementary section, pp. 11, 14.

[66]Los Angeles Study, 1923, "Los Angeles Federation," p. 5, "Jewish Aid Society."

[67]*BBM*, June 18, 1920.

[68]Charles F. Wilinsky, M.D., "A Survey of Jewish Health Services in Los Angeles" [1949], mimeographed, p. 19.

CHAPTER 11. THE BROADENED HORIZON OF WARTIME

[1]*BBM*, Sept. 25, 1914.

[2]*BBM*, Dec. 18, 1914.

[3]*BBM*, Aug. 27, 1915.

[4]*BBM*, Nov. 12, 19, and 27, 1915. Wise also spoke on the relations between religion and political reform.

[5]The movement is described in Oscar I. Janowsky, *The Jews and Minority Rights (1898-1919)* (New York, 1933), pp. 161-190; *Louis Marshall: Champion of Liberty,* ed. Charles Reznikoff (Philadelphia, 1956), II, 505-548.

[6]Sic; the Hebrew is faulty, and probably corresponds to "Community Association." Farber's essays on such topics as "Rivalry" (evidently among organizations), "A Communal Need," and "Need of a Central Jewish Organization," are in *BBM*, Apr. 26, 1912, Aug. 1, 1913, and Dec. 18, 1913. The Agudas Kehillah held its first meeting on June 16, 1912, at the Olive Street Synagogue (*BBM*, May 31, 1912).

[7]*BBM*, Dec. 18, 1914; the claim need not be taken too seriously.

[8]This was a period of extensive kehillah attempts in the United States, most notably in New York City, and also in Cleveland, Chicago, and elsewhere. A comparative study would be in order.

[9]*BBM*, Mar. 8, 1901.

[10]*BBM*, Mar. 13 and Apr. 24, 1903.

[11]*BBM*, Aug. 14, 1903. The YZA marked its fourth anniversary in 1906 (*BBM*, Aug. 31, 1906).

[12]*BBM*, Jan. 31, Mar. 11 and 25, and Apr. 8, 1910.

[13]*BBM*, Jan. 29, 1909.

[14]*BBM*, Aug. 16, 1912.

[15]S. Naumov in *Idisher Kemfer,* Dec. 20, 1935, p. 144; Bernard Schireson, "Jewish Life in Los Angeles," *BBM*, Mar. 28, 1913.

[16]*BBM*, Sept. 9, 1909.

[17]*BBM*, Apr. 8, 1910.

[18]Morris Kaufman, "The Hebrew Renaissance," Nathan Straus Palestine Advancement Society, *First Anniversary Year-Book* (1915), p. 17; "Why I am a Zionist," *BBM*, Apr. 18, 1913. The use of "Hebrew" rather than "Jew" suggests an intended distinction between Palestinian and Diaspora Jewry—a separation partly ideological and partly apologetic. In 1917 the YZA published Kaufman's interesting small pamphlet *Three Essays on Jewish Nationalism.* Its spirit is consistently that of Ahad Ha-Am. A copy was kindly made available by Hebrew Union College Library.

[19]*BBM*, Mar. 20, 1914; Louis J. Swichkow and Lloyd P. Gartner, *The History of the Jews of Milwaukee* (Philadelphia, 1963), pp. 184 and 413, *n.* 84.

[20]*BBM*, July 23, 1909.

[21]Bernard Schireson to "The Secretary of the Central Zionist Organization, Berlin," Mar. 4, 1913, in Central Zionist Archive, Jerusalem, Folder Z3/948. A report from the same year, giving similar details, is in the same Archive, Folder L18/251. Aid to Yemenites arriving in Palestine was a special Zionist fund, while the speaking of renascent Hebrew was, of course, a major cultural ambition.

[22]*BBM*, Jan. 31, Feb. 14, and July 4, 1913. The claim that $27,000 had been subscribed by the last of these dates must be dismissed as a hopeful fantasy. The Hebrew name would today be transcribed "ha-ahuzah," the biblical term for "the landholding."

[23]*BBM*, May 8, 1914.

[24]*BBM*, Nov. 23, 1917. The Society also published two *Year-Books*, in 1915 and 1916.

[25]"Civilization Rejoices," *BBM*, Mar. 30, 1917.

[26]*BBM*, Aug. 24, 1917.

[27]For similar open and subdued opposition, cf. Swichkow and Gartner, pp. 273-278.

[28]*BBM*, May 4, 1917; Jan. 25, 1918.

[29]*BBM*, Jan. 4, 1918.

[30]*BBM*, May 17 and 31 and June 14, 1918.

[31]The *BBM* weekly chronicled much of this activity; July 19 and Oct. 4, 1918.

[32]*BBM*, July 12 and 19, 1918.

[33]*BBM*, Jan. 26, May 4 and 18, 1917.

[34]*BBM*, June 15, 1917.

[35]Janowsky, pp. 245-246, 264-268.

[36]*BBM*, Dec. 28, 1917; Feb. 1, 1918; July 9, 1920.

[37]*BBM*, Oct. 26, 1917. On the Labor Zionist Farband, see Abraham Babitz, *Zichronoth & Feder-shpritzen* [Memoirs and pen-strokes] (Los Angeles, 1961), pp. 78-80.

[38]Statements of Mr. Aaron Riche, Feb. 1, 1962, and Mar. 21, 1966.

[39]Lynchik was from New York City, but his family moved to Los Angeles. There was talk of erecting a monument to the dead soldiers, but nothing came of it (*BBM*, June 3, 10, 24, and July 8, 1921).

CHAPTER 12. THE TRIALS OF DEPRESSION

[1]James Clifford Findley, "The Economic Boom of the 'Twenties in Los Angeles" (Ph.D. diss., Claremont Graduate School, 1958), pp. 196-197, 231-232.

[2]Margaret S. Gordon, *Employment Expansion and Population Growth: The California Experience: 1900-1950* (Berkeley and Los Angeles, 1954), pp. 121-127. Other estimates of unemployment ran even higher, viz. the Metropolitan Life Insurance Company's sample of its industrial insurance policyholders' families in December 1930 revealed a proportion of 20.9% wholly unemployed (p. 123).

[3]Louis B. Perry and Richard S. Perry, *A History of the Los Angeles Labor Movement, 1911-1941* (Berkeley and Los Angeles, 1963), pp. 226-229, 237-242.

[4]*BBM*, Aug. 29, 1930.

[5]*BBM*, Aug. 29, 1930; the group referred to is a Jewish carpenters' association.

[6]*BBM*, Feb. 28, 1930.

[7]*BBM*, Oct. 17, 1930.

[8]*BBM*, Oct. 24, 1930.

[9]Jewish Social Service Bureau, Case Committee, Minutes, Aug. 10, 1932.

[10]The story is told from a rather pro-Giannini standpoint in Marquis James and Bessie Rowland James, *Biography of a Bank: The Story of Bank of America N.T. & S.A.* (New York, 1954), pp. 230-233, 239-240, 299-300, 306-307, 313.

[11]This estimate derives from 82,000 to 85,000 Los Angeles Jews circa 1937 (*U.S. Census of Religious Bodies, 1936*, Vol. I [1941]; *American Jewish Yearbook*, XXXIX [1937-38], 700), and the local rate of 8% totally unemployed or on emergency work

and 2% employed part-time; U.S. Bureau of the Census, *Final Report on Total and Partial Unemployment 1937*, Vol. I (1938), Table I, p. 319.

[12]JSSB, Case Committee, Minutes, Dec. 14, 1932.

[13]JSSB, Case Committee, Minutes, July 5, 1934.

[14]JSSB, Case Committee, Minutes, Aug. 10, 1932.

[15]Miss Freda Mohr, oral statement, Jan. 18, 1966.

[16]Jacqueline Rorabeck Kasun, *Some Social Aspects of Business Cycles in the Los Angeles Area, 1920-1950* (Los Angeles, 1954), p. 10, Table I.

[17]*BBM*, Dec. 24, 1937.

[18]Samuel C. Kohs with Louis H. Blumenthal, "Survey of the Recreational and Cultural Needs of the Jewish Community of Los Angeles Conducted by the National Jewish Welfare Board, 1942," typescript, 19 parts, separately paged (hereafter cited as Kohs Survey), Pt. XVIII, p. 31, "Report on Emigre Service Committee" by Charles Mesnick, in "Jewish Congregations Secular Organizations and Citizenship Activities for Jews."

[19]American Jewish Committee, Los Angeles general file, "Questionnaire for Local Surveys," late 1939; oral statements, Miss Freda Mohr, Aug. 24, 1962.

[20]"Report on Emigre Service Committee," in Kohs Survey, Pt. XVIII, p. 31.

[21]Gordon, pp. 59-60, 104-106.

[22]*The Citizen*, Oct. 23, 1936.

[23]*Los Angeles Times*, Mar. 31, 1934.

[24]*The Citizen*, Feb. 9, 1934.

[25]Perry and Perry, p. 453, Table 7.

[26]Ibid., pp. 251-259, 264, 265, 278-285, 406, 412-415; Rose Pesotta, *Bread upon the Waters* (New York, 1944), pp. 332-345, 361-368, 374-388.

[27]The 1932 figures are derived from *City Directory* sampling; the method is outlined above in Ch. 6, note 41. For 1940, "Vocational and Educational Guidance together with an Analysis of the Occupational Distribution of Jews in Los Angeles," in Kohs Survey, Pt. IV, Sec. 19, p. 30, Table 6; the technique as refined in later surveys was first used by Dr. Kohs in this study.

[28]Los Angeles Jewish Community Council, Health Survey, 1938, mimeographed, p. 121, Tables XXV and XXVI; *BBM*, June 3, 1938.

[29]The figures are based upon a weekly column, "The Jewish Community of Los Angeles," by Raphael Konigsberg, director of the Health Survey, who provides the proportions of Jewish practitioners in these professions responding to a questionnaire. The figures given here may be regarded as close approximations.

[30]*BBM*, Apr. 1, 1938.

[31]A factual though biased account is in Guy W. Finney, *Angel City in Turmoil: A Story of the Minute Men of Los Angeles in Their War on Civic Corruption, Graft and Privilege* (Los Angeles, 1945), esp. pp. 29, 42, 63, 65, 81, 93-94, 99, 111, 121.

[32]*The Nation*, Mar. 21, 1934, p. 321.

[33]One may mention Harry A. Hollzer, Leon R. Yankwich, David L. Coleman, Lester W. Roth, Isaac Pacht, Benjamin Scheinman, Ben Rosenthal, and others.

[34]Robert E. Burke, *Olson's New Deal for California* (Berkeley and Los Angeles, 1953), pp. 39, 76, 123-126, 144-145, 178-181, 183-186. Another controversial official was Sidney G. Rubinow, director of the State Relief Administration (Burke, pp. 135-138, 162-164).

35The list follows: for Roosevelt, Lester W. Roth, Isaac Pacht, Rabbi Jacob Kohn, M. Saeta, I. B. Benjamin, M. Carter, Peter M. Kahn, J. Leavitt, T. Strimling, J. A. Rosenkranz, J. Y. Berman, B. Zukor, H. Bachrack, Charles Brown; for Willkie, M B. Silberberg, M. R. Newmark, Dr. E. M. Lazard, A. Riche, E. J. Loeb, M. M. Sieroty, G. L. Goldstein, H. H. Lissner, J. Goldstone, J. H. Rosenberg, A. Rosenblum, H. Kern, L. Greenbaum, H. Herzbrun (*BBM*, Nov. 1, 1940). Judge Roth styled himself a former Republican who had voted for Hoover in 1932. Several of the Willkie group were comparatively unknown, while all the Rooseveltians were more or less prominent. This balancing of the endorsements—15 to 14—may well have been done to substantiate the newspaper's insistence that "members of the Jewish community are divided on the issues of the campaign in virtually the same proportion and along the same lines as are members of other groups the country over."

36Nathan Glazer, *The Social Basis of American Communism* (New York, 1961), pp. 166-168.

37"Communist Activity among Social Workers," memorandum dated Oct. 15, 1953, from Seymour Soroky to Nathan Weisman, Los Angeles, Communal Issues File, American Jewish Committee; statement by the late Joseph Esquith, Aug. 8, 1962; Jewish Community Council, "Report of a Preliminary Investigation for Consideration by the Evaluation Committee," written by Irvin Stalmaster, Jan. 17, 1940, mimeographed.

38The YIVO Archive on Los Angeles contains numerous stationery headings for such organizations. An instance of numbers may be the 1,352 members of the Jewish Section of the International Workers Order in 1938 (Rubin Saltzman, *Der Internatsionaler Arbeter Ordn in Idishn Lebn* [Pittsburgh, 1938], p. 34).

39YIVO Archive, ICOR [Organization for Jewish Colonization in Russia] Collection posters.

40Harvey Carr, *Los Angeles, City of Dreams* (New York, 1935), p. 245.

41George W. Bemis and Nancy Basché, *Los Angeles as an Agency of Municipal Government* (Los Angeles, 1946), pp. 33, 37.

42These statistics are derived from data and techniques described above, Ch. 6, note 41.

43"Determining the 1941 Jewish Population of Los Angeles," Kohs Survey, Pt. II, p. 178, Table 70.

44Eshref Shevky and Marilyn Williams, *The Social Areas of Los Angeles: Analysis and Typology* (Berkeley and Los Angeles, 1949), p. 49.

45Quoted in Edwin M. Lembert and Judy Rosberg, *The Administration of Justice to Minority Groups in Los Angeles County*, Univ. of Calif. Publications in Culture and Society, Vol. II, No. 1 (Berkeley and Los Angeles, 1948), pp. 20, 26. The data given date from 1938.

46The material on "polite" anti-Semitism in Los Angeles is sparse. Most information is derived from oral tradition, particularly the recollections of well-informed individuals.

CHAPTER 13. THE COMMUNITY WEAKENED AND REJUVENATED: 1929-1941

1*U.S. Census of Religious Bodies, 1936* (1941), Vol. I, Table 31, p. 569.

2"Jewish Congregations Secular Organizations and Citizenship Activities for Jews," in Kohs Survey. Pt. XVIII, p. 4.

3*BBM*, Sept. 13, 1935, p. 3; this and other issues before each High Holiday season are replete with such advertising.

[4]Kohs Survey, Pt. XVIII, pp. 6-7.

[5]Ibid.

[6]*BBM*, Apr. 1, 1938.

[7]*BBM*, Sept. 13, 1935.

[8]We are indebted to the late Rabbi Kohn for an interview on Feb. 2, 1962.

[9]The Western Jewish Institute *Publications* appeared in 37 parts between 1934 and 1948. Almost all were popular pamphlets and sermons, except for numbers 20 (an alphabetization of the Mishnaic *Sayings of the Fathers*), 24 (a 19th-century commentary on the same), and 25 (a compendium of commentaries on Psalms).

[10]Cf. Jacqueline Rorabeck Kasun, *Some Social Aspects of Business Cycles in the Los Angeles Area, 1920-1950* (Los Angeles, 1954), pp. 85-87.

[11]*U.S. Census of Religious Bodies, 1936*, Vol. I, Table 31, p. 569.

[12]Data on Jewish education during the 1930's is scanty. This section is based on "Jewish Education," Kohs Survey, Pt. XVII, 41 pp., tables.

[13]Quoted in Kohs Survey, Pt. XI, p. 19.

[14]A comprehensive bibliography of Los Angeles Yiddish productions by S. Sekuler is in *Kalifornier Shriften*, I (Los Angeles, 1954), pp. 63-69. Occasional bulletins of the Peter M. Kahn Jewish Community Library supplement the list. A work of classical Jewish learning is Moses Jacob Feldman's Hebrew compendium, *Areshet Sefatenu: Source Book of Hebrew Prayer and Proverb*, 3 vols. (St. Louis, 1942; New York, 1949; Brooklyn, 1958); a combination dictionary, concordance, and commentary upon biblical passages used liturgically, it is composed in very good Hebrew.

[15]*Los Angeles Jewish Club Bulletin*, Vol. I, No. 2 (Feb. 1929).

[16]From untitled Yiddish brochure issued in 1935 by the Jewish Culture Club; in archive of YIVO Institute for Jewish Research.

[17]Statement of Mr. Gustave Goldstein, March 1966.

[18]Kohs Survey, Pt. VI, "Report on the Jewish Community Center and the West Adams Jewish Community Center of the Jewish Center Association of Los Angeles," pp. 18 ff., 22, 40, 43.

[19]Ibid., pp. 93-94.

[20]Ibid., pp. 31-33.

[21]Information on the Menorah Center is to be found in Kohs Survey, Pt. VII, "Report on the Menorah Center." The list given here is derived from the Report of the Chairman of the Adult Education Committee for 1938, on p. 19. The WPA Adult Education Supervisor's list, on p. 20, differs slightly.

[22]Ibid., p. 20; punctuation has been corrected.

[23]Ibid., pp. 20-21.

[24]Ibid., p. 12.

[25]Harry Carr, *Los Angeles, City of Dreams* (New York, 1935), p. 246.

[26]*BBM*, Dec. 19, 1930.

[27]*BBM*, Oct. 19, 1928.

[28]UJWF Minutes, Mar. 11, 1929.

[29]*BBM*, May 11, 1928.

[30]UJWF Minutes, Jan. 13, 1930.

[31]This account by Isaac Pacht, then president of the Jewish Community Council, was given to the Council at its Annual Meeting in 1950. He cited Marco Newmark as his authority (JCC Minutes, Jan. 22, 1950). In accordance with the division of communal functions which began in 1933, the newspaper's question might quite as readily have impelled the formation of the Jewish Community Committee.

[32]UJC Minutes, Nov. 25, 1936.

[33]Ibid.

[34]UJC Minutes, Jan. 19 and Feb. 17, 1937.

[35]Five of the signers, it bears mention, were film magnates: Pandro S. Berman, Samuel J. Briskin, Louis B. Mayer, David O. Selznick, and Jack L. Warner. Sol Lesser, also a man of importance in Hollywood, was not an incorporator but was always actively identified with the Jewish community.

[36]On Dec. 10, 1937, "definitely" was added as a qualifier to "Jewish" and "religious" was added to the purposes of the Council.

[37]On Dec. 10, 1937, the number was reduced to five.

[38]On Dec. 10, 1937, the number was raised to 61.

[39]JCC By-Laws, Article XIII, Sections 4, 5, and 6.

[40]A campaign in 1934 produced approximately $67,000, with the film industry the backbone then and subsequently. Such figures as Irving Thalberg, Louis B. Mayer, Harry and Jack Warner, Eddie Cantor, Henry Herzbrun, Phil Goldstone, Samuel J. Briskin, B. B. Kahane, Ernst Lubitsch, and Max Reinhardt were prominent. The studios were of considerable help in fostering the Jewish campaign among their employees (California Jewish Bulletin and Directory, I [1934]); information also provided by Mr. Julius Bisno.

[41]JCC Annual Meeting Minutes, Dec. 21, 1941.

CHAPTER 14. SOARING POPULATION AND ECONOMIC EXPANSION

[1]Jewish Centers Association, Minutes, June 28, 1945; Kohs Survey, Pt. III, "Determining the 1941 Jewish Population of Los Angeles."

[2]JCC Annual Meeting Minutes, Oct. 28, 1946.

[3]Report of Executive Director at JCC Annual Meeting, Jan. 11, 1948. A figure of 260,000 was reported later that year; JCC Minutes, Oct. 28, 1948.

[4]Carey McWilliams, California: The Great Exception (New York, 1949), pp. 18-23.

[5]JCC Annual Meeting, Jan. 28, 1945.

[6]JCC Minutes, Oct. 28, 1948.

[7]McWilliams, California: The Great Exception, p. 23.

[8]Fred Massarik, "A Report on the Jewish Population of Los Angeles," mimeographed (Los Angeles Jewish Community Council, 1951), p. 20, Table 13; cf p. 11, Table 6; p. 21, Tables 15 and 16.

[9]Judah Rubinstein, "Jewish Day of Atonement Census Studies" (Cleveland, 1963; unpublished paper used by kind permission of the author), p. 15.

[10]The "Distinctive Jewish Names" technique first used by Kohs in Los Angeles ten years before was employed. A sample of 1,419 Jewish names was carefully drawn from the unduplicated files of the United Jewish Welfare Fund, the most extensive

listing of Jews to be had. The method is set forth in Massarik (1951), pp. 4-10. A more recent methodological treatment is Fred Massarik, "New Approaches to the Study of the American Jew," *The Jewish Journal of Sociology*, VIII (1966), 175-191.

[11]Massarik (1951), p. 11, Table 6; p. 19, Table 12; note, however, Massarik's considerable reservations concerning the basis of this estimate.

[12]Charles Zibbell, Director of Research and Planning of the Los Angeles Jewish Community Council, to Max Weinreich, Nov. 3, 1949; in the YIVO Archives.

[13]Massarik (1951), p. 19, Table 12.

[14]Much of the data here is derived from a report contained in a letter from Charles Zibbell, Director of Research and Planning of the Los Angeles Jewish Community Council, to Max Weinreich, Nov. 3, 1949, in the YIVO Archives; Memorandum, Feb. 27, 1952, in American Jewish Committee Archive—Los Angeles—Membership Education.

[15]L. H. Frisch, Editor, *American Jewish World*, to authors, Apr. 26, 1963. Also, L. Simmonds, Editor, *Intermountain Jewish News*, to authors, Apr. 30, 1963; Harry Weingast, Editor, *The Jewish News* (Newark), Apr. 26, 1963; Edwarde F. Perlson, Editor, *The Wisconsin Jewish Chronicle*, to authors, May 20, 1963; Mrs. Geraldine Alter Jacobson, Pittsburgh, to authors, May 15, 1963; Philip Slomovitz, Editor and Publisher, *The Jewish News* (Detroit), to authors, Apr. 26, 1963.

[16]Charles Brown, Address at JCC meeting, Oct. 28, 1948. Compton is now predominantly Negro.

[17]Carey McWilliams, *California: The Great Exception*, pp. 14-16.

[18]JCC Board Minutes, June 12, 1956. Of this total, 591 were underwritten in 1948 under the provisions of the Displaced Persons Act. In 1954, 40 per annum were accepted; and 43 were undertaken in the wake of the Hungarian emigration of 1956-57.

[19]Intake Sub-committee, Emigre Service Committee Minutes, May 28, 1948.

[20]Emigre Service Committee Minutes, Nov. 4, 1947.

[21]Ibid., Oct. 24, 1947.

[22]Julius Bisno to JCC Annual Meeting, Jan. 19, 1953. The number seems much exaggerated. Five years later this number was repeated (JCC Annual Meeting, Jan. 26, 1958).

[23]Emigre Service Committee Minutes, July 15, 1947.

[24]Ibid., Sept. 30 and Oct. 31, 1947.

[25]M. F. Berg to JCC, Minutes, Nov. 2, 1949.

[26]*Newsletter* (of the 1939 Club), Vol. I, No. 1 (April 1961).

[27]Julius Bisno at JCC Annual Meeting, Jan. 19, 1953; the figure is exaggerated—see above, note 22.

[28]U.S. Bureau of the Census, *County and City Data Book 1962*, Table 3; idem, *1949*, Table 2, Nos. 35, 36; idem, *1947*, Table 2, p. 31; idem, *1952*, Item 20, p. 43.

[29]These estimates are based upon the category of "seeking work, experienced" males over fourteen in Los Angeles Census Tracts 126 and 128 (Boyle Heights), 76 and 77 (Beverly-Fairfax), and 199 (West Adams) for 1940. Thus, Tract 126 showed 292 seeking work to 1,334 at work; the figures for Tract 76 are 167 and 2,240, respectively. Hence, an estimate of 10% seems plausible. 16th Census of the United States, *Population and Housing. Statistics for Census Tracts. Los Angeles—Long Beach* (1942).

[30]Massarik (1951), p. 34, Table 28 [note that unemployment rate is 3% higher for men than for women]. Massarik, "A Study of the Jewish Population, 1959," mimeo-

graphed (Research Service Bureau, Jewish Federation-Council of Greater Los Angeles, 1959), p. 25, Table 24. In a communication to the authors, Dr. Massarik suggests that Jewish unemployment may have been somewhat higher.

[31]*United States Census of Population: 1950,* Vol. III, Ch. 28, Census Tracts Statistics: *Los Angeles, California, and Adjacent Area* (1952); Massarik (1951), p. 41, Table 36. The "Jewish" Census Tracts, however, show considerably lower incomes; thus, 76 and 77, mainly Beverly-Fairfax, report $3,403 and $3,452, respectively, as 1949 median incomes. To the Jewish enumerator of 1951, a sample of 108 persons in the same area used a technique of anonymous report to claim a median income of $5,370. No satisfactory reconciliation of these figures comes to mind, although rising income levels between 1949 and 1951 may account in part.

[32]Massarik (1959), pp. 22-23, Table 22.

[33]Massarik (1951), pp. 97-98, Table 91; figures of the 1950 census are, as noted (above, note 31), much lower, except for the Boyle Heights tracts.

[34]Massarik (1959), pp. 22-23, Table 22. The 1960 figures for three census tracts considerably inhabited by Jews more than confirm the Jewish communal estimates. In 2146 (Beverly-Fairfax) median family income was $7,713, to a figure of $8,191 in Tract 7008 (Beverly Hills) and $8,842 in Tract 1331 (San Fernando Valley). *U.S. Bureau of the Census and Housing: 1960. Census Tracts. Los Angeles—Long Beach, California* (1962).

[35]Thus, in Tract 126, part of Boyle Heights, the "proprietors, managers, and officials" decreased from 285 in 1940 to 208 in 1950, but "clerical, sales, and kindred" workers shrank in the same period from 297 to 274. In 76, another "Jewish" tract (part of Beverly-Fairfax), the 574 "proprietors, managers, and officials" of 1940 reached 676 in 1950, while 640 "clerical, sales, and kindred" dwindled to 539 within the ten years. Similar drastic changes are to be seen in Tract 199 (part of West Adams). To be sure, many economic climbers moved from the rather depressed Tract 126 to better neighborhoods like that of Tract 76 and were replaced by Gentiles, mainly Mexican. These data are derived from the 1940 and 1950 censuses, cited above.

[36]Massarik (1951), pp. 35-37, Tables 29-32.

[37]Charles Zibbell, Jewish Community Council, to Max Weinreich, Yiddish Scientific Institute, New York, Nov. 3, 1949; in YIVO Archives.

[38]Massarik (1959), p. 21, Table 20; Kohs Survey, Pt. XIX, "Occupational Distribution of the Jewish Labor Force in Los Angeles" (1940), p. 30, Table 6; census reports cited above, notes 29 and 31.

[39]Kohs Survey, loc. cit.; Massarik (1951), p. 37, Table 32, compared with pp. 94, 96, Tables 87, 89; Massarik (1959), pp. 20-21, Table 20. In the rather Jewish Tract 1331 in San Fernando Valley, composed mainly of younger families, 28% of employed males were professional and technical workers. Comparable figures in the older "Jewish" Tracts 2146 (Beverly-Fairfax) and 7008 (Beverly Hills) are 13% and 17%, respectively (*1960: Census Tracts,* loc. cit.).

[40]This suggestion is based on a comparison of the data in Massarik (1951), pp. 78, 94, Tables 74, 87; compare also the observations of Neil Morgan, *Westward Tilt: The American West Today* (New York, 1963), pp. 109-153.

[41]The 1945 figure is derived from the 999,492 of 1940 (16th Census of the United States, 1940, *Housing,* Part 2, California [1943], Table 2), plus tentative total of 54,919 for the next five years (*Statistical Abstract of the United States, 1946,* Table 887, p. 774). Cf. Massarik (1959), p. 22, Table 21.

[42]*Los Angeles Times,* undated clipping of a Sunday article in May 1965. Louis H. Boyar was another major figure in this industry.

[43]Mr. Weinberg to authors.

44Information provided by Mr. Goodkin, who finished high school in New Jersey and migrated to California in 1947.

45Personal information from members of the Familian family.

46Interview with Mr. Reuben Finkelstein, Apr. 26, 1965.

47Private information from Jewish businessmen.

48Statement of Mr. Louis Siegal, Executive Vice-President, Union Bank of America.

49Examples are: City National Bank, Fidelity Bank, Manufacturers Bank, Century Bank, Heritage Bank, Continental Bank, Silverlake Bank.

50JCC, UJWF Campaign Committee, Progress Summary, Aug. 2, 1944; later information supplied by the staff of the UJWF; information from Mr. Lawrence Weinberg.

51Cf. Carey McWilliams, *Southern California Country* (New York, 1946), p. 219. Jewish predominance may be appreciated from the fact that in 1944, 1,261 presumptively Jewish businessmen in the apparel trade contributed to the United Jewish Welfare Fund (UJWF, Progress Summary, in Campaign Committee Minutes, Aug. 25, 1944).

52*U.S. Census of Manufactures, 1947*, Vol. III: *Statistics by States*, s.v. California, Los Angeles Standard Metropolitan Statistical Area; idem for 1954 and 1958 (Title of Vol. III varies slightly); see the slightly earlier study by Charles S. Goodman, *The Location of Fashion Industries: With Special Reference to the California Apparel Market*, Michigan Business Studies, Vol. X, No. 2 (Ann Arbor, 1948), esp. pp. 27-39, 54-55, Tables XIII-XIV.

53Massarik (1951) and Massarik (1959) do not go beyond the rough "industrial distribution"; only under "occupational distribution" are workers and entrepreneurs separated, but without reference to industry.

54Interview with Mr. Allen Ziegler, Apr. 26, 1965; files of the *Bakery Business Letter* published by Westco.

55Jewish Personnel Relations Bureau Minutes, June 24, 1949, and Jan. 18, 1949.

56"A Survey of Operations, Programs and Developments" of Jewish Personnel Relations Bureau, in JCC Board Minutes, June 11, 1957.

CHAPTER 15. EQUAL RIGHTS AND THEIR DIFFUSION

1M. B. Silberberg to JCC Annual Meeting, Minutes, Jan. 10, 1943; see the stimulating article by James Q. Wilson, "A Guide to Reagan Country: The Political Culture of Southern California," *Commentary*, May 1967, pp. 37-45.

2Harry A. Hollzer to JCC Annual Meeting, Minutes, Jan. 28, 1945.

3These quotations from panel discussion of the problem, JCC Minutes, Apr. 19, 1951.

4American Jewish Committee Archive—Los Angeles, Committee & Officers, Minutes of Committee on Jewish Integration, Nov. 13, 1958.

5AJC—LA, Visits, Dec. 14-15, 1945.

6Community Relations Committee (hereafter CRC) Minutes, Mar. 28, 1947.

7House of Representatives, Committee on Un-American Activities, 81st Cong., 1st Sess., Hearings Regarding Communist Infiltration of Minority Groups—Pt. I, pp. 438-439, 441. Schultz was executive director of the American Jewish League against Communism.

8AJC—LA, Committees & Officers, Executive Minutes, Oct. 4, 1950.

[9]CRC Minutes, June 1, 1951.

[10]CRC Minutes, Apr. 13, 1951.

[11]AJC–LA, undated, about September 1952.

[12]AJC–LA, Reports, July 1952.

[13]CRC Minutes, Sept. 9, 1949, ff.

[14]CRC Minutes, Jan. 24, 1947; 1949, passim.

[15]Fred Herzberg, Executive Director of the CRC, in JCC Minutes, Nov. 12, 1950.

[16]JCC Annual Meeting Minutes, Oct. 28, 1946.

[17]CRC Minutes, 1950, passim.

[18]Jewish Centers Association Minutes, passim.

[19]Council for Civic Unity, Bulletin, Aug. 22, 1944. JCA Minutes.

[20]*U.S. Census of Population: 1950*, Vol. III, Ch. 28: *Census Tract Statistics: Los Angeles, California and Adjacent Area*, p. 9, col. 1; *U.S. Census of Population and Housing 1960. Census Tracts: Los Angeles–Long Beach, California*, p. 25, col. 2.

[21]AJC–LA, Communal Issues–Employment.

[22]AJC–LA, Communal Issues–Housing, F. A. Schreiber to Ed Howden, Council for Civic Unity of San Francisco, Apr. 25, 1952.

[23]AJC–LA, Feb. 24, 1950.

[24]AJC–LA, Visit, Report of Isaiah Terman, Dec. 14-15, 1945.

[25]AJC–LA, General File, F. A. Schreiber to L. Dawidowicz, June 3, 1958.

[26]AJC–LA, Communal Organizations, F. A. Schreiber to T. Leskes, Feb. 25, 1953.

[27]Jewish Personnel Relations Bureau Minutes, Apr. 29, 1947.

[28]AJC–LA, Committees & Officers, Legal and Civic Action, Minutes, Legal and Civic Action Committee, Mar. 31, 1948.

[29]Jewish Personnel Relations Bureau Minutes, Jan. 18, 1949.

[30]Ibid., June 24, 1948.

[31]Ibid., Jan. 18, 1949.

[32]AJC–LA, Reactions of Los Angeles Chapter to "A Fresh Look at Anti-Semitism in Your Community," Apr. 16, 1958.

[33]CRC Minutes, Dec. 7 and Nov. 18, 1949.

[34]"A Fresh Look" (see note 32 above).

[35]JCA Minutes, Sept. 22 and Nov. 1948; Mar. 20, 1951.

[36]AJC–LA, Communal Organizations, JCC–CRC, Joint Staff Meeting, June 6, 1950.

[37]Jewish Telegraphic Agency, Bulletin, Apr. 11, 1957.

[38]AJC–LA, Communal Issues, Religion and Schools, 1947-49 passim.

[39]CRC Minutes, Nov. 18, 1949.

CHAPTER 16. EDUCATION FOR LIFE AND JUDAISM

[1]Carey McWilliams, *California: The Great Exception* (New York, 1949), p. 18.

[2]Bureau of Research, Los Angeles JCC, "A Preliminary Study of the Jewish Community of San Gabriel Valley, California" (June 1948), p. 17.

3CRC Minutes, Dec. 16, 1949; AJC–LA, Committees & Officers, Legal and Civic Action, Minutes of Scientific Evaluation Committee, May 17, 1949.

4Report of Hillel Council Board, p. 18 of Member's Kit at JCC Annual Meeting, Jan. 25, 1953.

5JCC Board Minutes, Jan. 11, 1955, and July 10, 1956. Before the University Religious Conference, there had been a Jewish Women's Guild during the late 1930's to help Jewish students on local campuses. Mrs. Rose Berch was its leader.

6Fred Massarik, "A Report on the Jewish Population of Los Angeles," mimeographed (Los Angeles Jewish Community Council, 1951), pp. 113-115, Tables 100, 101, 102; pp. 63-65, Tables 61 and 62.

7JCC Special Committee on Support of Jewish Education in All Day Schools, Minutes, July 8, 1948.

8"Unaffiliated" refers to association with the Bureau of Jewish Education; Report to JCC, Annual Meeting, Jan. 20, 1947; ibid., Jan. 29, 1956; "Jewish Education of the Los Angeles Jewish Community Council" (1951).

9On IWO–JPFO schools in Los Angeles, see the testimony of Miss Riva Solotaroff in Jewish War Veterans, Joseph Solomonow, et al., Complainants, and Jewish People's Fraternal Order, Respondents . . . Proceedings, Vol. XI, p. 38, Nov. 7, 1950, at Jewish Federation-Council.

10A folder of this Committee dated Mar. 3, 1955, is in the Los Angeles archive of YIVO.

11"Memorandum on Operation of Hebrew Schools in the Centers," June 7, 1955, in JCC Board Minutes, June 14, 1955; Hebrew secular education apparently did not exist in Los Angeles.

12"A Preliminary Study of the Jewish Community of San Gabriel Valley, California," p. 21.

13Temple Beth Hillel (North Hollywood, Calif.), "Religious School and Its Program" (Feb. 1957), first page of text and passim. Other Reform Temples, including Emanuel and Isaiah, also conducted weekday schools during the 1950's.

14Temple Beth Zion, Annual Report 1956-57, mimeographed.

15Report of Community Planning Committee in JCC Board Minutes, June 12, 1956.

16See, for example, Samuel Dinin, "A Five-Year Plan for Jewish Education in Los Angeles," Jewish Education Pamphlets, No. 2 (Nov. 1950).

17JCA Minutes, Sept. 28, 1943; Nov. 29, 1944; Feb. 14, 1944.

18JCA Minutes, Apr. 19, 1948, and report attached, dated Mar. 26, 1948.

19Meyer E. Fichman in JCA Minutes, June 28, 1945.

20Constitution and By-Laws Committee Report in JCA Minutes, Dec. 2, 1943.

21JCA Minutes, Mar. 16, 1944.

22JCA Minutes, Oct. 30, 1943. Ten years later, the Health Club—i.e., Turkish baths —was opened on Saturdays (Minutes, Oct. 20, 1953).

23JCA Minutes, June 28 and Apr. 15, 1945.

24JCA Minutes, Sept. 22 and Nov. 23, 1948; Mar. 20 and Dec. 18, 1951.

25The "offending" report was Fred Massarik, "The Jewish Population of the West Adams Area: A Tentative Report" (Sept. 1948), mimeographed. This prescient report helped indirectly to establish a permanent Research Service Bureau.

26JCA Minutes, June 24, 1952.

CHAPTER 17. RELIGIOUS LIFE

[1]Fred Massarik, "A Report on the Jewish Population of Los Angeles," mimeographed (Los Angeles, Jewish Community Council, 1951), p. 45 et seq.; Massarik, "A Study of the Jewish Population of Los Angeles, 1959," mimeographed (Research Service Bureau, Jewish Federation-Council of Greater Los Angeles, 1959), p. 29, Table 28. With the increase in the size of the average dwelling unit from 3.03 in 1951 to 3.23 in 1959, the hypothetical number of persons in synagogally affiliated households would have risen from nearly 75,000 to 133,000.

[2]Many carried out these observances partially or on occasion (Massarik [1959], p. 30, Tables 30, 31).

[3]Discussion Group on Anti-Semitism, Apr. 1, 1952, AJC–LA Membership Education.

[4]JCC Annual Meeting, Jan. 11, 1948.

[5]Massarik (1959), pp. 8, 28, Tables 5, 27; p. 11, Table 6.

[6]"Charting a 5-Year Program of Growth for the Conservative Movement . . . 12th Annual Conference of the United Synagogue of America Pacific Southwest Region," mimeographed (June 2, 1957), pp. viii-ix. There are 8,200 families counted, of whom 600 were affiliated with congregations in Tucson, Ariz.

[7]Ben J. Lax in Pacific Southwest Region, United Synagogue of America, "Report of Activities," mimeographed (Jan. 1955), p. 6.

[8]Kashruth Committee of JCC, Minutes, 1952-55, passim.

[9]Massarik (1959), p. 29, Table 29.

[10]Dr. Kohn's major theological works were *Moral Life of Man* (New York, 1956) and *Evolution as Revelation* (New York, 1963).

[11]Southwest B'nai Zion Temple Center, *Nineteenth Annual Souvenir Journal and Memory Book Nineteen Fifty-Seven*, p. 43.

[12]Leon A. Ligier, "Sephardim among the Early Settlers in Los Angeles, California," typescript, pp. 4-5; kindly made available by Mr. Ligier.

[13]Temple Beth Hillel (North Hollywood, Calif.), "Religious School and Its Program," Part II: "Our Fundamental Attitudes on Religion."

[14]This tendency appears deducible from Massarik (1959), pp. 28-31, Tables 27-33; p. 34, Tables 37 and 38.

CHAPTER 18. COMMUNITY WITHIN METROPOLIS

[1]JCC Board Minutes, Oct. 13, 1942.

[2]Charles Brown to Annual Meeting, JCC Minutes, Oct. 28, 1948.

[3]Federation-Council Merger Committee Minutes, Mar. 8, 1955.

[4]JCC Minutes, Nov. 1, 1953.

[5]JCC Board Minutes, Apr. 10, 1951. A short-lived attempt was made in 1953 to establish a Synagogue Council composed of synagogues represented on the Council. Its purposes were to combat "mushroom" synagogues and to function as the local voice of the none-too-potent Synagogue Council of America (Synagogue Council Minutes, June 30 and July 16, 1953).

[6]On the other hand, the Council at about the same time joined other groups in unsuccessfully attempting to reopen the case of three physicians who were dropped

from the Cedars of Lebanon staff. It was generally believed that the physicians lost their positions on account of left-wing political views; the hospital's Board would not comment on its decision, and aroused wide resentment.

[7]JCC Board Minutes, Feb. 8, 1944.

[8]Address at Annual Meeting, Nov. 27, 1944.

[9]JCC Minutes, Jan. 28, 1945.

[10]Report of Finance, Office and Personnel Committee regarding new building, in JCC Board Minutes, June 19, 1946.

[11]Address to JCC, Oct. 28, 1948.

[12]Charles Brown at induction of new JCC officers, JCC Board Minutes, Mar. 11, 1952.

[13]JCC meeting, Nov. 1, 1953.

[14]M. F. Berg, First Vice-President, to JCC meeting, June 8, 1952.

[15]JCC Board Minutes, Apr. 9, 1946.

[16]JCC Board Minutes, Nov. 13, 1951.

[17]JCC Board Minutes, Feb. 25, Mar. 10 and 17, 1942.

[18]JCC Board Minutes, Feb. 9, 1943; Apr. 8, 1947; Oct. 12, 1943.

[19]JCC Board Minutes, Feb. 10, 1948.

[20]JCC Board Minutes, June 8, 1948.

[21]This is the analysis of Leo Gallin, Executive Director of the Fund, at JCC meeting (Minutes, Jan. 22, 1950).

[22]Cf. Stanley Mosk's Presidential Message, in JCC Minutes, Jan. 26, 1958.

[23]Report of Allocations Committee, Aug. 10, 1954, in JCC Board Minutes, Jan. 10, 1955.

[24]JCC Allocations Committee, July 7, 1948.

[25]JCC Allocations Committee, Aug. 22, 1949.

[26]Allocations Committee Report, JCC Board Minutes, Oct. 6, 1949.

[27]Report to Annual Meeting, in JCC Minutes, Jan. 31, 1954.

[28]Report of Ike Greenberg, Campaign Chairman (JCC Board Minutes, Apr. 12, 1955).

[29]JCC President's Cabinet Minutes, July 27, 1954.

[30]Report of Ike Greenberg (JCC Board Minutes, Apr. 12, 1955).

[31]JCC Program Plan and Scope Committee Minutes, May 27, 1948.

[32]JCC Board Minutes, June 8, 1948.

[33]JCC East Los Angeles Committee Minutes, Dec. 11, 1951.

[34]JCC Board Minutes, Aug. 3, Aug. 10, Oct. 28, Dec. 14, 1948; Nov. 9, 1954; June 12, 1956.

[35]A report to a major Jewish organization, June 22, 1956.

[36]JCC Board Minutes, Sept. 14, 1948.

[37]JCC Board Minutes, 1954-1955 passim, esp. Nov. 9 and Dec. 14, 1954; July 12, 1955.

³⁸Based on the Minutes of the Merger Committee, passim, and its report to the JCC Board in the latter's Minutes, Sept. 10, 1957. In practice the combined Board had 75 members, with 25 from each source.

³⁹JCC Board Minutes, Sept. 10, 1957.

CHAPTER 19. EPILOGUE

¹The data on Jewish population, neighborhoods, income, and religious affiliation have been most generously supplied by Dr. Fred Massarik, from research to be published by the Jewish Federation-Council. The *American Jewish Year Book, 1966,* estimates 1965 American Jewish population at 5,720,000; see pp. 83-84.

²Lucy S. Dawidowicz and Leon J. Goldstein, *Politics in a Pluralist Democracy* (New York, 1963), pp. 35-37. The precincts studied, however, are not quite representative. Jewish support for Hubert Humphrey in 1968 was as overwhelming as that received by his Democratic predecessors (Max Vorspan, "Los Angeles," in "Patterns of Jewish Voting, 1968," *Midstream,* Feb. 1969, pp. 43-48).

³These data are taken from "Report of Executive Director to the Bureau of Jewish Education, December, 1961," mimeographed, 7 pp., and "Jewish Education in Los Angeles: A Statistical Portrait of Bureau-Affiliated Schools 1966-1967," mimeographed, 26 pp.

⁴The recent and valuable work of Robert M. Fogelson, *The Fragmented Metropolis: Los Angeles, 1850-1930* (Cambridge, Mass., 1967) appeared too late to be fully utilized, but its fresh analysis and comprehensiveness have made it most helpful.

INDEX

INDEX

CONSTITUTION.

PREAMBLE.

Whereas : The Israelites of this City, being desirous of procuring a piece of ground suitable for the purpose of a Burying Ground for the deceased of their own faith, and also to appropriate a portion of their time and means to the holy cause of Benevolence—unite themselves, for these purposes, under the name and style of " The Hebrew Benevolent Society " of Los Angeles.

ARTICLE I.

The government of this Society shall be administered by a President, Vice President, Secretary and Treasurer, and three Trustees.

ARTICLE II.

The President, Vice President and the three Trustees shall constitute a Board of Trustees.

ARTICLE III.

The Election of Officers of this Society shall take place annually, on the first Sunday in the month of July, which shall be the Annual Meeting of this Society.

ARTICLE IV.

The President shall preside at all general meetings, and shall be Chairman of the Board of Trustees. It shall be his duty to appoint the following Committees, viz :

Committee on Charity,
Committee on Letters,
Committee on Accounts.

He shall have the privilege of the casting vote on joint ballot.

ARTICLE V.

The Vice President shall, in the absence of the President, take the Chair and assume all the duties of the President ; and in the absence of the President and Vice President any Trustee may take the Chair.

ARTICLE VI.

The Secretary and Treasurer shall unite in one person, whose duty it shall be to be present at all meetings of the Society, as well as meetings of the Board of Trustees. He shall take minutes of all meetings, and keep a regular set of books, viz : A book of " minutes " of general meetings ; a book of transactions of Board of Trustees ; a cash book, ledger, and a record of all deaths and burials. The Treasurer shall receive all monies due the Society, and honor all drafts on him signed by the President and one member of the Board of Trustees, and also by the Chairman of Committee on Charity, countersigned by the President, and in his absence by the Vice President. He shall summons or otherwise give notice to members of time and place of meeting, &c. He shall also submit at every quarterly meeting a balance sheet and an account of the Society.

The salary of the combined officers of Secretary and Treasurer shall be five per cent on all receipts; and for the faithful discharge of his duties he shall give two securities of five hundred dollars each, to be approved of by the Board of Trustees.

ARTICLE VII.

The Board of Trustees shall exercise a due regard for the interests of this Society, and it shall be their duty to invest, in their joint names, as Trustees for the " Hebrew Beneyolent Society of Los Angeles," all sums of money over and above one hundred dollars which may be in the hands of the Treasurer, in such a manner as will best subserve the interests of this Society. They shall also receive all applications for burial, and appoint suitable persons to perform the burial service and prayers at the house of mourning; and it is expressly enjoined that in all their decisions on religious questions they shall be guided by the Jewish rites.

If necessary the Board of Trustees shall have power to appoint a " Sexton," to take care of the burying ground, dig graves, and attend at all places where his services may be required.

ARTICLE VIII.

The Committee on Charity shall consist of three persons, the first named to be Chairman, whose duty it shall be, on application verbally or in writing to either of them for relief from this Society, that they render it promptly, provided in their opinion the applicant is deserving, and entitled to the same ; and in case of illness of the applicant they shall immediately repair to the place of abode and render such assistance, either with money or personal and medical attendance as the case may require. They shall have the power to call on any members of the Society to assist with their personal attendance if necessary.

ARTICLE IX.

The Committee on Letters shall recieve all applications for membership addressed to the President and members of the Society, and report to the President if favorable ; if otherwise no notice shall be taken thereof.

ARTICLE X.

The fee of admission to membership shall be five dollars, payable in advance.

ARTICLE XI.

The subscription of each member shall be one dollar per month, payable monthly in advance.

ARTICLE XII.

Any Israelite recommended by at least two members of the Society, may, on application by letter, be balloted for as member of this Society, when, if he recieves a majority of ballots, he shall be considered a member after he has paid his admission fee and signed the Constitution.

ARTICLE XIII.

The sons of members over eighteen years of age are not entitled to the benefits of this Society unless they become members.

ARTICLE XIV.

Any Israelite, a resident of this city, dying a non-member of this Society, shall not be entitled to burial in the grave yard of this Society, except there be paid by his friends or administrators the sum of one hundred dollars, or such less sum as the Board of Trustees may decide on.

ARTICLE XV.

No Israelite who has committed suicide, or has suffered death by the penalty of the law, can be interred within the walls of this Society's burying ground, but may with the consent of the

Board of Trustees, be buried outside in a place appropriated for that purpose.

ARTICLE XVI.

Any member neglecting to pay his arrears for six months, without giving satisfactory reasons to the Board of Trustees, shall no longer be considered a member, and lose all privileges of this Society.

ARTICLE XVII.

There shall be eight regular monthly meetings, three quarterly and one annual meeting, to be held on the first Sunday of every month.

ARTICLE XVIII.

The Board of Trustees have the power to call a meeting of this Society whenever occasion requires.

ARTICLE XIX.

Nine members shall constitute a quorum for the transaction of business.

ARTICLE XX.

This Constitution shall not be altered except by and with the consent of two-thirds of the members present. To attain this object, a special meeting for this purpose must be called, giving two weeks notice in writing to each and every member.

BY-LAWS.

ARTICLE I.—MEETINGS.

SECTION 1. Within fifteen minutes after the time appointed for meeting, the President will take the Chair, the members present will come to order and the Secretary will proceed to call the roll. If a quorum be present the meeting may then proceed to business.

SEC. 2. No member shall leave the meeting without permission from the Chair.

SEC. 3. All motions and resolutions must be reduced to writing.

SEC. 4. No member shall speak more than twice on the same subject, unless with permission of the Chair.

SEC. 5. None but members shall be present at the meetings.

ARTICLE II.—ELECTIONS.

SECTION 1. At Elections for Officers the President or presiding officer shall appoint two Tellers who, in conjunction with the President, shall also be the Judges of the election.

SEC. 2. The Secretary shall call the names of all electors, who on being called shall deliver their votes.

ARTICLE III.—President.

SECTION 1. The President shall have the power to vote upon a revision of the Constitution, By-Laws, or at an election; otherwise he shall only have the casting vote.

SEC. 2. He shall sign a permit for the burial of members, their wives, their unmarried female children, and their male children under eighteen years of age.

SEC. 3. He shall not have the right to sign any certificate of burial for any one who is not a member of this Society without the consent of a majority of the Trustees present.

SEC. 4. Any member who behaves improperly in a meeting may be fined by the President in a sum not exceeding ten dollars; but in such cases an appeal may be made to the Board of Trustees—the majority of whose judgment shall be final.

SEC. 5. Should the President neglect his duty by permitting transgressions to pass unpunished, the Board of Trustees shall have the power to fine him (the President) in a sum not to exceed ten dollars, ($10) nor less than five dollars ($5.)

SEC. 6. He shall keep a check book for the purpose of drawing regular orders, each of which must be numbered successively and contain an exact statement for which the money has been applied.

SEC. 7. The President and Secretary and Treasurer shall at the expiration of their term of office deliver up to their successors the books, monies, deeds, or other vouchers belonging to the Society, for which a receipt shall be taken in the receipt book of the Society.

ARTICLE IV.—Trustees.

SECTION 1. Every Trustee shall be liable to impeachment for neglect of his official duties, or any other offence while in office, if a written declaration to that effect shall have been made; in such case the whole meeting shall examine into the whole complaint and decide.

SEC. 2. They shall attend all meetings concerning the Society which the President shall think proper to call.

SEC. 3. Any member having accepted an honorary office and refusing to serve out his time without a sufficient excuse shall pay a penalty of ten dollars ($10.)

ARTICLE V.—Resignations.

SECTION 1. Any member wishing to leave the Society shall notify the President of the same by enclosing a certificate, signed by the Secretary, that he is not indebted to the Society.

SEC. 2. This Certificate shall be presented to the Trustees who shall take action on the same in a proper manner.

ARTICLE VI.—General Laws.

SECTION 1. Should any member offend an

officer while in discharge of his official duty, or should any member in any manner violate the laws of this Society, he shall be summoned to appear within ten days before a special meeting of the Society, who shall examine the allegations brought against the accused.

SEC. 2. Should they find the charges well founded and the offence well proven, they shall have the power to inflict a penalty on him of a sum not exceeding twenty dollars ; and in case the accused fails to appear to answer the allegations he shall be considered guilty of the offence, and be fined in the sum of twenty dollars—in default of which his name shall be stricken from the roll.

These By-Laws may be amended with and by the consent of two-thirds of the members present when two weeks notice previous has been given.

S. K. LABATT,	H. NEWMARK,	H. TISCHLER,
CHARLES SHACHNO,	M. POLLACK,	B. MARKS,
J. ELIAS,	L. HARRIS,	H. KRAUSHAAR,
H. GOLDBERG,	A. BRUNN,	J. ROSENBLUM,
S. LAZARD,	J. BRUNN.	J. HYMAN,
J. L. MORRIS,	ALEX. B. EPHRAIM,	S. ROSINSKI,
J. J. LABATT,	MORITZ B. EPHRAIM,	J. NEWMARK.
S. MEYER,	SIMON FERNER,	H. M. COHN,
E. LOEVENTHAL.	W. KALISCHER,	G. MAHLER,
C. BEHRENDT,	J. HELLMAN,	L. ROSENBACH.